“Here’s fresh honey fr[illegible] alms, from two of my favorite preachers and theologians. Drs. Akin and Smith share precise, textual exegesis accompanied by practical applications that help us all become people after God’s own heart.”

Steve Gaines, senior pastor of Bellevue Baptist Church, Memphis, Tennessee

“In *Exalting Jesus in Psalms 1–50* Danny Akin and Josh Smith have given to the church a resource that is multidimensional. Their commentary on the Psalter is exegetical, Christological, theological, devotional, and homiletical. Every pastor who aspires to exposit the riches of the Psalms will find much help in these pages.”

Al Jackson, Pastor Emeritus of Lakeview Baptist Church, Auburn, Alabama

“Here is a commentary that will give insight to preachers as they prepare to preach. It will explain the text in plain language to Bible class teachers as they develop their lessons. And it can also serve the layperson who can profit from it as Scripture-saturated devotional reading. Best of all, it will show the connections between each psalm and Christ. As a bonus, there are questions at the end of each chapter to help the reader consider the practical implications of the passage. There’s something here for everyone!”

Donald S, Whitney, professor of biblical spirituality and associate dean at The Southern Baptist Theological Seminary, Louisville, Kentucky; author of *Spiritual Disciplines for the Christian Life*, *Praying the Bible*, and *Family Worship*

CHRIST-CENTERED
Exposition

OT / COMMENTARY

AUTHORS J. Josh Smith and Daniel L. Akin
SERIES EDITORS David Platt, Daniel L. Akin, and Tony Merida

CHRIST-CENTERED

Exposition

EXALTING JESUS IN

PSALMS 1–50

NASHVILLE, TENNESSEE

Christ-Centered Exposition Commentary: Exalting Jesus in Psalms 1–50

B&H Publishing Group
Nashville, Tennessee

ISBN: 978-1-5359-6109-7

Dewey Decimal Classification: 220.7
Subject Heading: BIBLE. O.T. PSALMS—
COMMENTARIES\ JESUS CHRIST

[Copyright information continued on page 374.]

Printed in the United States of America
1 2 3 4 5 6 7 8 9 10 • 27 26 25 24 23 22
VP

SERIES DEDICATION

Dedicated to Adrian Rogers and John Piper. They have taught us to love the gospel of Jesus Christ, to preach the Bible as the inerrant Word of God, to pastor the church for which our Savior died, and to have a passion to see all nations gladly worship the Lamb.

—David Platt, Tony Merida, and Danny Akin
March 2013

AUTHOR'S DEDICATION

Dedicated to Tom Elliff, who has been a constant role model to me and many others on how to be a man of God. He is the Psalm 1 man.

— Danny Akin

This book is gratefully dedicated to Mike Maxey and the pastors search team of Prince Avenue Baptist Church: Teresa Allen, Amy Chisholm, Robert Coletti, Chan Deep, Blake Haas, Preston Henry, Ansley King, Clay Kitchings, Scott McCall, Nancy Miller, Lisa Peacock, Mike Power, Lisa Vaughn, and Ron Weldon.

And to the Prince family: I love you and I love being your pastor!

—J. Josh Smith

TABLE OF CONTENTS

Psalms 1–50

ACKNOWLEDGMENTS

Thank you to Devin Moncada, Kim Humphrey, and Kimberly Rochelle for their excellent and tireless assistance in helping me with my part of this volume.

Danny Akin

Very special thanks to Devin Moncada for your organizational assistance and to Dave Stabnow for your hard work in the editing process.

J. Josh Smith

SERIES INTRODUCTION

Augustine said, "Where Scripture speaks, God speaks." The editors of the Christ-Centered Exposition Commentary series believe that where God speaks, the pastor must speak. God speaks through his written Word. We must speak from that Word. We believe the Bible is God breathed, authoritative, inerrant, sufficient, understandable, necessary, and timeless. We also affirm that the Bible is a Christ-centered book; that is, it contains a unified story of redemptive history of which Jesus is the hero. Because of this Christ-centered trajectory that runs from Genesis 1 through Revelation 22, we believe the Bible has a corresponding global-missions thrust. From beginning to end, we see God's mission as one of making worshipers of Christ from every tribe and tongue worked out through this redemptive drama in Scripture. To that end we must preach the Word.

In addition to these distinct convictions, the Christ-Centered Exposition Commentary series has some distinguishing characteristics. First, this series seeks to display exegetical accuracy. What the Bible says is what we want to say. While not every volume in the series will be a verse-by-verse commentary, we nevertheless desire to handle the text carefully and explain it rightly. Those who teach and preach bear the heavy responsibility of saying what God has said in His Word and declaring what God has done in Christ. We desire to handle God's Word faithfully, knowing that we must give an account for how we have fulfilled this holy calling (Jas 3:1).

Second, the Christ-Centered Exposition Commentary series has pastors in view. While we hope others will read this series, such as parents, teachers, small-group leaders, and student ministers, we desire to provide a commentary busy pastors will use for weekly preparation of biblically faithful and gospel-saturated sermons. This series is not academic in nature. Our aim is to present a readable and pastoral style of commentaries. We believe this aim will serve the church of the Lord Jesus Christ.

Third, we want the Christ-Centered Exposition Commentary series to be known for the inclusion of helpful illustrations and theologically driven applications. Many commentaries offer no help in illustrations, and few offer any kind of help in application. Often those that do offer illustrative material and application unfortunately give little serious attention to the text. While giving ourselves primarily to explanation, we also hope to serve readers by providing inspiring and illuminating illustrations coupled with timely and timeless application.

Finally, as the name suggests, the editors seek to exalt Jesus from every book of the Bible. In saying this, we are not commending wild allegory or fanciful typology. We certainly believe we must be constrained to the meaning intended by the divine Author himself, the Holy Spirit of God. However, we also believe the Bible has a messianic focus, and our hope is that the individual authors will exalt Christ from particular texts. Luke 24:25-27,44-47 and John 5:39,46 inform both our hermeneutics and our homiletics. Not every author will do this the same way or have the same degree of Christ-centered emphasis. That is fine with us. We believe faithful exposition that is Christ centered is not monolithic. We do believe, however, that we must read the whole Bible as Christian Scripture. Therefore, our aim is both to honor the historical particularity of each biblical passage and to highlight its intrinsic connection to the Redeemer.

The editors are indebted to the contributors of each volume. The reader will detect a unique style from each writer, and we celebrate these unique gifts and traits. While distinctive in their approaches, the authors share a common characteristic in that they are pastoral theologians. They love the church, and they regularly preach and teach God's Word to God's people. Further, many of these contributors are younger voices. We think these new, fresh voices can serve the church well, especially among a rising generation that has the task of proclaiming the Word of Christ and the Christ of the Word to the lost world.

We hope and pray this series will serve the body of Christ well in these ways until our Savior returns in glory. If it does, we will have succeeded in our assignment.

David Platt
Daniel L. Akin
Tony Merida
Series Editors
February 2013

Psalms 1–50

What Do You Do When You Come to a Fork in the Road? (The Blessed Person Is the Righteous Person)

PSALM 1

Main Idea: True blessing comes through obeying and delighting in the Word of God.

I. Reach for the Life That Pleases God (1:1–3).
   A. Know when to say no (1:1).
      1. Don't walk with the wicked.
      2. Don't stand with sinners.
      3. Don't sit with fools.
   B. Know when to say yes (1:2–3).
      1. Say yes to God's Word (1:2).
      2. Say yes to God's wisdom (1:2).
      3. Say yes to God's will (1:3).

II. Run from the Life That Displeases God (1:4–6).
   A. Stay away from the useless life (1:4).
   B. Stay away from the senseless life (1:5).
   C. Stay away from the hopeless life (1:6).

Lawrence Peter "Yogi" Berra is one of the greatest catchers of all time in Major League Baseball. Elected to the Baseball Hall of Fame in 1972, he was a fifteen-time all-star and a three-time American League MVP. He played in fourteen World Series with the New York Yankees, and he is a member of baseball's All-Century Team. He also joined the Navy at age eighteen and participated in the D-Day invasion at Omaha Beach in World War II. Yogi Berra is deservedly known as a great baseball player, but he is equally known for his famous "Yogi-isms," becoming one of the most quoted personalities of the twentieth century. Yogi Berra said,

- It ain't over 'til it's over.
- It's like déjà vu all over again.
- Never answer an anonymous letter.
- I usually take a two-hour nap from one to four.

And perhaps his best of all:

- When you come to a fork in the road, take it! ("Yogi Berra's Most Memorable Sayings")

If you think about that last sentence, it has some truth. When you come to a fork in the road, you must take it. Life confronts us with many forks in the road:

- Where will I go to school?
- Will I marry or remain single?
- Whom will I marry?
- Will we have children?
- How many children will we have?
- Will I put my faith in Jesus Christ as my Lord and Savior?
- When I die, will I go to heaven or hell?

These are important and significant questions; indeed, they are unavoidable forks in the road. Each of us faces different circumstances and situations that confront us with decisions we must make, with forks in the road. Thankfully, in Psalm 1 God gives us a road map that can guide us so that when we come to a fork in the road, we will choose the right road and the wise road.

In Psalm 1 we are confronted with two men, two roads, and two destinies. The psalm shows how important some life decisions are. Eugene Peterson gives a creative and colorful paraphrase of the psalm in *The Message* that will benefit our study:

How well God must like you—
you don't walk in the ruts of those blind-as-bats,
you don't stand with the good-for-nothings,
you don't take your seat among the know-it-alls.
Instead you thrill to GOD's Word,
you chew on Scripture day and night.
You're a tree replanted in Eden,
bearing fresh fruit every month,
Never dropping a leaf,
always in blossom.
You're not at all like the wicked,
who are mere windblown dust—
Without defense in court,

unfit company for innocent people.
God charts the road you take.
The road they take leads to nowhere.

When you come to a fork in the road, what should you do? What does the wise person do?

Reach for the Life That Pleases God

PSALM 1:1-3

Psalm 1 introduces the entire Psalter. James Boice said,

> It stands as a magnificent gateway to this extraordinary ancient collection of Hebrew religious verse. . . . It is a text of which the remaining psalms are essentially exposition. (*Psalms,* 13–14)

It is a wisdom psalm reminiscent of the wisdom of Proverbs as it draws a contrast between two men, two approaches to life, two roads to travel, and two destinies. One way is the blessed road of those who follow God. The other is the tragic road of those who follow the ways of the wicked, the sinners, and the mockers.

Know When to Say No (1:1)

Wisdom is as much about knowing when to say no as it is when to say yes. It is knowing when to walk away, when to swim against the tide, and when not to follow the crowd even when they laugh at you and call you a fool. This psalm teaches about three areas where we must learn to say no.

Don't walk with the wicked. The word *happy* (ESV, "Blessed") describes a rewarding and fulfilling life. What kind of person lives the blessed, rewarding, and meaningful life? The psalmist answers by describing what the blessed person avoids. He gives three negatives of descending tragedy: association → identification → fixation.

> walk → stand → sit (habits of life)
> advice → pathway → company (people you listen to)
> wicked → sinners → mockers (company you keep)

First, the psalmist warns us not to follow "the advice of the wicked," who are mentioned four times in Psalm 1. Whom you follow will inevitably shape your conduct. It is difficult to avoid imitating and becoming like those we walk with daily. As Calvin wisely says, "By little and little, men are ordinarily induced to turn aside from the right path" (*Psalms 1–35*, 3). Following the advice of the wicked starts with simple association with people for whom the things of God matter little, if at all. Be careful where you go. Be wise about the people you listen to. Not all advice is good advice. Don't walk in the counsel of the ungodly.

Don't stand with sinners. The phrase *stand in the pathway* conveys the idea of staying a while, stopping to look and listen, and hanging around or hanging out with. The word *pathway* describes a manner of life, the way one lives. "Sinners" are those who miss God's mark. They are in the habit of standing on the opposite side from God. Instead of taking a stand for God, they take their stand with those who oppose him. Their way of life is more important than Christ's way of life. Sin becomes their pattern, and sinners become their partners. Instead of wisely imitating Christ, the ultimate blessed man (1 Cor 11:1), they foolishly imitate sinners.

Don't sit with fools. Finally, the psalmist warns us not to throw our lot in with or "sit in the company of mockers." The action from walking to sitting describes moving from thinking like the wicked to living like the rebellious and to ridiculing like the cynic. If we walk in the advice of the wicked, this way of life is now our home. This is where we sit. We are comfortable here. Not only do the things of God not matter, but we mock as fools those who think the things of God do matter. "Mockers" or "scoffers" describes the self-sufficient who pridefully say, "I don't need God; I will live my life my way." They laugh at and look down on those who live for God. Often these are the people with a quick wit and a sharp tongue. They are the kind who live for this life only, forgetting the life to come (see Prov 3:33–35; 15:12; 21:24). The psalmist warns us to be careful about what we love. Know when to say no.

Know When to Say Yes (1:2–3)

The psalmist now presents the positive case for the righteous, blessed, and God-honoring life. Contained in these two verses is both a plan and a promise for those who pursue the life that pleases God.

Say yes to God's Word (v. 2). We should "delight" in the "Lord's instruction." We should take joy and find pleasure in the Word of God.

We should be people who love the Bible. It is a joy, not a burden, to learn it and to live it. Spurgeon says, "'The [instruction] of the Lord' is the daily bread of the true believer" (*Treasury*, 2). The wise person gives his unreserved yes to the Word of God.

Say yes to God's wisdom (v. 2). The person who delights in the Word of God "meditates on it day and night." To *meditate* means "to think over something by talking to oneself." He or she carefully and continually ponders and weighs the Scriptures. Joshua 1:8 reminds us,

> *This book of instruction must not depart from your mouth; you are to meditate on it day and night so that you may carefully observe everything written in it. For then you will prosper and succeed in whatever you do.*

Here is the person who is preoccupied and consumed with the Word of God. It is his priority; it is her passion. We should ask ourselves some of these questions regularly:

- What do I think about when I daydream?
- What do I sing about when I take a drive or go on a walk?
- What comes to my mind and fills my heart when tragedy strikes and disappointment comes?
- In a 24-hour day, 10,080-minute week, 2,592,000-second month, how much time do I give to memorizing and meditating on God's Word?

What we love, we will spend time with.

Say yes to God's will (v. 3). Romans 12:2 says God's will is "good, pleasing, and perfect." The psalmist says God's will is fruitful and prosperous. In the arid desert of the Middle East, the picture of a beautiful, fruit-bearing tree located by streams of water would have been striking. This life is healthy, fruitful, and successful, maybe not in man's eyes but in God's! This life is worth living. It means something. It matters! The people who live this life trust God to plant them! They trust God to make them prosper. These are happy people because the road they travel pleases God. What then does a spiritually prosperous life look like? To answer, we can restate verse 1. Such a person walks in the advice of the godly, he stands in the pathway of the righteous, and he sits in the company of the hopeful. He studies the Word. He acts with wisdom. He is devoted to God's will. This life is the truly prosperous life.

Run from the Life That Displeases God

PSALM 1:4-6

Jesus said in Matthew 6:24,

> *"No one can serve two masters, since either he will hate one and love the other, or he will be devoted to one and despise the other. You cannot serve both God and money."*

Jesus also said in Matthew 7:13-14,

> *"Enter through the narrow gate. For the gate is wide and the road broad that leads to destruction, and there are many who go through it. How narrow is the gate and difficult the road that leads to life, and few find it."*

What is the way that leads to destruction? What is this road that I do not want to travel? Verses 4-6 give us the answers.

Stay Away from the Useless Life (1:4)

Verse 4 begins by contrasting the wicked person with the righteous person of verses 2-3. Unlike a strong, fruitful tree by rivers of water, the ungodly are chaff, straw, and dust in the wind. Derek Kidner says, "Chaff is . . . the ultimate in what is rootless, weightless . . . and useless" (*Psalms 1–72*, 49). The wicked are not like the blessed person of verses 1-3. They are spiritual lightweights. They have no roots, no foundation, and no substance. They lack the real stuff that gives meaning to their existence. It is the useless life—useless to God and useless to others. This word picture was familiar to the contemporaries of the psalmist. Every harvest they saw the grain being threshed and winnowed on the local threshing floor situated on some open, elevated site. During the winnowing, the grain that was still mixed with broken straw and husks was thrown into the wind. The wind blew the useless chaff away. "Chaff" provided a good description of all that is passing and useless.

Stay Away from the Senseless Life (1:5)

"The wicked will not stand up in [i.e., "survive"] the judgment." When it comes time to stand before God and give an account of their lives—something we will all do—the wicked will not be able to stand. Further, the psalmist writes that sinners will not be in the "assembly of the righteous." No place is saved for them among God's people. When they came to that ultimate fork in the road, they decided to avoid God's path, not realizing that on that day they were sealing their eternal destinies. They thought to themselves, *Go to the left, go to the right. What difference does it make? Run with those who draw me closer to God or run with those who push God aside. It's not that big a deal, is it?* The time is always right to do the right thing and choose the right road. Every day is such a day. Don't play the fool. Don't choose the senseless life.

Stay Away from the Hopeless Life (1:6)

Jesus often talked about two ways. He spoke of two gates, one narrow gate leading to life and one wide gate leading to destruction (Matt 7:13-15). He also spoke of two roads, two trees, two types of fruit, two houses, and two foundations (Matt 7:15-29). In each instance, one brought life and blessing; the other brought death and sorrow. Psalm 1:6 summarizes the end of every life based on whether one followed: the godly road or the ungodly road, the righteous road or the unrighteous road. The righteous road is God's road. Jesus stands at its beginning with a cross by his side. He knows and cares personally and intimately for every traveler on it. He sees. He watches. He cares. He knows. He will walk that road with you. The unrighteous road is the devil's road, where he and his demons wait. They promise life to the fullest here and now. But he is a liar and the father of lies (John 8:44). What he promises, he cannot deliver. In contrast, Jesus said in John 10:10, "A thief comes only to steal and kill and destroy. I have come so that they may have life and have it in abundance." The devil's road is the road to "ruin," one of death, destruction, sorrow, and regret. The wicked and ungodly may think it seems right, but as Proverbs 14:12 says, "There is a way that seems right to a person, but its end is the way to death." The way of the righteous, however, is the way of the Lord Jesus, who said, "I am the way" (John 14:6).

Conclusion

Arno C. Gaebelein, writing about Psalm 1, said, "The perfect man portrayed in the opening verses . . . is . . . the Lord Jesus" (*Psalms*, 18). Augustine said the same: "[Psalm 1], this is to be understood of our Lord Jesus Christ, the Lord Man" (*Expositions*, 1). I (Danny) completely agree! No one is truly like this wise and righteous man other than our

Lord. Some years ago, James Boice relayed the following story from a well-known and much-respected pastor:

> Harry Ironside, the Bible teacher, told of a visit to Palestine years ago by a man named Joseph Flacks. He had an opportunity to address a gathering of Jews and Arabs and took for the subject of his address the first psalm. He read it and then asked the question: "Who is this blessed man of whom the psalmist speaks? This man never walked in the counsel of the wicked or stood in the way of sinners or sat in the seat of mockers. He was an absolutely sinless man."
>
> Nobody spoke. So Flacks said, "Was he our great father Abraham?"
>
> One old man said, "No, it cannot be Abraham. He denied his wife and told a lie about her."
>
> "Well, how about the lawgiver Moses?"
>
> "No," someone said. "It cannot be Moses. He killed a man, and he lost his temper by the waters of Meribah."
>
> Flacks suggested David. It was not David.
>
> There was a silence for a long while. Then an elderly Jew arose and said, "My brothers, I have a little book here; it is called the New Testament. I have been reading it; and if I could believe this book, if I could be sure that it is true, I would say that the man of the first Psalm was Jesus of Nazareth." (Boice, *Psalms 1–41,* 19)

Jesus is the man of Psalm 1, and he challenges us all to follow him down the road that leads to life. This road will not disappoint!

Reflect and Discuss

1. How do you normally respond to forks in the road? Are you slow or quick to make decisions? Do you tend to avoid or include input from others? Are you ever overwhelmed by the decisions you must make? Why?
2. In what ways do the people around you shape how you think and what you do? How can Christians be a light to those who do not know God without becoming like them?

3. How does the idea of "blessing" shape the whole psalm? How would the psalm be different if it only said, "Don't walk in the advice of the wicked"?
4. What is necessary to have a "happy" life according to this psalm? Do you think the psalmist's requirements are easy or hard to follow?
5. What will happen if one tries to obey the Word of God without regularly delighting in and meditating on the Word of God?
6. This section says, "What we love, we will spend time with." Does your time with God's Word indicate that you love his Word? How can you continue to renew and increase your affection for God's Word when it feels like a burden or duty?
7. How would thinking about final judgment shape how you make decisions? In what ways can thinking about God's judgment both frighten and encourage you?
8. Describe how your thinking about a blessed life changed when you became a Christian. In what ways are you tempted now to believe that disobedience to God will bring blessing?
9. Why is it important to remember that Jesus is the ultimate picture of this wise and righteous man?
10. How does Psalm 1 shape how you will read the rest of the book of Psalms?

The Glory and Greatness of the Messiah-King

PSALM 2

Main Idea: Jesus is God's anointed Messiah-King who will rule decisively and sovereignly over all the nations.

I. See the Fools Who Rebel in Sinful Insurrection (2:1-3).
  A. Be careful when you scheme (2:1).
  B. Be careful where you stand (2:2).
  C. Be careful what you say (2:3).
II. See the God Who Ridicules with Scathing Indignation (2:4-6).
  A. God derides the senseless peoples (2:4-5).
  B. God declares his sovereign plan (2:6).
III. See the Son Who Reigns with a Supreme Inheritance (2:7-9).
  A. The Son will be revealed to the nations (2:7).
  B. The Son will rule over the nations (2:8-9).
IV. See the Blessed Who Respond to Salvation's Invitation (2:10-12).
  A. Be wise and instructed by the Lord (2:10).
  B. Serve and rejoice for the Lord (2:11).
  C. Honor and trust in the Lord (2:12).

Ever since the fall in Genesis 3, God's people have looked for the promised deliverer. As Scripture unfolds and history rolls on, step by step, piece by piece, God painted the portrait of this Savior:

- He will crush the head of the serpent (i.e., Satan; Gen 3:15).
- He will come from Abraham (Gen 12:1-3).
- He will be of the tribe of Judah, from whom the scepter shall not depart until Shiloh (peace) comes (Gen 49:8-12).
- He will be a prophet greater than Moses (Deut 18:15).
- He will be a Son of David and a Son of God whose throne and kingdom will be established forever (2 Sam 7:5-16; Isa 9:6-7).

Now in Psalm 2, against this marvelous backdrop, we gain further insight into a song that celebrates the coronation of the king and that celebrates the glory and greatness of the Messiah-King.

Psalm 2 is a royal psalm, a coronation psalm for the king, that was originally written at a specific time for a specific king. Acts 4:25 informs us the author is David. Perhaps he penned the psalm for, or in reflection of, his own ascension to the throne. Perhaps he wrote it for Solomon. Deposited in the sanctuary, it would have been retrieved for subsequent coronations or similar celebrations. Yet as the fortunes of the nation of Israel turned dark because of its sin, idolatry, and rebellion, and as it faced exile and foreign oppression, Psalm 2 began to function as a psalm of hope. The people of God looked not to the past and the glory days of David but to the future and the greater Son of David and his greater glory. They looked and longed for the great Messiah-King, the Christ, the Anointed One of God, who would usher in a cosmic and universal kingdom as the enthroned King, God (*Yahweh*) himself.

Psalms 1 and 2 serve as the preface to the Psalter. These twin songs begin and end with the theme of blessedness (1:1; 2:12). Michael Wilcock helpfully points out, "The private world of the first Psalm opens out into the public world of the second; the personal is followed by the cosmic . . . one is 'domestic' and the other 'international'" (*Message*, 23). Further, the blessed man of Psalm 1 is fulfilled in the Messiah-King of Psalm 2. The blessed righteous of Psalm 1 are the blessed humble who trust this king in Psalm 2. The wicked scoffers in Psalm 1 are the foolish rebels in Psalm 2.

Psalm 2 finds its ultimate and climactic fulfillment in the Lord Jesus Christ. Not surprisingly, it is one of the most quoted psalms in the New Testament. Willem VanGemeren notes the significance the first-century church attached to this psalm:

> The second psalm . . . was favored by the apostles as scriptural confirmation of Jesus' messianic office and his expected glorious return with power and authority. The writers of the synoptic Gospels alluded to Psalm 2 in their account of Jesus' baptism, when the Father proclaimed him to be his Son (v. 7; cf. Matt 3:17; Mark 1:11; Luke 3:22). With the words of verse 7, Jesus introduced the beginning of the messianic age.
>
> The first-century church applied Psalm 2 to the Messiah as an explanation of the crucifixion of Jesus by the rulers (Herod

> and Pontius Pilate), the nations, and Israel (the priests, teachers of the law, and Pharisees). They had conspired together against the Messiah of God (Acts 4:25-28). Paul applied it to Jesus' ministry: his sonship, resurrection, and ascension to glory, which confirmed God's promises in Jesus as *the* Messiah (Acts 13:32-33).
>
> Psalm 2:8 is similarly applied in Hebrews, where the glory of the Messiah as "the exact representation of [God's] being" is revealed in Jesus' suffering for sins, in his authority "at the right hand of the Majesty in heaven" (1:3), and in his authority over angelic beings (vv. 5-6). The apostle John reveals the greatness of the Messiah's victory. He was born of a woman but is destined to "rule all the nations with an iron scepter" (Rev 12:5). He is the Rider on the white horse who will "strike down the nations" in the day of God's wrath (Rev 19:15; cf. 11:16-18).
>
> The apostolic witness makes it clear that the second psalm has a messianic dimension. While it is preferable to understand the psalm first in its historical and literary setting as a royal psalm, the eyes of faith must look beyond it to the powerful message of the full establishment of God's kingdom in Jesus Christ. (*Psalms*, 90; emphasis in original)

This coronation psalm of celebration naturally divides into four stanzas of three verses each. In these stanzas David declares that the truly wise will humble themselves and submit to the Messiah-King's authority because God has appointed him and will put down anyone and everyone who opposes and rebels against his sovereign rule.

See the Fools Who Rebel in Sinful Insurrection

PSALM 2:1-3

God's people look forward to the time when all aspects of this psalm are fulfilled in the reign of the Messiah-King. However, not everyone feels this way. Sadly, most do not look forward to the Messiah's future reign. This has been true in the past, and it will be true until the end of time. David sees the nations and their leaders rising up against God and his anointed king. In the process he sounds a warning.

Be Careful When You Scheme (2:1)

The psalm begins with a rhetorical question: "Why do the nations rage and the peoples plot in vain?" David is amazed and astonished that the people on earth would rebel and conspire against the God of heaven (v. 4). Like the raging waves of the sea during a storm, the peoples of the earth rage and conspire against the Lord. In their rebellion they plot against the Lord. The word "plot" is the same root word that is translated as "meditate" in Psalm 1:2. The godly meditate day and night on the law of the Lord, but the defiant nations meditate in empty, foolish rebellion against God and his authority. Although the nations and their leaders are brilliant in the eyes of the world, they are foolish to conspire against the Lord of heaven. Shaking their fists in the face of God, the nations and their leaders plot, conspire, and scheme together in how to overthrow the Lord of heaven. Fallen, sinful humanity rebels against God's authority. God's Word is mocked, set aside, ridiculed, and scorned as antiquated and outdated. Could any people be more foolish in their rebellion and moral insanity?

In Acts 4:25-27 Peter saw this verse fulfilled in the murder of God's "holy servant Jesus," whom God anointed (2:2). Peter says that Herod, Pontius Pilate, the Gentiles, and the people of Israel all conspired together to crucify the Son of God in the ultimate act of defiant scheming against God. All who refuse to submit to the lordship of Jesus in their lives align themselves with these who foolishly reject God's authority.

Be Careful Where You Stand (2:2)

The leaders and rulers of the nations are now the specific focus of attention. Acting out the thoughts of their evil hearts, they take a public stand against Yahweh and his Messiah. The irony of the situation is breathtaking. "The kings of the earth" are setting themselves against the King of heaven! The counsel of the wicked in Psalm 1 is now the wicked council of the kings and rulers of the earth as they "conspire together." The thought of the great leaders of the earth coming together for counsel as they "take their stand" against some enemy would normally not seem unusual. However, in this scenario it is "against the Lord [*Yahweh*] and his Anointed One" (Hb *mashiach*/messiah). Standing in opposition and plotting evil against God's Messiah is nothing less than opposing and plotting against the Lord himself. What amazing folly and foolishness!

The righteous and blessed person of Psalm 1 is not wanted or desired by these political rulers and leaders. They take their stand against him. But these rulers are standing in the wrong place and thinking in the wrong way against the wrong persons.

Be Careful What You Say (2:3)

What was in the hearts of these rebels now flows freely from their mouths. With defiance and determination, they declare their intention to be free from this "sky God" and his puppet lacky. "Let's tear off their chains and throw their ropes off of us," they say. "Chains" and "ropes" suggest the yoke of a cart or plow placed on the necks of animals for service. This is how they see the authority of the Lord in their lives, and they will have none of it. His authority is not just rejected; it is thrown off. They cannot stand the idea of King Jesus having absolute lordship and authority over their lives. They declare freedom from the Lord and his anointed, and they are proud to do so.

See the God Who Ridicules with Scathing Indignation

PSALM 2:4-6

Those who scoff and mock God in Psalm 1:1 are now mocked themselves with divine laughter and derision in verse 4. They may laugh at God and his ways, but the Lord and his Messiah will have the last laugh. Verses 1-2 described the actions of the earthly kings, and verse 3 gave their speech. Now verses 4-5 describe the response of the heavenly King, and verse 6 gives his speech. Here is heaven's response to the arrogant earthlings. Hear the Father's roar from heaven's throne.

God Derides the Senseless Peoples (2:4-5)

God sits "enthroned" in heaven as sovereign Lord over all creation. He "laughs" and "ridicules" the foolish leaders of the earth and those who follow them. He is Lord over everything, and they are lords over nothing. He laughs and "holds them in derision" (ESV), in contempt. James Boice says, "He does not even rise from where he is sitting. He simply 'laughs' at these great imbeciles" (*Psalms 1–41*, 24).

In verse 5 God announces how he will deal with the rebels of the earth. He "speaks to them in his anger and terrifies them in his wrath" (cf. Rom 1:18-32). Horrifying judgment is on the way for all who trifle with this God.

God Declares His Sovereign Plan (2:6)

The rulers claim they will throw off the Lord's chains and sovereign rule over them (vv. 2-3). The Lord simply responds, "I have installed my king on Zion, my holy mountain." The ESV provides a strong contrastive: "As for me." The idea is, "They may do such and so, but as for me, I will do this" (Ross, *Psalms 1–41,* 206). The declaration "I have installed my king" is definitive and decisive. God has done this here and now, and it is fixed and settled. The place from which this king will rule is Mount Zion, the "holy mountain" on which David built his city and designated as the location for the temple. It is a holy mountain set apart by the Lord and for the worship of the Lord.

The rebellious and raging tribes of the earth may yell and scream, plot and plan, but God will see to it that a Davidic King will rule over the nations. Second Samuel 7:12-14 will come to pass. In those verses God said to David,

> *I will raise up after you your descendant, who will come from your body, and I will establish his kingdom. He is the one who will build a house for my name, and I will establish the throne of his kingdom forever. I will be his father, and he will be my son.*

God's promise to David cannot be thwarted.

See the Son Who Reigns with a Supreme Inheritance

PSALM 2:7-9

God's Messiah now responds to the nations who have rejected him and to the God who has chosen him. Hebrew kings, especially those in the Davidic lineage, used the language of adoption, indicating that their installation into the office of king placed them in a unique relationship to the God who sovereignly instated them. In this sense the words are figurative. Yet they take on a literal fulfillment in the greater Son, Jesus. What these Davidic kings were anticipating, the final King, the greatest son of David, would realize. In the fullest sense everything these words promise and foretell have come to fruition in Jesus the Messiah.

The Son Will Be Revealed to the Nations (2:7)

The divinely appointed King, God's Messiah, now declares the promise made to him by the Lord. "I will declare the LORD's decree. He said to Me, 'You are my Son; today I have become your Father'" (ESV, "I have begotten you"). This King has received a word from the Lord himself declaring a father-son relationship. This Davidic King is the Son of God by birth and by promise. In this psalm the Son repeats what God his Father told him. However, in Jesus's baptism, the Father declares from heaven for all creation to hear, "This is my beloved Son" (Matt 3:17; see Mark 1:11; Luke 3:22). But the voice from heaven does not stop. It adds "with whom I am well-pleased," echoing the words of Isaiah 42:1: "I delight in him." This statement is monumental. Jesus is the Lord's Anointed, the Messiah, the Christ. He is God's Son. And he is also the Servant of the Lord, the Suffering Servant of Isaiah's prophecy (see Isa 42; 49; 50; and especially 52:13–53:12). He will reign over a universal kingdom, but this kingdom does not come as one may expect. It is brought into existence by his suffering and work of redemption. Psalm 2 and Isaiah 42:1 are wed, and the portrait of the Messiah is filled out more fully and completely.

The phrase "today I have become your Father" is applied in the New Testament to our Lord's resurrection from the dead. Acts 13:33 interprets the resurrection as the Father's vindication of Jesus's divine sonship. Romans 1:3-4 declares that Jesus Christ is "our Lord, who was a descendant of David according to the flesh and was appointed to be the powerful Son of God . . . by the resurrection of the dead." Hebrews 1:5 unites the theme of resurrection with heavenly exaltation, quoting Psalm 2 with the same significance and declaring that in Christ's resurrection and exaltation, God has proclaimed the coronation of King Jesus who now sits at his right hand. Hebrews 5:5 further unites the kingly motif with the priestly one so that David's greater Son is now exalted and enthroned as a King-Priest, a Messiah-Priest, after the order of Melchizedek (cf. Ps 110). Here is the fulfillment of Ezekiel 34's "true shepherd," whom the Lord describes as "my servant David [who] will be a prince among them" (34:24). Here is the fulfillment of Isaiah 9:6-7:

> *For to us a child is born, to us a son is given. . . . Of the increase of his government and of peace there will be no end, on the throne of David and over his kingdom, to establish it and to uphold it with justice and*

> *with righteousness from this time forth and forevermore. The zeal of the* *Lord of hosts will do this.* (ESV)

"I have installed my king," says the Lord. Here is David's greater Son, God's Son, the Lord Jesus, established as the Lord's King now and forever.

The Son Will Rule over the Nations (2:8-9)

God tells his Son, "Ask of me, and I will make the nations your inheritance and the ends of the earth your possession." About those who oppose his Son, the Lord says, "You will break [or "rule"] them with an iron scepter; you will shatter them like pottery." The book of Revelation beautifully develops the themes and trajectories of Psalm 2. Because we are the people who trust and "take refuge" in the Son of God (2:12), Revelation 2:26-27 tells us we will share in his rule over the nations; Revelation 12:5 tells us this Son shares God's throne; and Revelation 19:11-16 tells us all of this will come to pass when the rider on a white horse, whose name is called "Faithful and True," returns as King over all kings and Lord over all lords. When he comes, his enemies will indeed be dashed like pieces of a potter's dry, clay vessel. Allen Ross observes about this imagery,

> This figure may be based on the Egyptian custom in which the name of each city under the king's dominion was written on a little votive jar and placed in the temple of his god. Then, if the people in a city rebelled, the pharaoh could smash that city's little jar in the presence of the deity. Such a symbolic act would terrify the rebellious—not that the city had much of a chance of withstanding the pharaoh in the first place. The psalmist may be drawing on that imagery to stress how easily the king, with all the authority of heaven behind him, will crush the rebellion swiftly. (*Psalms 1–41*, 210)

See the Blessed Who Respond to Salvation's Invitation

PSALM 2:10-12

The tragic destiny of all those who oppose the Lord's Messiah, who reject God's Son and his rule over them, provides the basis and motivation for our missionary and evangelism priorities. God's Son, the

Lord Jesus, will rule the nations. So the nations must know and be challenged to trust in God's Son the Lord Jesus. We must go. We must tell. We must warn.

Be Wise and Instructed by the Lord (2:10)

In the face of God's sovereign purpose (v. 6), plan (vv. 7-8), and power (v. 9), only one appropriate response exists according to David. Given that the kings and rulers of the earth were raging and plotting against God's Son, the psalmist addresses them specifically, though all persons should hear and heed these words. Irony hides here. Those who should be wise and well instructed are themselves viewed as inadequately wise and deficiently instructed. In light of the decreed purpose of God to honor, exalt, and prosper his righteous king (Ps 1:6), they should ("So now") "be wise" (act prudently) and "receive instruction." The "kings" and "judges" (ESV, "rulers") of the earth need to be educated like elementary schoolchildren. They need to be taught how to be wise decision makers so that they may be blessed and not destroyed. They need to become like the wise person of Psalm 1.

Serve and Rejoice for the Lord (2:11)

The wise person will worship and work for the Lord. He will serve him as he meditates on his law (1:2), and he will do so with a spirit of reverence. The title *servant of the Lord* is one of the greatest and most honored titles any of us can have. Our loyalty is to him and no other. He is our Lord and King, so we ought to serve him with fear ("reverential awe"). In our worship we must "rejoice with trembling" (with appropriate awe and respect), a holy adoration. We should not view worship as a pep rally for Jesus. The psalm does not call us to applaud God as if he were some cosmic performer. God is not one of our favorite sports teams! He is in a different category altogether. He is God. We must serve and rejoice. He is God. We should fear and tremble.

Honor and Trust in the Lord (2:12)

Verse 12 is an invitation to salvation. It is a call to be saved. It is universal in scope. It is personal in response. The wise and instructed in heart will "Pay homage to [ESV, "Kiss"] the Son." They will humble themselves and submit to his rightful lordship over their lives. They will indeed be like the blessed person of Psalm 1 because they put their trust in the

Son. In contrast, the wicked, like the ungodly of Psalm 1, will perish. The Son will be angry with them in judgment, and they will perish in the way (cf. 1:2). They did not heed the warning that "his anger may ignite at any moment" (NIV, "his wrath can flare up in a moment"; NLT, "in an instant").

Again we see a fork in the road. We see two lives, two ways to live and two ways to end. Those "who take refuge in him [the Lord] are happy." But those who refuse to bow the knee to his Son, King Jesus, will receive his anger and "will perish in [their] rebellion."

Conclusion

In Philippians 2:9-11 Paul speaks of God's exalted Messiah, the Lord Jesus Christ. The language is drawn from Isaiah 45:23, but the imagery is from Psalm 2. Philippians 2:10 says, "Every knee will bow." Psalm 2:12 says, "Kiss the Son" (ESV). What better place to begin than at his feet, in great gratitude for his salvation and sovereignty, his redemption and his reign. Kiss the Son and trust him. Kiss the Son and serve him. Kiss the Son and adore him. Bow the knee and kiss the Son.

Reflect and Discuss

1. How does placing a passage like Psalm 2 in the story line of Scripture help you understand the psalm better?
2. In what ways is your sin a rebellion against God, the King of heaven? In what ways do you minimize your sin instead of viewing it as rejecting God's authority?
3. Why does the psalmist say that the people plot "in vain"?
4. How does Psalm 2 emphasize the importance of walking like the "happy" one in Psalm 1?
5. If the wicked describe God's authority as "chains" and "ropes," how would the righteous describe God's authority? How could you explain to someone that God's authority is good?
6. Read Luke 6:44-45. What beliefs would be in these leaders' hearts that create their rebellion against God? How does this shape how you think of those who do not desire to submit to God?
7. Why is it important for Christians to remember that Jesus is their ultimate King? How would doing so shape how you think about your life in your current country? How would this shape how you interact with others across the world?

8. In what ways did Jesus live as the opposite of an anointed Messiah-King? Why did he do this?
9. How can God's rule over the earth give you confidence and peace in the midst of fear and uncertainty? How can it give you hope when earthly leaders do harm to you or others?
10. In what ways does Psalm 2 motivate us to go on mission with the gospel to the nations? How does Psalm 2 encourage us that God's mission will be accomplished?

When Your Enemies Are Too Many to Count

PSALM 3

Main Idea: The Lord cares about his people and will be their sustainer and Savior.

I. **Share Your Problem with God (3:1-2).**
   A. Tell the Lord what they do (3:1).
   B. Tell the Lord what they say (3:2).

II. **Shout Your Praise to God (3:3-4).**
   A. Exult in the character of God (3:3).
   B. Express your confidence in God (3:4).

III. **See Your Protection in God (3:5-8).**
   A. Trust the Lord to sustain you (3:5).
   B. Trust the Lord to strengthen you (3:6).
   C. Trust the Lord to save you (3:7-8).

We should not be surprised when we fight battles we cannot avoid. Sometimes the fighting is so fierce and the conflict so intense we are driven into the trenches. One of life's great blessings is to have company in the foxhole, people who will put their lives on the line for you and guard your back. Such friends are few, but they are a cherished possession. One of life's greatest disappointments and heartbreaks, however, is to be in that foxhole, receiving enemy fire, and to feel a sharp pain in your back. You turn and see that someone you were certain was a friend is actually an enemy who has just betrayed you. The disappointment is more than words can convey.

David felt such pain when his own son, Absalom, betrayed him (2 Sam 15–18). Absalom was a handsome and impressive figure. Second Samuel 14:25 says, "He did not have a single flaw." No doubt his parents were proud of him. He showed tremendous promise. He was loved by his father David; even after Absalom murdered his own half-brother Amnon for raping their sister Tamar (2 Sam 13), David forgave him and grew once again to trust him (2 Sam 14:33). Absalom, however, had a plan to revolt against David. Second Samuel 15:6 says, "So Absalom stole the hearts of the men of Israel." Absalom led a successful palace coup against David, who was forced to abdicate the throne and flee Jerusalem. The Bible says he wept and went barefoot as he fled (2 Sam 15:30). He also endured ridicule and rock pelting from a man named Shimei (2 Sam 16:5-14). And worst of all, his own son sought to take his life. During this tremendous trial and test of faith, David penned this psalm of lament.

This psalm displays one of the most painful hours of David's life. Being rich, famous, powerful, and influential did not keep David from problems and difficulties. He is running for his life. What can David do? What should we do when the shadow of death crosses our horizons and all seems lost? We can do only one thing: trust in the Lord and call out to him with confidence that he will deliver us.

Share Your Problem with God

PSALM 3:1-2

Psalm 3 is the first psalm with a superscription providing information about its context and occasion for writing. It is also the first psalm of lament, and it is the natural extension of Psalms 1 and 2 (Ross, *Psalms 1–41,* 216). Psalm 1 contrasted the righteous with the ungodly. Psalm 2 contrasted the righteous, anointed Son and the Lord with the wicked kings and rulers and those who follow them. Now the Davidic king is alone, faced with innumerable enemies that include family and friends. Interestingly, the promise of Psalm 2:12 is tragically fulfilled in the death of Absalom as recorded in 2 Samuel 18:14-15 (Cole, "Psalm 3," 4–5).

David is fleeing for his life. Finding a quiet moment of rest, David turns to God and pours out his heart in prayer. He does not invoke the general name for God (*Elohim*); instead, he uses the personal covenantal name *Yahweh* (LORD).

Tell the Lord What They Do (3:1)

"LORD, how my foes increase! There are many who attack me." David's numbers appear to be shrinking while those of his enemies multiply. His foes are increasing and rising up against him. David feels attacked from every side. Escape appears impossible. Everywhere he turns and everywhere he looks, he sees the enemy. Importantly, he tells the Lord about his troubles. He knows the Lord cares, so he brings his trials to him.

Tell the Lord What They Say (3:2)

David's adversaries are active (v. 1), and they are harsh (v. 2). The "many" of verse 1 are now the "many" of verse 2 who claim God is against David. "There is no help [ESV, "salvation"] for him in God." No doubt this attack wounded David deeply. Maybe he even wondered if what they were saying were true. He had murdered Uriah and stolen his wife Bathsheba (2 Sam 11–12). His family life was a disaster. A daughter raped, a son murdered, and now a son seeking to take his life. Perhaps this was God's judgment. Perhaps God had abandoned David. That is certainly what his enemies were saying. It is not, however, what God had said. Despite his sin, he was still God's anointed king, a king who had owned his sin and sought the Lord's forgiveness (see Pss 33; 51). These opponents of David may have fooled themselves into believing God was on their side as they sought to displace and remove his chosen servant. However, if you read 2 Samuel, Absalom and his enablers had violated the law of God, engaged in subterfuge, advocated immorality, and now wanted to murder the Lord's Anointed (2:2), God's king whom he had set on his holy mountain Zion (2:6). Treachery can happen in any life. People you think are your friends will betray you. When they do, check your heart, take an inventory of your actions, and give your problem to God.

Verse 2 ends with "*Selah*," as do verses 4 and 8. The word occurs seventy-one times in Psalms, but its precise meaning is not clear. It perhaps served as a musical interlude or marker (VanGemeren, *Psalms*, 65). The idea is perhaps to pause for a moment so you can carefully consider what you just read or sang.

Shout Your Praise to God

PSALM 3:3-4

David's complaint now takes a 180-degree turn. He gets biblical and theological. He takes his eyes off his enemies and directs his gaze to the power and promise of God. Despair gives way to confidence as he recalls and remembers who God is and what God is like.

Exult in the Character of God (3:3)

"But you" is a strong adversative, a powerful point of contrast. They may say, "There is no help for him in God," but David knows that the

"LORD" (*Yahweh*) is a "shield" around him, his "glory," and the one who lifts his head.

The word *shield* speaks of God as David's protector, and the image is repeatedly used in the Psalms (7:10; 18:2,30; 28:7; 33:20; 59:11; 84:9, 11; 91:4; 115:9-11; 119:114; 144:2). David, perhaps, recalled God's words to his forefather in Genesis 15:1: "Do not be afraid Abram. I am your shield; your reward will be very great" (see also Deut 33:29). What a blessing to know the command and promise of Ephesians 6:16: "In every situation take up the shield of faith with which you can extinguish all the flaming arrows of the evil one." The Lord is David's shield. He is also his "glory." Any praise and honor he possesses have come from the Lord. His own glory is worthless and useless. No, his glory and esteem are in the Lord. "The one who lifts up my head" informs us that David had a droopy head—a depressed, downcast countenance. The Lord, however, could fix that. Absalom had brought him shame and embarrassment. David fled from his throne with his head hanging down and his tail between his legs. Apart from the Lord, he was not much, but with the Lord, his honor, dignity, and reputation as God's man would be restored (cf. Jas 4:10). Ross writes, "God is the one who would exalt him. . . . The king knew that he would return to the royal city with head held high" (*Psalms 1–41*, 222).

Express Your Confidence in God (3:4)

David prayed, and he prayed hard! This verse and those that follow reveal God's answer to his prayer. It will take the form of a testimony. "To the LORD," he cried aloud. He is not ashamed if anyone overhears his desperate plea.

David received an answer from God's "holy mountain," the place God installed him as king (see 2:6). The people plot, the kings set themselves against him, and the rulers conspire. Even his own son joined their ranks and sought his ruin, but the Lord set him as king. The Lord laughs at and derides those who oppose him and his anointed. God made a promise to him, and God always keeps his word. David may have doubted, but no more! He cried; God heard. What more does he need? *Selah.*

See Your Protection in God

PSALM 3:5-8

The Bible promises us a peace "which surpasses all understanding" (Phil 4:7). Indeed, it says this peace "will guard [our] hearts and minds in Christ Jesus." David received this peace from the Lord. His response is both amazing and instructive.

Trust the Lord to Sustain You (3:5)

David went to sleep! Enemies are all around. His own son is seeking to murder him. David would tell us to read Psalm 121:3. Nothing needs to keep us awake at night because the Lord never slumbers. He can keep watch, and we can sleep! And what happened? David says, "I wake again because the Lord sustains me." A safe night's sleep was a sign, a pledge from the Lord, that he would protect and provide for David. If he will keep us safe through the night, he will keep us safe through this day as well.

Trust the Lord to Strengthen You (3:6)

The "many" of verses 1-2 are now the "thousands" (NIV, "tens of thousands") of verse 6. They are everywhere. David says they "have taken their stand against me on every side." David, however, after a good night's rest, begins his day by remembering the promises of God:

- The Lord is my shield (v. 3).
- The Lord hears my prayers (v. 4).
- The Lord sustains me (v. 5).

Trust the Lord to Save You (3:7-8)

Now comes David's actual petition. True to the form of most lament psalms, it includes a prayer for God to arise and a prayer for God to deliver (Ross, *Psalms 1–41,* 225). "Rise up, Lord!" is a prayer for God to come to the aid of his people in power and glory. The poetic parallelism is beautiful and balanced: "Save me, my God!"

David is so confident of God's rescue that he uses "a prophetic perfect." The perfect tense in Hebrew is generally translated with the past tense in English. The Lord's future vindication of his servant David is so certain that he can write as if it has already happened (Ross, *Psalms 1–41,*

226). Again, there is poetic parallelism as David's enemies, pictured as wild and dangerous animals, are described as receiving a crushing blow from the Lord: "You strike all my enemies on the cheek; you break the teeth of the wicked." He will smack the jaw and smash the teeth of the ungodly who have walked the path of the sinners of Psalm 1:1 and who have refused to kiss the Son of Psalm 2:12 (Cole, "Psalm 3," 9). All of this is God's doing. He may choose to use men or even "the tangled branches of a large oak" that captured Absalom's hair and ended his life and rebellion (2 Sam 18:9-15).

Like Jonah (2:9), David proclaims, "Salvation belongs to the LORD." Joining with Psalms 1:1 and 2:12, this third song affirms the blessing of the Lord on his people: "May your blessing be on your people." *Selah.* Yes, "the Lord knows the way of the righteous, but the way of the ungodly shall perish" (Ps 1:6 NKJV).

Conclusion

King David lay down to sleep with death all around him, but by God's grace he awoke and was restored to his throne on the holy hill of Zion. It is amazing that David's greater Son, the Lord Jesus, also lay down to sleep with death all around him. This Davidic King also cried to the Lord ("It is finished") and was heard ("Into your hands I commend my spirit"). Yes, he lay down and slept in death. Then he awoke! And he has been restored to his throne at the right hand of the Majesty on high (Heb 1:3). When your enemies are too many to count, cry out to our Lord. He heard David. He heard Jesus. He will hear you and me as well. With David we can rejoice and say, "Salvation, deliverance, rescue, it all belongs to the Lord. Your blessing truly is on your people."

Reflect and Discuss

1. Describe the various parts of David's prayer of lament. How are each of these important components of our prayers?
2. What does the psalm's encouragement to lament teach us about the character of God? What does it teach us about the power of God?
3. Have you ever told your problems to others without telling them to the Lord? If so, why? What often prevents you from telling the Lord about what is happening in your life?

4. Do you believe the Lord cares about you and desires to help you? How do Christians defeat the temptation to believe the taunt, "There is no salvation for him in God"?
5. Describe a time when you doubted God would help you. Did his help come? What did you learn about God during that time?
6. How should Christians respond to friends who betray them?
7. How can David have confidence in God (v. 6) when he is in the middle of such distress? What promises does Scripture give that provide the foundation of our confidence in God?
8. How can choosing to sleep be a form of trust and faith in the Lord? What does sleeping teach us about our abilities compared to God's abilities?
9. According to this psalm, what is our responsibility when we are betrayed and attacked? What is God's responsibility? What happens when we confuse our responsibilities with God's?
10. In what ways did Jesus show his trust in God when enemies were around him? How could he have been tempted to doubt God?

Now I Lay Me Down to Sleep

PSALM 4

Main Idea: God hears and gives rest to those who call on him with humility and faith.

I. **God Answers the Prayers of the Hurting (4:1).**
   A. God will act righteously.
   B. God will give relief.
II. **God Honors the Pure in Heart (4:2-5).**
   A. Avoid that which is shameful (4:2).
   B. Claim that which is sure (4:3).
   C. Flee that which is sinful (4:4).
   D. Sacrifice that which is sincere (4:5).
III. **God Prospers the Hopeful (4:6-7).**
   A. Seek the Lord's presence (4:6).
   B. Celebrate the Lord's provisions (4:7).
IV. **God Gives Peace to the Humble (4:8).**
   A. The humble rest in the Lord.
   B. The humble trust in the Lord.

Psalm 127:2 says, "He [the Lord] gives sleep to the one he loves." Eugene Peterson paraphrases it: "Don't you know he enjoys giving rest to those he loves?" (MSG). Sleep is a gift from the Lord. However, how often have you missed out on this gift? How often have you tossed and turned, stared at the darkness of the ceiling, or poured your tears into your pillow because insomnia enslaved you? People fail to get a good night's rest for many reasons. Physiological and personal issues can make us restless. But many times a spiritual reason keeps us awake. At least, that is what Psalm 4 would indicate.

Psalm 4 is an evening psalm and possibly a companion to Psalm 3. We can appropriately pray Psalm 3 when we get up (3:5). And we can appropriately pray Psalm 4 before we lie down (4:8). It is another psalm of lament, but it also has components of the psalms of trust or confidence (Ross, *Psalms 1–41*, 231). Although David aches with hurt, he expresses confidence that the Lord will not abandon him in his distress.

The Lord will restore him and bless him. The rebellion and treason of Absalom may again be in the background as it was in Psalm 3. Alec Motyer writes, "David is facing a second night under the stars! Allowing Absalom's forces another twenty-four hours to pursue and attack; therefore, increased threat!" (*Psalms by the Day,* 16). Because David believes God is a righteous God (v. 1) who has set him apart (v. 3), he will trust the Lord (v. 5), seek his face (v. 6), trust in his provisions (v. 7), and lie down for a good night's sleep knowing the Lord will keep him safe (v. 8).

God Answers the Prayers of the Hurting

PSALM 4:1

David is experiencing a grim time, as he makes clear in verses 2, 4, and 6. Circumstances beyond his control have overwhelmed him. He knows he can only look in one direction for help, and so he does. He looks to God. What does he know about the God to whom he prays?

God Will Act Righteously

Twice in this verse David asks God to hear him: "Answer me when I call . . . hear my prayer." He calls on the "God, who vindicates [him]" or "[his] righteous God" (NIV). God is righteous in his character and in his conduct. David focuses on the latter here. He can trust God to do the righteous thing, the right thing, on behalf of his people. Because the Lord has set us apart for himself (v. 3), we can be confident he will hear our cry and vindicate us. Sometimes we can see this vindication outwardly. Other times this vindication appears inwardly with peace, sleep, and security (v. 8).

God Will Give Relief

Psychological, physical, or spiritual distress (pressure)—perhaps all the above!—has put David under "affliction." The word for "affliction" or "distress" (ESV) implies being in a "tight corner" (Kidner, *Psalms 1–72,* 56). David finds himself in a tight spot, a tough spot. By a series of requests, he pours out his heart to the Lord, asking him for help. He presents his requests with confidence because he has experienced God's deliverance in the past. He makes five requests: answer me, vindicate me, free me, be gracious to me, and hear my prayer. David needs God to bring him some space. He needs from God what he knows he does not deserve: grace and mercy. Because he is God's child, he can call out to him. Because he is God's child, he can be confident that God will hear him and that he will receive mercy and experience relief. If you are his child, you have the same promise.

God Honors the Pure in Heart

PSALM 4:2-5

David is in trouble. Psalm 3 addressed physical danger. Psalm 4 describes personal slander. His enemies drag his reputation through the mud. People from every direction question his integrity. In a strange turn, David addresses his enemies. He asks them to examine their motives and actions. He challenges them to follow him in repentance from sin and to trust in the Lord (the name *Yahweh*, "the LORD," appears five times in vv. 3-8). His enemies could become his friends if they would listen to his counsel. David provides a four-part strategy for those who, having their sin exposed, now hunger for a pure heart.

Avoid That Which Is Shameful (4:2)

David raises a series of rhetorical questions designed to expose the shameful actions of his opponents. "Exalted ones," literally "sons of a man," refers to "men of high degree . . . distinguished and influential people" (Ross, *Psalms 1–41*, 235). These are prominent citizens, the powerful in Israel, the movers and shakers. The leadership has gotten on the wrong track, and David specifies their error. First, they have "insulted" the "honor" of God's anointed (Ps 2). They have despised the Lord's king and the glory, honor, and weightiness given to him by God. Second, they "love what is worthless" (ESV, "vain words") and "pursue a lie" (v. 2). Whenever we challenge God's plan and purposes, we chase after that which is false, worthless, and delusional. Before long, we traffic in lies, dishonoring God and deceiving ourselves. We slander those we envy. Such activity is foolish. It is shameful.

Claim That Which Is Sure (4:3)

The ways of the ungodly shall perish (1:6), but the way of the Lord is set apart and sure. "Know that the LORD has set apart the faithful [ESV, "godly"] for himself" (v. 3). Spurgeon says we are "*set apart* as God's own peculiar treasure" (*Treasury*, 35; emphasis in original). The Lord knows the faithful and godly person intimately; he has a personal fellowship with him. Because we belong to the Lord, we can be confident that "the LORD will hear when [we] call."

How beautiful are the sure things of verse 3 when contrasted with the uncertain things of verse 2! We belong to the Lord who hears us when we pray. Ultimately, the enemy cannot defeat us. The enemy will not succeed against us regardless of what he says or does.

Flee That Which Is Sinful (4:4)

Sometimes our feelings and emotions run high and out of control. David describes his enemies as wild animals in Psalm 3:7, and their rage and anger manifest here. What do we do when our temperatures rise, our necks get hot, and our cheeks flush with passion? David says, "Be angry and do not sin" (cf. Eph 4:26). "Tremble" (NASB) and do not sin. Get control of yourself. Bite your tongue. Better yet, get alone with God and let him deal with your heart. "On your bed, reflect in your heart and be still" (HCSB). Alone and undistracted, be still (NIV, "silent"), resting and listening to the Lord (cf. the wicked on their beds in Ps 36:4; Mic 2:1).

Getting quietly alone with God will clear our heads, remove the fog, and calm the angry and restless waves of our hearts. It puts us in a position where we can see our sin as God sees it. It is always wise to sleep on things before acting, no matter what it is. *Selah!* Pause and meditate on that.

Sacrifice That Which Is Sincere (4:5)

David now issues a call to action. "Offer sacrifices in righteousness and trust in the LORD." Right sacrifices come from a right heart. As Psalm 51:17 teaches, "The sacrifice pleasing to God is a broken [humble] spirit. You will not despise a broken and humbled heart, God." Our righteous God (v. 1) requires righteous sacrifices. Such sacrifices, whether ritual or practical, must be sincere. They can only come from those who "trust in the LORD."

Individual pursuits now give way to what is right before the Lord. Personal agendas must be set aside as worthless and false (v. 2). God's agenda must now become our agenda. Even if we do not fully grasp his plan and purposes, we must trust him and serve him from the heart and with sacrificial acts that agree with his character and his commands. It may not always be easy, but it will always be right (cf. Rom 12:2).

God Prospers the Hopeful

PSALM 4:6-7

Sometimes God's people become confused or depressed when hopes and expectations fail to materialize. We begin to question ourselves, our leaders, and even God. David certainly knew this truth. Those following him began to ask these questions. David responds with wonderful counsel. The wisdom he shares could not be more perfect.

Seek the Lord's Presence (4:6)

A large number ("many") are asking a good question given their difficult and troubling circumstances (vv. 2,4a): "Who can show us anything good?" With a downcast and defeatist attitude, the spiritual pessimists were questioning their leader and their Lord's goodness. David responds with a simple and direct prayer: "Let the light of your face shine on us, LORD." David draws from the great Aaronic benediction, which says, "May the LORD bless you and protect you; may the LORD make his face shine on you and be gracious to you; may the LORD look with favor on you and give you peace" (Num 6:24-26).

The phrase *light of your face* speaks of God's personal presence in "his covenantal blessings" (VanGemeren, *Psalms*, 111). David asks God to be faithful to his promises and to be faithful in the fullest measure. The Lord set him apart, so David trusts him. He simply asks the Lord to let him experience the blessing that he knows belongs to him by divine promise. We can ask the Lord to lift us up (3:3) and to let us see his face in glorious radiance and brilliance. Then we will see clearly once more that he is all we need.

Celebrate the Lord's Provision (4:7)

The presence of the Lord is all we need, and it is better than anything else we could ever hope for in this life. It puts abundant joy in our hearts. Basking in his presence gives "more joy" than all the material blessings this world could offer.

Using imagery his audience would find familiar, David says that an outstanding grain harvest and a remarkable abundance of wine pale in comparison to what people receive when the face of the Lord shines on them. Calvin says, "The sum is, that he had more satisfaction in seeing the reconciled countenance of God beaming upon him, than if he had possessed garners full of corn, and cellars full of wine" (*Psalms 1–35*, 48–49).

God Gives Peace to the Humble

PSALM 4:8

David has talked to God. He was with the Lord, he knelt in his presence, and he knows he has the Lord's favor. Nothing remains for him to do but to lie down for a good night's sleep. His enemies may attack him, but his Lord remains on his side. As Paul says in Romans 8:31, "If God is for us, who is against us?"

The Humble Rest in the Lord

We are set apart for the Lord. We plead for his mercy and put our trust in him. No matter what happens around us, we can "both lie down and sleep in peace." Our enemies may struggle on their beds (v. 4), but we can sleep on ours. They may lie awake in anger, but we can sleep with a peace that surpasses understanding because we trust in the Lord (v. 5).

The Humble Trust in the Lord

Our security cannot come from wealth or wisdom, position, or possessions. We are not safe if it depends on our efforts alone. We are only safe in the Lord. As David writes, "You alone, LORD, make me live in safety." Locked doors, security systems, and bodyguards will ultimately prove inadequate. Our safety comes from the Lord who will never leave us or abandon us (Heb 13:5). Our safety and security are found in a Savior who said, "I give them eternal life, and they will never perish. No one will snatch them out of my hand" (John 10:28). We are safe. We can sleep.

Conclusion

A sweet, little rhyme many of us learned as children says,

> Now I lay me down to sleep,
> I pray the Lord my soul to keep.
> If I should die before I wake,
> I pray the Lord my soul to take.

Considering the truths found in Psalm 4, I suggest slightly adjusting the rhyme:

> Now I lay me down to sleep,
> I *trust* the Lord my soul to keep.
> If I should die before I wake,
> I *trust* the Lord my soul to take.
> *I can trust him when I sleep.*
> *I can trust him when I die.*
> *I can trust him when attacked.*
> *I can trust him because I am his*
> *and he is mine.*

Go now and get a good night's sleep.

Reflect and Discuss

1. Does David *have to* ask God to "answer" him or "hear" him? Why does he pray in this way?
2. Describe a time when you could not sleep because of a spiritual reason. Why did this issue keep you sleepless? What did you learn about God and yourself from this experience?
3. Why does David habitually appeal to God's righteous character and conduct when he prays? Is this habit a part of your prayers? Why or why not?
4. Do you desire that your enemies trust God and repent? How should God's grace and mercy on you influence how you think about and pray for your enemies?
5. Why would a person "love what is worthless" or "pursue a lie"? In what ways have you seen Scripture change your view of sin from *valuable* to *worthless* and from *truth* to a *lie*?
6. Compare Psalm 3:2 with 4:3. What do these verses teach you about the necessity of reminding ourselves of God's promises in Scripture?
7. How can one be angry and yet not sin? Have you seen anyone exemplify this?
8. David draws near to God with sacrifices (v. 5). In what ways are you tempted to run from God during difficulties? Why should difficulties cause us to run *to* instead of *away from* God?
9. Why is God's presence all we need (v. 6)? And why is it the best thing we could ever hope for?
10. Why is it amazing that God listens to and answers our prayers?

How to Begin Each Day in a Good Way

PSALM 5

Main Idea: Because our righteous God cares for his people with promises of protection, we should begin each day seeking him, obeying his Word, and praising his name.

I. Talk to the Lord in Prayer (5:1-3).
- A. Seek the Lord in meditation (5:1-2).
- B. Seek the Lord in the morning (5:3).

II. See the Lord Evaluate the Wicked (5:4-6).
- A. God is displeased with them (5:4).
- B. God will not dwell with them (5:4).
- C. God will dishonor them (5:5).
- D. God disdains them (5:5).
- E. God will destroy them (5:6).
- F. God despises them (5:6).

III. Follow the Lord in His Righteous Ways (5:7-8).
- A. Pursue the worship of the Lord (5:7).
- B. Pursue the ways of the Lord (5:8).

IV. Watch the Lord Deal with the Rebellious (5:9-10).
- A. They are unfaithful with their speech (5:9).
- B. They are uncontrollable in their sin (5:10).

V. Shout to the Lord with Joy (5:11-12).
- A. Trust the Lord and he will protect you (5:11).
- B. Love the Lord and he will bless you (5:11-12).

Often we encounter people who have what I (Danny) call "a partly cloudy disposition with thunderstorms on the horizon." They are angry and discouraged. Concerning these kinds of people, we have created a popular saying: "He must have woken up on the wrong side of the bed this morning." In other words, such a person began the day in a bad way instead of a good way, and it has stayed with him or her all day long.

David knew it was important to begin each day in a good way. He also knew the best way to start each day is with prayer. Psalms 3–6 have prayers for the morning and evening. Psalm 3 is a morning prayer, and

Psalm 4 is an evening prayer. Psalm 5 is another morning prayer (v. 3), and Psalm 6 is another evening prayer (6:6). From the rising of the sun to its setting, a believer's entire day should be bathed in prayer.

In this morning prayer, David seeks the Lord with great intensity. The wicked oppose David and would harm him. Perhaps the background of Psalm 5, like Psalms 3–4, is the rebellion of Absalom (Motyer, *Psalms by the Day*, 15–18). David combines elements of lament and confidence. We see him asking for guidance in the midst of his enemies and their slander (vv. 8-9). This psalm gives us five morning-prayer principles as we start each day with the Lord, principles that can be summarized with five imperatives: talk, see, follow, watch, and shout.

Talk to the Lord in Prayer

PSALM 5:1-3

As the day begins, David turns his face to the Lord (*Yahweh*) in prayer. He addresses him both personally and respectfully: "my King and my God." The one we approach is "I AM WHO I AM" (Exod 3:14), the King, the one true and living God. How do we talk to such a great God?

Seek the Lord in Meditation (5:1-2)

The psalm begins with a trio of parallel imperatives: "listen," "consider," and "pay attention." David describes his prayer as "my words," "my sighing," and "the sound of my cry." "Sighing" can connote the idea of quiet murmuring, whispering to oneself or others. James Boice notes,

> Most often we pray by words. That is, we express ourselves in proper, well-reasoned terminology. Sometimes we are in such distress that our prayers are only desperate cries for God to help us. At still other times we cannot find words adequate to express our feelings or voice what we need, though we are nevertheless still praying. But here is the encouraging thing: God hears all kinds of prayers. (*Psalms 1–41*, 46)

Seek the Lord in the Morning (5:3)

At the beginning of each day, we should seek in prayer the one who is our King and our God. The phrase "in the morning" is repeated for emphasis. We should start the day in the presence of our Lord, King, and God.

Verse 3 ends with "I . . . watch expectantly." The NKJV translates it, "I will look up." The NIV has "I . . . wait in expectation," while the NASB has "I . . . watch." David says that we are to begin each day pleading with the Lord and presenting ourselves in prayer. We can eagerly expect that the Lord (*Yahweh*) himself will receive our prayers. Because he is our King and our God and because we are his faithful servants who seek an audience with him as each day begins, we can know that he will hear our prayers. What a wise and encouraging way to begin the day!

See the Lord Evaluate the Wicked

PSALM 5:4-6

Verses 4-6 contrast starkly with verses 1-3. Again, the righteous person and the wicked person of Psalm 1 appear in sharp opposition. God will hear one, but he hates the other. Six striking statements in these verses expose God's perspective on the wicked.

God Is Displeased with Them (5:4)

Our God does not delight in wickedness. He takes zero pleasure in evil. A holy God, who is just and righteous in who he is and in all that he does, has no pleasure in the wicked person. Such a person is seen as wicked in both character and conduct. Psalm 34:21 says such persons "hate the righteous." God is displeased with them.

God Will Not Dwell with Them (5:4)

"Evil [ones] cannot dwell" with our God. Even a temporary visit with him is impossible and out of the question. As Habakkuk 1:13 says of the Lord, "Your eyes are too pure to look on evil." Evil will never be welcomed or at home with God.

God Will Dishonor Them (5:5)

In verse 5 David focuses on "the boastful," the proud and "arrogant" (NIV). The haughty will not have an audience in God's sight (lit. "before your eyes"). The prideful and arrogant will never enjoy a face-to-face encounter with the Lord. They will only stand before him in judgment.

God Disdains Them (5:5)

The last phrase of verse 5 may catch us by surprise. It says our loving and gracious God "hates all evildoers." These words take my breath away. The God who loved the world (John 3:16) hates. This verse emphasizes actions done by the wicked. In their essence and essential being as imagers of God, the Lord loves his human creatures. But when they function as workers of evil and wickedness, God has nothing but wrath, righteous anger, for them. The wisdom of Proverbs 6:16-19 can help us understand this psalm since it also focuses on wicked actions. There we read,

> *The LORD hates six things; in fact, seven are detestable to him: arrogant eyes, a lying tongue, hands that shed innocent blood, a heart that plots wicked schemes, feet eager to run to evil, a lying witness who gives false testimony, and one who stirs up trouble among brothers.*

Sam Storms reminds us, "Have you considered that to pray 'Thy kingdom come' (Matt 6:10) is to invoke divine judgment on all other kingdoms and all those who oppose the reign of God?" ("Those Troubling Psalms of Imprecation"). James Adams adds, "When we pray as Jesus taught us, we cry out to God for his blessings upon his church and for his curses upon the kingdom of the evil one" (*War Psalms*, 52). Finally, Steve Lawson's comment is also helpful: "God rejects all who reject him. This is a Hebraism that contrasts love and hate, which communicates acceptance and rejection" (*Psalms*, 38). Jesus said it this way in Luke 14:26:

> *"If anyone comes to me and does not hate his own father and mother, wife and children, brothers and sisters—yes, and even his own life—he cannot be my disciple."*

To truly love God is to reject all that is evil. God hates sin, and so should we.

God Will Destroy Them (5:6)

Verse 6 addresses sins of the tongue again. Verse 5 addressed boastful and arrogant talkers. Here it is liars. The Lord will "destroy those who tell lies." Those who slander and speak falsely reveal the nature of their hearts through their tongues. God will not entertain them. He will not allow their wicked words to go unpunished. Simply put, he will destroy them in righteous, holy, and just judgment.

God Despises Them (5:6)

Our Lord (*Yahweh*) abhors "violent and treacherous people," both the bloodthirsty (lit. "the man of blood") and the deceitful. The bloodthirsty murder with their hands. The deceitful murder with their tongues. Both are violent and treacherous acts. The Lord hates and will destroy all who live lives of such evil and wickedness.

Follow the Lord in His Righteous Ways

PSALM 5:7-8

The word *but* in verse 7 places verses 7-8 in strong opposition to verses 4-6. David returns to discuss the one who seeks the Lord in prayer (vv. 1-3). We discover he is also the one who seeks the Lord's house, his mercy, and his guidance. The Lord will take pleasure in this kind of person.

Pursue the Worship of the Lord (5:7)

David says, "But I enter your house" and "I bow down toward your holy temple." Because the temple had not yet been built, Derek Kidner suggests it's possible "that David's language has been adapted to the use of later worshipers" (*Psalms 1–72*, 59). David comes, as should we, to the place where God's people come together. When the people of God gather for corporate worship, the gathering ministers to the heart and soul of a person. David says we find "the abundance of your [the Lord's] faithful love," which is also translated as "the multitude of thy mercy" (KJV), "abundant lovingkindness" (NASB 1995), and "abundance of your steadfast love" (ESV). "Faithful love" is the Hebrew word *chesed*. Finding himself to be the recipient of such undeserved mercy, David says that he will worship ("bow down") in humility and respect ("in reverential awe") toward the place where the Lord manifests himself ("your holy temple"). Only by mercy may we approach God. Only in worship should we draw near to God.

Pursue the Ways of the Lord (5:8)

We can—we should!—ask the Lord (*Yahweh*) to lead us. Because he is a God who takes no pleasure in, will not give an audience to, will not allow to stand, hates, will destroy, and abhors wickedness and all evil, we can be confident he will lead us in righteousness, in the right way, and along the right path. When we are faced with opposition and confronted by enemies who would do us harm, we can ask him to make his way straight before us. We can ask him to guide us around spiritual booby traps, theological quicksand, and personal land mines. We can ask him to keep us on a path that is straight, a path of integrity, honesty, and humility. We can ask him to direct us away from wickedness and evil (v. 4), pride and rebellion (v. 5), lies, murder, and deception (v. 6).

Watch the Lord Deal with the Rebellious

PSALM 5:9-10

David again addresses the wicked. Now he writes about the sins of the mouth, the evil words that flow from an evil heart. These people may be David's enemies (v. 8), but their sin and rebellion are ultimately against God.

They Are Unfaithful with Their Speech (5:9)

Concerning the wicked, David says, "There is nothing reliable in what they say." The NIV translates the first line, "Not a word from their mouth can be trusted." Eugene Petersen in *The Message* writes, "Every word they speak is a land mine; their lungs breathe out poison gas. Their throats are gaping graves, their tongues slick as mudslides." They are dishonest and destructive in their words. Death comes from their hearts and through their throats. The words are smooth and flattering, but their end leads to death and the graveyard. Paul cites this verse in Romans 3:13 in his catalog of sins that makes the case for the depravity of people and the wickedness of the human heart apart from God's saving grace. How often our tongues reveal the condition of our hearts.

They Are Uncontrollable in Their Sin (5:10)

David calls on the Lord for a judicial verdict of guilty: "Punish them, God." The evidence is overwhelming. Not only should God condemn them, but also their own counsel or "schemes" (NASB 1995, "devices") bring them down. Their judgment is divinely enacted and self-inflicted. Sin does its job on them. Sin begets sin. Because of "their many crimes," the "abundance of their transgressions" (ESV), they are cast out (NIV, "banished"). They have rebelled against God! Therefore, the Lord will condemn them in final judgment.

Shout to the Lord with Joy

PSALM 5:11-12

The perspective of those who seek God in prayer, cling to his mercy, and seek his guidance appears again in verses 11-12. These final verses, like the ones at the beginning of the psalm, look to the Lord. They consider the blessings that come to those who approach Yahweh as their King and their God. They can "rejoice"; indeed, they can "shout for joy forever."

Trust the Lord and He Will Protect You (5:11)

Those who put their trust in the Lord are called to rejoice. Why? Because the Lord will "shelter them." He will defend, protect, and "spread his protection" (NIV) over them. Those who trust the Lord can trust him to be their refuge, their divine protector. Like a great eagle spreading her wings over her young, so our great God and King spreads his covering of protection over those who seek him in prayer, depend on his mercy, ask for his guidance, and trust in his protection.

Love the Lord and He Will Bless You (5:12)

Those who trust the Lord and rejoice in his protection also love his name and see him as their shield (cf. 3:3). Because they love his name, they love him for who he is. They are joyful. They "boast" or "exult" (NASB 1995) in the Lord (v. 11). Because they love the one who is righteous (v. 8), they will pursue righteousness. This is the place of divine blessing. Such blessing is to be surrounded with God's favor like a shield, one that provides 360-degree protection.

Conclusion

Our God, our King, cares for his people with faithful love, with promises of guidance and protection. So we should seek him as we begin each day. We should talk to him in prayer. We should follow his righteous ways. We should shout to the Lord with joy because we love his name, that name that is above every name—the name of Jesus my Lord (see Phil 2:9-11).

Reflect and Discuss

1. What role does the time of day have in our spiritual devotions? What advantages does the morning offer? What prevents you from

seeking the Lord in the morning? How could you prioritize seeking him?

2. Boice says, "God hears all kinds of prayers" (*Psalms 1–41*). Do you ever set unhelpful expectations for the prayers you pray? What does this reveal about your view of God? How does the gospel give us freedom as we pray?
3. What is the difference between a *hateful* God and a God who *hates* wickedness? What is the object of God's anger? How is God's hate different from how people hate?
4. How does God's holiness shape his anger for the wicked and his pleasure for the righteous?
5. Why should the wicked care about dwelling in God's presence (v. 4)?
6. Should Christians hate the wicked? What all should you consider when it comes to having anger?
7. How should this psalm's focus on the words of the wicked serve as a warning to you? Why does God hate wicked words? What does the New Testament teach about the source of one's words?
8. Why does the psalm view boastfulness as wicked? What is the difference between the boasting of the wicked (v. 5) and the boasting of the righteous (v. 11)?
9. Why is the corporate gathering important for God's people? How does God's "faithful love" serve as the foundation for the gathering?
10. How does God promise to bless the righteous?

Trusting God When You Cannot Find Him

PSALM 6

Main Idea: When God is silent, cry out to him with honest prayers and rest on his mercy, knowing he loves to answer his people's prayers.

I. Ask God to Be Gracious While He Is Silent (6:1-3).
II. Ask God for Deliverance Because of His Faithful Love (6:4-5).
III. Ask God to Hear Your Cries and See Your Tears (6:6-7).
IV. Ask God to Accept Your Prayers and Handle Your Enemies (6:8-10).

Adoniram Judson is one of my (Danny's) missionary heroes. Following the deaths of his wife Ann and daughter Maria, Judson dug an empty grave, sat by it, and stared into it for days. Three years after his wife's death, he would write, "God is to me the Great Unknown. I believe in him, but I find him not" (Anderson, *To the Golden Shore*, 391).

Psalm 6 is the first of the seven "penitential psalms" (Pss 6; 32; 38; 51; 102; 130; 143) (Kidner, *Psalms 1–72*, 60). VanGemeren says David prays "in deep anguish" (*Psalms*, 123). Motyer describes the psalm as one of "deep danger, great deliverance" (*Psalms by the Day*, 19).

Superscriptions were added to the psalms later and thus are not inspired, but they may contain helpful information. The superscription in Psalm 6 attributes the psalm to David. The psalm's occasion is unknown. It is said to be "according to *Sheminith*." The term literally means "an eighth," most likely "reflecting either a type of eight-stringed instrument or a particular instrumental tuning" (Wilson, *Psalms*, 177). Four movements carry the psalm (vv. 1-3,4-5,6-7,8-10). Each provides spiritual insight on how we should respond when God is silent, cannot be found, and is long in responding to our pain.

Ask God to Be Gracious While He Is Silent

PSALM 6:1-3

No confession of sin appears in this psalm, but the psalmist senses that he is experiencing the discipline of the Lord. Evidence of God's discipline appears in the psalm's first few sets of parallel lines. Michael Wilcock reminds us, "Hebrew poetry 'rhymes' not in sound of its word-endings but in its meanings" (*Message*, 33). Using the covenant name of his God, Yahweh, David pleads with beautiful parallelism in verse 1:

> *Lord, do not* ***rebuke*** *me in your* ***anger;***
> *do not* ***discipline*** *me in your* ***wrath***. (emphasis added)

Verse 2 provides the positive corollary to verse one:

> ***Be gracious*** *to me, Lord, for I am* ***weak;***
> ***Heal*** *me, Lord, for my bones are* ***shaking***. (emphasis added)

Verse 3 intensifies what David experiences and feels in verses 1-2 and concludes with a cry of absolute brokenness at God's absence:

> *My whole being is shaken with terror.*
> *And you, Lord—how long?*

The abrupt ending is startling.

Rebuke and discipline. Anger and wrath (see Rom 1:18-32). Weakness and shaking. Terror and silence. If the Lord does not come soon with grace and healing, David will not make it. Yet, in the silence and seeming absence of God, he prays and waits. Kidner writes, "'All God's delays are maturings', either of the time . . . or of the man" (*Psalms 1–72*, 61). Allen Ross helpfully adds,

> So the psalmist was weak, terrified, and anxious; his suffering at the hands of his enemies had wreaked havoc with his health and well-being. What made it so frustrating was that the Lord was silent and apparently willing to let him languish in pain and depression. He knew his suffering was divine discipline, so all he could do was appeal for a gracious deliverance. (*Psalms 1–41*, 264).

Ask God for Deliverance Because of His Faithful Love

PSALM 6:4-5

Verses 4-5 contain the petition proper with an appeal to the Lord's "faithful love" (ESV, "steadfast love"), his *chesed.* David uses three imperatives to make his urgent request: "turn," "rescue," and "save." He pleads with the Lord to act and to act quickly. Only the grace and power of God can deliver him. David needs God, and he needs him now! David specifies in verse 5 why he needs the Lord to "be gracious" (v. 2) and to act according to his "faithful love." He needs grace because he faces humanity's great enemy, "death." Death robs us of the ability to acknowledge and to praise God. Death silences our voices. *Sheol* has several possible meanings depending on the context. It can mean the grave, death, extreme danger, hell, or hades (Ross, *Psalms 1–41,* 267). Here the idea is that of the grave or death. If the Lord does not hurry and deliver him, David will not be able to praise him for his rescue and salvation. Death would have muted his voice. I appreciate Calvin's helpful theological insight on verse 5:

> We know that we are placed on earth to praise God with one mind and one mouth, and that this is the end of our life. Death, it is true, puts an end to such praises; but it does not follow from this, that the souls of the faithful, when divested of their bodies, are deprived of understanding, or touched with no affection towards God. (*Psalms 1–35,* 71)

No, our voices may be silenced, but our existence continues on. We see this teaching in the New Testament, which further develops what we call "personal eschatology." Here we discover a wonderful promise for all who are in Christ. Paul summarizes it best in 2 Corinthians 5:8: "We are confident, and we would prefer to be away from the body and at home with the Lord." Death will silence your voice among the living, so praise the Lord while you can. But do not doubt that, although death may silence your praise, it cannot rob you of the Lord's presence if you know Christ!

Ask God to Hear Your Cries and See Your Tears

PSALM 6:6-7

These two verses of lament are descriptive and intense. The verbs and nouns are highly instructive. In verse 6 David says, "I am weary . . . I dampen . . . and drench." In verse 7 he says, "My eyes are swollen . . . they grow old." In verse 6 he speaks of his "groaning" and "tears." In verse 7 he speaks of his "grief" and his "enemies." He verges on the edge of a complete breakdown. And the darkness and silence of the nights are especially difficult. Those who battle depression or experience periods of grief and sorrow often find the nights to be more than they can bear.

Peter C. Craigie and Marvin E. Tate write, "For most sufferers, it [is] in the long watches of the night, when silence and loneliness increase and the warmth of human companionship is absent, that the pain and the grief [reach] their darkest point" (*Psalms 1–50*, 93–94).

If we are honest, we all have had times when we were . . .

- too tired to get out of bed and get dressed,
- too worn out to get into the car and go to work,
- too exhausted to get the kids off to school,
- too weary to clean the house,
- too depressed to go to church,
- too burdened to read the Bible, or
- too sluggish even to pray. (Boice, *Psalms 1–41*, 54)

You may feel no one cares or no one hears your cries of despair and pain. Be encouraged. You are in good company. David has felt despair. Other great saints have too. Rest assured, God is with you. He hears your cries. He sees your tears. How do I know? The rest of Psalm 6 tells me so.

Ask God to Accept Your Prayers and Handle Your Enemies

PSALM 6:8-10

David has suffered emotionally, physically, and spiritually. Some of it may have been his fault (v. 1). Some of it was the result of attacks from his enemies (v. 10). Interestingly, he does not retaliate. Instead, he warns them (vv. 8-9) and testifies to God's faithfulness (vv. 9-10). He tells them to "depart" (cf. Matt 7:23; Luke 13:27), calling them "evildoers." David does not specify their evil. He tells them they better run because "the Lord has heard the sound of my weeping. The Lord has heard my plea for help; the Lord accepts my prayer." Three times he references the Lord. Three times he affirms the Lord has answered his prayer. Spurgeon wisely counsels us in light of verse 10 when he says, "The best remedy for us against an evil man is a long space between us both" (*Treasury*, 58). To this we may add the words of Calvin:

> David, it is to be noticed, repeats three times that his prayers were heard, by which he testifies that he ascribes his deliverance to God, and confirms himself in this confidence, that he had not betaken himself to God in vain. And if we

> would receive any fruit from our prayers, we must believe that God's ears have not been shut against them. (*Psalms 1–35*, 74)

David ends the psalm with a note of confidence, grounded in the assurance of answered prayer. He makes four affirmations about the future of his enemies. "All my enemies": (1) "will be ashamed," (2) "shake with terror"; (3) "will turn back"; and (4) "suddenly be disgraced." H. C. Leupold summarizes this verse well: "Just as certain as [David] is that his prayers have been accepted, just so assured is he of the complete overthrow of his enemies" (*Exposition*, 89).

Conclusion

Patrick Reardon is theologically spot-on when he writes,

> The divine wrath is not some sort of irritation: God does not become peeved or annoyed. The wrath of God is infinitely more serious than a temper tantrum. It is a deliberate resolve in response to a specific state of the human soul. . . . Only the grace of God can deliver us from the wrath of God." (*Christ in the Psalms*, 11)

We can fill out Reardon's point a bit further and conclude our study of Psalm 6 like this: only the overwhelming *grace* of God can deliver us from the righteous *wrath* of God through the marvelous *mercy* of God because of the unfathomable *love* of God manifest in the incarnate *Son* of God. Trust God when you cannot find him. He is with you! Remember: sometimes he speaks loudest in his silence.

Reflect and Discuss

1. Describe a time when you felt God was silent. What was especially hard about this time?
2. Why does God discipline his people? How does God discipline his people?
3. How should Christians respond to the discipline of the Lord?
4. In what ways can God's delays mature us? What should Christians do so that they mature when God delays?
5. Should Christians consider their time on earth as a special opportunity to praise God? Why or why not? If you answered yes, are you taking advantage of this time?

6. Do you express your emotions to God like David does in verses 6-7? Why should we tell God about our sadness, anger, frustration, and heartbreak?
7. Do you know who in your church is lonely and suffering? How can you serve them to show God's love? What are some of the best ways others have loved you when you were experiencing grief and loneliness?
8. Why can you be confident that God hears your prayers (v. 9)?
9. How has God communicated to you even in his silence? What did you learn about him and about yourself?
10. Where in the Gospels do you see Jesus joining others in their pain and grief? What do these examples teach us about how we can love others?

The Lord My Savior

PSALM 7

Main Idea: As God's people call on him to fight for them, they trust in his righteous character and praise him for the victory won for them by the only righteous one, Jesus Christ.

I. **Call on the Lord (7:1-2).**
II. **Examine Your Life (7:3-5).**
III. **Ask the Lord to Act (7:6-9).**
IV. **Rest in Confidence (7:10-16).**
V. **Praise the Lord (7:17).**

In his excellent work *Christ in the Psalms*, Patrick Reardon says,

> The Psalter is not human merely because it speaks for man in general, but because it speaks for Christ. The underlying voice of the Psalms is not simply "man," but *the* Man. To enter into the prayer of this book is not merely to share the sentiments of King David, or Asaph, or one of the other inspired poets. . . . The foundational voice of the Psalms, the underlying bass line of its harmony is, rather, the voice of Jesus Christ, the only Mediator between God and man." (*Christ in the Psalms*, 13; emphasis in original)

Reardon is right. Though people may claim a provisional or relative "righteousness" (v. 8), our voice fails to claim anything like this righteousness in an absolute sense. Ultimately, "this is the prayer of someone whose hands are clean and mind undefiled. . . . The voice of this psalm is his of whom St. Peter wrote that he 'committed no sin, nor was deceit found in his mouth' (2 Pet. 1:22)" (Reardon, *Christ in the Psalms*, 14).

The psalm combines different genres. It contains personal lament (vv. 1-2), a solemn oath (vv. 3-5), a psalm of the Lord's sovereignty and kingship (vv. 6-13), and a thanksgiving hymn (v. 17) (VanGemeren, *Psalms*, 128). The psalm does not specify the occasion for its writing, but James Boice helpfully observes how the superscription hints at the psalm's background:

> The specific details of David's problem are alluded to in the psalm's title, which describes it as a lament sung "to the *LORD* concerning Cush, a Benjamite." We have no other information about Cush, but the fact that he was from the tribe of Benjamin fits well with what we know of the opposition David faced from this tribe. David's predecessor, King Saul, was a Benjamite. So when Saul was killed by the Philistines and David became king of Israel, a process that spanned nearly eight years, it was natural that the new king's chief source of opposition was Saul's tribe. (*Psalms 1–41*, 60)

Our study will examine the psalm in five movements. We can clearly recognize our Lord's voice in the psalm. However, as we follow in his footsteps, we may rightly pray the psalm in our personal devotion and corporate worship.

Call on the Lord

PSALM 7:1-2

David begins the psalm by appealing to his covenantal relationship with Yahweh ("LORD"), who is his God. Because of this tender relationship, he seeks [ESV, "takes"] refuge in him. He seeks protection, safety, and shelter from the Lord, his God. Specifically, he pleads for the Lord to "save me" and "rescue me." David's enemies, his "adversaries," pursue him (vv. 4,5,6). If they have the chance, they will tear him to pieces like a lion ripping apart its prey (v. 2). *The Message* paraphrases it like this:

> *God! God! I am running to you for dear life; the chase is wild. If they catch me, I'm finished: ripped to shreds by foes as fierce as lions, dragged into the forest and left unlooked for, unremembered.*

Believers in persecuted countries can easily identify with these words. These enemies had no regard for David's life. They would kill him brutally if they could. Perhaps his adversary was Saul and his men or Absalom and his warriors.

When it comes to the Lord Jesus, these words perfectly describe the intent of the religious leaders who persecuted him (John 5:16), tried to arrest him (John 7:30), and sought his death (John 7:1). Yet, being in the center of God's will, he was saved and rescued. He rested in his Father as a refuge until his hour arrived (John 7:30) to go to the cross as "the Lamb of God, who takes away the sin of the world" (John 1:29). Call on the Lord when you are under attack and in danger. He is available. He cares. He hears your cry for help.

Examine Your Life

PSALM 7:3-5

David references the "Lord" or "God" fourteen times in this psalm. For the second time, he calls him the "Lord my God." In the form of an oath, he declares his innocence and puts his life on the line. Today we may say, "If I am not telling the truth, may God strike me dead!"

David's enemies accuse him of unjust actions ("injustice on my hands") in verse 3. They claim that he has harmed his friend ("one at peace with me") and taken advantage of ("plundered") his "adversary without cause." They accuse him of being a bully, taking advantage of his power and influence, and hurting those who did not see it coming (i.e., friends) or who were incapable of withstanding his assault. These words have wounded David. So in verse 5 he responds. If he is guilty as charged, then he says, "May an enemy pursue and overtake me; may he trample me to the ground and leave my honor [ESV, "glory"] in the dust." Allen Ross correctly writes, "His protestation of innocence is compelling because he invokes death by his enemy's hand if he is guilty (v. 5)" (*Psalms 1–41*, 280). Examine your heart before asking God to deal with others on your behalf. Is your conscience clear?

David makes these claims in a specific situation and with a relative sense. The three uses of the word "if" in verses 3-4 support this conclusion. Yet it is true that only one *Man* could claim absolutely the moral innocence expressed here and in what follows (especially v. 8). This is the one who allowed his life to be "trampled to the ground" and "his honor laid in the dust" (cf. Gen 3:19) for sinners who rightly deserved such a fate. The King of glory, our Lord Jesus, allowed his glory to be buried in the dust so that ours would not. Though our best intentions struggle to escape hypocrisy and the damning effects of the fall, such was not the case with the sinless Savior of the world!

Ask the Lord to Act

PSALM 7:6-9

David uses three strong imperatives to call on the Lord to act: "Rise up," "lift yourself," and "awake" (v. 6). He calls on "the assembly of peoples" to gather around the Lord as he takes his "seat on high over it" (v. 7). God is called on to condemn the wicked in his "anger" as he opposes what David calls "the fury [NIV, "rage"] of my adversaries." Appealing to the righteous character of God, the psalmist declares, "You have ordained a judgment." God has declared he is just and will do what is just, and David is confident he will. And he will do it publicly as he sits enthroned as the sovereign Lord God.

Verse 8 is surprising. David knows "the Lord judges the peoples," the nations. An eschatological note rings here. But then David speaks personally. He asks the Lord to vindicate him according to his righteousness and integrity (v. 8). David believes, having searched his heart, that he has not wronged either his friend or his enemy (vv. 3-5). He does not claim to be sinless or morally perfect. He claims that, as far as he can tell, he has acted rightly and with integrity in this instance. Still, he entrusts the matter to God. Yes, he can pray in verse 9, "Let the evil of the wicked come to an end, but establish the righteous." But he will also acknowledge in all this, "The one who examines the thoughts and emotions [ESV, "minds and hearts"] is a righteous God." Spurgeon is correct:

> What a solemn and weighty truth is contained in the last sentence of the ninth verse! How deep is the divine knowledge! . . . How strict, how accurate, how intimate his search! . . . "All things are naked and opened to the eyes of him with whom we have to do." (*Treasury*, 69)

When we are right before God in how we think and act toward others, we do not have to fear the one whose eyes are "like a fiery flame" (Rev 19:12), seeing every act, every thought, and every emotion. We can confidently call on him to bring justice and right judgments.

Rest in Confidence

PSALM 7:10-16

Verses 10-16 continue to develop the theme of God as a just and righteous Judge. Once again, David sings a word of confidence and assurance: "My shield [i.e., protection] is with God." He is the one "who saves the upright in heart." The Lord "protects and delivers the righteous" (Ross, *Psalms 1–41*, 284). Verse 11 explains why David holds this confidence: "God is a righteous judge and a God who shows his wrath every day." Derek Kidner explains this verse well: "God himself is far from lukewarm on the matter [of righteousness]: indeed his *indignation every day* . . . is more constant than any human zeal, having no tendency to cool down into either compromise or despair" (*Psalms 1–72*, 64; emphasis in original). The apostle Paul provides the expanded New Testament complement to this truth in Romans 1:18-32.

The stark reality of certain and painful judgment unfolds in verses 12-16 for the one who "does not repent" (v. 12). Using a series of descriptive images, David says of the Lord,

he will sharpen his sword;
he has strung his bow and made it ready.
He has prepared his deadly weapons;
he tips his arrows with fire.

The righteous God is also a warrior God, and he does not ignore sin or fail to condemn it in the most severe manner. Unrepentant sins will be dealt with and ultimately destroyed. Of this truth we should have no doubt.

Verses 14-16, in language similar to James 1:14-15, paint a chilling picture of how sin works and how it ends. Two images are used: (1) conception and birth and (2) digging a pit and falling into it. Verse 14 describes a wicked person as being "pregnant with evil." Because evil has filled him up on the inside, he eventually "conceives trouble, and gives birth to deceit." VanGemeren notes,

> Jesus warned against having a heart from which come "evil thoughts, sexual immorality, theft, murder, adultery, greed, malice, deceit, lewdness, envy, slander, arrogance and folly" (Mk 7:21-22). (*Psalms*, 134)

Sin works its way from the inside out!

The second image in verses 15-16 shows us that sin does not produce the desired and intended results. It is like a person who "dug a pit and hollowed it out" only to fall into the hole he had made. All his "trouble comes back on his head." Reinforcing the point and putting it in its proper moral context, David writes, "His own violence comes down on top of his head" (v. 16). *The Message* says it well: "Mischief backfires; violence boomerangs." Wilcock provides a helpful Christological insight:

> What [God] does is "to direct the consequences of evil away from the innocent and turn them back upon their perpetrators" [Craigie, *Psalms 1–50*, 103]. The supreme

> instance is when he raises his Son from death, and his Son's people with him, and death itself is destroyed. (*Message*, 37)

Praise the Lord

PSALM 7:17

The psalm ends on a high, celebratory note. It closes with thanksgiving and praise. We should join David in thanking "the LORD for his righteousness." The righteousness of God has been acknowledged several times already in verses 8-9. It is a theme the people of God should continually celebrate. It gives us a certainty and confidence that in his time and in his way God, "the Judge of the whole earth," will do what is just (Gen 18:25).

Yes, we "thank the LORD for his righteousness." And we also "sing about the name of the LORD Most High." *El Elyon* is who our God is, and there is no one like him. The name *El Elyon* first appears in Genesis 14:18-22, the story of Melchizedek and Abraham. There he is called the "Creator of heaven and earth." VanGemeren says, "'Most High' is descriptive of the universal rule of God, to whom his subjects sing praise (cf. 9:2; 50:14; 92:1)" (*Psalms*, 135). This is the God we worship. This is the God we praise. This is the God, our Lord and Savior Jesus Christ, who "has a name written on his robe and on his thigh: KING OF KINGS AND LORD OF LORDS" (Rev 19:16).

Conclusion

In Dietrich Bonhoeffer's classic work *Life Together*, he addresses what he calls "the secret of the Psalter":

> The psalms that will not cross our lips as prayers, those that make us falter and offend us, make us suspect that here someone else is praying, not we—that the one who is here affirming his innocence, who is calling for God's judgment, who has come to such infinite depths of suffering, is none other than Jesus Christ himself. It is he who is praying here, and not only here, but in the whole Psalter. The New Testament and the Church have always recognized and testified to this truth. . . . The Psalter is the prayer book of Jesus Christ in the truest sense of the word. (*Life Together*, 54–55)

Bonhoeffer is right. If we apply this insight to Psalm 7, then we can pray verse 8 in Christ. But only Christ can pray it for himself! The Lord our Savior. His name is Jesus!

Reflect and Discuss

1. Many of the psalms arose because of danger, trouble, or persecution. What does the regular occurrence of these psalms teach us about our lives in this world?
2. How does your relationship to the Lord change how you call on him when in trouble? In what ways is our relationship to the Lord the foundation of every prayer? Describe prayer that does not begin with a relationship with the Lord.
3. Does being in God's will mean that you will be free of danger? What does Jesus teach about the presence of danger in the Christian life?
4. Why should you examine yourself before asking God to deal with others?
5. How does your culture view anger when it comes to God? How does the anger of God in this psalm show his goodness? If God never expressed anger, could he give justice?
6. If Christians are righteous in Christ, what is the role of personal righteousness in our lives? Should Christians be concerned about personal righteousness for the sake of their prayers? If so, why?
7. This psalm teaches that God examines thoughts, emotions, and the heart. What does this teach us about the level of righteousness God requires?
8. What do verses 15-16 teach you about sin's deception? What do they remind you about sin's promises compared to sin's results?
9. How are Christians blessed to know God as both their Father and their warrior who fights for them?
10. Where in your life do you see examples of God's righteousness for which you can praise him?

The Lord's Excellent Name

PSALM 8

Main Idea: Praise the majestic Creator who cares for and honors his people.

I. Praise the Lord for His Glory (8:1-2).
   A. He is glorious because he is our Lord (8:1).
   B. He is glorious because he is a majestic God (8:1-2).

II. Praise the Lord for His Grandeur (8:3-4).
   A. He created the big things (8:3).
   B. He cares for the little things (8:4).

III. Praise the Lord for His Goodness (8:5-8).
   A. We are crowned with honor (8:5).
   B. We are commissioned as rulers (8:6-8).

IV. Praise the Lord for His Greatness (8:9).
   A. He has a great name.
   B. He has a great reign.

Everyone has a worldview, a specific way of looking at life. Our worldviews help us answer the ultimate questions of life: Who am I? Why am I here? Is there a God? What's it all about? What will happen to me when I die? Is anything worth dying for? We can't avoid these questions. We have been asking them since time began and sin entered the world.

Deep within our souls we have a nagging and lingering sense that things are not quite right. Something has gone wrong. Something is amiss in our world and lives. The great church father Augustine (AD 354–430) saw our dilemma and directed our attention to God. He wrote, "You have made us for yourself, and our hearts are restless until they rest in you" (*Confessions*, 3). People are incurably religious, worshiping creatures. We look for a god to worship even if it is the wrong god who is destined to disappoint and not deliver, the wrong god who is nothing more than an idol. These gods can come in a variety of worldviews:

- Atheism—those who say there is no god often turn and worship themselves.
- Pantheism—those who worship creation and all that is.

- Deism—those who tip their hats toward God, convinced he is out there but doesn't care.
- Finite theism—those whose impotent god is hardly worthy of worship.
- Panentheism—those who think they sense a divine force running throughout the universe like an electrical charge we need to tap into.
- Polytheism—those who perceive a smorgasbord of gods for the picking and choosing, and the more the better.

In contrast to all these worldviews, the Bible teaches there is one and only one God who is personal, powerful, and perfect. He is the awesome God who made the universe and all that is in it. He is also the approachable God whom you can know by name and with whom you can have a life-changing relationship. Psalm 8 tells us all about this magnificent God!

Psalm 8 is a hymn of creation praise. Its origin, perhaps, comes from young David's life as a shepherd. When lying in the fields one night, gazing into the majestic night sky, he may have been filled with awe and wonder concerning God's marvelous creation. This God, and only this God, is to be worshiped and adored as the good and great Creator, the Ruler, and the Sustainer of all things. The psalm looks back to Genesis 1–2 and God's creative activity, especially his creation of man. However, it also looks forward in anticipation to the coming of a new Man, a second Adam, who will make right all that has gone wrong since sin entered the world through the first Adam's disobedience. That Man is the Messiah, the Lord Jesus, who regains for us paradise lost. A God who accomplishes all this truly has an excellent name, a magnificent name.

Praise the Lord for His Glory

PSALM 8:1-2

Psalm 8 has four major movements. The first (v. 1) and the fourth (v. 9) are identical, forming bookends that bracket the psalm. The entire psalm, every word and every truth, is to be understood in the light of the "magnificent name" of the Lord.

He Is Glorious because He Is Our Lord (8:1)

Believers have gathered for worship. As they contemplate who their God is and what their God has done, they break out in praise: O *Yahweh*

(LORD), our *Adonai* (Lord). *Yahweh* is his personal, covenant name revealed to the Hebrews (Exod 3:14). It occurs 6,828 times in the Old Testament. The name *Yahweh,* Gerald Wilson points out, conveys the idea of "the God who is and continues to be" (*Psalms,* 210). The name is "a powerful promise of continuing divine presence in their lives" (*Psalms,* 210). The psalmist begins in worship, as we should begin. He begins his theology as we should begin our theology: with God.

He Is Glorious Because He Is a Majestic God (8:1-2)

Michael Wilcock notes verse 1 is so familiar to us that we could miss the weight of its claim:

> We can easily miss its shameless political incorrectness. The Bible world, like ours, was pluralistic, awash with all sorts of different beliefs: in the view of any correctly thinking person, all of them valid, but none of them actually "right" in such a way as to make the rest wrong. Not so the psalmist. The Lord, the God of Israel and the Bible, is not just our Lord, he says, but the name, the only name, to be honored in all the earth and even above the heavens. Little Israel is right, and the rest are wrong. (*Message,* 39)

This God's name is "magnificent" (ESV, "majestic") "throughout the earth!" And he has "covered the heavens with [his] majesty." A missionary anthem pulsates in this affirmation. Creation cannot contain his greatness, his majesty. Yet his greatness is displayed in little things such as in the simple and even humiliating manner in which he dismisses his enemies: "From the mouths of infants and nursing babies you have established a stronghold." The greatness of creation proclaims his majesty, and so does the cry of the infant and the chatter of a small child. The weak silence the wicked. The tiny shut the mouths of God's enemy. A child in a crib will "silence the enemy and the avenger." Paul said something similar in 1 Corinthians 1:26-29:

> *Brothers and sisters, consider your calling: Not many were wise from a human perspective, not many powerful, not many of noble birth. Instead, God has chosen what is foolish in the world to shame the wise, and God has chosen what is weak in the world to shame the strong. God has chosen what is insignificant and despised in the world—what*

is viewed as nothing—to bring to nothing what is viewed as something, so that no one may boast in his presence.

Jesus applies verse 2 to himself in Matthew 21:15-16 as he made his great triumphal entry into Jerusalem. We must not miss the point that by applying Psalm 8:2 to himself, Jesus was claiming to be the majestic God of whom the babes and infants give witness. He is the God of Psalm 8!

Praise the Lord for His Grandeur

PSALM 8:3-4

David now considers the paradox of mankind's insignificance and the lofty status bestowed on him as an act of pure grace by the magnificent God. That God, in the expanse and grandeur of his creation, would pay attention to specks of dust like people is more reason to proclaim the excellence and majesty of his name.

He Created the Big Things (8:3)

David observes, he meditates on, the heavens that belong to God. He says they are the "work of your fingers." Creating billions of stars in billions of galaxies is child's play to God. He snaps or points a finger, and it is done. This is simple for *Yahweh*, our *Adonai.*

David takes note of the moon and the stars that God has "set in place." The innumerable points of light in the heavens and the clockwork precision with which the moon and stars turn and then return again and again to map out the days, weeks, months, and years of human existence are truly unfathomable. They are beyond our ability to comprehend. Humans come and go, but the moon and stars continue in their regular appearance. A person fails to show up for work. The number of his days ends. But the moon and stars appear once again undisturbed, ready to serve their Maker. Each is right where it should be all the time, every time, in perfect obedience to its Master who ordained its existence and assignment.

He Cares for the Little Things (8:4)

David now descends from the lofty heights of the heavens to the lowly regions of earth. He now thinks about humans in the context of this massive cosmic masterpiece called creation. All he can do is muster a single question: "What is a human being that you remember [NASB 1995, "take thought of"] him, a son of man that you look after [give attention to or care for] him?" Looking up into the grandeur of the heavens, David feels dwarfed and shamed into insignificance at the greatness of creation and the smallness of humanity. Humans are so small. We are dust (Gen 3:19). Each of us is a vapor that is here one moment and gone the next (Jas 4:14).

"Human being" is the translation of the Hebrew *enosh.* It speaks of our weakness and frail human existence. It highlights our mortality (Wilson, *Psalms,* 204). We come and go. We live fragile, troubled lives and leave quickly with little noticeable or lasting impact. The phrase "son of man" (Hb *ben adam*) likewise emphasizes our fragile mortality, but it also may point to our dependence on God and his attentiveness to us in our need of him (Wilson, *Psalms,* 204–25). People are earthly creatures. Yet, in grace, God has given them glory and honor (vv. 5-7). Infinite God cares for finite man. The God who created the big things also cares for the little things, even you and me. He is mindful of us. He is attentive to us. He has not forgotten us.

Praise the Lord for His Goodness

PSALM 8:5-8

God says to us today that we are not out of sight or out of mind. He sees you. He knows you by name. He has honored you, his image bearer. Looking back to the creation account in Genesis 1, David notes both the dignity and responsibility with which God has endowed mere mortals.

We Are Crowned with Honor (8:5)

The Bible tells humanity to look up to get the proper perspective on who we are. We are set apart from the animal world; we draw our dignity from God, not beasts. We were made a little less than *Elohim* (Hb). This is a difficult phrase in the context with a bundle of potential meanings. Note the following translations:

- A little lower than the **angels** (NIV, NKJV),
- A little lower than the **heavenly beings** (ESV),
- A little lower than **God** (NASB, NLT, CSB),
- A little lower than **you yourself** (CEV),
- A little less than **a god** (REB),

- Yet we so narrowly missed being **gods** (MSG).

Though the precise meaning is uncertain, the basic meaning is clear. We are described as a little lower than those in the heavenly realm, not a little higher than the animal realm. Evolution may say we are slightly above the animals, but God says we are just a little lower than him and his angels. Further, as his vice-regents with delegated authority on earth, we are crowned with glory and honor like God (cf. v. 1). This should shape our sense of what it means to be human. This should shape who and what we aspire to be. James Boice puts things in proper perspective:

> It is nevertheless humanity's special privilege and duty to look upward to the angels (and beyond the angels to God, in whose image women and men have been made), rather than downward to the beasts. The result is that they become increasingly like God rather than increasingly beast-like in their behavior. . . . But here is the sad thing. Although made in God's image and ordained to become increasingly like the God to whom they look, men and women have turned their backs on God. And since they will not look upward to God, which is their privilege and duty, they actually look downward to the beasts and so become increasingly like them. (*Psalms 1–41*, 71)

John Piper sees the significance of all this. Lose sight of who man is, and you lose sight of who God is in all his majesty. Lose sight of God and his majesty, and the world goes insane. All of it is supposed to hang together. The fallout when we get it wrong is enormous. Piper says,

> Now I hope you will agree from this psalm that the truth follows: You cannot worship and glorify the majesty of God while treating his supreme creation with contempt—whatever color or whatever age that creation might be.
>
> - You cannot starve the aged human and glorify the majesty of God.
> - You cannot dismember the unborn human and glorify the majesty of God.
> - You cannot gas the Jewish human and glorify the majesty of God.
> - You cannot lynch the black human and glorify the majesty of God.

- You cannot treat human pregnancy like a disease and glorify the majesty of God.
- You cannot treat the mixing of human ethnicities like a pestilence and glorify the majesty of God.
- You cannot worship and glorify the majesty of God while treating his supreme creation with contempt. (Piper, "What Is Man? Reflections on Abortion and Racial Reconciliation")

We are a little lower than heavenly beings crowned with glory and honor, and we must not lose this perspective. If we do, as Alistair Begg notes, we devolve into nothing more than a monkey or a machine, neither of which has inherent value, dignity, or worth ("How Majestic Is Your Name").

We Are Commissioned as Rulers (8:6-8)

The psalmist continues as he draws from the Genesis creation account of humanity. Highlighting the functional aspect of the image of God in man, which is also the emphasis of Genesis 1, he tells us we have been fashioned by God for dominion and rulership. We are made to rule over the works of his hands. God has put all things under our feet, a symbolic act in the ancient Near East to demonstrate superiority over a defeated enemy or foe. A king would stand and put his foot on the neck of his enemy lying on the ground at his feet. The king is exalted, and the enemy is humiliated. The king rules, and the enemy submits (Wilson, *Psalms*, 209). David illustrates this by noting how animals, birds, and fish are under human authority and dominion.

If we look back to a pre-fallen world, we see that this is the way things were. But this is not the world we live in. This is not the way things work. This is clearly not the way things are. Right now we do not live in a Psalm 8 world. Tragically, we live in a Genesis 3 world. Verses 6-8 direct us back to the idyllic scene of the garden of Eden, but they also force us to look to the future and ask if paradise can be regained. Can the fall be reversed? Can death be defeated? Can tears be dried up? Can sorrow, pain, and suffering be no more? Will a day come when "all things" are once again under the feet, the authority, of humanity? The book of Hebrews says yes! In Hebrews 2:6-8 the author quotes Psalm 8, acknowledging that "we do not yet see everything subjected. . . ." Before we become disappointed, the writer gives hope in the next verse: "But we do see Jesus—made lower than the angels for a short time . . . crowned with glory and honor" (Heb 2:9).

Paul saw a specific implication and application of Psalm 8 in Ephesians 1:22-23, where the "all things" under the feet of Christ includes "the church, which is his body, the fullness of him who fills all things in every way." Paul also saw the eschatological and Christological impulse pulsating through the heart of this psalm. In 1 Corinthians 15:24-28 Paul sees the last enemy, which is death, destroyed and all things brought under subjection to the Son of God, who will give it all back to the Father from whom it all came.

The sons of Adam and the daughters of Eve await a grand and glorious, bright and beautiful, marvelous and majestic future. Paradise lost will be paradise regained because of a man, a man of God's own choosing, Jesus our Lord. His crown of thorns was actually a crown of glory, and the glory of Psalm 8 is already his, with even death under his feet. And as coheirs with Jesus (Rom 8), his present reign is our future destiny.

Praise the Lord for His Greatness

PSALM 8:9

Psalm 8 ends as it begins: on a note of praise. Earlier the psalm affirmed that Yahweh is *our* Lord and a *majestic* God. Now it concludes by focusing on two additional truths contained in these magnificent affirmations of God.

He Has a Great Name

Yahweh, the self-existent one, the one whose own existence is contained within himself as Triune deity and sovereign—he has a magnificent and excellent name. Wilson again is our helper in grasping the greatness of this name: Yahweh "is a majestic name for a majestic God, who promises to be with us, continues to reveal himself to us in each and every new circumstance, and yet remains forever beyond our power to control or manipulate to our own purpose" (*Psalms*, 211). Our Lord possesses a magnificent, majestic, and mighty name.

He Has a Great Reign

Our Lord's name is "magnificent throughout the earth!" "Name" here stands for his authority. The whole earth belongs to him. All of it is under his lordship. In every square inch he is there and should be praised. Charles Spurgeon, a wonderful British Baptist and pastor in London, captured something of what the psalm is saying when he wrote,

> Descend, if you will, into the lowest depths of the ocean where undisturbed the water sleeps, and the very sand is motionless in unbroken quiet, but the glory of the Lord is there, revealing its excellence in the silent palace of the sea. Borrow the wings of the morning and fly to the uttermost parts of the sea, but God is there. Mount to the highest heaven, or dive into the deepest hell, and God is . . . justified in terrible vengeance. Everywhere, and in every place, God dwells and is manifestly at work. (*Treasury*, 79–80)

Conclusion

The wonderful theologian J. I. Packer says of the era in which we live, "We stand at the end of four centuries of God shrinking" in the public mind (*Engaging*, 275). He gets smaller while we get bigger. The Bible does not see it this way. David did not see it this way. We must not see it this way. We are small. God is great! Let us make his name magnificent throughout the earth!

Reflect and Discuss

1. Why are people's hearts "restless" until they find their rest in God? How does the gospel bring rest to all people?
2. In what ways does Psalm 8 counter the beliefs of your culture?
3. In what ways does Psalm 8 create a "missionary impulse"? How does it motivate and sustain missionary work?
4. Why does God often use the weak instead of the strong to accomplish his purposes? If God uses the weak, how does that both bring glory to God and honor to the person?
5. Does observing God's world move you to worship God with praise? What role should this act have in your spiritual disciplines?
6. What did creation teach David about himself and God? What else can creation teach you about God and about yourself?
7. Why do verses 4-5 create a surprising truth? How may we assume God should treat people in light of his ability to create everything?

8. How should verse 5 shape how we view and treat all people? How does it shape what we should aspire to be? How can it motivate our work on behalf of others in the world?
9. What are some examples of your culture taking too high or too low a view of people? How do verses 5-8 help you keep the right perspective of yourself and others?
10. How can our responsibility to rule over creation (vv. 6-7) point to Christ's ultimate rule over creation? How can our stewardship of creation now point to how Christ will ultimately fix all things?

I Will Worship the God Who Is on His Throne

PSALM 9

Main Idea: Celebrate the Lord's perfect justice for the righteous and his wondrous salvation for the oppressed.

I Will Praise the Lord Most High . . .

I. For His Wonderful Works (9:1-2).

II. Because He Is a Righteous Judge (9:3-6).

III. Because He Is a Refuge of Safety for His People (9:7-10).

IV. Because He Hears the Cry of the Oppressed and He Saves (9:11-14).

V. Because He Will Deal Justly with the Wicked (9:15-18).

VI. Because He Hears Our Prayers and Will Show Us Who We Are (9:19-20).

The reformer Martin Luther (1483–1546) painfully, but truthfully, said, "Some people confess [God] with their lips only. They are the ones who say one thing in the heart and another with the mouth, like the sinner who has evil intentions and sings to God nevertheless" (*First Lectures on the Psalms,* 92). Psalm 9 offers a corrective to such disingenuous worship. Here David declares that he will "thank the Lord" (v. 1) and "sing about [his] name" (v. 2) and that he will do so "with all [his] heart" (v. 1). He will worship the God who sits on his throne (vv. 4,7,11), and he will do so with genuine sincerity.

Psalm 9 is a psalm of thanksgiving to the "Lord" (9x), to God "Most High" (v. 2), for his just punishment of the wicked (vv. 5,16-17). It has an eschatological ring as God, the "righteous judge" (v. 4), justly judges the nations (vv. 5,15,19-20), who are "mere humans" (v. 19). Alec Motyer notes that "the evidence suggests that Psalms 9–10 were originally one psalm—a (very) broken alphabetic acrostic" (*Psalms by the Day,* 26). In most English Bibles they are two separate psalms. We will study them separately due to their length and their different tone. They are clearly related like fraternal twins. There are similarities, but there are also significant differences. In Psalm 9 David tells us why he praises and thanks his Lord.

I Will Praise the Lord Most High for His Wonderful Works

PSALM 9:1-2

Words of gratitude and worship dominate the first two verses of this psalm to "the LORD" (*Yahweh*), the God "Most High" (Hb *elyon*). David will "thank the LORD." David will "declare all [his] wondrous works." He will "rejoice" and "boast" and "sing." And he will do all this with "all [his] heart." With a full and overflowing heart, David thanks and praises the God who is the Most High. VanGemeren notes,

> "Most High" is an epithet of deity and first occurs in the interaction between Melchizedek and Abraham where El Elyon is the "Creator of heaven and earth" (cf. Gen 14:18-20, 22). . . . "Most High" is descriptive of the universal rule of God. (*Psalms*, 135)

This is a great God, and this great God has done great works, "wondrous works" of creation and redemption. But what about the phrase "with all my heart"? Charles Spurgeon wisely reminds us, "half heart is no heart" (*Treasury*, 97). Patrick Reardon adds, "The key to the proper praying of the psalms is purity of heart. Psalmody involves prayer from one's central core, a heart characterized by wholeness . . . living with an undivided heart" (*Christ in the Psalms*, 17). We should praise this great God with the integrity of our hearts, with all that we are, because he is worthy. He has done great things!

I Will Praise the Lord Most High Because He Is a Righteous Judge

PSALM 9:3-6

Two important themes appear in verses 3-6: the Lord's "enemies"—also called the "wicked"—and the Lord's "throne." The sovereign "Most High" God will act as the "righteous judge" against those who come against his people who have a "just cause" (v. 4). How will he do it? Note the actions that emanate from the throne of heaven:

- Our enemies retreat, stumble, and perish before the Lord (v. 3).
- The Lord upholds our just cause (v. 4). He defends the Psalm 1 person.

- The Lord rebukes the nations (v. 5). In this psalm the nations are like those in Psalm 2 and Revelation 20:7-10 who take their stand against the Lord and his anointed.
- The Lord destroys the wicked (v. 5).
- The Lord has "erased their name forever" (v. 5; cf. Rev 3:5; 13:8; 17:8), and "the very memory of them has perished" (v. 6).
- The Lord's enemies have "come to eternal ruin" (v. 6).
- The Lord's enemies see their cities destroyed (v. 6).

The righteous judge is swift and certain in his judgment against his wicked enemies. Derek Kidner provides a helpful insight on these verses when he writes, "The past tenses of verses 5f. are 'prophetic perfects,' a feature of the Old Testament: they describe coming events as if they have already happened, so certain is their fulfillment and so clear the vision" (*Psalms 1–72,* 69). God has dealt with these enemies in the past, and he will deal with them in the future. Their day of just judgment is coming. You can count on it.

I Will Praise the Lord Most High Because He Is a Refuge of Safety for His People

PSALM 9:7-10

The Lord Most High "sits enthroned forever" (v. 7). No one, demon or human, will ever usurp his throne. Further, "he has established his throne" for a specific purpose: "for judgment." And how will he judge from his throne in heaven? Verse 8 provides the answer with beautiful Hebrew parallelism:

> *he judges the* ***world*** *with* ***righteousness;***
> *he executes judgment on the* ***nations*** *with* ***fairness***. (emphasis added)

These truths bring comfort and hope to God's people, those who trust in his name (v. 10). Fleeing to the Lord, they discover that "the Lord is a refuge for the persecuted, a refuge in times of trouble." Ross says, "By virtue of his just rule he will be . . . a high tower, a place of refuge and security . . . for those who are crushed" (*Psalms 1–41,* 308). Because the Lord is a refuge, those who have a personal relationship with him trust him because he will "not [abandon]" those who seek the Lord. He is a place of safety for those who "know [his] name." I (Danny) love Spurgeon's word of encouragement in light of the truth of these verses:

> The Lord may hide his face for a season from his people, but he never has utterly, finally, really, or angrily, *forsaken them that seek him.* Let the poor seekers draw comfort from this fact, and let the finders rejoice yet more exceedingly. (*Treasury*, 99; emphasis in original)

When you are in trouble, run to the Lord. You will not be disappointed.

I Will Praise the Lord Most High Because He Hears the Cry of the Oppressed and He Saves

PSALM 9:11-14

The Lord who is "seated on [his] throne" (v. 4) in heaven (transcendence) is the same God "who dwells in Zion" among his people (immanence). He is both above us and among us. Such a great God should be praised as we "sing to the Lord" and "proclaim his deeds among the nations" (v. 11). Zion is the mountain on which Jerusalem was founded. It is where the temple would be built. God chose to actualize his omnipresence specifically in that place. Today he actualizes his presence in every believer in Jesus Christ as his temple (1 Cor 3:16; 6:19-20). This God has done "wondrous works" (v. 1) and "deeds" (v. 11). These deeds must be proclaimed "among the nations." Verse 12 gives one example of these deeds. God remembers those who shed blood, and he will require them to give an account. This God "does not forget the cry of the oppressed." God sees all and he can remember all. The murderer will give an account, and the oppressed will be vindicated. God is the avenger against evil and the rescuer of the hurting.

This truth leads David to voice a passionate and personal prayer in verses 13-14. "Be gracious . . . consider my affliction . . . Lift me up from the gates of death." He asks God to deliver him from death at the hands of his enemies, "those who hate me." In response he will both "declare all your praises" and "rejoice in your salvation." Where will David render his praise? It will be "within the gates of Daughter Zion." Do you see the beautiful and poetic contrast? After being lifted up and delivered from the "gates of death" in verse 13, David can now praise the Lord and rejoice at different gates, "the gates of Daughter Zion." God has saved him and transferred him from the doors of death to the doors of the Lord's holy city. What a reversal! What a joyful turn of events! He thought he was dead, but now he is alive! I cannot help but hear gospel bells ringing throughout holy Zion.

I Will Praise the Lord Most High Because He Will Deal Justly with the Wicked

PSALM 9:15-18

In the midst of political turmoil, social unrest, and economic uncertainty, it is easy to get discouraged. It is difficult not to feel anxious or to despair. Add to these the injustices and exploitations of the oppressed and the poor we see every day throughout the world, and a person can give up almost all hope. This is exactly when we need to hear the words of Psalm 9, especially the final six verses. A day of reckoning is coming. Divine justice is on the way. The Lord is going to make things right.

Verses 15-16 again use the prophetic perfect of the Hebrew language. Future events are described in the past tense as if they have already happened. These are sure and certain. David also uses several powerful images showing how God will use the wicked person's own devices to execute his judgment. The raging nations (Ps 2) will fall into a pit of their own making (9:15). The raging nations will be caught in the net they hid to catch others (v. 15). The Lord will appear, making himself known and executing his righteous justice (v. 16). The imagery of verse 15 continues into verse 16 as the Lord snares the wicked "by the work of their hands." What a surprise! What a reversal of fortune! What the wicked planned for others becomes their destiny and experience. "*Higgaion. Selah,*" meaning, "Meditate on that" (Ross, *Psalms 1–41*, 301).

The future judgment of the wicked is a signed, sealed, and settled reality. They will return to Sheol, the grave, dust, death (cf. Gen 3:19). They forgot God, and now they are remembered no more. They have been removed from the land of the living (Ross, *Psalms 1–41*, 312). In contrast, "the needy will not always be forgotten" and "the hope of the oppressed will not perish forever" (v. 18). God will remember them, and he will rescue them. Justice will be done! God's people may have to wait on justice, but they will not wait forever. "They do not wait in vain" (Spurgeon, *Treasury*, 101).

I Will Praise the Lord Most High Because He Hears Our Prayers and Will Show Us Who We Are

PSALM 9:19-20

The final verses of Psalm 9 are a prayer of petition or request (cf. v. 13). They almost have the feel of a taunt, as the Lord who sits on his throne is set in opposition to mere mortals. David pleads with Yahweh to act and intervene in judgment. Using an imperative, David calls on the Lord to "rise up!" This is a request for quick action. Specifically, he asks the Lord "not [to] let mere humans prevail." These earthly tyrants and criminals are mere mortals (frail humanity). David asks the Lord to judge these men and "nations" who foolishly reject him and his Anointed One (Ps 2). He wants God to judge the nations "in [his] presence." They will be called to give an account before God's divine tribunal (v. 19). Indeed, he says, "Put terror in them, LORD" and "let the nations know they are only humans" (NIV, "mortal"). Let these wicked men and the nations know once and for all, now and forever, that the Lord is God, and humans are not. *Selah*! Think on that!

Conclusion

Psalm 9 looks back to the Lord's "wondrous works" of creation and redemption. It also looks forward in anticipation to the Lord's work of salvation in Christ and his judgment at the great white throne (Rev 20:11-15), where God's enemies will "come to eternal ruin" (Ps 9:6) and "the wicked will return to Sheol" (v. 17). All of this will take place to honor his name, the name we alone can put our trust in (v. 10). Just what are these wondrous works we should keep before us? Reardon suggests the following:

> Our creation from nothingness, the Lord's constant provision for our lives, His promises with respect to our final destiny, His covenant with our forefathers and its fulfillment in Christ the Savior, our liberation from bondage to the satanic pharaoh through the shedding of the paschal blood of Jesus, our passage through the Red Sea of baptism, our journey through the wilderness where we are nourished with living water and the bread of angels. The "all Your wonders," then, has reference to the great mysteries of our redemption: the Incarnation, the atoning Passion and Death, the glorious Resurrection and Ascension, the sending forth of the Holy Spirit, and the founding of the Church. These manifestations of God's grace are the substance of the narrative inherent in the psalms. (*Christ in the Psalms*, 17–18)

This is the God who is on his throne. This is the God we will worship and praise for all eternity.

Reflect and Discuss

1. What does it mean to confess God with lips only? What characteristics mark disingenuous worship? Which characteristics of disingenuous worship are so subtle that someone may not realize them immediately?
2. Why is purity of heart the key to proper praying of the psalms?
3. Why is the Lord's judgment of the wicked so fierce (vv. 5-6)?
4. What are some areas where your culture desires to see fair and righteous judgments? In what ways does our longing for fair and righteous judgments indicate a longing for God?
5. How does one find refuge and safety in the Lord? How are prayer, Scripture, and the local church a means for his refuge and safety?
6. Why is singing an appropriate response to God's salvation (vv. 2,11)?
7. In what ways can 11b ("proclaim his deeds among the nations") summarize the work of the Great Commission (Matt 28:18-20)?
8. Why does the Lord care so deeply for the oppressed? How should his love motivate our love and our work for the oppressed now?
9. What ironic reversals does this psalm depict (vv. 13-14,15-16)? In what way does Jesus's life, death, and resurrection display the ultimate reversal of fortunes for the righteous and oppressed person?
10. This psalm emphasizes where God sits and dwells (vv. 4,7,11). Why is this important for the psalm's theme of justice and salvation?

An Honest Perspective on Our Fallen World

PSALM 10

Main Idea: The wicked will appear to succeed in their pride and wickedness for a time, but God knows the hurt of his people and will bring justice in his eternal kingdom.

I. **There Will Be Times When the Lord Cannot Be Found (10:1).**
II. **Expect the Wicked to Boast against the Lord and to Do Evil against the Helpless (10:2-11).**
III. **Trust the Lord to Hear Your Cries for Help (10:12-15).**
IV. **Acknowledge the Lord's Eternal Kingship over the Nations (10:16).**
V. **Know that the Lord Will Do Justice and End Wickedness Forever (10:17-18).**

Why do the righteous suffer and the wicked prosper? That question has perpetually plagued humanity. The prophet Jeremiah asked the same thing: "Why does the way of the wicked prosper? Why do all the treacherous live at ease?" (Jer 12:1). Job also asked, "Why do the wicked continue to live, growing old and becoming powerful?" (Job 21:7). And Asaph says in one of his psalms, "For I envied the arrogant; I saw the prosperity of the wicked" (Ps 73:3).

Psalm 10 may have originally been joined to Psalm 9. They share similar phrases and words, but their messages are significantly different. David gives thanks in Psalm 9 for God's punishment of his wicked enemies. "The tone of the song is victorious and hopeful," but Psalm 10 "is all prayer, concerned with violence and wickedness" (Ross, *Psalms 1–41*, 302–3). Here the wicked mistreat the poor, innocent, helpless, and fatherless, and it appears as if God is either unaware or does not care. This scenario is not theoretical. We see oppression almost daily in the news. In our fallen, broken world, there are times when the wicked win and the victims of their evil are crushed. This psalm honestly addresses the issue. It laments, but it ends on a note of confidence that justice will be done (vv. 16-18).

There Will Be Times When the Lord Cannot Be Found

PSALM 10:1

David begins the psalm with a cry of anguish, even despair. He laments with two rhetorical questions: "LORD, why do you stand so far away? Why do you hide in times of trouble?" *The Message* reads, "God, are you avoiding me? Where are you when I need you?" David, unlike his enemies, does not doubt God's existence (v. 4) or his omniscience (v. 11). He knows that God is there and that God knows what is going on. But God *seems* indifferent to the troubles of his children. He appears to be hiding so that he will not have to deal with all the injustice that is taking place. Leupold writes,

> The times are very disturbed. The wicked push on in their ungodly pride . . . the good Lord stands "afar off" like one who cares little as to what happens to those who have only Him as their Helper. (*Exposition*, 119)

In the world in which we now live, there are going to be times when God is silent. There are going to be seasons when he seems not to care. There are going to be days when we cannot find him except by the eyes of faith. Psalm 9:1 has a helpful word when evil seems to have won the day: "I will thank the LORD with all my heart; I will declare all [his] wondrous works." We will trust God even when we cannot find him.

Adoniram Judson was the great Baptist missionary to Burma, now Myanmar. He lost his first wife Ann to spotted fever and cerebral meningitis in 1826. Shortly thereafter he lost his little daughter Maria. On October 29, 1829, on the third anniversary of Ann's death, he wrote, "God is to me the Great Unknown. I believe in him, but I find him not" (Anderson, *To the Golden Shore*, 391). Keep believing even when you cannot find him.

Expect the Wicked to Boast against the Lord and to Do Evil against the Helpless

PSALM 10:2-11

Verses 2-11 catalog the attitudes and actions of the "wicked" (vv. 2,3,4,13,15). We discover they have big mouths, are filled with arrogance, and care only about getting their way. There is no place for God in their lives, and they have no concern whatsoever for the innocent victims of their evil agendas and deeds. Arrogantly they "relentlessly pursue their victims." The ESV says they "hotly pursue the poor." However, David asks the Lord to snare them in their own devices: "Let them be caught in the schemes they have devised" (v. 2). Do to them, Lord, what they are trying to do to their innocent and helpless victims.

Verses 3-7 highlight the boasting of the wicked. In verse 3 the wicked person boasts about his own cravings and desires, cursing and despising (ESV, "renounces") the Lord in his greed. In verse 4 he thinks arrogantly as he schemes, "There's no accountability, since there's no God." With a smug and haughty look, the wicked shout that they will never have to face a day of reckoning. They will get away with what they do because God isn't there in any meaningful sense. The God of the Bible does not exist! After all, as verse 5 declares, the wicked are convinced that their "ways are always secure." God's judgments have "no effect on [them]." The wicked man laughs, mocks, and "scoffs at all his adversaries." When considering whether God will call him to give an account, he says, "I will never be moved—from generation to generation I will be without calamity." The wicked believe their present prosperity will never end. They get what they want today, and they will get it tomorrow too!

Alec Motyer notes verses 7 and following are . . .

> not a mere recapitulation of verses 1-6. The focus is on the dangerous hostility of the wicked to the defenseless: i.e., the danger he constitutes in the actuality of daily life (verses 7-10) and its basis in practical atheism (verse 11). (*Psalms by the Day*, 29)

Once more the wicked man puts his character on full display as he opens his mouth. "Cursing, deceit, and violence fill his mouth; trouble and malice are under his tongue" (v. 7). *The Message* says, "Their tongues spit venom like adders." Verses 8-10 draw attention to the evil actions of the wicked with several striking images. First, an evil man waits in ambush, kills the innocent where no one can see, and looks for other helpless victims to harm (v. 8). Second, like a lion hiding in the thicket, "he lurks in order to seize a victim," grabs him, and drags him away (v. 9). As verse 10 summarizes, "The helpless are crushed, sink down, and fall by his might" (ESV). They don't have a chance. Verse 11 reminds us that the contempt and disregard the wicked have for the innocent and the poor ultimately comes from their contempt and disregard for God. The wicked "says to himself, 'God has forgotten; he hides his face and will never see.'" Spurgeon writes, "This cruel man comforts himself with the idea that God is blind or, at least, forgetful." He then adds, this is "a fond and foolish fancy, indeed" (*Treasury*, 113). A day of reckoning is coming. The wicked will not always prosper and win the day. There is a rider on a white horse. His name is "Faithful and True" (Rev 19:11). His name is Jesus, and he is on the way!

Trust the Lord to Hear Your Cries for Help

PSALM 10:12-15

George Müller (1805–1898), who directed the Ashely Down orphanage in Bristol, England, was known for his great faith in God's care and providence. He is reported to have said, "The beginning of anxiety is the end of faith, and the beginning of true faith is the end of anxiety." If David was troubled and anxious over the exploits and victories of ruthless terrorists, his attitude and disposition completely reverse in verse 12. Instead of focusing on the wicked, his eyes turn to God in faith, hope, and prayer. Verse 12 is a cry of faith: "Rise up, Lord God!" Take action! Do something! "Lift up your hand" and intervene. The wicked say God has forgotten (v. 11), but David knows that is not true. God does "not forget the oppressed," the innocent victims of injustice in verse 8. David says in verse 13, I know the wicked despise (ESV, "renounce") God. I know the wicked man "says to himself, 'You will not demand an account.'" But David would say in response, I know he is wrong!

> *But you yourself* [God] *have seen trouble and grief, observing it in order to take the matter into your hands. The helpless one entrusts himself to you; you are a helper of the fatherless.* (v. 14)

God does see, and God does know. God is aware, and God does care. The fatherless, the orphan, "perhaps the most vulnerable person, the one with the fewest resources," especially is on God's radar (Ross, *Psalms 1–41*, 329). Indeed, "He is able to do for [them] what they cannot do for themselves" (Ross, *Psalms 1–41*, 329). The plea of verse 15 complements the request of verse 12. The psalmist calls for God to "break the arm of the wicked, evil person, until you look for his wickedness, but it can't be found." Kidner notes, "Break . . . the arm, which may sound merely brutal, is an expression for the breaking of his power" (*Psalms,* 72). Take the wicked down, Lord! Wipe them out and don't leave a trace! The wicked denied human justice to the poor and helpless. David wants them to experience divine justice in the fullest measure.

Acknowledge the Lord's Eternal Kingship over the Nations

PSALM 10:16

The kingship of Yahweh repeatedly appears in Psalm 9, the companion of Psalm 10. The throne of the LORD is referenced in verses 4, 7, and 11. Now it is expressed in 10:16 with the declaration, "The LORD [*Yahweh*] is King forever and ever." This proclamation finds its New Testament echo in Revelation 11:15: "The kingdom of the world has become the kingdom of our Lord and of his Christ, and he will reign forever and ever." The wicked have their day, but not forever. They come and go, but God sits enthroned now and forever. The wicked and the nations who follow them in rebellion against the sovereign Lord (see Ps 2) "will perish from his land." They will be vanquished. Not a memory of them will remain. Verse 16 is a wonderful promise and word of comfort. Allen Ross is right: "This present evil age is temporary and limited, but the LORD's reign is eternal and universal" (*Psalms 1–41*, 331). Have faith in God! He's on his throne.

Know That the Lord Will Do Justice and End Wickedness Forever

PSALM 10:17-18

Psalm 10 ends on a note of assurance and confidence that our good God will bring justice. David is certain that the Lord has "heard the desire of the humble" and that he will "strengthen their hearts." He will encourage their souls, their inner persons. How will he do this? First, he "will listen carefully" to their cries for justice and their prayers of pain (v. 17). Second, he will accomplish this by "doing justice for the fatherless and the oppressed" (v. 18). The most vulnerable and the most mistreated will have their day in court, the divine court of the Lord who is "King forever and ever" (v. 16). Third, those who are "mere humans from the earth" (cf. "only humans" in 9:20) will "terrify them no more." The reign of terror of the wicked, the evil, the arrogant, the boastful, the greedy, the scoffer, the violent, the troublemaker, the malicious, the murderer, the oppressor is coming to an end forever! Tyranny is coming to an end. The King who is forever and ever has promised. The wicked believed themselves to be invincible. They could not have been more wrong.

Conclusion

Psalms 9 and 10 end on an eschatological note. A day of judgment is coming. A day of righteous reckoning before the divine King is in the future. He reigns on his throne. He is the Lord who is "King forever and ever," and he will break the power of the wicked. The wonderful truth is that the power of evil has already been broken at the cross of our Lord Jesus Christ. There, as Colossians 2:15 teaches, "He disarmed the rulers and authorities and disgraced them publicly." Be encouraged in a world where evil and wickedness seem to be winning the day. We do not fight *for* victory. We fight *from* victory. Calvary says it is so. The second coming of King Jesus will make it so!

Reflect and Discuss

1. Based on this psalm, how would you answer someone who asks you, "Why do good people suffer and bad people prosper?"
2. In what ways does God refine and mature believers during the moments when it appears the wicked are succeeding?
3. Compare your culture's concept of justice to the Bible's. What are some similarities and differences? In what ways is Scripture's hope for justice better than your culture's?
4. What is the relationship between pride and wicked actions in this psalm? How should this relationship shape how you approach your sin and the sin of others?
5. What does pride reveal about one's view of God?
6. How does the desire for justice require faith? What happens if we attempt to pursue justice without faith?
7. How does the way David begins and ends this psalm teach you how to lament?
8. How can 2 Peter 3:1-13 help you to understand why God allows wickedness to continue for a time before he brings complete justice?
9. Can unbelievers hope to experience true justice on earth? Why or why not?
10. How does Jesus's death and resurrection display God's faithfulness and justice even when it appears as if the wicked are winning?

What Do You Do When Everything Is Falling Apart?

PSALM 11

Main Idea: When the wicked attack, the righteous run to the Lord, who will protect perfectly and judge righteously.

I. Trust the Lord as Your Refuge in Times of Trouble (11:1-3).
II. Trust the Lord Who Is Sovereign over All Things (11:4-6).
III. Trust the Lord Who Is Righteous in Who He Is and What He Does (11:7).

Concerning Psalm 11, Derek Kidner writes, "This is a psalm that comes straight from a crisis" (*Psalms 1–72,* 72). Verse 3 supports this thesis when David cries, "When the foundations are destroyed, what can the righteous do?" While we cannot be certain of the occasion of this psalm of lament, a time when King Saul was seeking to kill David would make sense. In 1 Samuel 16:20 David says he is being hunted by Saul "as one who hunts a partridge in the mountains" (VanGemeren, *Psalms,* 160). Verse 1 of Psalm 11 could echo this situation. Psalm 11, as James Boice well says, "contains faith's response to fear's counsel" (*Psalms 1–41,* 91). In three movements David says, Trust the Lord, trust the Lord, trust the Lord! He is your refuge (vv. 1-3), he is on his throne and in absolute control (vv. 4-6), and he is righteous in all his dealings (v. 7).

Trust the Lord as Your Refuge in Times of Trouble

PSALM 11:1-3

Fear can drive us to flee in doubt or stand in faith. David begins this psalm on a note of faith: "I have taken refuge in the LORD." He takes shelter for protection and safety in his God. Allen Ross points out, "The present perfect nuance of the verb stresses that the psalmist's trust has continued throughout life" (*Psalms 1–41,* 338). He has taken his refuge, he is taking his refuge, and he will always take his refuge in the Lord (v. 1). Well-intended counselors may tell him to "escape to the mountains like a bird," but that is rarely the best option for the man or woman of faith. We don't have to run away in fear. We don't have to become evangelical monks and withdraw to a monastery.

In verses 2-3 David tells us why his advisors told him to flee. The "wicked" (vv. 2,5,6) "who love violence" (v. 5) are out to get him. Using the imagery of a hunter with a bow and arrow, David says they are stringing their bows, putting their arrows in place, and getting ready to shoot any righteous person they can find, any who are "upright in heart" (v. 2). Further, their attacks come "from the shadows." Their attacks come secretly in the dark, not out in the open. Their goal is to kill the righteous before they see it coming.

Verse 3 takes the crisis to a whole new level. From the personal level, we move to the societal and cultural level. In one of the most-quoted verses in Scripture, especially in an election year (!), we read, "When the foundations are destroyed, what can the righteous do?" When the foundations of a society (its laws, government, and justice) begin to crumble, what are the righteous to do? We do not flee like a bird to the pseudo-safety of the mountains. We flee to the Lord who is a sure and certain refuge. He is our place of safety no matter what is happening around us. We don't trust in any person or institution. We trust in a Savior who is a Warrior-King, who has a sharp sword coming out of his mouth to strike down the nations, and who will rule them with a rod of iron (Rev 19:15). Charles Wesley (1707–88), who wrote approximately 6,500 hymns and was used by God in the First Great Awakening, beautifully writes in the hymn "Jesus, Lover of My Soul":

> Other refuge have I none,
> Hangs my helpless soul on Thee;
> Leave, O leave me not alone,
> Still support and comfort me.
> All my trust on Thee is stayed,
> All my help from Thee I bring;
> Cover my defenseless head
> With the shadow of Thy wing.

Trust the Lord Who Is Sovereign over All Things

PSALM 11:4-6

David says we should flee to the Lord and trust him as our refuge even when all hell is breaking loose. But why? Verses 4-7 provide the answer. Two powerful affirmations appear in verse 4 that are fundamental and foundational. First, "The LORD is in his holy temple." Second, the Lord's "throne is in heaven." Ross notes, "Describing the LORD's temple as holy (Ps. 22:3) sets it apart from anything earthly, physical, or profane—it is the heavenly temple" (*Psalms 1–41*, 341). Ross also informs us,

> The word "holy" . . . is one of the most important words in Old Testament theology. . . . In the Bible this is one of the primary attributes of God. He is the holy one (Isa. 57:15); there is no one like him (Isa. 45:5, 11-13, 19); he is incomparably holy (Isa. 6:3). This means that he is set apart from all other; he is unique. There is no one like him in heaven or on earth. (*Psalms 1–41*, 532)

The prophet Habakkuk reminds us, "The LORD is in his holy temple; let the whole earth be silent in his presence" (Hab 2:20). The Lord is also on his throne in heaven. He reigns with sovereign authority over all that he has created. His authority is absolute and unrivaled. From his throne, "His eyes watch; his gaze examines everyone." From his heavenly throne God is above all and sees all. Nothing escapes his gaze. Nothing happens that he does not see. X-ray vision belongs to this sovereign Lord. With such omniscient power, "The LORD examines [ESV, "tests"] the righteous" (vv. 3,5,7). God uses the trials and upheaval of verses 1-3 to test and prove the faith of his people. As Spurgeon puts it, the righteous "are precious to him, and therefore he refines them with afflictions" (*Treasury*, 130). "But"—the contrast is striking—the Lord "hates the wicked and those who love violence" (v. 5). Ross again provides helpful insight:

> The word "violence" . . . refers to a variety of acts of violence, ranging from social injustices to injurious language. The wicked are people who ultimately promote such violence; they might call it something else—shrewd business dealings, social reformation, or even ethnic cleansing—but if it destroys people in the process, it is wicked violence. The psalmist declares that the LORD hates violence with all his being (literally, "his soul hates"). (*Psalms 1–41*, 342)

In light of the harm and suffering inflicted by the violent and wicked, David expresses his desire for justice in the form of a prayer in verse 6. He knows the wicked deserve condemnation, and he also knows judgment is in their future. He knows God hates their acts of violence (see Prov 6:16-19) and the pain it causes the innocent and helpless

(Ps 10:8). So he prays, "Let [the Lord] rain burning coals and sulfur on the wicked." This verse contains a textual issue—note the marginal reading of the CSB—but Motyer is correct when he notes that the Hebrew says, "He will rain down on the wicked traps" (or "snares") (*Psalms by the Day*, 33). The NASB 1995 translation is preferrable: "Upon the wicked He will rain snares; fire and brimstone and burning wind will be the portion of their cup." The psalm uses imagery from the destruction of Sodom and Gomorrah (see Gen 19:24). The scorching wind speaks of the hot desert winds of the Middle East whose . . .

> effects are devastating, as the beautiful vegetation changes overnight into parched, withered plants (cf. Isa 21:1; 40:7-8; Jer 4:11). The wicked will be like the flowers of the field, which are here today and gone tomorrow. (VanGemeren, *Psalms*, 163)

This is their lot, the "portion in their cup," their certain destiny. It is a signed, sealed, and settled reality. It will happen.

Trust the Lord Who Is Righteous in Who He Is and What He Does

PSALM 11:7

Verse 7 provides an appropriate conclusion to Psalm 11 and ends on a note of comfort and encouragement. "The Lord is righteous." In his nature he is good. He is the standard of all that is right and good. He forever opposes the wicked and violent. And he loves those who do "righteous deeds." The NLT says, "For the righteous Lord loves justice." Righteous deeds please our righteous God. People who do the right thing in the right way at the right time and for the right reason (the glory of God!) have the smile of heaven on them. And the psalm ends with a promise: "The upright will see his face." James Boice says this about verse 7:

> What can the righteous do? There is one more thing. David had looked around at the wicked. He had looked up to God. Now he looks ahead, to the future, concerned at this point not with the destiny of his enemies but with his own destiny and that of all who trust God. The last verse means: *because* "the *Lord* is righteous [and] loves justice, upright men will see his face" (v. 7).

> This last phrase is an anticipation of nothing less than the beatific vision, the ultimate aspiration of the Old Testament saints: to see God face to face. Strangely, many commentators seem reluctant to admit this, pleading the incomplete and uncertain view of the afterlife Old Testament believers are supposed to have had. But although Old Testament understandings are obviously less developed than those of the New Testament, based as the latter are upon the resurrection and explicit teaching of Jesus, and although the idea of seeing God's face could mean only that the light of his favor will shine upon the upright, it is nevertheless hard to suppose that David is not thinking here of the believer's ultimate reward and bliss. Why? He has just spoken of a future judgment on the wicked: "On the wicked he will rain fiery coals and burning sulfur" (v. 6). What is called for now is a parallel statement of what the same all-seeing and just God will do for those who are righteous. They will see God! How glorious. (*Psalms 1–41*, 96; emphasis in original)

Conclusion

The wicked drink the cup of God's wrath because of their violence on the earth (v. 6). Thankfully, Jesus drank the cup of God's wrath in our place. The cup of judgment has passed from us to him (Matt 26:39). Because he drank that cup, which we all rightly deserve, believers have a future that will not see his wrath. We will, instead, see his face! As 1 John 3:2 promises, "We know that when he appears, we will be like him because we will see him as he is." The just man of Psalm 11 "is ultimately Jesus the Lord, that Righteous One" (Reardon, *Christ in the Psalms,* 20). Because we are in him, we will be like him. Because we will be like him, we will see him! What a promise! What a hope when everything is falling apart!

Reflect and Discuss

1. When you experience crises, whom or what are you tempted to run to instead of God? Why do we run to anyone or anything other than God?
2. How can fear drive us to flee in doubt or stand in faith? What determines how you will respond to fear?

3. Does the Christian life mean faithful believers will not be afraid? Why or why not?
4. Why does living righteously not guarantee freedom from harm or fear?
5. Why must taking refuge in the Lord be ongoing instead of a one-time action?
6. In what ways does trusting in people or things other than God reveal a desire to be in control?
7. How does remembering that God is "in his holy temple" and on his throne in heaven (v. 4) affect how we respond to fear and temptation?
8. Why does the Lord test the faith of his people with trials? What passages in the New Testament can help you answer this?
9. What examples in the Old and New Testaments do we have of faith being tested? What was the result?
10. In what ways does verse 7 summarize the goal of Scripture's redemptive story?

When You Live in a Land of Liars!

PSALM 12

Main Idea: The Lord will rise up to protect the weak and to punish the wicked.

I. **Cry Out to the Lord Who Alone Is Faithful (12:1).**
II. **Ask the Lord to Silence the Duplicitous and Boastful (12:2-4).**
III. **Wait on the Lord Who Will Act on Behalf of the Oppressed (12:5).**
IV. **Trust in the Lord Because His Words Are Pure and Flawless (12:6).**
V. **Rest in the Lord's Promise to Protect His People amid Rampant Wickedness (12:7-8).**

God cares about how we use our tongues. He pays close attention to the words that come out of our mouths. He especially despises it when we use our mouths to speak lies rather than truth. Proverbs 6:16-19 tells us there are six things the LORD hates. Among them are "a lying tongue" and "a lying witness who gives false testimony." Proverbs 12:22 adds, "Lying lips are detestable to the LORD." Our Lord Jesus teaches us that the devil "is a liar and the father of lies" (John 8:44). And in Revelation 21:8 we are reminded that "all liars" will experience for all eternity "the lake that burns with fire and sulfur, which is the second death" (i.e., hell).

We do not know the circumstances that moved David to pen Psalm 12. It takes the form of a "community lament" asking the Lord for help and deliverance from all the liars, flatterers, and slanderers who stalk the land (VanGemeren, *Psalms*, 165). Although David is discouraged, he is still hopeful. He has the promise of the Lord himself in verse 5, which is the psalm's focal point. "'I will now rise up,' says the LORD. 'I will provide safety for the one who longs for it.'" What do we do when we live in a land of liars? David provides five words of counsel to help us navigate these shark-infested waters.

Cry Out to the Lord Who Alone Is Faithful

PSALM 12:1

Psalm 12 begins with an immediate cry for help and an explanation about why it is needed now. "Help, LORD" (ESV, "Save, O LORD").

The call for help is an imperative that conveys the urgency of the petition (Ross, *Psalms 1–41*, 353). David needs immediate deliverance. The reason for his request follows in beautiful Hebrew parallelism: "For no faithful [ESV, "godly"] one remains; the loyal have disappeared from the human race" (ESV, "the children of man"). People you can trust have vanished. People you once counted on have let you down. They turned their backs on you when you needed them most. Friends you thought you could trust to have your back turn out to be the ones who betray you. The pain of such betrayal is devasting. When it happens, turn to the Lord and cry out to him for help. Others may desert you, just as Paul's friends deserted him (2 Tim 4:16-18), but the Lord will not. Those you believed to be faithful and loyal may disappear, but the Lord will be there for you. As Hebrews 13:5 promises, "[He] will never leave you or abandon you."

Ask the Lord to Silence the Duplicitous and Boastful

PSALM 12:2-4

The faithful and loyal may have disappeared (at least it feels that way), but liars and deceivers are everywhere. "They lie to one another; they speak with flattering lips and deceptive hearts" (v. 2). *The Message* says, "Everyone talks in lie language; lies slide off their oily lips. They doubletalk with forked tongues." With duplicitous and dishonest hearts, they look you in the face and lie to you. They tell you what you want to hear with flattery, but their words are inflated at best and dishonest at worst. You cannot believe or trust a word that comes out of their mouths. They have an agenda and will say anything to see it accomplished. They have crafted a story and will not let facts get in the way.

David's cry for help gets precise in verse 3. He prays that the Lord would "cut off all flattering lips and the tongue that speaks boastfully." David wants the Lord to wipe out those who flatter and boast, to take out the big talkers who use smooth words to get their way with little or no regard for the well-being of others (see v. 5).

Verse 4 summarizes the thinking behind the boastful of verse 3. "They say, 'Through our tongues we have power; our lips are our own—who can be our master?'" These arrogant and conceited boasters claim no one has authority over their words or their actions. Alec Motyer helpfully rewords the verse like this: "With our tongues we will prove our strength; our lips are at our disposal. Who is our master?" (*Psalms by the Day*, 34). These men believe they can say whatever they want. They believe they answer to no one. They are their own propaganda machine with zero accountability. In our world their words would be their weapons and social media would be their tool. James Boice is right: "Words are both our glory and our shame" (*Psalms 1–41*, 98). Let's be sure to use words for God's glory (1 Cor 10:31). Otherwise, be prepared for him to silence you in his own time and in his own way.

Wait on the Lord Who Will Act on Behalf of the Oppressed

PSALM 12:5

David has spoken in verses 1-4. Now the Lord speaks. Derek Kidner points out, "This is the first psalm to contain an answering oracle from the Lord" (*Psalms 1–72*, 75). We now learn that the liars of verses 2-4 have used their words and power to oppress the hurting, specifically the poor. Their oppression has been so great the poor groan over the devastation they have experienced. Exactly how they are suffering is not stated. Michael Wilcock notes, "Destructive gossip, undemocratic legislation, language devalued by political correctness, the media's drowning of quality in quantity, are all [modern] examples" (*Psalms 1–72*, 49).

The Lord is aware of what is happening. The time has come for him to act, and act he will! "'I will now rise up,' says the LORD. 'I will provide safety for the one who longs for it.'" Gerald Wilson puts the Lord's actions in helpful context:

> Yahweh—the divine king who sits in judgment in Psalms 9–10, who from his heavenly throne examines both righteous and wicked in Psalm 11, who has given feeble *'enoš* great honor and authority in Psalm 8—will enforce limitations on that power and authority when he arises to protect the defenseless "from those who malign them." (*Psalms Volume 1*, 269)

The Lord will save his people. Their cries for help will be answered. When they are literally "panting" for help, their covenant God flies to the rescue and puts them in a place of safety and security. Spurgeon is right: "Nothing moves a father like the cries of his children" (*Treasury*, 143). In Psalm 50:15 our Father encourages us, "Call on me in a day of trouble; I will rescue you, and you will honor me." Be patient. Wait on the Lord. He will act on behalf of his people, his children. He promises!

Trust in the Lord Because His Words Are Pure and Flawless

PSALM 12:6

Many verses in the Bible testify to the Scriptures' faithful and truthful nature. Jesus affirmed his full confidence in the Bible's inspiration in Matthew 5:17-18; John 10:35; 17:17. Paul writes that all Scripture is inspired in 2 Timothy 3:16-17, and Peter adds his witness in 2 Peter 1:20-21. David wrote Psalm 19 and may have written the magnificent "Word of God Psalm," Psalm 119. Here he adds another word of confidence in the nature of the Word of God in verse 6: "The words of the LORD are pure words, like silver refined in an earthen furnace, purified seven times." Men lie, but God does not. Men speak with flattering words and deceptive hearts, but the Lord speaks with honest words and a heart of integrity. His words are "pure," without flaw or defect. Using a powerful illustration, David says they are like valuable silver that has gone through a refiner's fire seven times, the number of perfection. God's Word is perfectly pure and can be completely trusted. Wilcock is again helpful:

> The true shows up the false, and Scripture, which is God speaking, is guaranteed true . . . [and] those who preach from Scripture have the inestimable privilege of showing the way things really are—a great definition of preaching!—and thus of countering with words of truth the words of guile which would otherwise engulf today's world. (*Psalms 1–72*, 49)

Read the Word. Meditate on the Word. Study the Word. Preach the Word (2 Tim 4:1-5)! It is pure and without flaw. It is inspired, infallible, and inerrant. "It can be trusted completely in everything it says" (Ross, *Psalms 1–41*, 357).

Rest in the Lord's Promise to Protect His People amid Rampant Wickedness

PSALM 12:7-8

The Lord's Word is pure and flawless. His promises, therefore, are true and certain. He has promised in verse 5 to "provide safety." David takes him at his word and declares in verse 7, "You, LORD, will guard [ESV, "keep"] us; you will protect us from this generation forever." Those who are liars, deceptive, boastful, and arrogant (today and forever!) cannot ultimately harm God's people. VanGemeren puts it perfectly:

"God's guarding his people is a reality even when the wicked walk around like kings" (*Psalms*, 169). "The wicked prowl all around." That cannot be denied in a fallen world under Adam's curse. Further, we can expect that "what is worthless [will be] exalted by the human race" (ESV, "children of man," cf. v. 1). Yes, we can expect lost people to act like lost people. Yes, we can expect power to corrupt and absolute power to corrupt absolutely. But we can also expect God to act like God! He will provide for and protect those who know him, love him, and belong to him.

In a world that idolizes power and applauds deception and dishonesty, God's Word and his promises remain the only source of "true truth." If you want the truth, don't put your trust in ABC, CBS, or NBC. Don't count on CNN, FOX, or MSNBC. Ross is spot on: "People may not always like what the Bible says, but it tells the truth" (*Psalms 1–41*, 359).

Conclusion

When God chose to incarnate himself in the person of his "one and only Son" (John 3:16), he did so by means of his Word. This Word entered the world revealing himself to be "full of grace and truth" (John 1:14). There was not a taint of sin, impurity, or deception. When people saw Jesus, they saw God. When people heard Jesus speak, they heard gracious words of undiluted truth. The inerrant Word of God is often a wonderful pointer to the sinless Word! You can trust them both. You can count on them both. Both are pure. Both will protect. Both will provide, now and forever, all that you will ever need!

Reflect and Discuss

1. Why are words so significant? What do your words reveal about who you are and what you believe?
2. What are "flattering lips"? Why does the Lord hate them?
3. What should be your response to those who betray you?
4. How migh this psalm cause you to change the way you talk and the words you write online?
5. Why is it *not* excusable to lie, even for a righteous cause?
6. Why are you still responsible if you lie because you have spread rumors that you have not verified to be true?
7. What in this psalm should cause you to have a high concern for the words you speak?

8. Describe how "words are both our glory and our shame" (Boice, *Psalms 1-41*, 98).
9. Evaluate your words this past week. What do you need to repent of and to confess? Do that now.
10. How does Scripture help you change your words so that you speak truthfully? Why is it able to do that?

From Honesty to Intimacy

PSALM 13

Main Idea: Greater honesty with God cultivates greater intimacy with God.

I. Accusing God: Expressing How You Really Feel (13:1-2)
II. Asking God: Expressing What You Really Want (13:3-4)
III. Accepting God: Believing What Is Really True (13:5-6)

I (Josh) am not sure when it happened or even how it happened, but it seems that at some point Christians were taught that their emotions did not matter. Truth matters, but how we feel is irrelevant. At times, it seems many Christians are even afraid of emotions. We don't want to be too excited; someone might think we are charismatic. We don't want to be too happy; someone might think we are shallow. We don't want to be too sad because someone might think we don't trust the Lord. The result is that many Christians tend to either ignore their emotions or suppress them.

But ignoring and suppressing our emotions does not make them go away. Telling people to stop being sad rarely keeps them from being sad. And ignoring our emotions ignores the fact that we have been created in the image of God, and God is an emotional being. God is often happy, sad, angry, or jealous, and he even weeps. Just look at the life of Jesus. Not only does God's Word not tell us to bury our emotions, but it also tells us that how we feel matters to God.

Dan Allender and Tremper Longman, in their book *The Cry of the Soul*, say it this way: "Our emotions are the language of our soul. They are the cry that gives the heart a voice. To understand our deepest passions and convictions, we must learn to listen to the cry of the soul" (31). In other words, to ignore our emotions is to ignore what is really going on in our hearts.

The Psalms give us what the church often doesn't—the freedom to express how we really feel. The Psalms remind us that although God does not care for our meaningless repetition, he loves our honest emotions. He welcomes them. He hears them. And he shows us how greater honesty with him cultivates greater intimacy with him.

Psalm 13 is a lament. It is a cry of distress. It is an honest expression of the heart when it feels as if God has forgotten us. The lament in Psalm 13 can be summarized: "How long, LORD? Will you forget me forever?" (v. 1). Psalm 13 also serves as a great example of our freedom to be honest with God and how that freedom is an essential part of our movement toward greater intimacy. If we fail to be honest, we will fail to be intimate. In the course of six verses, David moves from accusing God, to asking God, to accepting God. This process serves as an important model for us as we learn to be honest with God.

Accusing God: Expressing How You Really Feel

PSALM 13:1-2

It's difficult to imagine anyone being more honest with God than David is in these first two verses. Four times he asks the simple question, "How long?" He is in a season of what feels like unrelenting suffering. He feels as if God has forgotten him, as if God is hiding from him (v. 1), as if God is ignoring him, and as if God has allowed his enemies to triumph over him (v. 2). These are feelings that all of us, if we are honest, have felt at some point in our lives.

When reading the Psalms, it is important to allow your heart to *feel* the emotion of the text. It is not enough just to understand the text; we must allow its emotion to capture us. Do you feel the emotion in these two verses? David is accusatory, frustrated, angry, irritated, and confused. He does not hesitate to express all of that to God. David looks to heaven and says, "Hey God, what's going on with you? Where are you? How long are you going to ignore me and allow me to suffer?"

We are not surprised that David feels that way (because we have all felt that way). We are surprised that David told God he felt that way. We are surprised by David's honesty. Something about it feels sacrilegious. But the irony of feeling that way and not expressing it to God is that God knows exactly how you feel. Psalm 13:1-2 shows us that God wants you to pour out your heart to him. He welcomes your honesty.

Asking God: Expressing What You Really Want

PSALM 13:3-4

If you look closely at the text, you will notice extra space between verses 2 and 3. That space matters. David is moving through a process of lament. As he does, it takes time for him to move from accusing God to asking God. It always takes time to move through this process. It cannot be rushed.

In verses 3-4 David moves from accusing God to asking God. He makes three requests. He asks God to listen, he asks God to restore, and he asks God to bless. When David says, "Consider me and answer" (v. 3), he is doing what my kids often do to me. They demand that I put aside any distractions, turn toward them, look them in the eyes, and give them my undivided attention. There have been times when one of my children will even put a hand under my chin and turn my head toward her. This is what David is doing to his Father. He is asking God to stop ignoring him, turn to him, and listen!

Then David asks the Lord to "restore brightness to my eyes" (v. 3). He is asking the Lord to wipe away the tears and return the sparkle. This is the same word used in 1 Samuel 14:27 when Jonathan, King Saul's son, ate honey and it brightened his eyes (Leupold, *Exposition*, 136). It means to restore, energize, and refresh. David understands the physical toll emotional strain can take, and he longs for God to restore him spiritually and physically.

Finally, David asks for the Lord's blessing. God had promised to bless David, but it feels as if the blessing of God went to his enemies (v. 4). They seem to be prevailing while David is suffering. David wants the Lord's blessing turned toward him.

It is clear in verses 3-4 that David begins to turn a corner. After feeling lost and ignored, he pours out his heart to God by stating not what he really feels but what he really wants. He has moved to longing. He longs for God to listen to him, restore him, and bless him. David is headed in the right direction. Whenever we move from accusing God to asking God, we are moving in the right direction. We are moving toward greater intimacy when the cry of our hearts is one of longing for more of God.

Accepting God: Believing What Is Really True

PSALM 13:5-6

Just as there was between verses 2 and 3, there is another pause between verses 4 and 5. Why? Because lamenting takes time. It cannot be rushed. And the process itself, not just the end result, matters to God. We have no idea how long it took David to move from verse 1 to verse 5, but he eventually worked his way to a place of acceptance. He starts with a simple "But" (v. 5)—but in spite of how I feel; but in spite of what appears to be true; but in spite of my circumstances—"I have trusted in your faithful love" (v. 5).

In these verses, for the first time, David feels confident and resolved. He is confident in the Lord's love; he is confident in the Lord's salvation (v. 5); he is confident in the Lord's blessing (v. 6). The confidence of verse 5 is a dramatic departure from the accusations in verse 1. Somehow, in this process of lament, the Lord has reminded David of what is true, and David has chosen to believe it.

But David is not only affirming his confidence in the Lord but also affirming his resolve to act on his confidence. This is always the nature of true faith. David says, "I have trusted," "My heart will rejoice," and "I will sing" (vv. 4-5). These are all acts of faith. It is not blind faith; it is faith rooted in his confidence in what he knows to be true about God. David is choosing to believe and respond to the truth he knows. God is answering David's prayers. God is bringing David back to a place of confidence and hope. David continues to make progress.

Conclusion

Do you think David really believed what he said in verses 1-2? Do you think he really believed God had forgotten him forever? Do you think he really believed God had hidden from him? I don't think he did. David is fully confident in verses 5-6 of everything he questioned in verses 1-2. But it took time for him to get from verses 1-2 to verses 5-6. We tend to be so quick to move to the acceptance of verses 5-6 (and even more quick to tell others to get moving), but we must not skip the process of verses 1-4. This process matters. The Lord does restore David to praise, joy, and confidence, but David gets there through the process of lament. In other words, we must give ourselves, and others, the freedom to be honest with God and the time to turn the corner from accusation, to asking, to acceptance.

Any one of us who has tried to cultivate meaningful, healthy, and deep relationships with others knows that honesty is the foundation of intimacy. If there is no freedom to be honest, there will never be any true intimacy. This is also true in our relationships with God. If you do not feel the freedom to be honest with God, you will never move toward greater intimacy with God. So when you feel as if God has forgotten you or hidden from you, tell him. Pour out your heart to God. Don't rush.

And as you begin to pour out your heart to God and honestly express your emotions, you will be on the pathway to greater intimacy with him.

Reflect and Discuss

1. Do you feel the freedom to be honest with God? Why or why not?
2. How do you think honesty with God cultivates intimacy with God?
3. When you feel as if God has forgotten you, what do you tend to do with those emotions? What would be a healthier way to deal with them?
4. Have you ever, thoughtfully or not, gone through a process of lamenting like David did in Psalm 13? Have you ever moved from accusing God to accepting God? Discuss that process with someone else.
5. What role does the Word of God play in David's transition in verses 5-6?
6. Verse 6 begins with "I will sing." There are times when we choose to sing even when we don't feel like it. What role has singing played in your own life as a way to move into greater confidence in God?
7. If you are in a season of struggle right now, what part of the lamenting process are you in? How do you feel that you can continue to move forward in that process?

Only Fools Deny There Is a God

PSALM 14

Main Idea: Fools deny God and live without him, but the wise follow Jesus and rejoice in him.

I. The Fool Opposes the Things of God (14:1-3).
- A. He does not serve God (14:1).
- B. He does not seek God (14:2-3).

II. The Fool Troubles the People of God (14:4-7).
- A. The fool acts wickedly (14:4-5).
- B. The Lord acts faithfully (14:5-7).

A small but vocal group of people surround us. Though few, they have extraordinary influence. We can hear their voice in major universities and colleges, the entertainment industry, and the media. They may also be your classmates, next-door neighbors, or even those sitting beside you in a church service. Who am I (Danny) talking about? Atheists.

In its simplest definition, atheism is a worldview that believes God does not exist. Paul Feinberg explains that four forms of atheism exist:

> 1. *Classical atheism* is not a general denial of God's existence but rejection of a particular god. Christians were repeatedly called atheists in this sense because they refused to acknowledge heathen gods.
>
> 2. *Philosophical atheism* may be contrasted with theism, which affirms a personal, self-conscious deity (not a principle, first cause, or force).
>
> 3. *Dogmatic atheism* is absolute denial of God's existence. This [position] has been rarer than one might think; people more often declare themselves agnostics or secularists. There have, however, been those who claimed to hold this view (the eighteenth-century French atheists).
>
> 4. *Practical atheism* does not deny God, but lives as if there is no God. (Feinberg, "Atheism," 193)

When it comes to *dogmatic atheism*, a list of impressive advocates exist who teach with colorful and thought-provoking rhetoric. For example, German atheist philosopher Ludwig Feuerbach (1804–1872) wrote,

> My only wish is . . . to transform friends of God into friends of man, believers into thinkers, devotees of prayer into devotees of work, candidates for the hereafter into students of this world, Christians who, by their own procession and admission, are "half animal, half angel" into persons, into whole persons. (*Lectures*, 285)

The American astronomer Carl Sagan (1934–1996) is reported to have said,

> The idea that God is an oversized white male with a flowing beard who sits in the sky and tallies the fall of every sparrow is ludicrous. But if by God one means the set of physical laws that govern the universe, then clearly there is such a God. This God is emotionally unsatisfying . . . it does not make much sense to pray to the law of gravity.[1]

And the popular scientist and atheist Richard Dawkins (1941–) adds,

> If you have a faith, it is [probably] the same faith as your parents and grandparents had. No doubt soaring cathedrals, stirring music, moving stories and parables help a bit. But by far the most important variable determining your religion is the accident of birth. (*A Devil's Chaplain*, 143)

Elsewhere Dawkins says,

> Faith is the great cop-out, the great excuse to evade the need to think and evaluate evidence. Faith is belief in spite of, even perhaps because of, the lack of evidence. ("Editorial," *The Independent*, 17)

These men are passionate in their beliefs, dogmatic in their convictions, and rock-solid in their commitments. Yet one wonders if they truly arrived where they landed by pure reason and rational processes as they claim. If you were to dig beneath the surface of the affirmations

---

[1] This quote is often attributed to Carl Sagan, but no citation could be found for it. However, he did use similar wording elsewhere (see Sagan, *Broca's Brain*, 330).

of these priests and prophets of atheism, you would find honest admissions of the emotions and the heart supporting the beliefs of the atheistic agenda. Famous atheist and novelist Aldous Huxley (1894–1963) describes the underlying reasons behind his philosophy in *Ends and Means*:

> For myself, as, no doubt, for most of my contemporaries, the *philosophy of meaninglessness was essentially an instrument of liberation.* The liberation we desired was simultaneously liberation from a certain political and economic system and liberation from a certain system of morality. We objected to the morality because it interfered with our *sexual* freedom; we objected to the *political* and economic system because it was unjust. The supporters of these systems claimed that in some way they embodied the meaning (a Christian meaning, they insisted) of the world. There was one admirably simple method of confuting these people and at the same time justifying ourselves in our political and erotic revolt: we could deny that the world had any meaning whatsoever. (Huxley, *Ends and Means*, 316; emphasis added)

Consider the straightforward confession of Thomas Nagel, professor of philosophy at New York University:

> I speak from experience, being strongly subject to this fear myself: I want atheism to be true and am made uneasy by fact that some of the most intelligent and well-informed people I know are religious believers. It isn't just that I don't believe in God and, naturally, hope that I'm right in my belief. It's that I hope there is no God! I don't want there to be a God; I don't want the universe to be like that. My guess is that this cosmic authority problem is not a rare condition and that it is responsible for much of the scientism and reductionism of our time. One of the tendencies it supports is the ludicrous overuse of evolutionary biology to explain everything about human life, including everything about the human mind. . . . This is a somewhat ridiculous situation. . . . [I]t is just as irrational to be influenced in one's beliefs by the hope that God does not exist as by the hope that God does exist. (*The Last Word*, 130–31)

And hear the heart cry of eighteen-year-old Tara Fritsch:

> I was taught that God was the Almighty and was good, but the past few months have set me straight. There is no God. At least, not the God everyone is talking about. If He/She was real, then there wouldn't be so much disease, death, hurt and heartbreak in the world. In December, one of my friends lost her mother. In January, a friend was killed on his way to school. In April, a friend of the family lost his long battle with AIDS. And in May, one of my best friends also lost her mother. What god would want to do this to anyone? None that I know of or believe in. (Fritch, "'Do You Believe in God?'" 117)

If we examine why people choose atheism, we will discover the problem for many does not reside in their minds but in their hearts. Many do not believe God exists because they do not want God to exist—at least, not a God like the one revealed in the Bible. But by saying no to this God and rejecting this God, we play the fool. The wisdom of King David in Psalm 14 addresses this foolish thinking.

The Fool Opposes the Things of God

PSALM 14:1-3

Psalm 14 is almost identical to Psalm 53. It is a psalm of lament and a psalm of wisdom. The fool of Psalm 14 epitomizes the ungodly sinners of Psalm 1. To him the things of God do not matter at all. They count for nothing. Intellectually and practically, he lives an anti-god, atheistic life where he is the center of his own universe. Allen Ross correctly notes, "The description of the depravity in this psalm refers to unbelievers who persist in living as if there were no God" (*Psalms 1–41,* 373).

He Does Not Serve God (14:1)

The Hebrew word for *fool* here is *nabal.* The story of Nabal in 1 Samuel 25 tells of a real-life fool, a real *nabal.* The emphasis of this foolishness in Psalm 14:1 is more on his will than his mind. This fool is the practical atheist. With wicked and evil motives, he intentionally and boldly asserts his independence and autonomy from God. In his soul he says God has no place. In his heart and in his life, there is no God *for* him or *to* him.

If God is there, this person does not care. This person is self-consumed and self-absorbed to the core.

David quickly diagnoses such people's spiritual condition: "They are corrupt" (i.e., morally perverse, wicked, depraved in character), and "they do vile deeds." David adds a comprehensive judgment: "There is no one who does good." To them, serving God is of no concern at all.

He Does Not Seek God (14:2-3)

David describes the Lord as looking "down from heaven on the human race" (lit. "sons of man" or "sons of Adam"). He looks down to see if "there is one who is wise, one who seeks God." Verse 3 provides the tragic answer: "All have turned away; all alike have become corrupt. There is no one who does good, not even one." Alec Motyer says the phrase "become corrupt" connotes the idea "of milk turning sour" (*Psalms by the Day*, 36).

Yahweh, the Lord of heaven, surveys planet Earth to find someone who understands the *ways* of God and who seeks the *will* of God. Although verse 1 has the fool in view, verse 3 now scrutinizes all humanity. What the Lord saw in David's day, and what he sees now, is astonishing. What God saw in the garden of Eden (Gen 3–4), before the flood (Gen 6:5), at the tower of Babel (Gen 11:5), and in Sodom and Gomorrah (Gen 18:21) continues. The foolish want to be their own god (Gen 3) rather than confess Jesus as Lord and God. They would prefer to murder their brothers than submit to God's Son (Gen 3). They desire to pursue every form of wickedness with an evil heart (Gen 6) rather than give their hearts to Christ. They build for themselves a monument to the heavens (Gen 11) and extol humanity's greatness rather than look up to a Savior on a cross, drop to their knees, and bow their heads at the feet of a crucified King. They would rather lust after strange flesh in sexual immorality (Gen 18) than live for the Lord Jesus in purity and holiness. No, the wicked, foolish, and self-centered person will neither serve God nor seek God. The fool opposes the things of God.

The Fool Troubles the People of God

PSALM 14:4-7

Committed to a world without God, the fool of Psalm 14 actively opposes the things of God and the people of God. In some places of the world, active persecution and oppression exist. Death, imprisonment, torture, and loss of home and job daily threaten believers. In countries like North Korea, China, Indonesia, Saudi Arabia, and Sudan, devoted disciples of Jesus follow their Master knowing it could mean great loss. In other places opposition comes in a different form. Most often it is verbal. Christians are ridiculed and lampooned. They are excluded from the public square, denied a voice on educational platforms, and asked (not so politely) to keep their views to themselves. Foolish and blind to reality, the wicked fail to see the tragic end of their worldview. What does David say of these who trouble God's people?

The Fool Acts Wickedly (14:4-5)

David calls these persons "evildoers" who "never understand" (NLT, "never learn"). They lack godly wisdom and insight, the ability to see things as God sees them. They eat ("consume") with an insatiable appetite the people of God as one eats bread, the daily food requirement for life. They feed on God's people. They treat others as only a useful means to their evil ends and goals. They consume others like bread while avoiding the bread of life that truly satisfies (John 6). Further, "they do not call on the Lord." Why? They think they do not need him, nor do they want him. But they will not always think or feel this way. A day is coming when "they will be filled with dread" (v. 5), "overwhelmed with dread" (NIV), and "in great terror" (ESV) because they do see something divine in the redeemed community. Amazingly, the psalmist says they act against and oppose what they clearly see, that "God is with those who are righteous."

Albert Einstein saw this truth on display in Germany prior to World War II:

> Being a lover of freedom, when the [Nazi] revolution came, I looked to the universities to defend it, knowing that they had always boasted of their devotion to the cause of truth; but no, the universities were immediately silenced. Then I looked to the great editors of the newspapers, whose flaming editorials in days gone by had proclaimed their love of freedom; but they, like the universities, were silenced in a few short weeks. . . . Only the Church stood squarely across the path of Hitler's campaign for suppressing truth. I never had any special interest in the Church before, but now I feel a great affection

> and admiration for it because the Church alone has had the courage and persistence to stand for intellectual and moral freedom. I am forced to confess that what I once despised I now praise unreservedly. (Piper, "Religion: German Martyrs")

Yes, the fool fails to see where life without God will lead. Remove God from the earth, and the earth becomes hell.

The Lord Acts Faithfully (14:5-7)

Blaise Pascal (1623–1662) was a brilliant mathematician and Christian philosopher. Many people still admire and contemplate his insights about God. Considering how God reveals himself and works in our midst, he wrote some perceptive and challenging words:

> If there were no obscurity, man would not feel his corruption: if there were no light, man would not hope for a remedy. Thus, it is not only just, but useful for us, that God should be concealed in part and revealed in part, since it is equally dangerous for man to know God without knowing his misery and to know his own misery without knowing God. (Pascal, *Thoughts*, 328)

The fool does not feel his corruption, but the person in Christ does. The fool does not perceive the light of salvation, but the person in Christ does. The fool does not know his own wretchedness as he ought, but the person in Christ does. This person in Christ, despite the attacks and opposition of the wicked, can rest in the reality that the Lord will act faithfully on his behalf.

Verse 5 informs us that the Lord is with those who are "righteous." When someone opposes God's people, they oppose the God who is with his people. Verse 6 indicts the wicked fool who frustrates "the plans of the oppressed." The NIV says, "Evildoers frustrate the plans of the poor." In positions of power and prominence, they ridicule, harass, and do their best to keep God's people down. However, the Lord is believers' refuge, their fortress of protection, and their place of security in times of trouble.

The prayer of Psalm 14 finally comes in verse 7. The psalmist pleads for deliverance and rescue from Zion, the place where Messiah-King is enthroned as God's anointed (2:6)! He looks forward to "when the Lord restores the fortunes of his people." Such a day would bring rejoicing and gladness to God's people. Such a day would come with the obedience and submission of the nations to God. Such a day was seen when Jesus the Messiah-King, who joined his people, came out of Zion and struck terror in the hearts of the wicked, delivered his own through the cross, and brought joy and gladness to all who flee to him for refuge.

Conclusion

On June 11, 2001, six years, one month, and twenty-three days after destroying the Murrah Federal Building in Oklahoma City, killing 168 people and wounding hundreds more, Timothy McVeigh was executed. He made no statement, but he left a handwritten note quoting a section of the poem "Invictus," written by William Ernest Henley (CNN, "Timothy McVeigh Dead"). The words of the poem sum up well how the fools of Psalm 14 view life.

> Out of the night that covers me
> Black as the Pit from pole to pole,
> I thank whatever gods may be
> For my unconquerable soul.
> In the fell clutch of circumstance
> I have not winced nor cried aloud.
> Under the bludgeonings of chance
> My head is bloody, but unbowed.
> Beyond this place of wrath and tears
> Looms but the Horror of the shade,
> And yet the menace of the years
> Finds, and shall find, me unafraid.
> It matters not how strait the gate,
> How charged with punishments the scroll,
> I am the master of my fate:
> I am the captain of my soul.

Each one of us must carefully examine his or her heart and life to make certain we are not playing the fool of Psalm 14. We are often closer to acting as a fool than we may think. When we persist in sin, closing our ears and heart to God, we are fools. When we attempt to live without the guidance of the Holy Spirit, we are fools. When we attempt to live without prayer, we are fools. When we attempt to satisfy ourselves with anything or anyone other than Jesus Christ, we are fools. When we claim to be the masters of our own destinies, we are fools. The fool has said in his heart, "There is no God." The wise has said in his heart, "There is a god, my God, and his name is Jesus."

Reflect and Discuss

1. What similarities can you find between the various atheist scholars that this section mentions? Do you know someone who is an atheist? What reasons does he or she give for not believing in God?
2. Does being an atheist mean a person will do only bad things? Why or why not? If you answered no, how do you explain any positive things atheists do?
3. Could someone claim to be a Christian but practically live as an atheist? Explain. What are some ways you act that do not match with what you believe?
4. Why do those who oppose God also want to trouble his people?
5. Do you have compassion for people who do not believe in God? Why should the gospel give us compassion for those who act like fools?
6. What does it take for an atheist to begin believing that God exists? Can you convince someone with arguments to become a Christian? Why or why not?
7. This section teaches that "the fool does not feel his corruption, but the man in Christ does." How has your life in Christ changed how you view corruption in yourself?
8. Paul uses this psalm in Romans 3. What does Paul say one must do in response to humanity's lack of righteousness?
9. How will the Lord restore the fortunes of his people? What promises does Scripture give? How does this hope help us live now?
10. Why should God's people rejoice (v. 7)? What does a lack of joy indicate about your beliefs?

A Heart Cry for God's Presence

PSALM 15

Main Idea: We can only enjoy God's presence because of Christ's righteousness.

I. God Stirs in Our Hearts a Longing for His Presence (15:1).
II. God Reveals Our Inadequacy for His Presence (15:2-5).
III. God Makes a Way for Us into His Presence.

Our conversations with God reveal a lot about our relationships with God. This general concept is true in any relationship. If you were to eavesdrop on a long conversation between two people you have never met (which is probably not a good idea), you would discern things about the nature of their relationship. Our conversations with God reveal the health and depth of our relationships with him. Our conversations with God reveal what we really think of him and what we really want from the relationship. Our prayers are a good indicator of where we are in our relationships with God.

In Psalm 15 David is talking with the Lord. More accurately, he is crying out to the Lord. He begins with one word: "Lord." David's brief conversation with God reveals a lot about his relationship with God. That one word is not simply the way he chooses to address God; it is a cry of the heart to God. With that one word David reveals that the greatest longing of his heart is to experience and know more of God's presence. In Psalm 15 David reveals that the God who stirs up a longing for his presence is also the only one who can satisfy that longing. He also reveals that we will only be able to enjoy God's presence by his righteousness, not our own.

God Stirs in Our Hearts a Longing for His Presence

PSALM 15:1

David begins this psalm with two questions directed toward the Lord. Both reveal his longing for God's presence. "Lord, who can dwell in your tent? Who can live on your holy mountain?" With these words

David paints a picture of the earthly places in which God's people meet with him. The "tent" (or tabernacle) represents God's dwelling place that went with the people as they journeyed to the promised land (Exod 25–40). The tent represented the centrality of God's presence in the lives of the people. It reminded the people that if God did not go with them, they would never make it to the promised land (Exod 33:15). When David asks, "Who can dwell in your tent?" he is asking, "Who can be in your presence?"

In the next phrase David asks the same thing in a different way. The "holy mountain" of the Lord points us back to the garden of Eden, God's dwelling place. We infer the garden was elevated on a hill because of one river flowing into it and four rivers flowing out of it (Gen 2:10-14). These rivers symbolize God's presence flowing into the garden and that presence flowing out to the ends of the earth so that his glory might spread to all people (Beale and Kim, *God Dwells*, 20–23). The "holy hill" represents a longing for the perfect, uninterrupted, unhindered experience of God's presence. And David did not want to just "sojourn" there; he wanted to "live" there.

Psalm 15 is a longing for intimacy, nearness, communion with God. It is the cry of the heart of someone who longs for God more than anything else in life (Ps 27:4). And it is a longing that only God can initiate. When we long for God's presence, it is a clear sign that God is inviting us into his presence. It is the summons of the Lord. It is a clear sign that the Lord is stirring in our hearts. In the same way that a doctor asks us about our appetites to determine if we are healthy, our appetites for God reveal the health of our relationships with him. This kind of longing for God is one we do not ever want to ignore. But the question still remains: Who exactly can enter into his presence?

God Reveals Our Inadequacy for His Presence

PSALM 15:2-5

In Psalm 15:2-5 David answers the question he asked in verse 1. He asks and answers the most important question of life: Who can be restored back to life as God intended for it to be? Who can enjoy God's presence? David then gives ten qualifications for the one who can enjoy God's presence. These ten qualifications do not serve as a checklist so that we might be confident in our worthiness of entering; rather, they remind us that without divine help, we will never enjoy his presence.

Verse 2 tells us that to enter his presence we must live blamelessly, practice righteousness, and acknowledge the truth in our hearts. The last phrase clarifies that it is not enough to have an external form of religion or to be able to articulate the truth with our mouths. God demands that we speak the truth in our hearts, meaning our desires and motivations are true. To enter his presence we must do, think, and say what is right.

In verse 3 the list of qualifications grows. The one who can enter God's presence must be one "who does not slander with his tongue, who does not harm his friend or discredit his neighbor." This means that you must not speak badly of others, gossip, or tell lies. You must also not bring pain to anyone, ridicule them, mock them, of make fun of them. The point is, we must not think, say, or do anything unloving to another. How are we doing so far? Feeling good about ourselves?

In verse 4 David says the qualified person is one "who despises the one rejected by the LORD but honors those who fear the LORD, who keeps his word whatever the cost." This is a picture of one who grieves over evil, despises wickedness, and is committed to doing and upholding what is right, no matter the cost. Finally, as if we were not all disqualified already, verse 5 addresses how we deal with money. In order to enter the presence of the Lord we must uphold absolute integrity in all areas of finance.

Although these verses do feel like a list of ten qualifications for entering God's presence, they are not a list of do's and don'ts. These verses reveal the kind of person who can enter God's presence. "The one who does these things will never be moved" (v. 5 HCSB). In other words, this is not a call for us to strive to meet all these qualifications; rather, it is a picture of the kind of person we must be in order to enter his presence—a kind of person that doesn't look much like any of us at all!

God Makes a Way for Us into His Presence

Psalm 15 ends in a rather hopeless way. David has reminded us that we were created for God's presence and will only experience the fullness of life in God's presence, even while making it abundantly clear that absolutely none of us can enter God's presence. If a pastor closed in prayer and sent everyone home right here, this would be a hopeless sermon.

In some ways Psalm 15 should stir up a bit of hopelessness in us. Verses 2-5 should actually terrify us. When we read these qualifications, we should realize that they are not here to help us but to condemn us. What if that's actually the point of Psalm 15? What if this psalm serves to remind us that we will never be the kind of people who can enter God's presence? What if this psalm exists to make us cry out for mercy? What if this psalm was meant to point us beyond ourselves to the only one who is qualified to enter God's presence? This is exactly the point of Psalm 15.

There is only one man who has ever met the qualifications to enter the presence of God. Only one man has been pure in all his thoughts, motives, actions, and responses—the man who knew no sin, Jesus Christ (2 Cor 5:21). Jesus is "the one" of Psalm 15:5.

The truth of the gospel is that we were created for God's presence, but like Adam and Eve, we were removed from God's presence because of our sin. The problem is not just that we have committed sins but that we are sinful people to our core. None of us can ever be "the one" who is qualified. So God, who longs to restore humanity back into his presence, sent Jesus to live a perfect life and die a criminal's death. He died, not for his sins but for ours, so that through his perfect life and sacrificial death, and through our faith in him, his righteousness might be credited to our accounts (Rom 4:22-25). That means we will never enter God's presence by our righteousness but by the righteousness of Jesus Christ. Jesus entered the "holy mountain" so that through faith in him we also might enter.

Conclusion

How do we respond to Psalm 15? First, we must **receive** the righteousness of Christ. We must confess our sins, feel the weight of condemnation, and throw ourselves at the mercy of God. We must call on the name of the Lord and ask him to forgive us of our sins and give us his righteousness.

We must also **rejoice** in the righteousness of Christ. We must see Jesus as our only hope and the ultimate picture of God's love and desire for us. When we see ourselves as we truly are and Christ as he truly is, we should sing like never before and rejoice with all our might because of the goodness of God.

Finally, we must **rest** in the righteousness of Christ. The righteous requirements of the law were fully met in Jesus (Rom 8:3-4). God's affection for you is not based on how well you did on the qualifications test of Psalm 15. God's affection for you is based on the fact that he sees you through the perfect righteousness of Christ. You cannot win his favor or earn his favor; you must simply rest in the finished work of Jesus Christ on your behalf. This is what it means to have faith in Jesus Christ.

Reflect and Discuss

1. Do you hunger and thirst for righteousness as David does in Psalm 15:1? Do you remember specific times when you have felt an overwhelming sense of longing for God? If so, how did you respond to that? How should you respond to that?
2. Although verses 2-5 are not given for us to try to meet the requirements, they still point us to the Christlike character we have been called to imitate. Look through verses 2-5 carefully and ask the Lord to reveal any areas of your life in which you might be walking in sin.
3. Carefully consider areas of your life that you need to ask God, and others, to help you with. For instance, as you look at verse 3, do you tend to slander others or take up an offense against someone else? If so, confess this to the Lord and a trusted believer who can hold you accountable, and ask the Lord for help to change.
4. Did the truths from Psalm 15 help you understand more of the gospel? If so, take the time to share the gospel with another believer. Then challenge one another to share the gospel with an unbeliever.

Satisfied in the Lord

PSALM 16

Main Idea: God himself is the Christian's ultimate good, and the bodily resurrection of Jesus Christ is the Christian's ultimate hope and peace.

I. We Have the Protection of the Lord (16:1-4).
- A. The wise person will run to God and find satisfaction (16:1-3).
- B. The unwise person will run from God and find sorrow (16:4).

II. We Have the Provisions of the Lord (16:5-6).
- A. The Lord is our sustenance (16:5).
- B. The Lord is our inheritance (16:6).

III. We Have the Presence of the Lord (16:7-8).
- A. The Lord counsels us (16:7).
- B. The Lord comforts us (16:7-8).

IV. We Have the Promises of the Lord (16:9-11).
- A. We experience his peace (16:9).
- B. We experience his power (16:10).
- C. We enjoy his presence (16:11).

I (Danny) know of no one who has challenged us to be more God focused and more God centered in all that we do than John Piper. Again and again he reminds us, "God is most glorified in us when we are most satisfied in him" (Piper, *When I Don't Desire God,* 13). Jonathan Edwards (1703–1758), a major figure in the First Great Awakening and the first president of Princeton University, also believed our delight and God's glory were connected. He said, "God is glorified not only by his glory's being seen, but by its being rejoiced in. When those that see it delight in it, God is more glorified than if they only see it" (Edwards, *Works,* 495). These words capture the heart of King David in Psalm 16. He not only saw the Lord's glory, but he was also satisfied in that glory. He delighted in the Lord. In a psalm of trust, perhaps in the midst of danger or a threat to his life, David focuses on all his blessings and benefits from God. He says with a resounding confession, "I am satisfied in the Lord." He says to his God, "You are my refuge (v. 1), you are my goodness (v. 2), you are my portion and cup (vv. 5-6), you are my counsel (v. 7), you are at my right hand (v. 8), you are my security (v. 9), you are my guide (v. 11), you are my fullness of joy (v. 11), and you are pleasures forevermore (v. 11)." He is satisfied in the Lord.

From this list of bountiful blessings, David proclaims his confidence in his God (v. 1), his *Adonai* (v. 2), Yahweh (v. 5), through four movements within the psalm. They highlight why we should forever be satisfied in the Lord.

We Have the Protection of the Lord

PSALM 16:1-4

Verses 1-4 look back to the prologue of the Psalter and Psalm 1, which contrasted the righteous and the ungodly. That same scenario occurs again in these verses. The Godward life brings joy. The idolatrous life brings sorrow.

The Wise Person Will Run to God and Find Satisfaction (16:1-3)

David asks God to "protect me," (ESV, "preserve me; NIV, "keep me safe"). He will "take refuge" in the Lord. "Protect" could be rendered "watch over." We can flee to God and ask him to protect and deliver us. In verse 2 David addresses "the LORD" (*Yahweh*) and exclaims, "You are my Lord [*Adonai*]; I have nothing good besides you." The personal pronouns are important. The sovereign Lord and Master of creation is David's good. Apart from the Lord, he has no good. God is his delight, his treasure, and his refuge. To look for goodness, true goodness, elsewhere would be foolish. It would be idolatrous. It would mean pursuing another god, a false god. As James 1:17 reminds us, "Every good and perfect gift is from above." Now we understand why Jesus says to the rich young ruler in Mark 10:18, "Why do you call me good? . . . No one is good except God above." To see the wrong thing as a good thing plunged the human race into sin. Adam and Eve convinced themselves they knew what good was better than God (Gen 3). We frequently, yet foolishly, follow in their footsteps.

Verse 3 addresses one of the good things we receive from the Lord: brothers and sisters in Christ. David makes a distinction between the "holy ones" in the heavens (the angels; Ps 34:9) and the "holy ones" he has in view here. These he calls "the holy people who are in the land." He says of these holy ones, "They are the noble [ESV, "excellent"] ones."

Of these men and women who love and obey the Lord, David says, "All my delight is in them."

David sees no contradiction between saying that God is his only good and that he delights in God's people. When we delight in the fellowship of believers, we do not take anything from God's glory because God has given them to us as a good gift. You are God's gift to me, and I am God's gift to you. We are God's gifts to one another. To delight in God's people is to take delight in the Lord's goodness. This is God's plan for his people. To be practical, there are seven reasons we need other saints:

1. We need the *fellowship* of God's good gift.
2. We need the *instruction* of God's good gift.
3. We need the *accountability* of God's good gift.
4. We need the *rebuke* of God's good gift.
5. We need the *comfort* of God's good gift.
6. We need the *love* of God's good gift.
7. We need the *presence* of God's good gift.

Without God's people, we stumble and falter, grow cold and cynical, lose our passion, and miss out on the blessings God provides in and through these "noble" or "excellent" ones. Do you delight in the saints? Do you love and enjoy fellowship with your brothers and sisters in Christ? We need to be around people who have been around God!

The Unwise Person Will Run from God and Find Sorrow (16:4)

The unwise of verse 4 contrast starkly with the wise in verses 1-3. The unwise do not trust the Lord, nor do they enjoy the community of believers. Tragically, they will have their sorrows multiplied. Why? Because they "take," or hasten after (ESV, "run after"), another god.[2] They multiply their sorrows by chasing after idols, false gods of the head and the heart, false gods of silver and gold, and false gods of power, prestige, position, and possessions. They chase empty dreams, clouds without water, illusional aspirations and goals, and hopes that will never materialize.

What they believe will bring joy only brings sorrow. Matthew Henry well said, "Those that multiply gods multiply grief to themselves; for, whoever thinks one God too little, will find two too many, and yet hundreds not enough" (*Commentary*, 288). David says that he will have nothing to

---

[2] The word *god* is implied in the Hebrew text.

do with the works of those who do not love the Lord. He will not join them in pagan worship ("pour out their drink offerings of blood"), nor will he even allow the names of false gods to flow from his lips.

"Offerings of blood" may refer to the actual drinking of pagan blood sacrifices, either animal or human. It also may be a metaphor for guilt due to the bloodshed of the innocent (Anderson, *Psalms*, 142–43; Wilson, *Psalms*, 309). The shedding of the blood of the innocent for any reason will sear the conscience, scar the soul, and increase sorrow and trouble. The gods of this world only offer empty promises. They make promises but never deliver. "David," as Allen Ross says, "did not recognize the divinity or power of any 'god' other than Yahweh" (*Psalms 1–41*, 404). He would not join them. He would never speak of them.

We Have the Provisions of the Lord

PSALM 16:5-6

In verses 5-6 David again addresses God (v. 2) in terms of his covenant name "LORD" or *Yahweh*. Drawing on language related to Joshua's conquest of the promised land, David praises the Lord for who he is. The provision of Yahweh is Yahweh himself (Belcher, *Messiah*, 163).

The Lord Is Our Sustenance (16:5)

Refusing the cup that pours out drink offerings of blood and worships the names of mere idols (v. 4), David confesses Yahweh as his God and the Lord as his portion and cup, a cup that Psalm 23:5 says "overflows." What he needs for life is the Lord, not the things of the Lord. God is David's drink and food. The Lord is his nourishment. All he will ever need, he finds in the Lord now and in the future. What a blessing to know the God who holds the whole world in his hands holds our futures too!

The Lord Is Our Inheritance (16:6)

The Lord is also David's inheritance. Using promised-land imagery again, he says, "Boundary lines have fallen for me in pleasant [or delightful] places." What David has, he has from the Lord. God gave it. He did not earn it or work for it. And the inheritance remains safe and secure because the Lord provides it, places it, and protects it. It is, David says, a "beautiful inheritance," a delightful inheritance, because it was marked out by the Lord. God gives himself to us, his saints. He gives us pleasant and good things because he is the source and origin of everything good. We have the Lord. Why would we clamor for anything else?

We Have the Presence of the Lord

PSALM 16:7-8

David continues to meditate on the greatness and goodness of God. His theocentric (God-centered) focus balances beautifully with the personal response of adoration and praise of a humble worshiper. Indeed, we must approach the Lord in this manner if we want to truly worship him as we ought.

The Lord Counsels Us (16:7)

We live in the day of the counselor, psychiatrist, psychologist, psychoanalyst, and therapist. When mental health professionals make right use of God's Word in their work, they are invaluable. But many try to fix problems without God and Scripture. In fact, it was by means of an evil counselor that the world was ruined by sin. The serpent gave Eve wicked counsel, Adam joined in, and together they plunged the whole world into insanity. David, however, says the Lord is his counselor. Isaiah tells us of a "Wonderful Counselor" (Isa 9:6). David blesses the Lord because of his counsel that comes "even at night when my thoughts trouble me." Proverbs 2:6-7 says, "For the LORD gives wisdom; from his mouth come knowledge and understanding; he stores up sound wisdom for the upright" (ESV). David receives wisdom and direction from the Lord. He receives it day and night, in good times and troubling times.

The Lord Comforts Us (16:7-8)

Because the Lord fills David's mind with counsel, the Lord also guides his life so that he "will not be shaken." The Lord guides his mind and his heart. At night, when the mind can run wild, David's mind runs to the Lord. At night, when the heart worries and frets easily, the Lord brings calm and rest. The believer, the disciple of Jesus, can say of this Wonderful Counselor and instructor, "I have set the LORD always before me" (ESV). The Lord is my constant companion, a friend who sticks closer than a brother. This God rules and sustains the universe, but he is also the same Lord who always stays right in front of me. Indeed, we can say with the psalmist, "Because he is at my right hand, I will not be shaken." We have the Lord's presence. Why would we ever think of moving? Why would we let anything shake us from the joy we can find only in him?

We Have the Promises of the Lord

PSALM 16:9-11

David has put his trust in the Lord. God has sovereignly provided all that he needs and has carefully mapped out his inheritance. He is David's counselor and confidant, always in sight, ever at his side. Enemies may come against him, and death may even threaten him, but David rests in the Lord who completely satisfies him.

We Have His Peace (16:9)

The Lord is always with us (v. 8). Therefore, like David, we can be glad in heart, and our whole being can rejoice! David not only rejoices inwardly, but he also rejoices outwardly. He shouts, "My whole being rejoices." What is the result? He says, "My body also rests securely." David is secure in body and soul. He has inward and outward peace. He has spiritual and physical peace. He is whole in the Lord. But how can David make such a stunning claim? Verse 10 gives the answer.

We Experience His Power (16:10)

David now looks forward to the future. Although Old Testament eschatology was not highly developed at this point, hints and anticipations of an eternal, bodily existence in the presence of the Lord appear here. Job 19:25-27 has already taught us,

> *But I know that my Redeemer lives,*
> *and at the end he will stand on the dust.*
> *Even after my skin has been destroyed,*
> *yet I will see God in my flesh.*
> *I will see him myself;*
> *my eyes will look at him, and not as a stranger.*
> *My heart longs within me.*

Scholars who reject the presence of a belief in immortality or bodily resurrection in Psalm 16 inadequately interpret verse 10. That David is confident of immediate divine intervention to preserve his life is not in doubt. However, we can find much more here than that. A look at the companion to this psalm, Psalm 17, will help clarify things. There, verses 13-15 clearly contrast the destiny of the wicked with the destiny of the righteous:

> *Rise up, Lord!*
> *Confront him; bring him down.*
> *With your sword, save me from the wicked.*
> *With your hand, Lord, save me from men,*
> *from men of the world*
> *whose portion is in this life:*
> *You fill their bellies with what you have in store;*
> *their sons are satisfied,*
> *and they leave their surplus to their children.*
> *But I will see your face in righteousness;*
> *when I awake, I will be satisfied with your presence.*

Note how 1 John 3:2 echoes this.

David is confident that the Lord "will not abandon me to Sheol," which is the grave or the place of the dead (16:10). The ESV translates this verse, "For you will not abandon my soul to Sheol." Nor, David adds, will the Lord "allow your faithful one to see decay." The NASB, AMP, and NKJV translate the words *faithful one* as "Holy One." The capitalization is significant. It recognizes rightly the Christological promise in verses 10-11. The Spirit of God moves David to consider God's plan and purpose for David's greater Son, the Lord's anointed of Psalm 2, the prototypical Son of Man of Psalm 8, and the Righteous Sufferer of Psalm 22. David, by the Spirit, looks down the corridors of history, and he sees Jesus delivered out of the corruption of the grave through his glorious bodily resurrection!

Peter interprets this passage in his sermon on the day of Pentecost (Acts 2:24-32). There he teaches us Psalm 16:8-11 is about Messiah Jesus! Belcher helpfully comments,

> Psalm 16 is considered a Messianic psalm because verses 9-11 are used in Acts 2:24-32. The passage from 16:9-11 is quoted and then applied directly to the resurrection of Christ. The justification for this is that 16:10 could not have been about David because he was dead and buried in a tomb, thus he experienced corruption. David was not speaking of himself but of one of his descendants. His statement is based on the

> oath of the covenant promise that one of his descendants would sit on the throne. Peter says that David was a prophet and thus foresaw and spoke about the resurrection of Christ. Christ did not see the corruption of the grave because God raised him from the dead. (*Messiah*, 164)

Paul would also reference this psalm in Acts 13:35-38 as he proclaimed the resurrection of Jesus at Antioch in Pisidia. Derek Kidner rightly says, "Both Peter and Paul insisted (Acts 2:29ff.; 13:34-37), this language is too strong even for David's hope of his own resurrection. Only 'he whom God raised up saw no corruption'" (*Psalms 1–72*, 86). Only Jesus can ultimately fulfill the promise of these verses! We have the experience of his power, the power that raised God's Son, David's Son, from the grave.

We Enjoy His Presence (16:11)

David's confidence in the Lord is perfect. He has complete trust in a God who can bring life out of death. The God we can trust for our future is a God we can trust today no matter what. Therefore, we should live in the reality of verse 11 every day. David says, "You reveal the path of life to me." The Lord determines the way, and we will walk in it. Proverbs 15:24 reminds us, "For the prudent the path of life leads upward, so that he may avoid going down to Sheol." Back in Psalm 16:11 we also see, "In your presence is abundant [ESV, "fullness of"] joy." Where? The Lord's presence. What? "Abundant joy." Truly "better a day in your courts than a thousand anywhere else" (Ps 84:10). Amazingly, the Lord does not promise *one* day in his house. He promises *eternity* in his house and in his presence. As Psalm 23:6 promises, God's people "shall dwell in the house of the Lord forever" (ESV).

David concludes the psalm with a simple and beautiful affirmation: "At your right hand are eternal pleasures." In verse 8 the Lord is at David's right hand with his perfect presence. Now we are at his right hand with "eternal pleasures." Because all these pleasures come to us through Messiah, Jesus, we can shout, "I am satisfied in the Lord!"

Conclusion

Jesus's bodily resurrection brings us all the promises of Psalm 16. Because of Jesus's resurrection, we can call God "my Lord" (vv. 1-2), we are united with brothers and sisters who are our delight (v. 3), we have a beautiful inheritance in Jesus's eternal kingdom (vv. 5-6), we have a faithful Counselor who will teach us and be at our right hand (vv. 7-8), we will not be abandoned (vv. 9-10), and we have fullness of joy (vv. 11). In response to all these blessings, we should never stop praising God. The words of the wonderful hymn "The Day of Resurrection" by the Byzantine monk John of Damascus (ca. AD 675–749) are appropriate words to conclude with:

> Now let the heav'ns be joyful! Let earth her song begin!
> The world resound in triumph, And all that is therein!
> Let all things seen and unseen Their notes of gladness blend,
> For Christ the Lord hath risen, Our joy that hath no end.

Reflect and Discuss

1. Why would God be glorified by us when we are satisfied in him? What does it look like to be satisfied in God?
2. If you believed that God is your ultimate good, how would that shape how you live? How could you examine your life to determine if you believe it?
3. What does a lack of delight in God's people reveal about a person's love for God? How can delight in God's people help fuel your love for God?
4. Have you ever wanted something *from* God instead of God himself? What is the difference between these two desires?
5. Why does David need to remind himself of his blessings and inheritance (vv. 5-6)? How may he be tempted to leave the Lord like others have done (v. 4)?
6. In what ways does the Lord give counsel to his people? How can you discern whether the counsel you receive and give is good or bad?
7. Describe a time when you experienced peace in the Lord despite terrible circumstances. What led to and sustained this peace?
8. Read 1 Corinthians 15. How does Jesus's bodily resurrection give us hope and rest?
9. How does a bodily resurrection differ from popular beliefs in culture about heaven? How does a bodily resurrection bring us back to the hope of Genesis 1–2?
10. In what ways does prayer help us experience the Lord's presence now?

Persevering Faith

PSALM 17

Main Idea: A life of persistent trials demands a life of persevering faith.

I. The Reality of Persistent Trials
II. The Marks of Persevering Faith
   A. Persevering Prayer
   B. Persevering Holiness
   C. Persevering Confidence

If you have been part of a local church for any extended period of time, you have certainly seen Jesus's parable of the soils played out in real life. In Mark 4 Jesus tells about four groups of people who have the seed of the gospel sown in their lives. The first group is equated with a hard path where seed fell; but Satan, like a bird, came and took it away so it did nothing. When seed fell on rocky soil, those represented by that soil type heard the word and received it with joy, but tribulations and persecution came, and they immediately fell away. More seed fell among thorns. People represented by that soil type heard and received the word, but the cares of the world and the deceitfulness of riches choked it out. Only the seed that fell on the good ground took root and bore fruit.

This parable reminds us that the primary mark of a genuine follower of Christ is perseverance. Anyone who has ever been actively involved in a church knows of people who have made a profession of faith, but because of the trials of life, they have fallen away. Although it is incredibly sad, it should not be all that surprising. Jesus not only told us of those who would fall away, but he also told us that only those who persevere to the end will be saved (Matt 24:12-13). This is one of the reasons we need Psalm 17. It reminds us of both the reality of persistent trials and the need for persevering faith.

In Psalm 17 David is crying out for God to help him. He feels as if he has been unjustly accused, and he wants the Lord to fight for him (vv. 1-2). He is looking for vindication. He wants the truth to be made known. He is not afraid of the truth being known because he is confident in his own integrity (vv. 3-5). He is not without sin, but the accusations against him are not true. He has been tried and tested, and nothing has been found. He then prays again (vv. 6-9). Once again, he asks the Lord to deliver him. He talks about his enemies and the violent things they are doing to him (vv. 9-12). Then he prays again (vv. 13-14). For the third time he asks the Lord to intervene, to step in, to take action, and to vindicate him. He ends the psalm with a statement of confidence. In verse 15 he says, "But I will see your face in righteousness; when I awake, I will be satisfied with your presence."

A pattern emerges in Psalm 17. It goes something like this: prayer, problem, prayer, problem, prayer, problem, prayer, confidence (VanGemeren, *Expositors*). And through that pattern two themes emerge: persistent trials and persevering faith. David is under attack, falsely accused, hunted, and wanted. The trials are intense. Yet, in the midst of the trials, he keeps walking with the Lord. He keeps talking with the Lord. He keeps trusting in the Lord. And his trials actually prove the authenticity of his faith. David shows us how the life of persistent trials demands persevering faith.

The Reality of Persistent Trials

PSALM 17

One of the most helpful things about the psalms is that they often remind us we are not alone in our trials and feelings of despair. David's trials were persistent and painful. Those who had come against him were uncaring and unkind (v. 10). They came against him, surrounded him, and were determined to take him down (v. 11). They were like a lion, eager to tear him apart, waiting for the right moment to ambush him (v. 12). Although our situations might not be the same, every believer faces seasons of persistent trials. Psalm 17 is not just for those who are falsely accused or under the threat of physical attack. Psalm 17 is for all of us. We all suffer. We all struggle. And we are all tempted to drift away in the midst of our trials (Heb 2:1-4).

Because I (Josh) am a pastor, people often tell me their problems. I'm glad they do. It is a privilege to know what is going on in their lives. But when my family went through a series of deep struggles, I found that people were more hesitant to bring their problems to me. When they did, they would often say, "Well, I know this is nothing like what you are going through, but . . ." The reality is, it doesn't work that way. All of our trials, even those that seem insignificant to others, are significant. If they feel heavy to you, then they are heavy. Every person's trials should matter to each of us within the church family (see 1 Cor 12:26).

The reality is, we each live a life of persistent trials. Some are massive, some are small, but they do persist. It is part of living in a broken world, being followers of Christ, and submitting our lives to the one who is intent on conforming us into the image of Jesus Christ. As Jesus said in John 16:33, "You will have suffering in this world." This was a guarantee. And Jesus did not tell us that to discourage us but to prepare us. We should be reminded by the promise of persistent trials, and the temptation to give up in the midst of them, that these kinds of trials demand a deep faith. If we want to make it to the end and finish well, each must have a persevering faith like David's in Psalm 17.

The Marks of Persevering Faith

PSALM 17

Psalm 17 not only shows us what persistent trials look like but also what persevering faith looks like. It shows us how to respond when these trials come. It shows us what to do when we feel like giving up or giving in. It shows us what to do when we feel as if the trials are too much and we are in over our heads. Psalm 17, through the example of David, gives us three marks of persevering faith.

The first mark of persevering faith is **persevering prayer**. Three times in this psalm David goes back to prayer. The entire structure of the psalm shows us that David prays and prays and prays. As the situation worsened, his prayers strengthened. David's response brings to mind the widow in Luke 18 who keeps praying and does not lose heart. David just keeps going back. He says, "Lord, hear" (v. 1), "I call on you, God" (v. 6), and "Rise up, Lord!" (v. 13). He just keeps going back to the Lord.

There really is a lesson in David's response. Instead of allowing his trials to increase his anxiety, they increase his cries to the Lord. He does not just pray once; he goes back over and over again. David realizes that prayer is not just about getting something from the Lord; prayer is about gaining the strength to persevere in faith. David prays as if his faith depends on it.

The second mark of persevering faith is **persevering holiness**. Trials make us tired. When we are tired, we tend to be more susceptible to temptation. But David remained steadfast in his holiness. He asked the Lord to test his heart, examine him at night, and try him (v. 3). He remained determined that he would not even allow his words to be sinful while he is being falsely accused (v. 3). David understands the real source of his holiness. He says in verse 4, "Concerning what people do: by the words from your lips I have avoided the ways of the violent." How has David remained steadfast in holiness? Through remaining tethered to God's words. There is no life of holiness without the Word of God. In the inside cover of his Bible, John Bunyan wrote, "Either this book will keep you from sin, or sin will keep you from this book." David, through his commitment to God's words, kept his steps on the right path, and his feet did not slip (v. 5).

The third mark of persevering faith is **persevering confidence**. What kept David persevering in prayer and holiness? His confidence that God had remained faithful to him. His confidence that God was able to help him. He says, "I call on you, God, because you will answer me" (v. 6). That is confidence. Verse 8 is a precious verse. David says, "Protect me as the pupil of your eye; hide me in the shadow of your wings." To be the pupil or apple of someone's eye is to be cherished above all else (Deut 32:10-11). Being hid under the Lord's wings means that the Lord cares for us and cherishes his people. David knows that he is under the shelter of the Lord's wings.

One of the ways you see David's confidence in Psalm 17 is by his consistent use of anthropomorphisms. He speaks of the Lord's lips (v. 4), ear (v. 6), hand (v. 7), eye (v. 8), wings (v. 8), and face (v. 15). God's lips mean that he speaks to us, his ears mean that he hears us, his hands mean that he helps us, his eyes mean that he sees us, his wings mean that he covers us, and his face means that he looks at us (Goldingay, *Psalms 1–41*, 245). The point is that God is real. He is alive and near and active in our lives. Our confidence in him lies in his active involvement in our lives and awareness of all our trials.

Our confidence is not rooted in the depth of our faith but the depth of God's love for us. In the context of these types of trials, Paul writes Romans 8 to assure us of the love that is ours in Christ Jesus and of his eternal commitment to ensure us that those whom he justifies will also be glorified. While our trials demand we persevere in prayer, holiness, and confidence, our ultimate assurance is found in the gospel of Jesus Christ.

Conclusion

Like David's, our trials will persist. Like David, we must fight to persevere. And like David, we must rest in the reality that our perseverance is rooted and grounded in who God is for us and in all that he has promised us. David responds to his trials with the appropriate action. So must we. We must not passively wait for the trials to end but rather aggressively pray, seek holiness, and deepen our confidence through his Word. Yet, while doing all those things, we rest in who God is for us. We rest in his promises and his character. As we do, we gain the assurance that God will work all these things out for our good and his glory.

Reflect and Discuss

1. What is your greatest temptation in times of trials? How do you feel your faith being attacked, and what is your normal response?
2. Which of the three responses (prayer, holiness, confidence) are the most difficult for you? Why?
3. Which one of these responses do you need to cultivate in your life the most?
4. How do the promises of Romans 8 encourage you in your seasons of trials?

Salvation Is of the Lord!

PSALM 18

Main Idea: The Lord rescues his anointed king and gives him victory over his enemies.

I. The Lord Is Worthy of Our Love and Praise (18:1-3).
II. The Lord Rescues Those in Whom He Delights (18:4-19).
III. The Lord Blesses the Righteous and Blameless (18:20-30).
IV. The Lord Equips with Strength the One He Calls to Lead (18:31-45).
V. The Lord Exalts and Demonstrates His Steadfast Love to His Anointed King (18:46-50).

Psalm 18 is a magnificent, but neglected, psalm by King David. At fifty verses, it is the fourth longest psalm after Psalms 119, 78, and 89, which may be part of the reason it is neglected.[3] But it is a magnificent song. It is a royal psalm (see also Pss 2; 20; 21; 45; 72; 89; 132) that calls David the Lord's "king" and "anointed" (Belcher, *Messiah,* 118). It is also a psalm of thanksgiving that looks back at how the Lord delivered David from his enemies and "the power of Saul" (superscription). Yet a prophetic note in the psalm also looks to the distant future and the Lord's final anointed King, the Lord Jesus Christ. Michael Wilcock agrees and writes,

> The Israel whom God had saved from Egypt is known to the Old Testament as God's servant, as God's firstborn son in whom he delights, and as a nation of kings and priests and therefore God's anointed. It cannot escape us that this same calling, in almost every respect, is according to Psalm 18 also that of one particular Israelite, who is likewise God's servant (in the heading) and God's anointed (v. 50), in whom God delights (v. 19); and with the anointing comes also the sonship, as we shall see.

---

[3] Psalm 18 is virtually an exact reproduction of 2 Samuel 22.

> And here we begin to [catch sight of] something even more astounding as we look into the future than what we have seen in linking David with his past. For there will be another of the same nation, even the same family, who will be his heir in all these respects. Luke, who speaks within a few verses of both God's servant Israel and his servant David, speaks in another place, also within a few verses, of both his servant David and his servant Jesus. And Jesus is of course God's anointed, his Christ, and his firstborn son in whom he delights, and we know into how spacious a place he has been raised from his *distress* and *the cords of the grave* (vv. 5-6). (*Message*, 64; emphasis in original)

So in this psalm we will celebrate with David his deliverance, note the preview of the coming attraction in Messiah-King Jesus, and see the promises that are also ours because we are in him.

The Lord Is Worthy of Our Love and Praise

PSALM 18:1-3

David begins the psalm with confession and praise. He boldly says, "I love you, LORD" (v. 1) The word "love" "describes a deep feeling of compassion and tender affection . . . [and] usually refers to the LORD's tender compassion for his people" (Ross, *Psalms 1–41,* 441). David truly, genuinely, and devotedly loves his Lord. And just who is this Lord that David loves so fervently and passionately? Like assembling a beautiful necklace, David strings together nine powerful images that display the Lord's power and protection in his life. Note the repetition of the personal pronoun "my" before each one. The Lord is "my strength," "my rock" (2x), "my fortress," "my deliverer," "my God, "[my] refuge," "my shield," "the horn of my salvation," and "my stronghold" (vv. 1-2). The accumulative power of these word pictures caused John Calvin to write, "David . . . furnishes the faithful with a complete suit of armour, that they may feel that they are in no danger of being wounded" (*Psalms 1–35,* 261–62). This is our God. We can be confident that when we call, he hears.

Verse 3 gives David's testimony to this truth. The God we love and praise hears our prayers, answers us, and delivers us. These verses have their ultimate fulfillment in Hebrews 5:7. There we read about the Lord Jesus: "During his earthly life, he offered prayers and appeals with loud cries and tears to the one who was able to save him from death, and he was heard because of his reverence." Jesus prayed. God heard his Son, and he was saved from the greatest enemy, death. Yes, our Lord is worthy of our love and praise. He is a powerful and truly wonderful God.

The Lord Rescues Those in Whom He Delights

PSALM 18:4-19

David catalogs the gracious and supernatural intervention of the Lord on his behalf. The images are picturesque and striking. They are similar to Jonah's prayer from the belly of the great fish (Jonah 2:1-9). They are also similar to the passion of our Lord Jesus and his Father's rescue of his Son. Matthew 27 is foreshadowed throughout Psalm 18.

The psalmist had walked through the "valley of the shadow of death" (Ps 23:4 ESV). Indeed, "The ropes of *death* were wrapped around me; the torrents of *destruction* terrified me. The ropes of *Sheol* entangled me; the snares of *death* confronted me" (18:4-5; emphasis added). These four parallel constructions draw our attention to the terrifying power of death and its almost inescapable hold. The enemies of the Lord's king (v. 50) wanted him dead, and they were almost successful.

David responded as we must when we are at the end of our ropes. He prayed (v. 6). God answered and divinely intervened with amazing supernatural power (vv. 7-19). David sings, "I called to the Lord [cf. v. 3] in my distress [GNT, "trouble"], and I cried to my God for help." God was David's only hope, his only possible deliverer. The Lord heard the prayer of "his anointed" (v. 50; cf. Ps 2). "From his temple," his heavenly throne and sanctuary, "he heard my voice, and my cry to him reached his ears" (v. 6; Ross, *Psalms 1–41*, 446). Look at how Yahweh answered! "The earth shook and quaked; the foundations of the mountains trembled; they shook because he burned with anger" (v. 7). Matthew 27:51 informs us that when our Lord Jesus was crucified, "the earth quaked, and the rocks were split."

This apocalyptic description of the Lord's rescue continues in vivid, poetic detail in verse 8. Ross notes, "These are symbols of divine wrath being breathed out. The language of a volcanic eruption is reminiscent of the end of Sodom" (Gen 19; *Psalms 1–41*, 448).

Verses 9-12 describe the Lord's coming to save his anointed king as a chariot ride on the angels within a canopy of darkness. "He bent the heavens and came down, total darkness beneath his feet" (v. 9; see

Matt 27:45). "He rode on a cherub [an angel; see Gen 3:24; Ezek 10:1-20] and flew, soaring on the wings of wind" (v. 10). "He made darkness his hiding place, dark storm clouds his canopy around him" (v. 11). "From the radiance of his presence, his clouds swept onward with hail and blazing coals" (v. 12). This is how "the Divine Warrior" announces his coming to those who have abused and rejected his king (VanGemeren, *Psalms,* 205). Spurgeon says, "Suddenly the terrible artillery of heaven [is] discharged" (*Treasury,* 240). This artillery barrage continues in verses 13-15. "The LORD thundered from heaven; the Most High [see Ps 7:17] made his voice heard" (v. 13). Some Hebrew manuscripts add the phrase "with hail and blazing coals" (see NASB). God's apocalyptic intervention includes his powerful, purifying, and thunderous word. "Out of this storm," Ross notes, "God sends down bolts of lightning like arrows (see also Ps. 77:17; 144:6; and Hab. 3:9-11) to scatter the enemy" (*Psalms 1–41,* 449).

The Lord's enemies flee as Yahweh flexes his sovereign muscles (v. 14). The impact of this cataclysmic judgment is felt on the earth (v. 15, cf. v. 7). In what may be another slap at the pagan mythologies of the ancient world, Yahweh simply speaks the word and exposes the natural things humans often fear and worship. "The depths of the sea become visible, the foundations of the world were exposed [ESV, "laid bare"], at your rebuke, LORD, at the blast of the breath of your nostrils" (v. 15). Michael Wilcock correctly writes,

> Much of what these verses portray had once happened quite literally in the experience of his people Israel. We have only to recall the events of the exodus to realize that the plagues of Egypt possibly, the crossing of the Red Sea probably, and the descent of God on Mount Sinai certainly, are all in mind here. Exodus 9, 10, and 15, and especially 19, are the chapters to link with the verses of this section . . . what happened to David was an exodus-type deliverance. (*Message,* 63)

The final verses of this section (vv. 16-19) record the actual rescue of Yahweh's anointed king. David says, "He reached down from on high and took hold of me; he pulled me out of deep water" (v. 16), just like the Lord rescued baby Moses (Exod 2:10). "He rescued me from my powerful enemy and from those who hated me, for they were too strong for me" (v. 17). God did for his anointed king what he could not do for himself. David's enemies viciously attacked him. He says, "They confronted me in the day of my calamity, but the Lord was my support" (GNT, "the Lord protected me"; v. 18). All seemed lost, but then the Lord showed up!

In fact, "he brought me out to a spacious place; he rescued me" (v. 19). And why did the Lord do this for his anointed king? David says, "Because he delighted in me." Proverbs 8:30 records the words of God's eternal wisdom: "I was his delight every day, always rejoicing before him." In Isaiah 42:1 Yahweh says of his servant, "This is my chosen one; I delight in him. I have put my Spirit on him." In Matthew 3:17 God speaks from heaven and says of Jesus, "This is my beloved Son, with whom I am well-pleased [AMP, "delighted"]." Each of these texts ultimately refers to the Son of God, Jesus Christ our Lord. In him God delights as in no other. David certainly is a foreshadow, but he is not the climactic focal point, as the following verses will make clear. There is one and only one to whom verses 20 and following can finally and ultimately apply.

The Lord Blesses the Righteous and Blameless

PSALM 18:20-30

These verses, especially 20-24, are why we must understand this hymn Christologically. No mere human could say or sing verses 20-24 except in the most tempered and relative sense. No doubt this is how David could apply them to himself. The person described here can say, "The Lord rewarded me according to *my righteousness*; he repaid me according to the *cleanness of my hands*" (v. 20; emphasis added). Further, "I have *kept the ways of the* Lord and have *not turned from my God* to wickedness" (v. 21; emphasis added). Verses 22-23 continue this song of a completely holy and righteous life: "Indeed, I let *all* his ordinances guide me and *have not disregarded his statutes*" (v. 22; emphasis added). "I was blameless toward him and *kept myself from my iniquity*" (v. 23; emphasis added). Verse 24 climactically concludes this wonderful declaration of personal righteousness: "So the Lord repaid me according to *my righteousness*, according to *the cleanness of my hands in his sight*" (emphasis added). God has dealt with his anointed king according to the attitude of his righteous heart and the actions of his righteous and holy life. These words can only apply in an absolute sense to one who "did not know sin" (2 Cor 5:21) and who "has been tempted in every way as we are, yet without sin" (Heb 4:15). This is a portrait of Messiah Jesus!

Verses 25-30 turn to address the character and actions of the God who rescues (v. 27) and who is perfect in his ways (v. 30). David says, "With the faithful [ESV, "merciful"] you prove [ESV, "show"] yourself faithful, with the blameless you prove yourself blameless, with the pure you prove yourself pure, but with the crooked [NIV, "devious"] you prove yourself shrewd" (vv. 25-26). God is loyal and true to those who are loyal and true to him. But with the wicked who are crooked, twisted, devious, perverse, God deals shrewdly (ESV, "you make yourself seem tortuous"). He outwits them and uses their own perverse and twisted ways against them.

In contrast to the crooked of verse 26, verse 27 informs us that the Lord will "rescue [ESV, "save"] an oppressed people." He also will "humble those with haughty eyes." James 4:6 sounds a similar note: "God resists the proud but gives grace to the humble." God raises the humble, but he lowers the haughty.

God alone gives his people victory against their enemies. Verses 28-30 drive this truth home. When things seem dark and hopeless, the Lord "light[s] my lamp" and "illuminates my darkness," my circumstances (v. 28). He shows me how things are and guides me on the right path. In verse 29, "the writer grows superlatively bold in the confidence of faith" (Leupold, *Exposition*, 171). With the Lord, "I can attack a barricade [ESV, "run against a troop"], and with my God I can leap over a wall." We can fight any enemy with our God by our side! All of this is so because God's "way is perfect; the word of the Lord is pure. He is a shield to all who take refuge in him" (v. 30). God's presence and Word are an unbeatable combination in the lives of his children. It is all we will ever truly need. Spurgeon comments, "Every way of God is complete in itself, and all his ways put together are matchless in harmony and goodness. . . . No armour of proof or shield of brass so well secures the warrior as the covenant God of Israel protects his warring people" (*Treasury*, 245).

The Lord Equips with Strength the One He Calls to Lead

PSALM 18:31-45

The Lord both equips and prepares his servants for battle. This is especially true of his king, his anointed (v. 50). He alone does this. Verse 31 affirms this precious truth by means of two rhetorical questions that have clear answers. "For who is God besides the Lord [*Yahweh*]?" Answer: no one! "And who is a rock," our source of protection, security, and strength? Answer: "Only our God."

David applies these truths in verses 32-45. The imagery is picturesque and comprehensive. Verse 32 is a simple and straightforward declaration: "God—he clothes [ESV, "equipped"] me with strength and makes my way perfect [ESV, "blameless"]." *The Message* paraphrases it: "Is not this the God who armed me, then aimed me in the right direction?" And how exactly does God do this? He gives us both speed and stability, strength and sure-footedness (v. 33; VanGemeren, *Psalms*, 210). He also trains us with the necessary skills for battle (v. 34). Furthermore, in verse 35 the psalmist is blessed with the Lord's "shield of . . . salvation," "right hand" of power and protection, and "gentleness" (ESV) that "exalts" him or makes him "great" (ESV). Everything this anointed king accomplishes is made possible by the favor of the God he trusts.

The warrior-king is now prepared for battle. He is confident that he is ready because God "make[s] a spacious place [ESV, "wide place"] beneath me for my steps, and my ankles do not give way" (v. 36). He has room to maneuver in the battle, and he is "always able to keep standing and to keep fighting" (Bratcher and Reyburn, *Handbook*, 181). The evidence is plain for all to see in the verses that follow. A simple listing of the evidences of victory is instructive. They are in the form of personal, eyewitness testimony. As we note them, think of the past victories God gave Israel and King David, but also look forward to the victory of the "King of Kings and Lord of Lords" at Christ's second coming (Rev 19:11-21).

First, the anointed king says, "I pursue my enemies and overtake them; I do not turn back until they are wiped out." Victory will be complete.

Second, he says, "I crush them [ESV, "thrust them through"], and they cannot get up; they fall beneath my feet" (v. 38). The sounds of Psalm 110 and Romans 16:20 call out! Defeat is both certain and humiliating for the king's enemies.

Third, he says, "You have clothed [ESV, "equipped"] me with strength for battle; you subdue my adversaries beneath me" (v. 39). God has made his king ready, and God also is responsible for the victory.

Fourth, he says, "You have made my enemies retreat before me; I annihilate those who hate me" (v. 40). The marginal reading of the CSB says, "You gave me the necks of my enemies" (also see Motyer, *Psalms by the Day*, 48). Ross says the idea may be, "He destroyed them [as] he placed his foot on their backs [necks?] as they groveled before him" (*Psalms 1–41*, 457). Those who hate God's anointed king hate the God who raises him up. They now face his righteous wrath.

Fifth, "they cry for help, but there is no one to save them—they cry to the Lord, but he does not answer them" (v. 41). There is no help, no deliverance, no salvation for those who oppose and wage war against the Lord's anointed (again, see Ps 2).

Sixth, he says, "I pulverize them like dust before the wind; I trample them like mud in the streets" (v. 42). The enemies of the king have been reduced to nothing more than dirt, than "dust," nothing more than mud in an ancient street to be walked all over. This is what God does for his king in whom he delights (v. 19).

Seventh, he notes, "You [Yahweh] have freed me from the feuds [ESV, "strife"; NIV, "attacks"; NASB, "contentions"] among the people" (v. 43). The battle is over. It is finished! Victory belongs to the Lord's king!

Eighth, he says, "You have appointed me the head [Hb *rosh*] of nations; a people I had not known serve me." There is a universality to the reign of this king (Ps 2 again!). Kidner notes,

> The Accession Decree of Psalm 2:7-9 offers "the ends of the earth" to the Lord's anointed, and while these verses take up the stern aspect of this, others will dwell on the prospect of Gentile conversions (cf. 22:27; also Isa 55:5 with our verse 43). The New Testament endorses both these emphases (e.g., Rev. 2:26f.; 7:9ff). (*Psalms 1–72*, 96)

This King will rule the nations, and he will do so forever (v. 50).

Ninth, the speaker says, "Foreigners submit to me cringing; as soon as they hear they obey me. Foreigners lose heart and come trembling from their fortifications" (vv. 44-45). Gerald Wilson notes of these verses, "The picture is of a conquering king receiving the submission of his enemies" (*Psalms*, 351). Indeed it is! As Paul will say of the Lord Jesus in Philippians 2:10, "Every knee will bow—in heaven and on earth and under the earth." Humans, demons, and angels all will join in total submission to this great King. You can count in it! It is a signed, sealed, and settled reality!

The Lord Exalts and Demonstrates His Steadfast Love to His Anointed King

PSALM 18:46-50

This magnificent royal psalm ends on a word of praise and worship as the anointed king celebrates all that Yahweh his God has done for him.

David begins on a doxological note declaring, "The LORD [*Yahweh*] lives—blessed be my rock [cf. v. 2]! The God of my salvation [i.e., deliverance] is exalted." We should not pass too quickly the personal pronoun "my" in verse 46 or the many others in verses 47-50. The Lord is my rock (protection and strength). The Lord is my salvation. He is rightly lifted up and exalted in my praise and worship.

Verses 47-48 explain how Yahweh brought his king salvation. They summarize verses 37-42 well. David says, "God—he grants me vengeance and subdues peoples under me. He frees me from my enemies. You exalt me above my adversaries; you rescue me from violent men." God grants, subdues, frees, exalts, and rescues his king. God defeats peoples, enemies, adversaries, and violent men for his king. All of this is the Lord's doing on behalf of his anointed Davidic king! "Therefore," in light of all that the Lord has done, the Lord's anointed says, "I will give thanks among the nations, LORD; I will sing praises about your name" (v. 49). James Boice notes, "Verse 49 is the verse Paul uses in Romans 15 to show that Jesus brought salvation to the Gentiles as well as to the Jews" (*Psalms 1–41*, 157). Paul read Psalm 18 Christologically too.

The psalm concludes with an eschatological ring of assurance and hope. "He [*Yahweh*] gives great victories to his king; he shows loyalty [ESV, "steadfast love"] to his anointed, to David and his descendants forever" (v. 50). Many Davidic kings would rightly claim the promises of Psalm 18. But ultimately, the psalm finds its climactic fulfillment in Jesus. Leupold says it well: "David was given victory to make possible the greater victories of his Greater Son" (*Exposition*, 174).

Conclusion

When David wrote Psalm 18, he wrote out of his own experiences of his enemy's opposition and persecution and his Lord's deliverance. Yet he wrote about more: the future of God's final anointed King. James Boice is right: "Some of the kingship psalms have elements that look beyond the earthly king to God's promised Messiah. That is the case here" (*Psalms 1–41*, 145). Derek Kidner notes Paul's use and application of the psalm, specifically verse 49, as proof that the Messiah would come for both Jew and Gentile in his mission of salvation. His words fittingly conclude our study of this majestic psalm:

> Paul quotes verse 49 as the first in a series of four prophecies to show that Christ came for the Gentiles as well as the Jews

> (Rom. 15:8-12). While David may have thought only of Yahweh's fame spread abroad, his words at their full value portray the Lord's anointed (50), ultimately the Messiah, praising Him *among*—in fellowship with—a host of Gentile worshippers. Although every Davidic king might make this psalm his own, it belonged especially to David whose testimony it was, and to Christ, who was his "offspring" . . . *par excellence.* (*Psalms 1–72*, 96–97; emphasis in original)

Reflect and Discuss

1. Describe some of the reasons in your life that God is worthy of love and praise. In what ways has he been your rock, deliverer, and stronghold?
2. What does Jesus's life teach us about God's plans to deliver his people?
3. Verses 4-5 describe the power of death. Where else does Scripture discuss God's power over death?
4. How does the description of God in verses 7-15 compare to typical descriptions you hear about him? What feelings do these descriptions evoke in you? How can these descriptions of God provide hope?
5. How did the Father reward Christ according to his righteousness (v. 20)?
6. Why was it necessary for Christ to perfectly obey God the Father?
7. How did God the Father prove himself faithful to Christ (v. 25)?
8. Who are the enemies that God's anointed king defeats (vv. 37-45)? Why is the defeat of God's enemies so significant to the psalmist?
9. What is the victory that Christ has won for himself and his people (v. 50)?
10. What role does the Word of God have in providing protection and strength to his people?

God Is There and He Is Not Silent

PSALM 19

Main Idea: God has revealed himself through creation, through Scripture, and ultimately through Jesus, the Word of God, so that people may know him and be saved.

I. Listen to God Speak through Nature (19:1-6).
- A. The heavens speak of his glory (19:1-4).
- B. The sun speaks of his glory (19:4-6).

II. Listen to God Speak through Scripture (19:7-14).
- A. It is perfect and strengthens (19:7).
- B. It is sure and gives wisdom (19:7).
- C. It is right and brings joy (19:8).
- D. It is pure and provides direction (19:8).
- E. It is clean and endures forever (19:9).
- F. It is true and righteous altogether (19:9).
- G. It is valuable and priceless (19:10).
- H. It is delicious and sweet (19:10).
- I. It is helpful and rewarding (19:11).
- J. It is instructive and cleansing (19:12).
- K. It is protective and liberating (19:13).
- L. It is transforming and saving (19:14).

Francis Schaeffer (1912–1984), one of the Christian intellectual giants of the twentieth century, taught us that you can be a Christian without abandoning your mind. In his book *He Is There and He Is Not Silent*, Schaeffer makes a crucial and thought-provoking statement: "The infinite-personal God is there, but also he is not silent; that changes the whole world. . . . He is there and is not a silent, nor far-off God" (*He Is There and He Is Not Silent*, 276).

God has revealed himself to us in two books: the book of nature and the book of Scripture. Francis Bacon, a fifteenth-century scientist who is credited with developing the scientific method, said, "There are two books laid before us to study, to prevent our falling into error: first the volume of the Scriptures, which reveal the will of God; then the volume of the creation, which expresses his power" (*The Advancement of Learning,* 72).[4]

Psalm 19 addresses both of God's books: the book of nature in verses 1-6 and the book of Scripture in verses 7-14. The beauty, poetry, and splendor of Psalm 19, described as a wisdom psalm, led C. S. Lewis to say, "I take this to be the greatest poem in the Psalter and one of the greatest lyrics in the world" (*Reflections,* 73). God is there and he is not silent. How should we hear and listen to the God who talks?

Listen to God Speak through Nature

PSALM 19:1-6

God has revealed himself to every rational human on the earth in at least two ways: through nature and conscience. We call this type of revelation natural or general revelation (see Rom 1–2). In verses 1-6 David addresses the wonder of nature and creation.

The Heavens Speak of His Glory (19:1-4)

"The heavens declare the glory of God." *The Message* paraphrases verse 1 as "God's glory is on tour in the skies." The heavens, referring to the moon, sun, planets, and stars, announce or speak of the greatness and awesomeness of God. "And the expanse [ESV, "sky above"] proclaims the work of his hands." The "expanse" refers to the lower atmosphere where the clouds float and the birds fly. They show or "proclaim" the masterpiece of the divine craftsman. The words "declare" and "proclaim" express continuous, ongoing revelation. "The heavens keep on declaring . . . the skies keep on proclaiming" (VanGemeren, *Psalms,* 215).

Verse 2 expands on the idea of constant revelation from creation: "Day after day they pour out speech." The words *pour out* can mean to bubble up and overflow (Ross, *Psalms 1–41,* 475). Revelation keeps bubbling up and overflowing like a river flooding day and night. And "night after night they communicate knowledge." Without the night

---

[4] The quote is a popular paraphrase of the original: "For our Saviour saith, You err, not knowing the Scriptures, nor the power of God; laying before us two books or volumes to study, if we will be secured from error; first the scriptures, revealing the will of God, and then the creatures expressing his power."

we would not see the stars, the Milky Way, or the great galaxies with the naked eye. The night shouts to us that God is there. What a glorious God he is! Indeed, verse 3 further informs us, "There is no speech; there are no words; their voice is not heard." This wordless "word" appears visibly to every hemisphere, every continent, every nation, every people. The message is for all. No one is excluded. Verse 4 caps off the universality of this revelation from the skies: "Their message has gone out to the whole earth, and their words to the end of the world." All have seen it. All have heard it. I love how Charles Spurgeon puts it: "Although the heavenly bodies move in solemn silence, yet in reason's ear they utter precious teachings" (*Treasury*, 271). The heavens truly speak of God's glory!

The Sun Speaks of His Glory (19:4-6)

David now speaks of the greatest stellar light from earth's perspective: the sun. Although it is ninety-three million miles from the earth, we are dependent on its regularity and its faithfulness for our existence. David uses two striking metaphors to describe how the sun appears to us mortals on planet Earth. First, with the sky, likened to a tent, as its backdrop (v. 4), the sun is like a bridegroom coming out of his bridal chamber on his wedding day headed for his bride. It is brilliant, joyful, and exuberant. It is radiant and magnificently adorned. It is something to see, something to behold. Second, the sun is like "an athlete [NIV, "champion"] running a course" (v. 5). "It rises from one end of the heavens and circles to their other end" (v. 6). And "nothing is hidden from its heat." Everyone sees its brilliance. All feel its warmth. God's glory, power, wisdom, and greatness shine bright for all to see and feel.

From these amazing verses we can draw at least five important applications. First, from creation we can know God exists. Creation points us to the Creator. Second, all people everywhere have this visual knowledge. Nature bubbles with the knowledge of God day and night. This knowledge is not verbal but visible. It is "heard" with the eyes, not the ears. Third, creation informs all that God is a powerful and glorious Creator. The magnitude and wonders of creation display his omnipotence. Fourth, the superstitious, who are enslaved to the worship of nature and the deception of astrology, see more in the stars than is there. They look to the sky for knowledge that can only be found in Scripture. Fifth, the modern secularist and atheist actually see less than the heavens reveal. Although they may see creation with amazing insight, they remain blind to the Creator it points to. We should listen to God through nature, but we must listen clearly and carefully, accurately and truthfully. He is saying a lot, but he is not saying everything we need to hear and know. To know him savingly, we need his Word!

Listen to God Speak through Scripture

PSALM 19:7-14

Revelation from nature leaves everyone without excuse (see Rom 1:18-20). It is enough to condemn them, but it is not enough to save them. The theoretical person isolated on the island is neither safe nor innocent. He is a condemned, lost sinner. He needs the gospel. He needs the Scriptures, which proclaim the good news of salvation found in Jesus the Son of God.

It is an interesting and instructive exercise to scan the Bible and see what various persons say about the inspiration and inerrancy, the authority and sufficiency of Scripture. Here is the starting point for building our theology of the Bible.

> ***Peter:*** *Above all, you know this: No prophecy of Scripture comes from the prophet's own interpretation, because no prophecy ever came by the will of man; instead, men spoke from God as they were carried along by the Holy Spirit.* (2 Pet 1:20-21)
>
> ***Paul:*** *All Scripture is inspired by God and is profitable for teaching, for rebuking, for correcting, for training in righteousness, so that the man of God may be complete, equipped for every good work.* (2 Tim 3:16-17)
>
> ***Jesus:*** *Don't think that I came to abolish the Law or the Prophets. I did not come to abolish but to fulfill. For truly I tell you, until heaven and earth pass away, not the smallest letter or one stroke of a letter will pass away from the law until all things are accomplished.* (Matt 5:17-18)
>
> ***John:*** *The Scripture cannot be broken.* (John 10:35)
> *Sanctify them by the truth; your word is truth.* (John 17:17)

Now, here in Psalm 19:7-14, David adds his witness with no less than twelve marvelous truths about the Holy Scriptures. Six stand out like beacons of light in verses 7-9. Six more are beautifully and devotionally embedded in verses 10-14. In the first six we find declarations that tell us what the Bible is and does: six nouns, six adjectives, six verbs. The focus is on the identity, the quality, and the function of Holy Scripture.

It Is Perfect and Strengthens (19:7)

First, "the instruction of the LORD is perfect, renewing one's life" (v. 7a). Instruction is the "law" (ESV). It is the *Torah.* It is all that God wants us to know about him. It is the Lord's teaching. David says this instruction is "perfect." Alec Motyer writes that God's instruction is "'perfectly complete, completely perfect,' neither needing addition nor permitting subtraction" (*Psalms by the Day*, 51). And this perfect Word does a perfect work, "renewing one's life." It refreshes, revives, and brings the soul back to where it belongs. It restores and renews my life, my inner self.

It Is Sure and Gives Wisdom (19:7)

Second, "the testimony of the LORD is trustworthy, making the inexperienced wise" (v. 7b). Derek Kidner writes that "testimony . . . is its aspect as truth attested by God himself" (*Psalms 1–72*, 99). The Word of God is "sure" (ESV), true in principle, and trustworthy. It is never fallible, unstable, or undependable. You can always trust God's Word to lead you in truth. The phrase "making the inexperienced wise" (ESV, "making wise the simple") is instructive. The Bible takes undiscerning, naïve, and gullible people and makes them wise. We need wisdom for wise decision making, and it comes from the Bible. It allows us to see life as God sees life and act accordingly. John Piper says, "Wisdom is a life that makes sense in the light of reality. And the light of reality shines from the Bible" ("Sweeter than Honey, Better than Gold").

It Is Right and Brings Joy (19:8)

Third, "the precepts of the LORD are right, making the heart glad" (v. 8a). "Precepts" means rules, regulations, and guidelines for living (cf. Ps 119:16,97,111; Jer 15:16). "Right" tells us they are never wrong. They can always be counted on to provide truth and accuracy. "Making the heart glad" tells us that if our hearts need joy, we should dive into God's Word. In it is joy and gladness evermore!

It Is Pure and Provides Direction (19:8)

Fourth, "the command of the LORD is radiant, making the eyes light up" (v. 8b). Holy Scripture is "radiant" (ESV, "pure"). It is absent of sin, malice, and corrupting influence. It is not dark, vague, or contaminated. VanGemeren says, "The Bible is an open book" (*Psalms*, 218). And what does this open book do? It "enlighten[s] the eyes" (ESV). It brings understanding so that we can see how to live and what to do (cf. Ps 119:105).

It Is Clean and Endures Forever (19:9)

Fifth, "the fear of the LORD is pure, enduring forever" (v. 9a). "Fear of the LORD" references the fear of God that the Bible produces in us, a right and holy reverence and respect for God. It is honoring God for who he is. "Pure" (ESV, "clean") speaks of Scripture's quality in terms of its essence. And this pure Book endures forever. Its power and purpose never end! We can always count on God's Word to do its work because God's Word never changes; it is never out of style or out of season.

It Is True and Righteous Altogether (19:9)

Sixth, "the ordinances of the LORD are reliable and altogether righteous" (v. 9b). "Ordinances" are divine decisions about human conduct. They are ordinances of Yahweh. "Reliable" means "true" (ESV), never false, and never off the mark. God's Word is the only measure for reality. "Altogether righteous" amplifies the previous phrase. The Word of God provides us with the standard of righteousness because it flows from the nature of God himself. A righteous God will only speak a righteous word!

It Is Valuable and Priceless (19:10)

Scripture is "more desirable than gold." It is more desirable than "an abundance of pure gold." Take the best this world can offer. Take what this world values most. It is nothing compared to the Word of God. Scripture exists in a class by itself.

It Is Delicious and Sweet (19:10)

David says the Bible is "sweeter than honey dripping from a honeycomb." Honey tastes sweet to the tongue. The Bible tastes sweet to the soul. Honey satisfies our taste buds for a moment. The Bible satisfies the deepest desires and longings of the heart forever. Ross writes, "God's Word is sweet in the enrichment and satisfaction of life that it brings to the faithful believer, and its sweetness increases its desirability day by day" (*Psalms 1–41*, 481).

It Is Helpful and Rewarding (19:11)

David now addresses the specific benefits he receives from the perfect, precious Scriptures. The Bible alerts us to sin. It warns the servant of God of spiritual danger. Like a perfect spiritual watchdog, it barks furiously at the sight of evil and wickedness. The Word informs us how to live and not live, how to walk and not walk, and how to find joy and avoid sorrow. And obeying the Word brings "abundant reward." Obedience always reaps abundant blessing and fruit.

It Is Instructive and Cleansing (19:12)

David addresses two avenues of sin in verses 12-13. He follows each by providing a strategy for overcoming them. Verse 12 provides the first way to sin: "Who perceives his unintentional sins? Cleanse me from my hidden faults." This way of sinning has two characteristics. First, it is confusing or baffling. That is what David means when he says, "Who can discern his [own] errors?" (ESV). Who can figure out his own sinning? Who can fathom the tangled web of self-deceit? Sin deceives and fools us. We look at ourselves in hindsight and say, "What was I thinking? I cannot believe I said that. I cannot believe I did that."

The second characteristic of this way of sinning is "hidden faults" or ignorance (Ross, *Psalms 1–41*, 482). This sin is often hidden from us. It is unintentional or inadvertent (Ross, *Psalms 1–41*, 482). Thus David prays, "Cleanse me from my hidden faults." This doesn't mean our sin is hidden from others, though. Others may see it clearly. It means sin is hidden from us, the offenders. We don't sense its sinfulness. We don't see our sin as sin. We need the light of God's Word to reveal it, to bring it into the light of day.

It Is Protective and Liberating (19:13)

Verse 13 reveals the second way of sinning. John Piper addresses this well:

> "Keep back your servant from presumptuous sins." So David sees a difference between, on the one hand, sins that we commit because they baffle us and sneak up on us, and on the other hand, sins that we commit because we presume to know better than God or presume that sin is no big deal. The point is not that there is a special category of extra-bad sins, like murder, rape, treason, etc. The point is that there is a special

> category of sinning—namely, sinning in arrogant defiance of a known law. It's not so much what you do that puts sinning in this category as whether you do it with forethought and defiance and rebellion. This is what David calls presumptuous sins. They are fully intentional, with our eyes open, and with a heart that says, "I know God says this is wrong and harmful, but I just don't care what God thinks; I am going to do it anyway." (Piper, "The Heart You Know and the Heart You Don't")

How do we combat and defeat this type of sin? David shares several insights from his prayer. First, he says, "Do not let them rule me." We must pray for spiritual strength and power. Second, he says, "Then I will be blameless and cleansed." We must confess confidence in God's gracious and full forgiveness. Third, he says, "[I will be] cleansed from blatant rebellion" (ESV, "innocent of great transgression"). We must declare our assurance that great sin will not be able to slap a guilty sentence on us or cut us off from the community of God's people (cf. Num 15:30-31).

It Is Transforming and Saving (19:14)

Verse 14 is one of the most memorized verses in the Bible. It is a beautiful and appropriate prayer to close out this great psalm. Gerald Wilson says it is both a plea and model of life in submission to the will of God (*Psalms*, 372). "The words of my mouth and the meditation of my heart" speaks of all of a believer's being. We hold nothing back, not one thing. We give all of ourselves to our Lord! They must be acceptable (NIV, "pleasing") in his sight. The eyes of God are the only eyes that matter. Ultimately, how he sees us is all that matters. And why only his eyes? Because they are the eyes of Yahweh, the eyes of David's "rock," the eyes of his "Redeemer" (Hb *goel*). The Lord is our sure foundation of protection and security. The Lord is our Redeemer, Deliverer, and Savior. We have this God and his Word. What more do we need?

Conclusion

In his superb book *The Messiah and the Psalms*, Richard Belcher Jr. captures beautifully the Christology that is veiled but woven throughout this majestic psalm:

> Just as the law was central to the Mosaic covenant as God's word to his people, so Christ is central to the new covenant as

God's final word to his people (Heb. 1:1). Christ inaugurates the new covenant. He not only teaches the word of God but is the Word of God (John 1:1) and the revelation of God (John 1:18). The Old Testament focuses on the law as the heart of the Mosaic covenant, whereas the New Testament focuses on Christ as the heart of the new covenant. This does not diminish the law, but the law must be read in light of Christ. The words [of the psalm] describe the character of the law, [but they] also describe Christ. The word "perfect" (*tāmim*) means whole, complete, without blemish. This term is used of the wholeness and completeness of the sacrificial offerings in that they are without blemish (Lev. 1:3). So Christ is without blemish and offers himself as such to God (Heb. 9:14; 1 Peter 1:19). He is perfect in the ultimate sense (Heb. 4:15). Christ is "sure," a concept that stresses faithful, which is used absolutely of Christ in 2 Timothy 2:13. Christ is also a faithful witness (Rev. 1:5), a faithful high priest (Heb. 2:17), and faithful over God's house as a son (Heb. 3:6). Christ is "right" in the sense of righteous and upright. . . . Christ is pure and clean (1 John 3:3) and has the power to make us clean (Matt. 8:2-3) by his word (John 15:3). Christ has the same effect as the law; he is the one who brings restoration (Acts 3:21), who is the true wisdom of God (1 Cor. 1:24; Col. 2:3), who is the source of true joy (John 15:11; Phil. 4:4), who enlightens the eyes (John 9:26, 39; 1 John 5:20), who endures forever (Heb. 13:8), and who is true (1 John 5:20; Rev. 3:7) and righteous (2 Tim. 4:8; 1 John 2:1). Christ is the fullness of God's revelation. . . . Psalm 19 as a prayer of Jesus would extol the glory of God's revelation in creation and the law. On a different level, because he is the Creator, he would be delighting in his own creation (vv. 1-6), and because he is the final revelation, he would be magnifying his own word (vv. 7-11). As our *human* mediator he would pray to be kept from sin to maintain his innocence in order to accomplish his work as our Redeemer. He is the only one who can ultimately be declared innocent from hidden faults, and whose words are completely acceptable in the sight of God (vv. 12-14). (*Messiah*, 53–54; emphasis in original)

Reflect and Discuss

1. What does creation teach us about God? What does Scripture teach us about God that creation cannot?
2. Describe a time when seeing God's creation helped you better understand his power and glory.
3. In what ways can you use creation to talk to nonbelievers about God? How could you use Scripture to affirm and build on that aspect of creation?
4. What is the purpose of Scripture? In what ways might you read or use Scripture that deviate from its purpose?
5. How is having Scripture an example of God's mercy and grace?
6. Which of the twelve truths about Scripture from Psalm 19 encourages or challenges you the most? Why?
7. Do you always believe these twelve truths about Scripture? Do you ever believe Scripture does not bring joy, is not sweet, or is not liberating? How do we fight against devaluing Scripture?
8. Where do people in your city go to find wisdom, direction, or liberation? How and why is Scripture better than any of those things?
9. Why should you be concerned about unintentional sins? How do you become aware of your own unintentional sins? How should your heart respond when you become aware of these sins? How could your flesh tempt you to respond?
10. Psalm 19 reminds us that Christ is the true Word of God. Why is this truth good news? How does this truth make Christianity different from every other religion?

Where to Look in Times of Trouble

PSALM 20

Main Idea: Our victory is tied to the victory of King Jesus!

I. The People Look to the King (20:1-5).
II. The King Assures the People of Victory (20:6).
III. The People Rise and Stand Firm (20:7-9).

One of the most important lessons I (Josh) learned in driver's education class was learned through a rather dramatic moment. I was sitting in the back seat of the training car, the teacher was in the front passenger seat, and another student driver was in the driver's seat. As she drove down a crowded two-lane road, we were quickly approaching a moment in which a semitruck would be on our left and a man on a bicycle would be on the right. The girl driving was visibly nervous and white-knuckled. The teacher just kept saying, "Keep your eyes looking straight ahead, and you will be fine." He first said it calmly, but the closer we got to the situation, the louder and faster he began to say it. Eventually, it was clear the girl driving could not stop looking at the cyclist and worrying about hitting him. As she focused her attention on him, she drifted toward him; and as she passed him, she nudged him with the rearview mirror, making him almost fall off his bike and crash. I saw the entire thing from the back seat, and thirty years later I still remember it.

The teacher pulled the car over and taught us a lesson I will never forget. He simply said, "Your car always tends to drift toward where your eyes are looking." I don't remember anything else that teacher ever said, but I have never forgotten that one statement. Over the years, it has been a helpful truth not only in navigating tight driving situations but also in navigating tough life situations. The truth is, our hearts always tend to drift to where our eyes are focused. If your eyes continually look at all the troubles around you, your heart will follow. That is why we need Psalm 20, which teaches where to look in times of trouble.

Even a surface reading of the Old Testament will show that the people of Israel were almost always under attack. Growing up in America, I always felt as if we were the world's greatest superpower and could defend ourselves against anyone. Israel never knew that feeling. They were easy to pick on. Although we don't know the exact context of Psalm 20, we know there is a battle raging and a nation attacking them. The people are in troubled times. The question is, Where will they look for help?

At first glance Psalm 20 seems like it could be a personal blessing. A blessing is like a prayer; but instead of looking up toward the Lord, blessing givers look straight ahead at a person. Blessing is a means both to cry out to God on behalf of another person and to empower and encourage him or her. This is certainly a statement of blessing, but it is not a blessing directed toward us individually. Look at verse 9. It says, "LORD, give victory to the king!" Psalm 20 is a statement of blessing on the king! In troubled times, the people looked to the king.

The People Look to the King

PSALM 20:1-5

Take note of the number of second-person pronouns as you read verses 1-5. Ten times there is a reference to "you" and "your." The "you" and "your" of Psalm 20 is the king. Just imagine this moment. The king (most likely David) is facing a large invading army. He knows he is outmatched in every way, but he also knows he has been called to fight. So he goes into the temple, gets on his knees, calls on the name of the Lord, offers a burnt offering, then leaves. As he does, the people are waiting to send him off with the blessing of verses 1-5. If you were the king, this would fire you up. What an encouraging and affirming moment!

But why all the attention on the king? Verse 5 gives us the reason: "Let us shout for joy at your victory and lift the banner in the name of our God. May the LORD fulfill all your requests." For the first time, the first-person pronoun (us) is joined with the second-person pronoun (your). If the king wins the battle, the people get the joy. If the king gets the victory, the people raise their banner, the symbol of victory.

The people looked to the king because they knew their success was tied to his. In the same way that we raise a banner and join in the victory of a favorite sports team, the people would share in the joy and lift a banner for the victory of the king even though, in reality, they had not done anything. If the king loses, they all lose. If the king wins, they all win.

The King Assures the People of Victory

PSALM 20:6

An obvious switch of speakers occurs in verse 6. This psalm is a dialogue (Goldingay, *Psalms 1–41,* 301). The people speak to the king (vv. 1-5), and now the king responds to the people (v. 6). He begins with a statement of absolute confidence: "Now I know that the LORD gives victory to his anointed; he will answer him from his holy heaven." David has met with the Lord, he has heard the blessing of the people, he is confident in the one who has called him, and he is confident in the promises of God. He knows that the Lord will give him victory. This is not arrogance; this is a faith-filled assurance that God will hear him and give him the victory. The king assures the people of victory.

The People Rise and Stand Firm

PSALM 20:7-9

In verse 7 the dialogue continues. The people share not only the king's confidence but also the foundation for the king's confidence. Their confidence was in the character, the promises, and the person of the Lord himself.

Although we do not know the specific circumstance of this psalm, it reminds us of a situation King Saul faced in 1 Samuel 13. The Philistines had gathered together against Israel and had three thousand chariots, six thousand horseman, and troops as numerous as the sand of the seashore (1 Sam 13:5). On the other side was King Saul and his six hundred men. Israel could not "take pride" in their chariots and horses. Their only hope was to take pride in the name of the Lord. As they did, they won the battle.

David reminds us that if we allow our eyes to drift toward the enemies and troubles that surround us, our hearts will follow, and we will certainly be discouraged. Instead, then, we must take pride in the Lord. We must remember his character and his promises. You can't help but wonder if David was thinking about his own run-in with an intimidating enemy when he wrote these words. When David approached Goliath, he was mocked and told that his flesh would soon be food for the birds. But David stood up to Goliath and declared that, although Goliath had a sword, spear, and javelin, David came in the name of the Lord. David, trusting in the name of the Lord, then killed Goliath and removed his head.

David's own experiences as well as his deep-rooted confidence in the Lord caused him to know that the Lord's enemies will "collapse and fall" while the people of God "rise and stand firm" (v. 8). This picture of God's people rising and standing is important. Their posture points to their faith. They are confident and assured of their ultimate victory. They will rise and stand firm.

The most beautiful thing about this moment is that the people did nothing and yet gained everything. When it was time for battle, they looked to the king, the king led them in victory, and they received all the joy of victory.

Every time we read a psalm about the king, it points us beyond King David. David was the anointed king of Psalm 20, but as with Psalms 2; 18; 20; 24; and many others, our eyes are directed beyond King David to King Jesus. Jesus is the ultimate anointed King. Psalm 20 was written to point us to *that* King. Jesus is the one who went to battle and won the victory while we did nothing. He was the victorious one who defeated all our enemies through his life, death, and resurrection. Our sins are buried, and we have new life because of his death and life (Col 2:12). We are seated with him in the heavenly places not because of our victory but because of his (Eph 2:6). The reason we need Psalm 20 is that we too live in troubled times, and Psalm 20 reminds us of what we must keep doing in them.

First, in troubled times we must **keep looking at King Jesus**. Our hearts *will* drift toward where our eyes are focused. Therefore, while our troubles seem overwhelming and our tendency is to look at them, we must turn our eyes away from our troubles to King Jesus. The more troubles we encounter, the more we must discipline ourselves to spend more time in God's Word, more time with God's people, and more time seeking God's face. As troubles arise, turn your eyes to King Jesus.

Second, in troubled times we must **be constantly assured of his victory**. The refrain of verse 6 needs to be constantly in our minds: "I know that the Lord gives victory to his anointed." Say it out loud. Say it often. Jesus will win. His victory is assured. And for those who have chosen to trust and follow him, our victory is as assured as his. We will raise our banner. Our enemies will fall.

Third, in troubled times we must **rise and stand firm with King Jesus**. The posture of our minds, hearts, and mouths says a lot about our faith. Our troubles tend to cripple us and cause us to be defeated, scared, discouraged, or even paralyzed with fear and anxiety. Instead, we must rise and stand firm. In troubled times the world needs to see in believers the confidence that Jesus is greater than the trouble.

Conclusion

Psalm 20 is not about the power of positive thinking. Psalm 20 is about confidence that those who have trusted Jesus Christ are united with him in his death, burial, and resurrection. Our victory is assured because our King's victory is assured. Because of that, we must sing, rejoice, and raise our banner. Our King has won, and so have we.

Reflect and Discuss

1. Our hearts tend to drift toward where our eyes are looking. How have you seen that prove true in your life? Do you notice a difference in your heart when you spend more time looking to Jesus? If so, explain.
2. Practically speaking, how can you keep your eyes on Jesus more consistently throughout the day? What do you need to stop looking at, and what do you need to look at more frequently?
3. How should knowing your victory is certain change the way you respond in troubling times?
4. Psalm 20 calls us, who have been assured victory through Jesus, to rise and stand upright. How should your victory change your disposition? How should it change your actions? How can you rise and stand firm as someone who has been assured victory?

The Lord's King Will Reign Forever

PSALM 21

Main Idea: The Lord richly blesses his messianic King who trusts and rejoices in him.

I. The Lord's King Trusts the LORD Completely (21:1-7).
   A. He rejoices in the Lord's deliverance (21:1).
   B. He is blessed with the Lord's answer to prayer (21:2).
   C. He is anointed with the Lord's authority (21:3).
   D. He is granted life by the Lord forever (21:4).
   E. He is exalted by the Lord with majesty and splendor (21:5).
   F. He is blessed by the Lord with his joyful presence (21:6).
   G. He is established by the Lord's faithful love in his reign (21:7).

II. The Lord's King Will Destroy the LORD's Enemies Totally (21:8-12).
   A. The Lord will capture and destroy his enemies (21:8-9).
   B. The Lord assures us the works of the wicked will not succeed (21:10-12).

III. The Lord's King Leads Us to Worship the Lord Fully (21:13).
   A. We exalt the Lord.
   B. We sing to the Lord.
   C. We praise the Lord.

The psalms, especially those written by King David, can be understood in three ways. First, David sang them in his historical context and experiences. Second, successive kings would sing them and apply them to their experiences. Third, and climactically, Messiah Jesus will sing them as the final fulfillment of their themes. This is especially true of Psalm 21, a royal psalm of praise of which John Calvin says,

> Above all, it was the design of the Holy Spirit here to direct the minds of the faithful to Christ. . . . What is here stated was only fully accomplished in Christ, who was appointed by the heavenly Father to be King over us, and who is at the same time God manifest in the flesh. (*Psalms 1–35*, 343, 356)

The theme of victory in battle dominates this psalm. Ross notes that the victory "was a direct answer to prayer, probably the prayer of Psalm 20" (*Psalms 1–41*, 509). We cannot be certain of David's historical context, but the battle on the horizon is clearly eschatological and resonates with the second coming of King Jesus in the book of Revelation, especially 19:11-21. We will examine the psalm in three movements.

The Lord's King Trusts the Lord Completely

PSALM 21:1-7

Nehemiah 8:10 says, "The joy of the LORD is your strength." Psalm 21 says the strength of the Lord is our joy! Because of the Lord's great strength, the king "relies on the LORD" (v. 7). The king is certain that this powerful God will meet his every need, especially in battle. This absolute confidence of the king appears in seven affirmations of trust in verses 1-7.

He Rejoices in the Lord's Deliverance (21:1)

"The king finds joy in [the Lord's] strength." This enables him to rejoice greatly in the "victory" (ESV, "salvation") the Lord has given him. God's power is the cause of his victory. God did it for his anointed (Ps 2). VanGemeren writes, "The theocratic king knows that the 'victories' are God's gracious 'gifts' and that they are the evidence of God's 'strength'" (*Psalms*, 230). From the psalm's beginning the king serves his people as a worship leader! The Lord has delivered his king in victory. An exuberant and enthusiastic celebration is the rightful response.

He Is Blessed with the Lord's Answer to Prayer (21:2)

David sought the Lord in prayer from a sincere heart, and God answered. The king prayed, and God gave him "his heart's desire." Praying aloud with "the requests of his lips," he was "not denied" by his God. The king's desires lined up with God's, and God gave a wonderful answer to his prayer. We can follow this verse to the garden of Gethsemane where Jesus prayed to his Father, "Not as I will, but as you will" (Matt 26:39). The wills of the Son and the Father were in perfect harmony in the great drama of redemption. When our desires align with God's, we can expect an affirmative answer. We can also expect our Lord to do great things.

He Is Anointed with the Lord's Authority (21:3)

The Lord's pleasure rests on his anointed king. As a result, God "meet[s] him with rich blessings." But there is more! God "place[s] a crown of pure gold on his head." Spurgeon, looking down the corridors of messianic history, says, "Jesus wore the thorn-crown, but now wears the glory-crown" (*Treasury*, 313). This regal recognition is the Father's doing. Jesus humbled himself, but God has highly exalted him (Phil 2:9-11). The Lord truly meets his king "with rich blessings"!

He Is Granted Life by the Lord Forever (21:4)

Verse 4 is difficult to fathom except in messianic categories. The view of some scholars that the phrase "length of days forever and ever" "meant no more than 'many years'" is unconvincing; that "there is no ground here for interpreting the psalm as messianic" is shortsighted (see Taylor, *Psalms*, 113). The psalm looks back to God's covenant promise to David in 2 Samuel 7:12-16, and it looks forward to the glorious resurrection of the Lord Jesus in the Gospels. The king "asked [the Lord] for life, and [he] gave it to him—length of days forever and ever." What a request! What an answer! Calvin is right, and his understanding of the text is much preferred: "The course of [David's] life was too short to be compared to this *length of days*, which is said to consist of many ages. . . . David, therefore, without doubt, comprehends the Eternal King" (*Psalms 1–35*, 346–47; emphasis original). This is resurrection language. This is eternal-life theology. We will read the text in its plain and straightforward sense and celebrate its truth with King Jesus.

He Is Exalted by the Lord with Majesty and Splendor (21:5)

The Lord gave his king life unto the ages in his victory against his enemies and the forces of evil. In response God makes his glory great; "He confer[s] majesty and splendor on him." What powerful words. Glory! Majesty! Splendor! God is delighted by his king in the most supreme and exalted way. He gave him a great victory, and his glory is made evident in that victory. In making application to the Lord Jesus, Spurgeon beautifully writes,

> The whole weight of sin was laid upon him; it is [right] that the full measure of the glory of bearing it away should be laid upon the same beloved person. A glory commensurate

> with his shame he must and will receive, for well he has earned it. It is not possible for us to honour Jesus too much. (*Treasury*, 314)

He Is Blessed by the Lord with His Joyful Presence (21:6)

The "length of days forever and ever" in verse 4 is now complemented with "blessings forever." The Lord gives these blessings to the king. The Lord also cheers him (ESV, "make[s] him glad") with joy in the Lord's presence. *The Message* says, "You pile blessings on him; you make him glad when you smile." The intimate, loving relationship between the king and his Lord is tender, precious, and real. Verse 7 will make this even more clear.

He Is Established by the Lord's Faithful Love in His Reign (21:7)

This verse is the focal point of the psalm. Everything moves toward it and from it. "The king relies on the LORD." He completely, totally, and fully depends on him. He trusts in this Lord and no other. And this trust is honored. He is blessed with the *chesed* of Yahweh! The "faithful love" (CSB), "steadfast love" (ESV), "constant love" (GNT), "unfailing love" (NIV), "lovingkindness" (AMP) of Yahweh, "the Most High," is the promise and guarantee that "he will not be shaken" (NIV; ESV, "moved"). The king's kingdom is secure because his relationship with Yahweh is certain. The love of our Lord is a sure and steadfast anchor for the souls of all who trust in him. Just ask the King!

The Lord's King Will Destroy the Lord's Enemies Totally

PSALM 21:8-12

These verses look forward to a sure and certain victory of the king over his enemies. It is again the Lord's work, and he accomplishes it through his king. Notice the repetition of the phrase "you will" in the English text (vv. 9,10,12). Add to that the double use of "your hand" in verse 8. The end of the enemies of God and his king is on the way. God has been faithful in the past to his people. We can count on his faithfulness in the future as he vindicates his King, his Son, at the end of the age. Kidner sets the table for these verses when he writes, "The scale of events calls once more for the Messiah. Second Thessalonians 1:7b-9 may owe something to this passage, with its theme of Christ's appearing and of attendant fire and judgment" (*Psalms 1–72*, 104).

The Lord Will Capture and Destroy His Enemies (21:8-9)

Verse 8 is set in Hebrew parallelism:

> *Your* ***hand will capture*** *all your enemies;*
> *Your* ***right hand will seize*** *those who hate you.* (emphasis added)

The king will powerfully and decisively deal with his foes. The evil agenda of the nations, who rage against the Lord's anointed king and who plot in vain against him (Ps 2:1), is ending. Their end will be apocalyptic! David writes, "You will make them burn like a fiery furnace when you appear; the LORD will engulf them in his wrath, and fire will devour them" (v. 9). When the Lord's king shows up for battle, the war will be over. Ross rightly notes, "The extravagant language will be literally and historically fulfilled when the Messiah destroys all the wicked in the final judgment" (*Psalms 1–41,* 517). That the second coming of Jesus is in view is almost certain (see Matt 24:29-31; 2 Pet 3:10; Rev 19:11-21).

The Lord Assures Us the Work of the Wicked Will Not Succeed (21:10-12)

Verses 10-12 explain why verses 8-9 will happen. Verse 10 uses strong and startling language: "You will wipe their progeny from the earth and their offspring from the human race" (v. 10). God will remove the wicked from the earth, and he will finally and totally stop their evil deeds. No trace of the king's enemies will remain anywhere. They will vanish forever. "Though they intend to harm" and also "devise a wicked plan, they will not prevail" (v. 11). This psalm echoes Psalm 2. The wicked enemies did their best to stop the Lord's king and to destroy him, but they failed miserably. Their treachery will turn back on them, and the Lord will expose them for the evil fools that they are. Verse 12 ends the rout of the king's enemies. The king "will put them to flight" as he readies his "bowstrings to shoot at them" (v. 12). The GNT says, "He will shoot his arrows at them and make them . . . run." The Lord's king always hits his target. He never misses. Run where you will, hide as best you can; it will all be in vain when the King pulls closed the curtain of history (see Rev 6:12-17). It will be a great day of rejoicing for all who love and submit to King Jesus. It will, however, be a tragic day of judgment for all who oppose him.

The Lord's King Leads Us to Worship the Lord Fully
PSALM 21:13

A God who cares for his king, leads him to victory, and showers him with "faithful love" (*chesed*) is more than worthy of our total devotion, praise, and worship. His strength becomes our song. His power becomes our praise. As the doxology proclaims, "Praise God from whom all blessings flow" (Thomas Ken). Three common verbs of worship bring our psalm to a perfect end.

We Exalt the Lord

"Be exalted, LORD," the king sings. He declares exclusivity to this worship. The Lord and only the Lord is to be exalted. *The Message* provides an interesting paraphrase: "Show your strength, GOD, so no one can miss it." Every child of God should make a regular habit of exalting the name of the Lord. Praise him when you speak to others. Praise him when you pray. Praise him when you sing. Praise him every day.

We Sing to the Lord

The psalms were meant to be sung, and they were meant to be sung by God's people. This God has blessed his King and blessed us through his King. A heart overflowing with gratitude and thanksgiving cannot help but sing. Psalm 100:1-2 reminds us, "Let the whole earth shout triumphantly to the LORD! Serve the LORD with gladness; come before him with joyful songs."

We Praise the Lord

The psalm ends as it began with a note of praise for the Lord's "strength" (ESV, "power"). The Lord is mighty on behalf of his Messiah-King and his people. Notice it is "we" who "sing and praise [his] power." The eschatological vision of the church in heaven in Revelation 7:9-12 provides a perfect New Testament commentary to this verse. Spurgeon again puts it beautifully: "For a time the saints may mourn, but the glorious appearance of their divine Helper awakens their joy. . . . He wrought our deliverance alone, and he alone shall have the praise" (*Treasury*, 317).

Conclusion

David penned Psalm 21, but Jesus Christ fulfills it. He is its *telos*, its completion, its end. He is the Lord's King who will reign forever. Michael Wilcock is right: "Psalm 21 celebrates the unity between the King and his Father God. He emerges from the bitter conflict of Calvary, and from every other conflict, crowned with glory and victory (21:3, 5). The *length of days for ever and ever* (21:4) . . . is for him literal truth" (*Message*, 77; emphasis in original). King Jesus reigns forever, and so will our praise!

Reflect and Discuss

1. Describe some spiritual victories God has won in your life for which you can praise him. Why should you regularly praise God for victory over sin and your flesh?
2. If God gave you the desires of your heart, what would happen? Would any big prayers be answered?
3. How can you know if your desires line up with God's? What is the difference between praying your will and praying God's will? What fears or temptations keep you from wanting to pray God's will?
4. Why is it not possible for us to honor Jesus too much? What does appropriate honor of the Lord look like?
5. How does joy in the Lord's presence fulfill the victory that God has won for us in Christ?
6. What does complete trust in the Lord look like compared to partial trust? In what places are you tempted to put your trust?
7. How do we strengthen our trust in the Lord? How can we strengthen the trust of other believers in the Lord?
8. Are you confident that your life is physically and spiritually secure because your relationship with the Lord is certain? Why or why not?
9. How can you praise/exalt the name of the Lord when you speak to others?
10. How should an eschatological vision of Jesus's coming victory over death cause you to live?

The Psalm of the Cross

PSALM 22

Main idea: Jesus the messianic King suffered and died so that, like him, people from every nation could be rescued for the praise of the Lord.

I. Meditate on the Passion of Our Lord (22:1-18).
 A. Our Lord suffered spiritually (22:1-5).
 B. Our Lord suffered personally (22:6-10).
 C. Our Lord suffered physically (22:11-18).

II. Meditate on the Prayer of Our Lord (22:19-21a).
 A. Our Lord prayed for God's help (22:19).
 B. Our Lord prayed for God's deliverance (22:20-21a).

III. Meditate on the Praise of Our Lord (22:21b-31).
 A. Because of what God has done, the people of God will worship the Lord (22:21b-26).
 B. Because of what God has done, the nations of the world will worship the Lord (22:27-31).

When reading Psalm 22, you can imagine its author, King David, standing beneath the cross of the Lord Jesus as he penned it. Many throughout church history have described the importance and value of Psalm 22 for our portrait of Jesus's death. James Boice described it as "the best description in all the Bible of Jesus Christ's crucifixion" (*Psalms 1–41*, 191). Martin Luther said,

> This Psalm is a kind of gem among the Psalms that contain prophecies concerning Christ and his Kingdom, and is peculiarly excellent and remarkable. . . . This Psalm contains those deep, sublime, and heavy sufferings of Christ, when agonizing in the midst of the terrors and pangs of divine wrath and death, which surpass all human thought and comprehension. And I know not whether any Psalm throughout the whole Book contains matter more weighty, or from which the hearts of the godly can so truly perceive those sighs and groans, inexpressible by man, which their Lord and head, Jesus Christ, uttered when conflicting

> for us in the midst of death, and in the midst of the pains and terrors of hell. (Luther, *Manual*, 66)

Charles Spurgeon adds,

> This is beyond all others *The Psalm of the Cross*. . . . It is the photograph of our Lord's saddest hours, the record of his dying words . . . the memorial of his expiring joys. David and his afflictions may be here in a very modified sense, but, as the star is concealed by the light of the sun, he who sees Jesus will probably neither see nor care to see David. Before us we have a description both of the darkness and of the glory of the cross, the sufferings of Christ and the glory which shall follow. Oh for grace to draw near and see this great sight! We should read reverently, putting off our shoes from off our feet, as Moses did at the burning bush, for if there be holy ground anywhere in Scripture it is in this Psalm. (*Treasury*, 324)

Augustine, speaking of the whole psalm, simply states, "Now what follows is spoken in the person of The Crucified . . . our old man was nailed together with Him to the Cross" (*Expositions*, 58). Finally, Sidney Greidanus informs us,

> In response to the reading of Isaiah 52:13–53:12 (The Suffering Servant) the *Revised Common Lectionary* assigns the reading of Psalm 22 for Good Friday in all three years. Psalm 22 is quoted more frequently in the New Testament than any other psalm. On the cross, Jesus himself cried out the opening line of this psalm, "'*Elōi, elōi, lema sabachthani?*' which means, 'My God, my God, why have you forsaken me?'" (Mark 15:34; Matt 27:46). . . .
>
> For when Jesus quotes the first line of the psalm, 'My God, my God, why have you forsaken me?' he has the whole psalm in mind. (*Preaching Christ from Psalms*, 405)

Some wish to identify the Righteous Sufferer in the psalm with David or another ancient writer prior to the time of Christ. I, however, would concur with Calvin who said,

> Although David here bewails his own distresses, this psalm was composed under the influence of the Spirit of prophecy concerning David's King and Lord. . . .

> The heavenly Father intended that in the person of his Son those things should be visibly accomplished which were shadowed forth in David. (*Psalms 1–35*, 362, 376)

Richard Davidson observes how Christ himself would have viewed this magnificent psalm:

> I have become convinced that Christ conquered at Calvary, at least in part, because he had seen the battle plan in advance of the OT scriptures, and in particular Psalm 22, as it links with the prediction of his death in Daniel 9. He recognized what David described under inspiration in Psalm 22, was to happen to the New David, the Messiah, in his death. ("Psalm 22," 10)

Indeed, Psalm 22 is about our crucified and risen King, Jesus Christ.

The New Testament references Psalm 22 some twenty-four times (Wilson, *Psalms*, 424). The psalm does not describe a sick man or a weary warrior; the words of Psalm 22 are the words of a man enduring execution, depicted with language so graphic and brutal that the pictures conjured disturb us.

Psalm 22 is part of a magnificent trio (Pss 22–24). Each psalm emphasizes an aspect of the Lord's anointed, the Messiah-King. In Psalm 22 we have a portrait of our suffering King. In Psalm 23 we have a portrait of our Shepherd-King. In Psalm 24 we have a portrait of our sovereign King. It is also instructive to read Psalm 22 in light of what precedes it in Psalms 20 and 21. In Psalm 20:6 we read,

> *Now I know that the* L*ORD* *saves his anointed;*
> *he will answer him from his holy heaven,*
> *with the mighty victories from his right hand.*

And in Psalm 21:1-7 we read,

> L*ORD*, *the king finds joy in your strength.*
> *How greatly he rejoices in your victory!*
> *You have given him his heart's desire*
> *and have not denied the request of his lips.* Selah
> *For you meet him with rich blessings;*
> *you place a crown of pure gold on his head.*
> *He asked you for life, and you gave it to him—*

length of days forever and ever.
His glory is great through your victory;
you confer majesty and splendor on him.
You give him blessings forever;
you cheer him with joy in your presence.
For the king relies on the Lord;
through the faithful love of the Most High he is not shaken.

Now, in stark contrast, Psalm 22:1 surprises us and startles our expectations as God's anointed is forsaken. God is absent; he does not answer him.

Although the psalm can be studied under the two categories gleaned from 1 Peter 1:10-11—suffering (vv. 1-21) and glory (vv. 22-31)—our meditation will concentrate on three dominant themes of suffering and deliverance: (1) the passion of the Messiah-King (vv. 1-18), (2) the prayer of the Messiah-King (vv. 19-21), and (3) the praise of the Messiah-King (vv. 21-31).

Meditate on the Passion of Our Lord

PSALM 22:1-18

Allen Ross says, "The psalm is for the most part an extended lament psalm" (*Psalms 1–41,* 528). It contains prayers of both petition and praise. Immediately the cry of the righteous Sufferer confronts us. How do we know he is righteous? In the psalm he does not confess personal sin. He has none. Further, he does not hurl a vindictive or vicious word at the enemies who taunt him and seek his death. No, the one suffering the abandonment of heaven and earth endures his passion as an innocent victim and as a trusting servant of the Lord. In what ways does this righteous one suffer? Verses 1-18 highlight three aspects of his suffering.

Our Lord Suffered Spiritually (22:1-5)

The psalm begins with a deeply personal threefold cry to God. The one to whom the righteous Sufferer cries is "My God" (vv. 1-2). He painfully petitions, "My God, my God, why have you abandoned [ESV, "forsaken"] me?" This petition is the fourth saying of Jesus on the cross recorded in Matthew 27:46 and Mark 15:34. This prayer is intensely personal. The personal pronouns *my* and *me* appear five times in verse 1. The psalm's initial question is followed by a second: "Why are you so far from my deliverance [ESV, "from saving me"] and from my words of groaning?" The word translated "groaning" is a "strong word [and] is used in verse 13 of a roaring lion" (Motyer, *Psalms by the Day*, 57). Here is the Lion of the tribe of Judah (Gen 49:9-10) roaring to his God, "Why? . . . Why are you nowhere to be found?"

Verse 2 illuminates the intensity of Messiah's isolation and sense of separation. No answer. No rest. Despite his nonstop seeking, he remains in distress. His cry is one "of utter distress, but not of distrust" (Storms, "The Agony and the Ecstasy"). Verses 3-5 move from complaint to confidence as David recalls God's past faithfulness. Five times he uses the personal pronoun *you* in reference to God. The righteous Sufferer knows that, despite what he is experiencing at the moment, the Lord (*Yahweh*, vv. 8,19,23,26,27,28) answers prayer. His confidence stands firm on the character of God and on the acts of God.

In verse 3 our Savior declares that there is no god like God, and his covenant people rightly praised and worshiped him. They also "trusted [him]" (three times in verses 4-5). Indeed, David writes, "our ancestors trusted in you; they trusted, and you rescued [ESV, "delivered"] them." You were their salvation. Verse 5 reinforces the truth of verse 4; then it adds, "They cried to you and were set free," which perhaps refers to the exodus. And again, "they trusted in you and were not disgraced" (ESV, "put to shame"). The Lord did not disappoint his people or let them down.

However, our Lord Jesus experienced death, not salvation, as the following verses make clear. He was shamed more than any man (cf. Isa 52:13–53:12). He was not delivered; he was forsaken. His suffering, however, had a purpose. As Paul writes, God "made the one who did not know sin to be sin for us, so that in him we might become the righteousness of God" (2 Cor 5:21). Christ suffered in every way so that we who believe in him would not have to suffer eternally. He was shamed so that we would not be shamed in our sin. He was abandoned so that we would not be abandoned by God forever in our depravity. He was not delivered so that we could be delivered from judgment. In some real sense that will forever remain a divine mystery, the Son was abandoned by his Father as he bore the sins of the world (John 1:29; 1 John 2:1-2). The Son, who for all eternity had been in a perfect, loving fellowship with his Father, was forsaken for us. I (Danny) cannot explain it, but I thank God for it.

Our Lord Suffered Personally (22:6-10)

This psalm makes a clear connection to the great Suffering Servant song of Isaiah 52:13–53:12. When given the opportunity to share the gospel with a Jewish person, I make a beeline to Psalm 22 and Isaiah 53. Both read as if they had been penned at Golgatha's hill. What does our suffering Savior say of himself as he hangs on the cross bearing the curse of sin (Deut 21:23; Gal 3:13)?

Verses 6-8 reflect our Lord's experience of humiliation on the cross. "But I am a worm and not a man" (v. 6) is a metaphor expressing how he feels insignificant and how close he is to death (Wolde, "A Network," 648). He feels worthless and of no value. He has been dehumanized; no one cares about him. He is "scorned by mankind and despised by people." He is ridiculed and held in contempt. He is, as the prophet Isaiah writes, "despised and rejected by men" (Isa 53:3).

"Everyone who sees me mocks me; they sneer and shake their heads" (v. 7; see Matt 27:39-43) indicates that with derisive words and insulting gestures, they taunt him and make faces at him. Verse 8 may be the most insulting and painful of all. They call to mind the psalmist's own words in verses 3-5, but they are used here against him: "He relies on the LORD; let him save him; let the LORD rescue him, since he takes pleasure in him." These words sound like those the mocking crowds hurled at Jesus (Matt 27:39-43). Willem VanGemeren well says, "Out of sheer disregard for his feelings, they apply their 'theological' measuring sticks to his situation and conclude, that if he truly were to trust God, he would not suffer" (*Psalms*, 239). The suffering one, however, did trust the Lord. He declares four affirmations of confidence in the Lord in verses 9-10. From the beginning of life, he learned to trust and rely on God. The Lord has been his God (cf. vv. 1-2) all these years, and he will continue to trust him even now.

Our Lord Suffered Physically (22:11-18)

The psalmist trusted in the Lord. This trust leads him to plead in verse 11, "Don't be far from me, because distress [ESV, "trouble"] is near, and there's no one to help." The righteous Sufferer refers to the enemies who have surrounded him (vv. 12,18). These vicious opponents are described with powerful images: many bulls (v. 12), mauling and roaring lions (vv. 13,21), dogs (vv. 16,20), and wild oxen (v. 21). The bulls of Bashan "were proverbial for their size. . . . Bashan is the region known today as the Golan Heights" (VanGemeren, *Psalms*, 242). The goal of the four packs of animals is to trample him and tear him apart.

Verses 14-18 are some of the most amazing in the Bible. They transport us into the world of prophetic wonder in terms of their specificity. Although death by crucifixion would not come into existence for several hundred years, these words accurately describe the sufferings a victim of crucifixion would experience. Again, the authors of the Gospels interpreted the psalm in this way.

Our Lord, through David, cries out, "I am poured out like water, and all my bones are disjointed" (v. 14). Pain racks his body and his bones; they are stretched to the breaking point and dislocated from their proper places. "My heart is like wax, melting within me" (v. 14) indicates he can sense his life ebbing away.

Verse 15 describes total dehydration and looks back to the curse of Genesis 3:19. "My strength is dried up like baked clay [ESV, "a potsherd"]; my tongue sticks to the roof of my mouth. You put me into the dust of death." This last phrase leads us to Isaiah 53:10: "Yet the LORD was pleased to crush him severely." This suffering—and eventual exalting—is the Lord's doing and will. The evil enemies of the righteous Sufferer are called "a gang of evildoers" in verse 16. To inflict even more pain on the Lord's servant, the psalmist writes, "They pierced my hands and my feet" (cf. Isa 53:5; Zech 12:10; John 20:24-27). I appreciate Spurgeon's expositional and pastoral counsel at this point: "This can by no means refer to David, or to any one but Jesus of Nazareth, the once crucified but now exalted Son of God. Pause, dear reader, and view the wounds of thy Redeemer" (*Treasury*, 330).

Verses 17-18 conclude the psalmist's testimony of his brutal sufferings. He is emaciated like a tragic victim of a Holocaust concentration camp. He can count his ribs one by one (v. 17), which appears to describe well what his enemies do as they "look and stare [ESV, "stare and gloat"] at me." Finally, in words found in all four Gospels (Matt 27:35; Mark 15:24; Luke 23:34; John 19:23-24), "They divided my garments among themselves, and they cast lots for my clothing." John tells us our Lord's death fulfills Psalm 22:18. As far as his enemies are concerned, the righteous Sufferer is as good as dead already. After all, a dead person has no need for clothes. Suspended naked between heaven and earth for all to see, the Lord's Servant endures his last humiliation.

Meditate on the Prayer of Our Lord

PSALM 22:19-21A

Now we arrive at the actual prayer of the Lord's Servant. It is direct and simple, and it recalls verse 11. He makes four requests. Despite all he has suffered, the righteous Sufferer still trusts in the Lord. James Boice is on target when he writes, "The climax of the first part of Psalm 22 and the turning point between part one and part two comes in verses 19-21, as the suffering Savior finds his communion with God restored" (*Psalms 1–41*, 196).

Our Lord Prayed for God's Help (22:19)

The prayer of confidence and faith begins with a strong and emphatic adversative, "But you." He addresses God as "LORD" (*Yahweh*) and "my strength." His request is twofold: "Don't be far away" and "Come quickly to help." Only the Lord can give him the strength he needs to endure the horrid torture he is suffering. Because his life is almost at an end, only the Lord can help him remain faithful. That is why the Lord must "come quickly."

Our Lord Prayed for God's Deliverance (22:20-21a)

The psalmist continues to pray for help in verses 20-21, and he expands it. Having addressed the Lord in faith, the psalmist glances one final time at his enemies. King David repeats, in reverse order, the enemies noted in verses 12-13 and 16. Previously, the strong bulls, raging lions, dogs, and band of evil men attacked. Now, in verses 20-21, the sword, dogs, lions, and wild oxen approach. The pattern of Psalm 2 is in play, as the nations rage and the kings of the earth and its ruler take counsel against Yahweh and his Messiah (2:1-2). The evil men not only oppose the Messiah but also oppose God! The metaphors again are picturesque and striking. A beautiful parallelism and symmetry also occur in verses 20-21 but with a striking turn at the end of 21. The righteous Sufferer again cries out for God's help (v. 20). In context "the sword" is a human instrument of execution and death. He also asks for rescue of "my only life from the power of these dogs." Verse 20 pictures wild scavengers who bite and tear at his body. These are "hounds . . . a pack of dogs [who move] in for the kill" (Belcher, *Messiah*, 169).

In verse 21 the psalmist makes his final request: "Save me from the lion's mouth; from the horns of the oxen" (v. 13; cf. v. 12). His time is almost up. The end is here. He has only one place to look, the place he has looked all his life: to his God, the Lord.

Meditate on the Praise of our Lord

PSALM 22:21B-31

In my (Danny's) Bible I have written the word *resurrection* between verses 21 and 22. Alec Motyer ends his devotional commentary at verse 21 with, "YOU HAVE ANSWERED ME!!" (*Psalms by the Day*, 59). The phrase "You answered me" ends the prayer of verse 21. But it is the key that opens the door to the praise of verses 22-31. It may be the most wonderful hinge verse (or part of a verse) in the Bible.

God, in sovereign power and glory, saved this righteous one not *from* death but *out of* death. He did not *rescue* the suffering King from death; he *resurrected* him out of death. God came through and answered his prayer. So the psalmist must honor him and praise him. With conviction and undeterred resolve, he will see to it that an assembly of his people praise the Lord. He will ensure that all the nations praise the Lord. A missionary and evangelistic mandate pulsates in the heart of the Messiah-King. That same mandate must seize our hearts as well.

Because of What God Has Done, the People Will Worship the Lord (22:21b-26)

The righteous Sufferer, King Jesus, declares through the prophet David, "You answered me!" Belcher is correct:

> The statement "you have answered me" (v. 22) indicates that Christ has been delivered from the power of death. The event that redeems his people from the power of death and begins the process of the restoration of creation deserves exuberant and world-wide praise. (*Messiah*, 171)

The Messiah now proclaims the name *Yahweh* to his brothers and sisters in "the assembly" (ESV, "the congregation"). Hebrews 2:12 puts these words in the mouth of the Messiah, the Lord Jesus. The author of Hebrews viewed Psalm 22 as messianic, and those to whom the Messiah declares and praises the name of the Lord as believers, members of the family of God.

Previously surrounded by a congregation of "evildoers" (v. 16), he is now surrounded by those who "fear the LORD" and "praise him" (v. 23), "descendants of Jacob" who honor him, and all descendants of Israel who revere him (v. 23). The rationale for proclaiming the Lord's name, praising him, fearing him, honoring him, and revering him is given in verse 24: "For he [Yahweh] has not despised or abhorred the torment [ESV, "affliction"] of the oppressed" (ESV, "afflicted"). Further "he did not hide his face from him but listened when he cried to him for help" (see vv. 19-21).

When the righteous one cried, the Lord heard. He had mercy and showed his favor. He looked on him and answered his prayer. Jesus prayed, and his Father heard him. Therefore, the Messiah will praise him in "the great assembly" (v. 25), for the Lord is both the source and object of his praise. Further, the Messiah will pay or fulfill his "vows" as a witness to those who "fear" the Lord. A new day has dawned with the Lord's vindication of King Jesus. "The humble will eat and be satisfied." Indeed their Shepherd-King will "prepare a table for [them] in the presence of [their] enemies" and "[their] cup overflows" (23:5).

Seeking him, we will praise him for all that he is and all that he has done. Our hearts will not melt like wax as was the case with our suffering King when he bore the full measure of the wrath of God and the scorn and abuse of sinful humanity (v. 14). No, our hearts will "live forever" through the one who James Boice says, "was thinking of you and me just before he committed his spirit to the Father" (*Psalms 1–41*, 202). We will worship the Father and his Son and be satisfied in our God forever and ever!

Because of What God Has Done, the Nations of the World Will Worship the Lord (22:27-31)

Commenting on verse 27, Spurgeon writes, "In reading this verse one is struck with the Messiah's missionary spirit" (*Treasury*, 333). John Stott says, "We need to become global Christians with a global vision, for we have a global God" ("The Living God Is a Missionary God," 9). This verse, like Revelation 5:9-10 and 7:9-10, contains a great missionary promise. With beautiful Hebrew parallelism, Messiah Jesus declares, "All the ends of the earth will remember and turn to the LORD. All the families of the nations will bow down [ESV, "worship"] before you." Why? Verse 28 provides the answer. The Lord and no other is King of the universe, a kingship he gladly bestows on his Son (see Rev 19:16). John Sailhamer notes that the clause "all the families of the nations will bow before you [NIV, "him"]" (v. 27b) "uses an image that recalls the 'Son of Man' in Da 7:13-14" (*NIV Compact Bible Commentary,* 319).

Verse 29 begins, as Ross notes, with a repetition of the idea of "feasting in worship" (*Psalms 1–41,* 547). Note the universality of this worship: "All who prosper on earth will eat and bow down [ESV, "worship"]; all those who go down to the dust will kneel before him—even the one who cannot preserve his life." Note the repetition of the word "all" in verses 27-29. From the healthy and wealthy to the weak and dying, all will worship the Lord because he is the one who took Jesus to the dust of death so that, although dust we may become (Gen 3:19), dust we will not remain!

Verse 30 informs us that a posterity ("their descendants") will serve the Lord because the old, old story of Jesus and his love will be recounted generation after generation. God, in Christ, was reconciling the world unto himself (2 Cor 5:19). We must be faithful to tell "the next generation" about the Lord.

The psalm's ending in verse 31 contrasts with its cry of abandonment in verse 1. The telling of redemption's story will not end until the kingdoms of this world become the kingdoms of the Lord and his Messiah. We will tell others, who will tell others, who will tell others. When people today, a hundred years from now, and a thousand years from now hear that the one true God answered the prayer of his righteous one and delivered him out of death in resurrection power so that sinners may be saved, then the nations will turn to him and worship him. They will submit to him, enjoy him, and tell all the ends of the earth, "He has done it!" "It is finished" (John 19:30). Yes! "They will come and declare [ESV, "proclaim"] his righteousness; to a people yet to be born they will declare what he has done."

Conclusion

German pastor and theologian Dietrich Bonhoeffer (1906–1945) wrote about Psalm 22:

> If David himself once prayed this psalm in his own suffering, he did it as the king anointed by God and therefore persecuted by men. From this king, Christ was to come. He did it as the one who bore in himself the Christ. But Christ appropriated this prayer, and for the first time it acquired its full meaning. (*Life Together,* 166)

Derek Kidner adds,

> No Christian can read this without being vividly confronted with the crucifixion. It is not only a matter of prophecy minutely fulfilled, but of the sufferer's humility . . . and his vision of a world-wide ingathering of the Gentiles. (*Psalms 1–72*, 105)

Psalm 22 is the psalm of Christ's crucifixion. Psalm 22 is the psalm of the Savior's resurrection. Psalm 22 is the psalm of the church's mission. Our Lord has done his work! Now let the church do hers.

Reflect and Discuss

1. How does Psalm 22 deepen your understanding of Jesus's suffering? Are we ever at risk of minimizing or forgetting Jesus's suffering? If so, how?
2. If someone does not realize the depths of Jesus's suffering, how will his or her view of the gospel be affected?
3. Why is it important to recognize that Jesus suffered spiritually, personally, and physically? How does Jesus's suffering in each of these ways allow those who follow him to be blessed spiritually, personally, and physically?
4. In what ways has sin affected us spiritually, personally, and physically?
5. Does asking God "Why?" signal a lack of faith? Why or why not?
6. Is complaining to God in prayer always sinful? If not, what would be the difference between righteous complaint and unrighteous complaint?
7. The psalmist pairs his complaints to God with his remembrance of God's past faithfulness. How does this act shape his prayer? How would our prayers be weakened if we never voiced our concerns to God or never remembered God's faithfulness?
8. How does God's rescue (vv. 22-31) provide the answers to the psalmist's problems (vv. 6-18)?
9. How does the truth that God did not rescue Jesus *from* death but *out* of it shape how you view God's will for his people?
10. What does the psalm's end (vv. 22-31) reveal about Jesus's thoughts on the cross when he quoted this psalm?

Portrait of Our Shepherd-King

PSALM 23

Main Idea: Whether we walk through green pastures or dark valleys, God, the divine King, rules as a good shepherd over his people, and he promises to be with us and to bless us for his name's sake.

I. Our Shepherd-King Provides for Us What We Need (23:1-3).
- A. He gives us nourishment (23:1-2).
- B. He gives us rest (23:3).
- C. He gives us guidance (23:3).

II. Our Shepherd-King Protects Us Where We Are (23:4-5).
- A. He is with us when we face death (23:4).
- B. He is with us when we face the enemy (23:5).

III. Our Shepherd-King Promises Us What We Will Have (23:6).
- A. We will always have his gracious love.
- B. We will someday enjoy his gracious acceptance.

Holy Scripture overflows with metaphors, pictures, and images of our great and awesome God. They help us understand his character and nature, his holiness and goodness, and his power and love. Herman Bavinck, in his work *The Doctrine of God,* lists the various ways God is described in the Bible. For example, he is compared to a lion, an eagle, a lamb, the sun, a light, a fire, a fountain, a rock, a hiding place, a tower, and a shield; the Bible also gives more personal and intimate images to help us comprehend the incomprehensible God. He is called a bridegroom, a husband, a judge, a king, a man of war, a builder and maker, a physician, and of course a father (*Doctrine of God,* 86–89). And yet another image appears in the Bible that portrays with wonderful clarity our Lord's compassion and concern, his protection and guidance. It is the image of a shepherd—actually, the image is of a Shepherd-King. We discover this Shepherd-King imagery in the beautiful Twenty-third Psalm, a psalm that forms a glorious trilogy with Psalms 22 and 24. In Psalm 22 we meet our suffering King. In Psalm 24 we see our sovereign King. In Psalm 23 we witness our Shepherd-King.

Each of these psalms has the Lord Jesus Christ in view. The Bible describes the Lord Jesus as a shepherd three times. In John 10:11 he is the "good shepherd" who gives his life for his sheep. In Hebrews 13:20 he is the "great Shepherd of the sheep" who shed his blood to inaugurate and ratify the new and eternal covenant. In 1 Peter 5:4 he is the "chief Shepherd" who provides for his faithful servants the crown of glory that does not fade away.

Each of these, no doubt, finds its origin in Psalm 23, which Charles Spurgeon called "the pearl of Psalms" (*Treasury*, 353). James Boice wrote, "The twenty-third Psalm is the most beloved of the 150 psalms in the Psalter and possibly the best-loved (and best-known) chapter in the entire Bible . . . [it] is a masterpiece throughout" (*Psalms 1–41*, 207). J. P. McBeth said, "The 23rd Psalm is the greatest poem ever written" (*Twenty-Third Psalm*, 3).

In Psalm 23 we find words of faith, confidence, and assurance. Jesus voiced Psalm 22 to his Father, and it would not be surprising if these words were on his lips too. These words should also be on the lips of every servant of God as we trust our good shepherd, the Lord Jesus, to lead us in the paths of righteousness and to walk with us through the valley of the shadow of death. Much of the imagery in the psalm also echoes the exodus, when Yahweh shepherded his people through the wilderness. This shepherd has a history. This shepherd has proven his faithfulness to his sheep in the past. Therefore, we can trust him in the present and the future.

As we give our lives in service and dedication to our Shepherd-King, the Lord Jesus, what can we be completely confident that he will do in our lives? Three precious truths emerge from these six verses.

Our Shepherd-King Provides for Us What We Need

PSALM 23:1-3

A sheep has only one shepherd. Jesus is a shepherd who knows his sheep by name, and they follow him. Further, as John 10:27-28 teaches, he gives them eternal life, and they will never perish. If that is what he will do in eternity, what will he do today and tomorrow?

He Gives Us Nourishment (23:1-2)

David affirms, "The Lord [*Yahweh*] is my shepherd; I have what I need" (NIV, "I lack nothing"; NLT, "I have all that I need"; *The Message*, "I don't need a thing"). The personal pronoun is crucial. A total of seventeen personal pronouns appear in the six verses of this psalm. The one true and living Lord is our shepherd. The great I AM of Exodus 3:14, who is not bound by time or space and who is not limited in power or knowledge, this one is my Shepherd. He is ours through faith and trust in his perfect work of salvation, and we are his in absolute trust and surrender. In this life we may not have all that we want, but we will always have everything we need for joy and the fulfilling of the Lord's perfect will for our lives (Rom 12:2). In the exodus the Lord shepherded his people through the wilderness into the promised land, meeting every single need they had. Left to themselves, sheep lack everything, but cared for by a good shepherd, they lack nothing.

Verse 2 describes the nourishment he gives as "he lets me lie down in green pastures; he leads me beside quiet waters." Unlike a hireling, he thinks first and foremost of his sheep's welfare. He will see to it that they have what they need for life. This is what Jesus does for you and me. He will feed us and satisfy our hunger because he is the bread of life (John 6:35). He will quench our thirst because he is the living water (John 4:14; 7:38).

He Gives Us Rest (23:3)

David says the Lord "renews my life." The Hebrew word *nephesh* is often translated as "soul" or "life." The Lord revives us when we need strength. The Lord "renews" us and puts us back on our feet and into the fight when we stumble and fall. The Lord puts life in proper perspective and helps us see things with a Godward, eternal perspective. The Lord restores us and refreshes us through his personal presence and his powerful Word. As Psalm 19:7 reminds us, "The instruction of the LORD is perfect, renewing [ESV, "reviving"] one's life."

How different life is for those who do not have the Lord Jesus as their shepherd or for the believer who forgets Jesus Christ is his shepherd. In her poem, Marcia Hornok captured the endless frustration and disappointment so many experience:

> "Psalm 23, Antithesis"
> The clock is my dictator, I shall not rest.
> It makes me lie down only when exhausted.
> It leads me to deep depression.
> It hounds my soul.

It leads me in circles of frenzy for activity's sake.
Even though I run frantically from task to task,
I will never get it all done.
For my "ideal" is with me.
Deadlines and my need for approval, they drive me.
They demand performance from me, beyond the limits of my
 schedule.
They anoint my head with migraines.
My in-basket overflows.
Surely fatigue and time pressure shall follow me all the days of
 my life,
And I will dwell in the bonds of frustration forever.

Thankfully this poem does not reflect the life of the one who walks with the great Shepherd of the sheep. No, the good shepherd restores, renews, and revives the soul. He gives us nourishment. He gives us rest. He gives us what we need.

He Gives Us Guidance (23:3)

The Lord also "leads [us] along the right paths for his name's sake." God gives constant and compassionate care. "He leads [NIV, "guides"] me." He does not drive or coerce. He does not manipulate or trick. And he leads us right where we need to go: "paths of righteousness" (ESV).

He always leads in the right and proper direction. He leads us by his Spirit and through his Word to do the right thing, to think the right thing, to say the right thing, and to live the right way. As Psalm 119:105 wonderfully reminds us, "Your word is a lamp for my feet and a light on my path." I like John Piper's thoughts here: "A path of righteousness is a right path followed with the right attitude" ("The Shepherd"). Doing the right thing in the right way signals true spiritual maturity, and righteousness is essential for a fruitful life (cf. Ps 1). This insight prepares us for the last phrase of verse 3.

God leads us "for his name's sake." Do you see what is here? Do you grasp the power and promise of this statement? He meets my needs, renews my life, and leads me in the right paths, putting his reputation on the line. His name. His glory. Psalm 106:8 says of God's deliverance of Israel, "Yet he saved them for his name's sake, to make his power known." God wants everyone to see his glory and good character. God, in his sovereignty, works in all things to display his greatness and his glory for the joy and blessing of his people, his children, his sheep. John Piper again hits the nail on the head:

> God is the beginning and God is the end of all my righteousness. The path of righteousness has *his* grace as its starting point (for *he* leads me into it) and it has *his* glory as its destination (because his leading is for his name's sake). ("The Shepherd"; emphasis in original)

How could this affect our prayer lives? Our approach to life? Our service? We will speak to God like this:

- Lord, use me for your name's sake.
- Lord, make me holy for your name's sake.
- Lord, keep me from evil for your name's sake.
- Lord, make me like you for your name's sake.

Our Shepherd-King provides what we need. What a wonderful shepherd he is!

Our Shepherd-King Protects Us Where We Are

PSALM 23:4-5

Russell Moore makes an interesting observation about heroic figures and "wild things" in the Bible. He writes,

> Heroic figures in Scripture are often pictured as heroic slayers of dangerous animals, like David or Samson. . . . [In] the shepherd imagery of the Bible . . . [t]he shepherd's primary duty is to protect his flock from predators, by fighting them off. That's why the Psalmist is comforted by the Good Shepherd's rod and staff. It's not that they look cool and shepherd-like. It's that they are used to knock the teeth out of wolves and big cats. . . . [T]he shepherd-warrior imagery in the Bible is then applied to the Davidic king of the people of God: "The good ruler, like the bold shepherd, devotes himself, to exterminating predators whenever and wherever they can be found." ("Where the Wild Things Are, Part One")

This is exactly what David has in mind when he affirms our Shepherd-King is about the business of protecting his people from threats like wolves and big cats, including the biggest threat of all: death.

He Is with Us When We Face Death (23:4)

David writes, "Even when I go through the darkest valley, I will fear no danger." In a sense, we are walking in "the darkest valley," the valley of the shadow of death, of deep shadow and darkness. Green pastures or restful waters do not exist here. Here it is unclear and uncertain. Life can often be like this. Yet David can say, "I fear no danger" (ESV, "evil"). When we move through the deep and dark valleys of life, when death itself peeks over the horizon and stares us in the face, we do not need to be afraid. How can we say this? The next line gives us the answer.

"For you [God] are with me; your rod and your staff—they comfort me." Do not miss the message David has for us. It can radically change your life and your service to the Lord. We are going through the deep, dark valleys *because* our good shepherd is leading us! The dark valley is part of the path of righteousness. Why would the good shepherd lead us through a place of danger and death? To get us to a better place! We may lack many things in life if we follow our good shepherd, but we will never lack anything the good shepherd knows is good for us. Psalm 84:11 reminds us, "For the Lord God is a sun and shield. The Lord grants favor and honor; he does not withhold the good from those who live with integrity." Two of the instruments our shepherd uses to lead us and "comfort" us are the "rod" and the "staff." The rod is an instrument to protect us and provide safety. It guards us. The staff is an instrument to comfort us and provide support. It guides us. In death-valley days, do not fear. You have the One you need, and he has the resources to lead and guide you to a better and more wonderful place. In the darkest moments of life, you and I have *whom* we need. We have the Lord.

He Is with Us When We Face the Enemy (23:5)

The imagery changes suddenly in verse 5. We move from that of a shepherd to the host of a great banquet. Yet it is not a completely new image so much as it is an extension and development of the Shepherd-King picture. This King is constantly with us and caring for us in the fields and in the valleys as a shepherd. But he also seats us at his table and in his house (v. 6). He has brought us from the fields, through the valley, and into his home! Here we are both safe and satisfied.

David says, "You prepare a table before me in the presence of my enemies." The Shepherd-King serves his sheep. Enemies may surround us; yet God sustains us. This says something both to us and to them. We can be confident we will lack nothing we need when we are walking in the paths of righteousness in complete trust and dependence on our Shepherd-King. To our enemies this is a witness, a testimony, to the favor of God in our lives and his faithfulness to his sheep, his children. They would harm us, but God protects us. They would starve us, but God feeds us and honors us. He "anoint[s] my head with oil." He publicly acknowledges us as honored guests with an ancient ritual of hospitality: oil, mixed with perfume, would smooth the skin and give off a sweet fragrance. It is a mark of friendship, acceptance, and celebration, "a pleasing provision of hospitality for an honored guest" (Ross, *Psalms 1–41*, 567).

There is more: David says, "My cup overflows." Indeed, our shepherd gives us more than we need in a gracious and lavish display that all can see. The Lord's cup never runs empty or even half filled. It is always filled to the brim and running over. Our enemies pale in comparison and fade fast away in the presence of the good shepherd and all the good things he has and does for us.

Our Shepherd-King Promises Us What We Will Have

PSALM 23:6

For some, Psalm 23 may recall images of a funeral. Psalm 23 can certainly comfort us at a time of death. However, a careful and balanced reading of Psalm 23 will reveal it is not about death. It is about life! It is not about dying. It is about living (now and forever!). It is life more abundant as described by the good shepherd Jesus in John 10:10. He laid down his life that each believer may have life, eternal life, a God-quality kind of life, a life lived in his presence forever.

We Will Always Have His Gracious Love

John Piper describes God like a heavenly highway patrolman ("The Shepherd"). He is always in hot pursuit of us with "goodness and faithful love" (ESV, "goodness and mercy"). Instead of being pursued by your enemies who angrily watch you feast at a great banquet prepared in your honor (v. 5), it is the "goodness [*tob*] and faithful love [*chesed*]," the loving-kindness of our Shepherd-King, that constantly run after you. God's goodness and covenant faithfulness aggressively chase after you. You cannot outrun or outlast God. Our Shepherd-King is swift.

We Will Someday Enjoy His Gracious Acceptance

A popular praise song says that a single day in God's courts is better than a thousand days anywhere else (Matt Redman, "Better Is One Day"; see Ps 84:10). I have no doubt that is true, but the Word of God has a much better promise than that: David writes, "And I will dwell in the house of the LORD as long as I live" (ESV, "forever"). Notice the psalm begins (v. 1) and ends (v. 6) with "the LORD." Life from beginning to end should be about the Lord.

In this life you may be a nomadic servant of the good shepherd. You may live overseas in another country. You may serve Christ in relative obscurity. His call on your life may take you far away from family, friends, and familiar surroundings. But you may rest assured that the good shepherd will feed you and lead you, protect you and provide for you. And when he finishes using you for his good purposes, he will bring you into his house as his child forever. What greater privilege could be imaginable than to dwell in the house of the Lord, our Shepherd-King, forever! Neither death nor life or any other thing will be able to separate us from the love of God in Christ Jesus our Lord (Rom 8:35-39).

Conclusion

Everyone needs a shepherd. In Ezekiel 34:23 God says to his people, "I will establish over them one shepherd, my servant David, and he will shepherd them." This verse promises a future Shepherd-King in the mold of Psalm 23. Couple this with Micah 5:2-4, which promises that from Bethlehem "one will come . . . to be ruler over Israel for me [the Father]. . . . He will stand and shepherd them in the strength of the LORD, in the majestic name of the LORD his God." And note, "His origin is from antiquity, from ancient times." You have a Shepherd-King who is God and man! Here is a shepherd for life and a shepherd for eternity. Why do we need such a shepherd? First Peter 2:25 helps provide the answer: "For [we] were like sheep going astray." Sin had confused you, deceived you, and had made promises it did not deliver. Then Jesus came looking for you. He found you and rescued you by laying down his life for you as the good Shepherd. He rescued you from sin, Satan, death, and hell. He rescued you from yourself. Now you have returned to the one the Bible calls "the Shepherd and Overseer of your souls" (1 Pet 2:25).

And what does this Shepherd promise for those who are his sheep? Revelation 7:16-17 says,

> *They will no longer hunger; they will no longer thirst* [Ps. 23:2]*; the sun will no longer strike them, nor will any scorching heat. For the Lamb* [the Lord Jesus] *who is at the center of the throne will shepherd them; and he will guide them to springs of the water of life* [Ps 23 again]*, and God will wipe away every tear from their eyes.*

This is our good shepherd. This is our great Shepherd of the sheep. This is the Shepherd-King who will receive, lead, love, and care for all who will say, "The Lord (Jesus) is my shepherd, in him I have everything I will ever need."

Reflect and Discuss

1. What do the various metaphors for God teach us about his character and being? How does the shepherd metaphor help you understand God?
2. What does the psalmist mean when he says, "I have what I need"? How does this statement pair with the truth that the psalmist will still experience "danger" and "the darkest valley" (v. 4)? How do we define "needs" and "wants" in the Christian life?
3. Does the poem "Psalm 23, Antithesis" ever describe you? If yes, how so? How can you know when you have replaced God with something or someone else as your source of nourishment and rest? How do you make God your source for these things?
4. What role does Scripture play in how God leads you?
5. Why is it a blessing that God has tied his name and glory to his people? How does this give us security during "dark-valley days"?
6. Why should God, as Piper states, be both the starting point and the destination of our righteousness? How does our righteousness depend on God? How does our righteousness bring God glory?
7. In what ways has God designed the local church to be one of the primary means through which he shepherds us?
8. What lies would Satan have you believe about God when you experience danger and dark valleys? What substitutes for God does Satan

tempt you to believe you need? How do you defeat these lies and trust that God is with you?

9. What promises does this psalm give that encourage you to follow God and put your trust in him?
10. How do Christ's life, death, and resurrection confirm that God will fulfill the promises he makes in Psalm 23?

Meet the King of Glory

PSALM 24

Main Idea: Jesus, the mighty King of glory, has made a way by his perfect life and perfect atonement for every person to enter God's presence.

I. Acknowledge His Creation (24:1-2).
  A. The earth is completely his (24:1).
  B. The earth is rightly his (24:2).
II. Hear His Challenge (24:3-6).
  A. You must come cleanly (24:3-4).
  B. You can come expectantly (24:5-6).
III. See His Coming (24:7-10).
  A. Look for the King who is mighty (24:7-8).
  B. Look for the King of glory (24:9-10).

First Timothy 3:16 contains a beautiful one-verse hymn that wonderfully captures in succinct simplicity the career of Jesus Christ:

> *He was manifested in the flesh, vindicated in the Spirit, seen by angels, preached among the nations, believed on in the world, taken up in glory.*

Many in the early church saw in that last phrase, "taken up in glory," a reference to our Lord's ascension back into heaven (Luke 24; Acts 1), depicted in Psalm 24 (Geljon, "Didymus the Blind," 70). The psalm's background is perhaps the return of the ark of the Lord to Jerusalem under David in 2 Samuel 6 (Motyer, *Psalms by the Day*, 62). Psalm 24 fits the context of a liturgy of worship as the people of God gather to celebrate the Lord as their Creator-God (vv. 1-2), their Holy God (vv. 3-6), and their Warrior-God (vv. 7-10) (Ross, *Psalms 1–41*, 575–76). Each of these Old Testament themes finds full and clear voice in the New Testament when "the Word became flesh" (John 1:14). The ark of the Lord was the presence of the Lord *symbolized.* The Word made flesh was the presence of the Lord *realized.* John says, "We observed his glory" (John 1:14). Let's meet this King of glory of Psalm 24. He is glorious indeed.

Acknowledge His Creation

PSALM 24:1-2

The first two verses function as a prelude of a hymn that celebrates Yahweh as the great and victorious Warrior-King. Anyone who attempts to claim any part of creation invites the Lord to become his enemy. Why?

The Earth Is Completely His (24:1)

Verse 1 literally reads, "To Yahweh [is] the earth and the fullness of it, the world and those who live in it." Everything belongs to the Lord. The land and the seas, the nations and the individual, all people and every single thing belong to him. He stamps all creation with the word *Mine!*

The Earth Is Rightly His (24:2)

Verse 2 explains why verse 1 is true. Why is the earth completely his? He created it. He made it. Of his own sovereign will and pleasure, God brought something out of nothing, an *ex nihilo* act of creation. Nature is not divine; Yahweh is. Nature is not eternal; the Lord is.

And just who is this Lord who created all that is? Listen to the Word of God.

> *In the beginning was the Word, and the Word was with God, and the Word was God. He was with God in the beginning. All things were created through him, and apart from him not one thing was created that has been created.* (John 1:1-3)

> *He is the image of the invisible God, the firstborn over all creation. For everything was created by him, in heaven and on earth, the visible and invisible, whether thrones or dominions or rulers or authorities—all things have been created through him and for him.* (Col 1:15-16)

> *Long ago God spoke to our ancestors by the prophets at different times and in different ways. In these last days, he has spoken to us by his Son. God has appointed him heir of all things and made the universe through him.* (Heb 1:1-2)

Who is this Creator-God (vv. 1-2) and King of glory (vv. 7-10)? It is the Lord Jesus Christ, the Son of God. He is the King of glory.

The language of verses 1-2 look back to the primal creation of Genesis chapters 1–2, particularly Genesis 1:9. Yet the words also anticipate that new and eternal creation of the new earth of Revelation 21–22, where we are promised by our God, "I will freely give to the thirsty from the spring of the water of life. The one who conquers will inherit these things, and I will be his God and he will be my son" (Rev 21:6-7). We should acknowledge his creation because he has promised his children that we will enjoy it with him forever.

Hear His Challenge

PSALM 24:3-6

Such an awesome and sovereign God may not be approached lightly or irreverently. He is not our pal, our buddy, or some cosmic cheerleader committed to our happiness and self-fulfillment. No, this God, the God of the Bible, is an altogether different God. He is a holy and righteous God, of whom Habakkuk 1:13 says, "Your eyes are too pure to look on evil, and you cannot tolerate wrongdoing."

In many ways Psalm 15 is a companion or commentary on verses 3-6. Read the words of David in that wisdom psalm:

> *Lord, who can dwell in your tent?*
> *Who can live on your holy mountain?*
> *The one who lives blamelessly, practices righteousness,*
> *and acknowledges truth in his heart—*
> *who does not slander with his tongue,*
> *who does not harm his friend or discredit his neighbor,*
> *who despises the one rejected by the Lord*
> *but honors those who fear the Lord,*
> *who keeps his word whatever the cost,*
> *who does not lend his silver at interest*
> *or take a bribe against the innocent—*
> *the one who does these things will never be shaken.*

Charles Spurgeon said,

> There should be some preparation of the heart in coming to the worship of God, and to the hearing of the gospel. Consider who He is in whose name we gather, and surely we cannot rush together without thought. Consider whom we profess to worship, and we shall not hurry into his presence as men run to a fire. (*Metropolitan*, 350)

What preparation must we make? What is the challenge we must hear?

You Must Come Cleanly (24:3-4)

Verses 3-4 consist of two rhetorical and poetically parallel questions. First, "Who may ascend the mountain of the LORD?" This is a reference to Mount Zion and looks back to Psalm 2:6 and the place where the Lord has installed his Messiah, his Anointed, as King. Second, "Who may stand in his holy place?" The idea is not only who can come into his presence but also who can remain and serve there? This looks back to the righteous person of Psalm 1 and anticipates the answer of verse 4 in our text.

Four things must be true of the person who would enter into the presence of the Lord and remain there. First, he must have "clean hands" (right actions). He must be free from sinful actions and clean in what he does, "literally, innocent, free from guilt" (Ross, *Psalms 1–41*, 580). Second, he must have "a pure heart" (right attitude). He must be blameless, free from impure motives, thoughts, and emotions. Third, he must not appeal "to what is false" (right actions). He does not disgrace God or dishonor him by being a hypocrite (VanGemeren, *Psalms*, 260). Fourth, he must not swear "deceitfully" (right attitude). No deception or false motives fill his heart, his soul. He knows nothing of dishonesty or deceit.

James Boice is correct: "Verse 4 answers the important question of verse 3 in terms of the worshiper's inner character and outward actions. It also answers it in terms of his relationships to God and to other people" (*Psalms 1–41*, 216). Charles Spurgeon also is right: "It is uphill work for the creature to reach the Creator. Where is the mighty climber who can scale the towering heights?" (*Treasury*, 375). Indeed, who among us could perfectly meet the fourfold requirements of verses 3-4? There is only one who had such clean hands that it is said of him in Acts 10:38, "[He] went about doing good." There is only one whose heart is so pure and dedicated to God that he can say in John 8:29, "I always do what pleases him [the Father]." There is only one so devoted to the glory of God that he alone can say in John 17:4, "I have glorified you on the earth by completing the work you gave me to do." Yes, there is only one whose words were of such truthfulness and integrity that the Bible says in 1 Peter 2:22, "He did not commit sin, and no deceit was found in his mouth." Yes, there is only one man who can ascend the holy hill of Zion and stand forever in the holy place. That one is Jesus. Now, by his perfect work of atonement, we can be found in him. We can be found with a righteousness not our own but an alien righteousness, his righteousness, imputed to us by faith. Now, in him I can come to the Lord clean, pure, undivided in loyalty, and with integrity. Yes, in him, I can come cleanly into his holy presence. I come in the righteousness of the King of glory!

You Can Come Expectantly (24:5-6)

Verses 5-6 promise marvelous things to the one who can meet the requirements specified in verses 3-4. First, "He will receive blessing from the LORD." Blessing (Hb *berakah*) carries the idea of a gift, enrichment; favor physically, spiritually, or both (Ross, *Psalms 1–41*, 581). It is grounded in the covenant promises of God to his people and finds eloquent expression in Aaron's high priestly blessing in Numbers 6:24-26. Calvin is a helpful teacher when he writes,

> When he speaks of *blessing*, he intimates that it is not those who boast of being the servants of God, while they have only the name . . . but those only who answer to their calling with their whole heart, and without hypocrisy. . . . God has in reserve for them a blessing which cannot fail them. (*Psalms 1–35*, 407)

Second, he receives the righteousness from the God of his salvation. The word *righteousness* (Hb *tsedaqah*) here could be affirming the doctrine of imputed righteousness developed more fully by Paul in Romans and Galatians. Vindication, even victory, may also be in view (Ross, *Psalms 1–41*, 582). The God who saves pronounces us to be right in character and conduct. We are acceptable in his sight, vindicated to stand in his presence. We have this only in Christ.

Third, he declares that those who receive the Lord's blessing and righteousness are like Jacob and his generation, those "who inquire of him, who seek the face of God." Genesis 32:24-30 says that Jacob wrestled with God. He wrestled or sought the Lord all night until the Lord blessed him (v. 29). Jacob named the place *Peniel*, "Face of God," for "I have seen God face to face, . . . yet my life has been spared" (v. 30). If we seek the Lord with all our hearts, we will find him (Jer 29:13). If we each seek the Lord with clean hands and a pure heart, we will see him. *Selah!* We should pause and meditate on that.

See His Coming

PSALM 24:7-10

Some questions exist about the precise meaning of these final verses. The voices of worshipers are clearly present, but what is the context of their praise and adoration? It could be the ark of the Lord's return from battle. Others believe it is specifically the ark's return to Jerusalem under the leadership of David (2 Sam 6; 1 Chron 13; Wilcock, *Message*, 88). Still others view this as a liturgical hymn celebrating the Lord's kingship over his people and his presence with them as they gather for worship on the hill of the Lord, Jerusalem (v. 3), and in his holy place, the tabernacle or temple (v. 4).

Yet, like the early church, I believe the earthly enactments point to something greater and more transcendent. This entry of the King of glory does not happen on earth. It transpired in heaven. As Geljon says, summarizing the view of the early church, "The gates in heaven are commanded to open themselves for the entrance of the king of glory, who is Christ, after his resurrection" ("Didymus the Blind," 70). Human hands did not make this holy hill and holy city. Nor do only human persons inhabit it. As Hebrews 12:22 instructs us, "Instead, you have come to Mount Zion, to the city of the living God (the heavenly Jerusalem), to myriads of angels, a festive gathering." This grand entrance is in heaven, as the ascended Lord Jesus is met by the hosts of heaven welcoming home the victorious warrior Christ, the mighty King of glory. This is why Spurgeon called Psalm 24 "The Song of the Ascension" (*Treasury*, 374).

Look for the King Who Is Mighty (24:7-8)

"Lift up your heads, you gates! Rise up, ancient doors!" The psalmist addresses the gates leading to the sanctuary. They are told to raise their tops and to throw open their doors as wide as possible. Why? Because the "King of glory" has arrived, and it would be insulting to have him stoop and bow to enter into his sanctuary.

This great King is described with a powerful and striking accolade in response to the question, "Who is this King of glory?" (v. 8). He is "The LORD (*Yahweh*), strong and mighty, the LORD (*Yahweh*), mighty in battle." This King is the Lord God! This King is a warrior, a warrior who is strong, not weak. Start the battle, and when the dust settles, he will be standing victorious over death, hell, and the grave.

Look for the King of Glory (24:9-10)

Five times in verses 7-10, the Lord Jesus is called the "King of glory," the glorious King. He is "strong and mighty, . . . mighty in battle" (v. 8), because he is also the Lord *Tsabbaoth*, the "LORD of hosts" (ESV), the "LORD of Armies" (v. 10). For a second time (v. 9) the gates, the "ancient doors," are commanded to "lift up" and "rise up"! They are to prepare for the King of glory. Interestingly, verse 10 repeats the question from verse 8: "Who is he, this King of glory?" The answer is basically the same with a slight change. It is the "King of glory," the "LORD of Armies."

Our Warrior-King, the Lord's anointed Son, has engaged the forces of evil and destroyed death by his death. Having finished the enemy off on the field of battle, he took a brief repose in a throne room of a tomb before bursting forth in glorious resurrection. Remaining for forty days to prepare his troops for further battles, he then climbed the hill known as Mount Olivet. He ascended from the earth into heaven (Luke 24; Acts 1). He took "the captives captive; he gave gifts to people," and he "ascended far above all the heavens, to fill all things" (Eph 4:8-10). Ascending into the presence of the holy sanctuary in heaven, he has entered in as our high priest, "holy, innocent, undefiled, separated from sinners, and exalted above the heavens" (Heb 7:26). Here is our ascended King-Priest after the order of Melchizedek (Ps 110). Here is the King of glory, the Lord of Armies. This is the King of glory you must meet so that you too may enter the presence of God. He is the way, and there is no other.

Conclusion

A hymn entitled "The Earth, with All That Dwell Therein" (1635), which is based on Psalm 24, provides a fitting conclusion to this psalm.

> The earth and all that dwell there-in,
> with all its wealth untold,
> belongs to God, who founded it
> upon the seas of old,
> upon the seas of old.
>
> O who shall stand before the Lord
> On Zion's holy hill?

The clean of hand, the pure of heart,
the just who do God's will,
the just who do God's will.

O everlasting doors, give way,
Lift up your heads, O gates!
for now, behold, to enter in,
the King of glory waits,
the King of glory waits.

Who is this glorious King that comes
to sit upon the throne?
All hail the Lord of Hosts, who is
our glorious King alone,
our glorious King alone. (Psalter 1912)

If I could add a fifth verse, it would be this:

So we proclaim his glory now
and celebrate his fame.
The Lord of might in battle reigns,
King Jesus is his name,
King Jesus is his name.

Who is this Creator-God and King of glory? It is the Lord Jesus Christ, the Son of God. He is the King of glory.

Reflect and Discuss

1. Why do many psalms acknowledge God as the Creator? How does this shape how you read the rest of this psalm?
2. Why is it important to remember that you are one of God's creations? In what ways is your sin an attempt to be the creator instead of the creation?
3. This section argues that verses 1-2 anticipate the new creation. How will the new creation be similar to and different from the current creation? How does the promise of a new creation contrast with popular views about heaven? How does the new creation complete the redemptive story of the Bible?
4. Why should you prepare your heart to worship God? How can you do this? What is the result of not preparing your heart?

5. How can you prepare your heart before, during, and after the weekly church gathering?
6. Why should verses 3-4 cause some level of fear in us? How does the gospel relieve these fears?
7. Why are both right *actions* and right *attitude* necessary to enter God's presence?
8. What are the blessings that verse 8 refers to?
9. In what ways is seeking God's face both the daily pursuit and the final reward of the Christian life (cf. 1 John 3:2)?
10. How does this psalm's warrior language comfort the Christian?

Enjoying the Lord's Leadership

PSALM 25

Main Idea: Those who allow the Lord to lead enjoy the Lord's leadership.

I. Allowing the Lord to Lead (25:1-11)
II. Enjoying the Lord's Leadership (25:12-21)

When Jesus invited people to himself, he did so with one simple statement: "Follow me." There were no spiritual laws, steps to peace, or Romans road. He simply made one demand: Follow me. That really is the all-encompassing demand of Christ. Those two words not only are a call to faith but also define the nature of our relationship with Jesus: he leads and we follow. We submit our entire lives to his leadership.

Those two words, "Follow me," sound simple, but think about their implications. They are not just a call to add Jesus to an already busy life. They demand that Jesus become one's life. They demand that we believe Jesus to be the only way, truth, and life, and in response we give ourselves fully to him. Our marriages, work, hobbies, decisions, business, leisure—everything is now submissive to him. Becoming a follower of Jesus Christ means that we, by faith, choose to let him lead.

Bill Bright, founder of Campus Crusade for Christ, built his entire ministry on one core message: the Christ-controlled life. He believed this was the first step of the Christian life. He illustrated this with an image that shows a throne in the middle of a circle. The throne is the control center of your life. It represents your intellect, emotions, and will. Only one person can be on the throne of your life. You and Christ cannot both sit there. The Christian life is all about keeping Jesus on the throne of life, living completely under his leadership (Bright, *Handbook*, 60).

Psalm 25 is about the leadership of the Lord. It is a cry of the heart to let the Lord lead in every way. It is an alphabetic acrostic, meaning each line begins with a successive letter of the Hebrew alphabet. This was normally a poetic device used to help memorize a psalm, and this psalm is certainly worthy of memorization. Although there are many great verses and themes throughout this psalm, the primary lesson is clear: those who allow the Lord to lead enjoy the Lord's leadership.

There is no clear indication of the exact context David found himself in when he wrote Psalm 25, but the general circumstances are certain. David is in danger, and he doesn't know what to do, where to go, or whom exactly to call. He needs deliverance (v. 2), direction (v. 3), forgiveness (vv. 7-11), and encouragement (v. 16). He is overwhelmed by his circumstances and feeling the weight of the moment. But what David needs most is leadership.

The theme of Psalm 25 is clearly that of guidance. It appears as the consistent cry throughout the psalm (vv. 4,5,8,9,10,12,14). The strongest indication is in verses 4-5. David says, "Make your ways known to me, LORD; teach me your paths. Guide me in your truth and teach me, for you are the God of my salvation; I wait for you all day long." David is in need of clear direction, and he knows that only the Lord can give it.

The primary lesson of Psalm 25 sounds simple, but it is worth our careful meditation: those who allow the Lord to lead enjoy the leadership of the Lord. Most believers *want* the leadership of the Lord. They long for the Lord to give them wisdom and direction. They want the Lord to supernaturally show them the way to go. But few believers actually *allow* the Lord to lead. Psalm 25 gives us a great picture of what it looks like to let the Lord lead as well as a picture of the joy of being led by the Lord.

Allowing the Lord to Lead

PSALM 25:1-11

Verses 1-2 set the tone for the entire psalm: "LORD, I appeal to you. My God, I trust in you. Do not let me be disgraced; do not let my enemies gloat over me." David is in need. He is crying out to the Lord for help and leadership. But beyond the obvious, these verses are a statement of complete surrender to the Lord's leadership. The simple phrase, "I trust in you," is a statement of submission to the Lord. He is lifting up his soul to the Lord in allowing the Lord to lead.

This is where all of us must begin. A life in Christ begins in faith and surrender. When we come to see Jesus Christ as the only way, our response is to then surrender to his way. We must take all that we have—all of our past, present, and future—and lift it up to the Lord. We must say, "OK, Lord, here it is: all that I have and all that I am. I am letting you lead." What David did in verse 1 is what every one of us must do—lift up everything to the Lord in surrender.

If we are honest, we will admit that this feels risky. David seems to feel that. He says, "Do not let me be disgraced" (v. 2). He is saying, "OK, Lord, I'm going all-in with you. I am putting all my trust in you. Now please, don't let me be humiliated." But immediately after those words come out of his mouth, he reminds himself that there is no risk in allowing the Lord to lead. He says, "No one who waits for you will be disgraced; those who act treacherously without cause will be disgraced" (v. 3). In other words, there is no risk in allowing the Lord to lead; the risk is in not allowing the Lord to lead. Those who wait for him (trust in him and allow him to lead) will never be disgraced (Isa 49:23). This is what it means to have the Lord on the throne of your life. Having confidence that those who let him lead will never be put to shame.

There is so much to learn from David's attitude here. The evidence of David's inward decision to trust the Lord's leadership is manifested in verses 4-5. "Make your ways known to me, Lord; teach me your paths. Guide me in your truth and teach me, for you are the God of my salvation; I wait for you all day long." David has no idea where to go and what to do next, but he knows that he wants to go where the Lord wants him to go. All he wants is to follow the Lord as the Lord thinks is best.

The truth is, we don't have a clue what to do with our own lives. None of us have the wisdom or knowledge to lead ourselves in the way that is right. Jesus is the way, and we cannot lead ourselves in the way of Jesus; we must let him lead. The reason there are so many references to waiting is because the only hope we have is to look to the Lord. And the Lord's goal is not just to lead us in a direction but to lead us to a person. Jesus does not *have* the way; Jesus *is* the way. Following the leadership of the Lord is about keeping Jesus central in our lives. Our response is to look to him all day long (v. 5).

Verses 8-9 give us much-needed confidence in our pursuit of allowing the Lord to lead. We can be confident that if we are humble and look to him, he will lead us (v. 9). God has no intention of hiding his way from us. He wants us to follow him. And we can always trust him because he is "good" and "upright" and "faithful" and forgiving. Our God loves to show sinners the way (v. 8). Even when we sin and fail to follow him the way we should, he still loves to lead us in the way. God is so good and so faithful and so kind and so patient. If all those things are true, there is no reason to try to lead ourselves. We must allow the Lord to lead. As we do, we experience the joys of his leadership.

Enjoying the Lord's Leadership

PSALM 25:12-22

Why would we accept the Lord's invitation to allow him to lead our lives? Psalm 25 answers that question in many ways. To say it most plainly, those who don't allow the Lord to lead are ultimately put to shame (v. 3). Their lives will be a disgrace. They will lose everything because they simply cannot lead themselves. But Psalm 25 gives us more than that. It gives us four specific benefits of following the Lord's leadership.

First, those who follow the Lord's leadership are shown the right way. Verse 12 says, "Who is this person who fears the LORD? He will show him the way he should choose." When the Lord leads, you know where to go. Because we tend to be stubborn and proud, we often wait until we are lost before we ask the Lord to lead. We don't like to admit we are lost until it is obvious to everyone that we are. But the Lord is inviting us to follow him and let him lead us in the right paths before we are too far lost. Without his leadership we will never find the way.

Second, those who follow the Lord's leadership receive the blessing of the Lord. Verse 13 says that the one who follows the Lord "will live a good life, and his descendants will inherit the land." The Lord blesses those who follow him. This is not an isolated reference to this truth; this is the testimony of all Scripture (Pss 1; 40:4; 119:1; Jer 17:7). When God is leading, our souls are at rest; and when our souls are at rest, we experience the blessing of the Lord. We must believe what the father longed for the son to believe in the book of Proverbs—God's way is the only way of blessing, and this way not only benefits us but will also benefit our children after us (v. 13; 20:7).

Third, those who follow the Lord's leadership know the secrets of the Lord. One of the most precious verses in the Psalms is found in Psalm 25. Verse 14 says, "The secret counsel of the LORD is for those who fear him, and he reveals his covenant to them." This is amazing! There appears to be an inner circle—a secret counsel—made up of those who fear him and allow him to lead. To those he makes himself known. He shares intimate communion with them. What an amazing motive for allowing the Lord to lead every day!

Finally, those who follow the Lord's leadership are promised the Lord's help. In verse 15 David says, "My eyes are always on the LORD, for he will pull my feet out of the net." When you are allowing the Lord to lead, you can rest in the protection of the Lord along the way. He looks to those who are his, and he will not let them slip. He will help them when trouble arises.

Psalm 25 gives us two options. We can lead ourselves, end up in a mess, and then when we are desperate, we can hope that the Lord will help. Or we can allow the Lord to lead from the start and live with the confidence that the eyes of the Lord are always on us and his hands are always there to help us. When we let the Lord lead, we receive his help.

Conclusion

PSALM 25:16-22

The psalm ends with a final cry for the Lord to lead, but more than that, it is a final statement of confidence that God will in fact lead. At times it may not feel like the Lord is leading. It might feel as if the Lord has left us to ourselves. Those are the times when he calls us to wait for him (v. 21). As we wait for him, we will see him make himself known to us.

One of the questions that plagues Christians the most is, How can I discern the will of God? Psalm 25 reminds us that God's will is not a place; God's will is a person. When we allow the Lord to lead, he always leads us to himself. What God is looking for is a relationship with us. He is not just a compass to be followed; he is a person to be known. When we accept his invitation to follow him, it is just that. As we come to him by faith, trusting in his death as the payment for our sins and his resurrection as the way to new life, he leads us moment by moment into a greater intimacy with him. In all of that, we will discover that what our hearts have longed for the most is not his direction but him.

Reflect and Discuss

1. Consider what Jesus means by the simple invitation, "Follow me." How do you know if someone is actually following Jesus? What are the implications on your life as you accept that invitation?
2. What would it require from you to follow the Lord more closely every day? What sins or attitudes are a hindrance to your following him?
3. Which one of the benefits of allowing the Lord to lead motivates you the most?
4. As a response, pray David's prayer in Psalm 25:1-2. Tell the Lord that you trust him and want him to lead. Make sure Christ is seated on the throne of your life.

Walking in Integrity before God

PSALM 26

Main Idea: Those who live for the approval of God and not of man walk with integrity before God and not just before man.

I. Be Committed to Openness (26:1-3).
II. Have Hatred for Wickedness (26:4-5).
III. Have Love for Righteousness (26:6-8).
IV. Be Resolved for Faithfulness (26:11).
V. Be Aware of Neediness (26:9-12).

Anyone familiar with the life of Christ knows about his ongoing conflict with the religious leaders. The Pharisees in particular played a huge role in his life, ministry, and death. Much of the conflict arose out of one primary issue: their hypocrisy. A hypocrite is an actor, someone who plays a part. The religious leaders of Jesus's day had mastered the art of hypocrisy. They knew the way to pray, fast, give, and act that made them appear to be holy. They were good at it. They had fooled the masses. They had become religious leaders. But they did not fool Jesus.

When Jesus began his ministry, he saw right through the Pharisees. He saw beyond the act, right to their hearts. Jesus even knew what they were thinking. That was the worst-case scenario for them. The one thing that destroys the game of a hypocrite is seeing beyond the act, into the heart. When they met Jesus, they met their match. They could not fool him. As a result, he exposed them for what they really were and warned the people to avoid them (Matt 23:27-28). In his Sermon on the Mount, he specifically warns the people *not* to be like the religious leaders of the day (Matt 6). Throughout his ministry he publicly called them out. This entire interaction reminds us that, even though it is relatively easy to fool others, it is impossible to fool the Lord.

This is really the heart of Psalm 26. The psalm reminds us that how we live shows whom we want to please. The longing of the Pharisees was to please man through living in hypocrisy. The longing of Psalm 26 is to please God through a life of integrity. Psalm 26 shows us how to walk with integrity before God.

As is the case in many of David's psalms, he is in a situation in which many people have arisen to bring false accusations against him, so David asks the Lord for vindication (v. 1). The word *vindicate* is a legal term that means to make a favorable judgment. He is asking the Lord to examine him, look at the facts, and decide the case. He is asking the Lord to test him like one would test gold (v. 2). David feels as if he has nothing to hide. He is inviting the Lord to examine his heart and mind (v. 2). David invites this kind of investigation because he has "lived with integrity" (v. 1). According to Mark Futato ("Book of Psalms," 112), *integrity* is the key word in Psalm 26; the psalm begins and ends with integrity (vv. 1,11).

Integrity means wholehearted devotion. It refers to an undivided heart. It is a commitment to walk in a way that is pleasing to the Lord. Integrity means that what others see is what they get. There is no act. There is no show. To walk with integrity means to be the real deal. What people see is what you really are. David's emphasis on his own integrity shows us that he was a man who was not living for the approval of others but the approval of God. He knew that the only thing that really mattered was how he stood before God. In so doing, David reveals that those who live for the approval of God and not of man walk with integrity before God and not just before man.

This is a word we all desperately need, not only for instruction but also for examination. If we only care about the approval of man, hypocrisy will be enough for us. But if we care about how God sees us, only integrity will work. Integrity is not just a character trait to be developed. Integrity is the result of a heart that really longs to live a life that is pleasing to the Lord. Integrity matters to God. He delights in the truth in our inward bring (Ps 51:6). The book of Proverbs is filled with promises for those who walk with integrity. Psalm 26 shows us five marks of walking with integrity.

Be Committed to Openness

PSALM 26:1-3

The heart of integrity is a willingness to be known for who you really are. David models that for us. He invites the Lord to examine him. "Test me, Lord, and try me; examine my heart and mind" (v. 2). David has a heart that is willing to be examined (139:23-24). He wants to be known. For some of us, this might be a scary prayer to pray. We may not actually want the Lord to examine us in that way. But the motive for this type of examination is a desire for the Lord to expose anything that would keep us from being all that God wants us to be. Truthfully, we will never walk with integrity unless we are first willing to be exposed. We must be willing to be truly seen and truly known. Without that kind of openness, there will never be integrity.

One of the biggest challenges of the local church is how easy it is for people to hide. A person can attend the Sunday service and even participate in a small group yet still not be known. As in Adam and Eve's case, sin makes all of us want to hide. But the Lord wants us to invite investigation—not to humiliate us but to ensure that we are walking with integrity before God and others. Are you willing to be known? Are you ready to be open with the Lord to invite his investigation? That openness is the first key to integrity.

Have Hatred for Wickedness

PSALM 26:4-5

As David opens himself up to investigation, he affirms his deep hatred for wickedness. He does not "sit with the worthless or associate with hypocrites" (v. 4). He hates the "crowd of evildoers," and he does not "sit with the wicked" (v. 5). He is staying as far away from evil as he can. He is not going to "sit" or "associate" with those who walk in evil. Why? Because he literally hates the hypocrisy of evildoers. He is sickened by them and their schemes.

As we begin to walk with integrity and our hearts are more fully open to the Lord, the Lord begins to fill us with his affections. We begin to hate the things he hates. Questions we must continually ask ourselves are, "Do I hate the things the Lord hates? Am I repulsed by the things that repulse the Lord?" True integrity does not take sin lightly. True integrity hates sin.

Have Love for Righteousness

PSALM 26:6-8

Not only does a heart of integrity hate what God hates, but it also loves what God loves. The more we walk in purity before him, the more his passions become ours. David experienced that in verses 6-8. He went into the temple, washed his hands, raised his voice in song, and declared the wonderful works of God. He longed to be with the people of God in the house of God (v. 8). The Lord's presence brought joy to his heart. He loved God's people, God's house, and God's glory.

It is often said that you should not trust people who say they love Jesus but don't love the church. The reality is, the more we love Jesus with pure and sincere hearts, the more we love the things Jesus loves, and Jesus loves his church. Those who walk with integrity are not just involved in the church for the outward show; they are involved in the church because they love what Jesus loves. As we seek to live with integrity, we must ask ourselves if we love righteousness as Jesus does.

Be Resolved for Faithfulness

PSALM 26:11

Integrity is not an accident. Integrity is developed in those who want it and seek it. Those who have integrity before God are those who have resolved to walk in faithfulness. David says, "I live with integrity." That is a great statement. He is not just hoping or wishing; he is taking his resolute stand. In verse 1 he says, "I have lived," and in verse 11 he says, "I live." He is resolved to continue to live with his integrity no matter what.

We often struggle with the apparent conflict between our role and God's role in sanctification, but we really shouldn't. Philippians 2:12-13 tells us that we should work out our salvation. We cannot "work in" our salvation. Only God can do that. But we must choose to work out what God has worked in. People are only saved by placing their faith in Jesus Christ alone as the payment for their sins and by surrendering their lives to him. As a result of doing that, we now use our Spirit-empowered wills to resolve ourselves to greater holiness. Integrity, like holiness, does not just happen. It is developed in the life of the one who is resolved to have it.

Be Aware of Neediness

PSALM 26:9-12

As you meditate on Psalm 26 and look for the ways David cultivated integrity, you notice from beginning to end his dependence on the Lord. The Lord's faithfulness guides him in all this (v. 3). The truth of God's Word leads him (v. 3). He is fully aware of his own need for God's redemption and grace and blessing (vv. 11-12). He is wholly dependent on the gracious work of God on his behalf. He knows that anything good that comes will be the result of God's gracious work in him.

Seeing this attitude in David reminds us that integrity is not only a result of a resolve of the will to walk honestly before the Lord, but it is also a humble awareness of our need for God's grace. We are fully dependent creatures, and we are all naturally drawn to personal hypocrisy. Hypocrisy is easier. But we are not after what is easier. We want to please the Lord in every respect. So with great resolve and deep dependence, we seek to be right in the eyes of the Lord.

Conclusion

Like most of David's psalms, Psalm 26 ends with a declaration of confidence. He concludes by saying, "My foot stands on level ground; I will bless the LORD in the assemblies." David is not sinless—he knows that. Neither are we. We all fall short. But like David, we each long for a life of integrity. We fight the constant temptation to live only for the approval of man. We seek to live in a way that is right before the eyes of God. We long to be people of integrity.

Integrity is more than just an admirable virtue. The call to integrity is a call to Christlikeness. God's purpose is to conform us to the image of Christ, and he does that from the inside out. God works in us in order to work through us. That work in us is the work of integrity. While we tend to be so concerned with what others think, the Lord whispers to us from Psalm 26 and says, "What matters most is how I see you, not how others see you." Psalm 26 reminds us that those who live for the approval of God and not of man walk with integrity before God and not just before man.

Reflect and Discuss

1. Why is it such a continual temptation to live for the approval of man more than God?
2. Are there any areas in your life in which you are not living in openness before God and others? If so, explain why.
3. Can you confidently pray David's prayer in verses 1-3? Why is it important to invite the Lord in to examine you and expose you? Take some time to do that now.
4. Which one of the five marks of integrity do you need to give more effort to?

The Lord Is My Light and My Salvation: A Wonderful Missionary Promise That Sustained Darlene Deibler Rose through Many Trials and Tribulations as She Served King Jesus among the Nations

PSALM 27

Main Idea: God's presence will sustain, save, and satisfy those who call out to him and wait on him.

I. **We Can Be Confident the Lord Will Save and Deliver Us (27:1-3).**
II. **We Can Be Confident the Lord Will Protect and Lift Us Up (27:4-6).**
III. **We Can Be Confident the Lord Will Hear and Guide Us (27:7-12).**
IV. **We Can Be Confident the Lord Will Sustain and Strengthen Us (27:13-14).**

Remember one thing, dear: God said he would never leave us nor forsake us." Those words were spoken on March 13, 1942, and would be the last words Darlene Deibler would ever hear from her husband Russell as they were permanently separated in Japanese prison camps during World War II. Darlene was a missionary in her early twenties. She did not even have a chance to say goodbye to him. Listen to her own words and thoughts as she honestly and hopefully reflected on that heartbreaking day:

> Everything had happened so fast and without the slightest warning. Russell had said, "He will never leave us nor forsake us." No? What about now, Lord? This was one of the times when I thought God had left me, that He had forsaken me. I was to discover, however, that when I took my eyes off the circumstances that were overwhelming me, over which I had no control, and looked up, my Lord was there, standing on the parapet of heaven looking down. Deep in my heart He whispered, "I'm here. Even when you don't see Me, I'm here. Never for a moment are you out of My sight." (Rose, *Evidence*, 46)

Psalm 27 was a favorite of Darlene Deibler and became increasingly so during more than four years of her imprisonment for being a Christian missionary and an American. This Davidic psalm of adoration (vv. 1-6) and lament (vv. 7-14) forms part of a trio (Pss 26–28) that instructs us on seeking and finding the Lord, especially when "an army deploys" against us, when "war breaks out" against us (v. 3), and when "false witnesses have risen against" us, breathing violence (v. 12) (Kidner, *Psalms 1–72*, 117). Our study will follow the four movements of the psalm, a psalm that is confident that (1) the Lord saves and delivers (vv. 1-3), (2) the Lord protects and lifts up (vv. 4-6), (3) the Lord hears and guides (vv. 7-12), and (4) the Lord sustains and strengthens (vv. 13-14; see VanGemeren, *Psalms*, 281).

We Can Be Confident the Lord Will Save and Deliver Us

PSALM 27:1-3

The psalm begins by exclaiming confidence in the saving power of Yahweh: "The LORD is my light and my salvation." Interestingly, the Septuagint translates the word "salvation" as "Savior" (Ross, *Psalms 1–41*, 621). Since the Lord is *my* light and *my* salvation, "whom should I fear?" Since he is "the stronghold [refuge, strength] of my life—whom should I dread?" Verse 1 is a beautiful example of Hebrew parallelism as the second line reinforces the first. It is also a great missionary verse for those taking the gospel of Jesus Christ into the difficult and dangerous places of the world where opposition is intense and even life-threatening.

It is significant that the Lord is our "light." Light appears at the beginning and the end of the Bible (Gen 1:3-4; Rev 22:5). Its source is God, and it overcomes and defeats darkness (John 1:4-5). It is the source of life and allows people to see. It is also a symbol of purity, holiness, goodness, and blessing. It finds its grand fulfillment in a person, the Lord Jesus, who said, "I am the light of the world" (John 8:12).

In verses 2-3 David speaks of evildoers, enemies, foes, and an army that deploy against him to devour his flesh and who break out against him with war. There is no escape. Yet he can say at the end of verse 3, "I will still be confident." Why? Verse 2 provides the answer: "My foes and enemies stumbled and fell." His enemies will be defeated by his God. The Lord who is his light and Savior takes them down. They may try to overcome him, they may surround and enclose him, but his God can handle them all!

Darlene Deibler found all this to be true. Darlene Mae McIntosh was born on May 17, 1917. Her father was not physically well; her mother was a hardworking lady. At the age of nine, Darlene put her trust in the Lord Jesus Christ as her light and salvation. One year later, at the age of ten, during a revival service, she sensed God's calling to give her life to missions (Rose, *Evidence*, 131). On that night she promised Jesus, "Lord, I will go anywhere with You, no matter what it costs" (Rose, *Evidence*, 46). How could that little girl know what the Savior had planned for her?

Darlene would marry a pioneer missionary to Southeast Asia named Russell Deibler on August 18, 1937. She was only twenty years old; he was twelve years her senior. Later she would write, "My ignorance of the future held no cause for anxiety, for my spirit witnessed within me that God was and would be in control" (Rose, *Evidence*, 135).

After six months of church meetings in North America and six months of language study in Holland, the Deiblers eagerly returned to Russell's pioneer missionary work in the interior of New Guinea. Darlene accompanied Russell into the jungle to establish a new mission station near a previously unevangelized tribe that had been discovered just a few years earlier. Darlene, the first white woman any of them had ever seen, grew to deeply love these primitive people she was ministering to for King Jesus.

World War II broke out in that part of the world in 1941 and engulfed the missionaries in January 1942. The Deiblers had served in New Guinea for three years. Though they could have left and returned safely home, they and many others chose to stay. Ten Christian Missionary Alliance (CMA) missionaries and one child would die in captivity during the war because the Japanese soon took control of the area and put them under house arrest. Later they herded all foreigners into prisoner-of-war camps, placing the men in one location and the women and children in another. Darlene had pledged as a ten-year-old that she would follow Jesus anywhere regardless of the cost. She never could have imagined what that meant. "Anywhere" would cost her unbelievable suffering. Over four years Darlene would endure separation from her husband, widowhood, and the brutal conditions of a WWII Japanese internment camp. She would experience near starvation, forced labor, inhumane conditions, false accusations of espionage, many serious illnesses, solitary confinement, and torture. But through it all, God sustained Darlene. He never left her or forsook her, just as he had promised. He remained her light and salvation. With time he would cause her adversaries to stumble and fall.

We Can Be Confident the Lord Will Protect and Lift Us Up

PSALM 27:4-6

David now expresses the soul's desire of all who have experienced the Lord's strength and his salvation. He says, "I have asked one thing from the Lord; it is what I desire" (v. 4). What is that "one thing"? "To dwell in the house of the LORD all the days of [his] life, gazing on the beauty of the LORD." This beauty, he says, is found in "the house of the LORD" (v. 4), "his shelter" (v. 5), and "his tent" or tabernacle or temple (vv. 5-6). It is found in his presence, wherever that may be.

"The temple was the visible expression of God's presence" (VanGemeren, *Psalms*, 283). The one thing that matters most is to be in the presence of the Lord, beholding his beauty and pursuing him with one's whole heart. In Jeremiah 29:13 God promises, "You will seek me and find me when you search for me with all your heart." To see his beauty is to see his glory, know his love, and enjoy his presence as Father, Savior, Protector, and Sustainer. David saw this protection as he depended on the Lord to "conceal" him in his shelter "in the day of adversity" (ESV, "trouble"), to "hide" him under the "cover of his tent," and to set him high on a rock of safety and security (v. 5). David saw this sustaining power as the Lord lifted his head up above his enemies (v. 6). The only proper response to this great God is worship! That's why David says, "I will offer sacrifices in his tent with shouts of joy. I will sing and make music to the LORD."

To sacrifice, shout, sing, and rejoice in the Lord is easy when everything is going well. It is something else when your heart is broken and God seems silent and distant. Nothing illustrates this like the day, when at the tender age of twenty-seven, this faithful missionary received news of her husband's death. On a Sunday evening in November 1944, Darlene was informed that Russell had died after having been critically ill for some time. He had been dead for months by the time the news reached her. She writes,

> I was stunned—Russell is dead. He'd been dead three months already! It was one of those moments when I felt that the Lord had left me; He had forsaken me. My whole world fell apart. . . . In my anguish of soul, I looked up. My Lord was there, and I cried out, "But God . . . !" (Rose, *Evidence*, 109)

Immediately he answered, "My child, did I not say that when thou passest through the waters I would be with thee, and through the floods, they would not overflow thee?" (Rose, *Evidence*, 109).

Prayer, memorized Scripture, and song would be a three-cord spiritual rope that held Darlene during those terrible days. She writes,

> Much time was passed repeating Scripture. Starting with [the letter] *A*, I would repeat a verse that began with that letter, then on through the rest of the alphabet. I discovered that most of the songs we had sung when I was a little girl were still hidden in my heart, though I hadn't consciously memorized many of them.
>
> As a child and young person I had had a driving compulsion to memorize the written Word. In the cell I was grateful now for those days in Vacation Bible School, when I had memorized many single verses, complete chapters, and Psalms, as well as whole books of the Bible. In the years that followed I reviewed the Scriptures often. The Lord fed me with the Living Bread that had been stored against the day when fresh supply was cut off by the loss of my Bible. He brought daily comfort and encouragement—yes, and joy—to my heart through the knowledge of the Word. (Rose, *Evidence*, 143)

God has often used that same trio of encouragers for those who have suffered in a similar fashion to Darlene. However, in the midst of her sorrow, on that day, something truly remarkable and providential occurred, the full outcome of which would not be known for many years.

As the news of Russell's death spread throughout the camp, Darlene was summoned to Mr. Yamaji's office; he was the prison camp commander. He was a hard and brutal man who had beaten a male POW to death in another camp. He was standing behind his desk when the following conversation took place:

> "Njonja Deibler, I want to talk with you," he began. "This is war."
>
> "Yes, Mr. Yamaji, I understand that."
>
> "What you heard today, women in Japan have heard."
>
> "Yes, sir, I understand that, too."
>
> "You are very young. Someday the war will be over and you can go back to America. You can go dancing, go to the theater,

> marry again, and forget these awful days. You have been a great help to the other women in the camp. I ask of you, don't lose your smile."
>
> "Mr. Yamaji, may I have permission to talk to you?" He nodded, sat down, then motioned for me to take the other chair.
>
> "Mr. Yamaji, I don't sorrow like people who have no hope. I want to tell you about Someone of Whom you may never had heard. I learned about him when I was a girl in Sunday School back in Boone, Iowa, in America. His name is Jesus. He's the Son of Almighty God, the Creator of heaven and earth." God opened the most wonderful opportunity to lay the plan of salvation before the Japanese camp commander. Tears started to course down his cheeks. "He died for you, Mr. Yamaji, and He puts love in our hearts—even for those who are our enemies. That's why I don't hate you, Mr. Yamaji. Maybe God brought me to this place and time to tell you He loves you." (Rose, *Evidence*, 111)

Mr. Yamaji uncharacteristically jumped from his chair and left the room in tears. Darlene respectfully waited and then quietly left when she realized he would not return to the room. The God who saves and delivers, who protects and lifts up, had proven himself present. He was working, as we will see before we are finished.

We Can Be Confident the Lord Will Hear and Guide Us

PSALM 27:7-12

Verse 7 changes mood significantly. Some have speculated that we have two psalms joined together (vv. 1-6 and vv. 7-14). However, there is literary and rhetorical evidence that supports the original unity of the psalm. In a sense, verses 7-14 provide the context from which verses 1-6 arose. Our God is a promise-keeping God, and we can rejoice and rest in that. David highlights several areas where we can count on the Lord to keep his word.

The voice that shouts and sings to him in worship (v. 6) can be confident that the Lord will hear that same voice when it prays (v. 7). A merciful and gracious answer can be our confident expectation.

Speaking to the Lord means seeking the Lord. What David does in verse 4, he is instructed to do in verse 8. His response is what ours should be: obedient and immediate. "LORD, I will seek your face." Four negative requests in verse 9 complement David's petition: (1) "Do not hide your face from me." (2) "Do not turn your servant away in anger." (3) "Do not leave me." (4) "[Do not] abandon me." These requests also contain words of hope and confidence. David says, "You have been my helper" and you are the "God of my salvation" (v. 9). His parents may abandon him (in death or desertion), but the Lord will extend adoptive parental love and care. "The LORD cares for me" (v. 10). This care, David says, is enough.

Psalm 119:105 teaches us, "[God's] word is a lamp for my feet and a light on my path." We need the light of God when we face difficult and trying times. We must not rely on our emotions or feelings. We dare not trust our hearts or experiences. We must stand firmly on Christ our Rock and the rock-solid direction of his Word.

David asks the Lord to "show me your way" (v. 11). He wants to live and respond to whatever he may face as the Lord would. David also asked the Lord to guide his life sovereignly, providentially, precisely, and specifically. He says, "Lead me on a level [NIV, "straight"] path" because of my "adversaries," my enemies (v. 11). "Do not give me over to the will ["desire," NIV, NASB; "the hands," NLT] of my foes." Why? "For false witnesses [liars] rise up against me, breathing violence." They would do him harm. Eugene Peterson in *The Message* paraphrases it this way: "Show my enemies whose side you're on. Don't throw me to the dogs, those liars who are out to get me, filling the air with their threats."

On May 12, 1944, the Kempeitai, the Japanese secret police, came for Darlene. They falsely accused her of being a spy. The Kempeitai took her to a maximum-security prison where they kept her in solitary confinement. They took her Bible away from her. Over the door of her cell, in Indonesian, were the words, "This person must die." After the guard unlocked the door and shoved her inside, she knew she was on death row. She was imprisoned to face trial and the sentence of death. She sank to the floor. Never had she known such terror. She prayed, "O God, whatever You do, make me a good soldier for Jesus Christ" (Rose, *Evidence*, 125). But suddenly she found herself singing a song she had learned as a little girl in Sunday School:

> Fear not, little flock, whatever your lot,
> He enters all rooms, "the doors being shut,"
> He never forsakes; He never is gone,
> So count on His presence in darkness and dawn.

> Only believe, only believe;
> All things are possible, only believe. (Paul Rader, "Only Believe")

She would later write, "So tenderly my Lord wrapped his strong arms of quietness and calm about me. I knew they could lock me in, but they couldn't lock my wonderful Lord out. Jesus was there in the cell with me" (Rose, *Evidence*, 126).

She was kept for weeks in a cell about six feet square and had only small amounts of rice to eat each day. She spent a great deal of time killing mosquitoes, saying, "I was tortured by hordes of them at night. They clung to the wall, too full of my good red blood to do anything else" (Rose, *Evidence*, 137). Frequently she would be taken to an interrogation room where two Japanese officers, whom she dubbed the "Brain" and the "Interrogator," would accuse her of spying, of having a radio, of getting messages to the Americans, and of knowing Morse code. They claimed to have proof of her treachery. All this she would deny. But in the process they would strike her at the base of her neck or on her forehead above her nose. There were times she thought they had broken her neck. She walked around often with two black eyes. Her beautiful black hair turned gray and white. "Bloodied but unbowed," she never wept in front of them (Rose, *Evidence*, 141). But when she was back in her cell, she would weep and pour out her heart to the Lord. When she finished, she would hear him whisper, "But my child, my grace is sufficient for thee. Not *was* or *shall be*, but it *is* sufficient." "Oh, the eternal, ever-present, undiminished supply of God's glorious grace!" (Rose, *Evidence*, 141).

The Kempeitai did not believe anything Darlene said. They informed her they had sufficient proof of her involvement in espionage—she knew she would be condemned without formal trial and be beheaded as an American spy. However, in her autobiography she writes of one of the ways the Lord had prepared her for the ordeal she now faced:

> Just two weeks before I was brought to this prison, the Lord had laid it on my heart to memorize a poem by Annie Johnson Flint. Now I knew why. After drying the tears from my face and mopping the tears from the floor with my skirt, I would sit up and sing:
>
> > He giveth more grace when the burdens grow greater.
> > He sendeth more strength when the labors increase.

To added afflictions He addeth His mercy,
To multiplied trials, His multiplied peace.
When we have exhausted our store of endurance,
And our strength has failed ere the day is half done,
When we reach the end of our hoarded resources,
The Father's full giving is only begun.
His love has no limits, His grace has no measure.
His power no boundary known unto men.
For out of His infinite riches in Jesus,
He giveth, and giveth, and giveth again.

> Strength came, and I knew I could go through another interrogation, and another, and another. I was physically weak, and desperately frightened, but God gave me the courage to deport myself like a good soldier for my Lord before those cruel men. (Rose, *Evidence*, 141–42)

One day Darlene pulled herself up to the window of her cell and began watching some women who were in the courtyard. One woman's actions intrigued her. The woman inched toward a fence covered with vines. When she was close enough and the guard wasn't looking, a hand clutching a small bunch of bananas thrust through the vines; the woman grabbed the bananas, folded them into her clothes and walked calmly back to another group of women. After that . . .

> Darlene began to crave bananas. She got down on her knees and said, "Lord, I'm not asking You for a whole bunch like that woman has. I just want one banana." She looked up and pleaded, "Lord, just *one* banana."
>
> Then she began to think—how could God possibly get a banana to her? There was really no way it could happen. She couldn't ask anyone to do it. It was impossible for her to get a banana. She prayed again, "Lord, there's no one here who could get a banana to me. There's no way for You to do it. Please don't think I'm not thankful for the rice porridge [her daily ration had changed because she suffered from dysentery and could not handle rice.] It's just that—well, those bananas looked so delicious!"
>
> The morning after she saw the bananas she had a surprise visitor—Mr. Yamaji. [He had warmed toward her following her

> husband's death.] When her door was opened and she saw Mr. Yamaji's smiling face she clapped her hands and exclaimed, "Mr. Yamaji, it's just like seeing an old friend!" Tears filled his eyes and he didn't say a word but walked back into the courtyard and talked to the officers for a long time.
>
> When he returned Mr. Yamaji was sympathetic. "You're very ill, aren't you?"
>
> "Yes, Sir, Mr. Yamaji, I am."
>
> "I'm going back to the camp now. Have you any word for the women?"
>
> The Lord gave her the confidence to answer, "Yes, sir, when you go back, please tell them for me that I'm all right. I'm still trusting the Lord. They'll understand what I mean, and I believe you do."
>
> "All right," he replied, and turning he left.
>
> When Mr. Yamaji and the other officers left Darlene realized she had not bowed to the men! "Oh Lord, they'll come back and beat me," she thought. When she heard the guard coming back she knew he was coming for her. She struggled to her feet and stood ready to go to the interrogation room. The guard opened the door, walked in and with a sweep of his hand laid at her feet—bananas! "They're yours," he said, "and they're all from Mr. Yamaji." Darlene was stunned as she counted—there were ninety-two bananas!
>
> In all my spiritual experience she said, I've never known such shame before my Lord. I pushed the bananas into a corner and wept before him. "Lord, please forgive me; I'm so ashamed. I couldn't trust You enough to get even one banana for me. Just look at them—there are almost a hundred."
>
> In the quiet of the shadowed cell, He answered back within my heart: "That's what I delight to do, the exceeding abundant above anything you ask or think." I knew in those moments that nothing is impossible to my God. (Rose, *Evidence*, 148–50).

Time and time again God showed himself to be powerful and faithful to Darlene. Shortly after this, she was moments from being beheaded as a spy only to be taken from the Kempeitai back to the prison camp in Kampili. The Lord again had heard her prayers and led her to a "level path" against her enemies.

We Can Be Confident the Lord Will Sustain and Strengthen Us

PSALM 27:13-14

This psalm concludes on a high note of confidence and assurance, even triumph and victory. Because of the power and might of the God who is our light and salvation, we can trust and rest in the Lord no matter what may come.

Verse 13 reads, "I am certain that I will see the LORD's goodness in the land of the living." How awesome it is that we can pray these words in full confidence, absolute faith, and complete certainty. The greater Son of David, the Lord Jesus, prayed such a prayer on the cross as his enemies surrounded him (v. 3), slandered him (v. 12), and violently took his life (v. 12). He commended his life, his destiny, into the hands of a heavenly Father. He knew with full confidence that he would see the goodness of the Lord three days later in the land of the living through glorious and powerful resurrection. In faith he waited on the Lord (v. 14). He was strong in the Lord (v. 14). His heart took courage (v. 14), trusting in the perfect and sovereign plan of a good and gracious and great heavenly Father.

The God who sustained and strengthened Jesus and David will sustain you and me. He certainly sustained and strengthened the wonderful missionary Darlene Deibler Rose throughout her life.

God sustained and strengthened her in her salvation at nine years of age.

God sustained and strengthened her call to be a missionary at the age of ten—yes, ten!

God sustained and strengthened her as a young bride at age twenty.

God sustained and strengthened her when she headed to the jungles of New Guinea at twenty-one!

God sustained and strengthened her when placed under house arrest by the Japanese when she was twenty-five.

God sustained and strengthened her when she and her husband Russell were separated into different prison camps in 1942, never to see each other again in this life.

God sustained and strengthened her as she ate rats, tadpoles, dogs, runny oatmeal, maggots, and other unimaginable foods.

God sustained and strengthened her as she and others were forced to present sixty thousand dead flies a day to Mr. Yamiji because they bothered the pigs they tended, pigs who were treated better than the POWs.

God sustained and strengthened her through dengue fever, beriberi, malaria, cerebral malaria (Rose, *Evidence*, 142), dysentery, beatings and torture, attacks of rabid dogs, false charges of espionage, the promise of beheading, solitary confinement, Allied bombings, and many other inhumane abuses.

God sustained and strengthened her when she was told of the death of her beloved husband Russell and his own tortures and sufferings.

God sustained and strengthened her when she and the other POWs were finally released, and she was allowed to visit the grave of her husband. She weighed all of eighty pounds.

God sustained and strengthened her when he brought her home to America and kept the fire of missions burning in her heart.

God sustained and strengthened her when he brought another missionary into her life, Gerald Rose, whom she would marry (1948) and then return with him to New Guinea in 1949.

God sustained and strengthened her as she labored on the mission field of Papua, New Guinea and the Outback of Australia for over forty years of evangelizing, teaching, building landing strips, delivering babies, facing down headhunters, and loving them to Jesus.

No wonder she could write, "The twenty-seventh Psalm was a great comfort to me. . . . I knew that without God, without that consciousness of his presence in every troubled hour, I could never have made it" (Rose, *Evidence*, 154–55).

Conclusion

On February 24, 2004, Darlene Deibler Rose quietly passed away and entered into the presence of the King she so dearly loved and faithfully served. She was eighty-six years old. According to her obituary in the Chattanooga, Tennessee, newspaper, "Together, Darlene and Jerry were used of God to bring hundreds of Aborigines to the Lord and disciple them to Christ. They were also instrumental in beginning several indigenous churches that are pastored by natives" ("Rose, Darlene").

One person came to Christ through her faithful witness that stands out as a testimony to the mysterious plans and providences of God. Following the end of World War II, Mr. Yamaji, the prison camp commander where Darlene was imprisoned, was tried and sentenced to be executed for the brutal beating to death of a man, which had happened while he was in another POW camp at Pare Pare. His sentence was later commuted to life imprisonment with hard labor. Later that sentence was also commuted, and he was released. Many years later, in 1976, Darlene would learn from a friend that Mr. Yamaji had been heard on Japanese radio. He was heard sharing the gospel of Jesus Christ with the Japanese people, testifying to his cruelty in World War II but also bearing witness that he was now a different man because of Christ (Rose, *Evidence*, 224). It was Darlene who had first told Mr. Yamaji of the gospel, and she did so on the day she learned of her husband's death.

Throughout her life, when sharing her story, Darlene would say, "I would do it all again for my Savior." No doubt many in New Guinea are grateful for her devotion. No doubt Mr. Yamaji is grateful too! You never know what the Lord who is our light and Savior is going to do when you say and obey, "Lord, I'll go anywhere with You, no matter what it cost" (Rose, *Evidence*, 47). He will be with you, as Psalm 27 promises. Are you willing to go?

Reflect and Discuss

1. What parts of Darlene's life challenge and encourage you the most? Why?
2. What sustained Darlene and gave her hope when, as she says, her whole world fell apart? Have you ever felt that your world was falling apart? If so, how did you respond? How did God speak to you during that time?
3. Why is suffering *not* an indicator that God has abandoned his people? How can the character of God and the work of Christ help you answer this question?
4. Are you willing and ready to suffer as a Christian? Why or why not? What steps can you take to make your heart hardship ready?
5. What is the goal of the Christian life? How does this goal shape how you perceive suffering?
6. Why were songs and hymns such powerful tools for Darlene during her suffering? Are hymns and songs a part of your daily time with the Lord? In what ways can you include hymns and songs more in your life?
7. In what ways does God's presence bless his people?

8. What does the banana story teach you about God's abilities to provide?
9. What does Mr. Yamaji's conversion remind you about God's work and will in our lives?
10. Are you willing to pray today, "Lord, I will go anywhere with You, no matter what it costs"? If so, take time now to pray this to the Lord. Do you have any fears about praying this type of prayer?

A Cry for Help

PSALM 28

Main Idea: God helps those who cannot help themselves.

I. A Cry for Help (28:1-5)
II. The Lord Hears His People, So Call on Him (28:6).
III. The Lord Helps His People, So Trust in Him (28:7).
IV. The Lord Holds His People, So Run to Him (28:8-9).

There are few biographies in Scripture more amazing than that of Moses. From beginning to end, his life was one of constant divine intervention. He was born a Hebrew at the moment in which all the Hebrew boys were ordered to be killed. He was hidden in a basket by his mother and rescued by Pharaoh's daughter. Instead of being killed like the rest of the Hebrew boys, he was raised in Pharaoh's home. Because of the love he had for his own people, he was eventually exiled and left homeless in a foreign land. But every step of the way he saw God's supernatural intervention.

When Moses needed a home, God provided a home and a wife. When he needed direction, God called him to lead his people and then led them by a cloud by day and pillar of fire by night. When he needed deliverance, God parted the Red Sea, and he walked across on dry land. When he needed food, God gave him bread from heaven and water from a rock. It is almost as if every moment of Moses's life was one of deep desperation and divine intervention.

When you understand the life of Moses, it makes sense that when he had a son, he named the son "Eliezer." *El* means "God," *i* means "my," and *ezer* means "help." *Eliezer* means, "my God is help." The entire life of Moses is a reminder that God loves to help his people—for their good and for his glory. That is the heart of Psalm 28.

Psalm 28 is a cry for help. If you have ever found yourself in a moment of deep desperation and in need of divine intervention, Psalm 28 is for you, not only because you will be able to relate to the sense of desperation but also because of the hope found here. This psalm, like most psalms of lament, moves from despair to delight, from the valley to the mountain, from a cry to a song. Psalm 28 moves from "God, please don't ignore me" to "God always hears me!" And most of all, Psalm 28 reminds us that God helps those who cannot help themselves.

A Cry for Help

PSALM 28:1-5

Verses 1-2 set the initial tone for the psalm. David is calling, pleading, and crying out to the Lord. He is desperate. He is desperate for the Lord to hear him and pay attention to his cries. He pleads with the Lord not to be deaf or remain silent. He is certain that if the Lord does not hear him, he won't make it through this situation. He knows if the Lord does not help him, his fate will be just like the fate of the wicked. So he cries to the Lord and lifts up his hands.

When we read a passage like Psalm 28:1-2, we must also picture it and feel it. When David says, "I cry to you for help," it is the same phrase Jonah uses while in the belly of the whale (Jonah 2:2). He is desperate. Yet, even in his desperation, he knows where to look. He looks to the sanctuary, to the place where God's presence dwells. He is going directly to the Lord for help. Psalm 121:1-2 says, "I lift my eyes toward the mountains. Where will my help come from? My help comes from the LORD, the Maker of heaven and earth." This is what David is doing: he is lifting his eyes and his hands to the only one who can help him.

One thing that drives David to seek the help of the Lord is that he is aware of the fate of those who fail to look to the Lord for help. He does not want to be dragged away with the wicked (v. 3) or torn down like those who reject the Lord (v. 5). Those who do not look to the Lord for help are dragged away to face his judgment. David knows, if the Lord does not help him, his fate will be the same as the wicked's. But David knows he does not belong to the wicked. So he looks to the Lord with hope. The feel of verses 1-5 is one of absolute desperation.

After five verses of deep desperation and cries for help, the most amazing thing happens. In verse 6 David begins to praise the Lord. And to the same degree we feel the desperation in verses 1-5, we begin to feel the praise in verse 6. In a moment his entire disposition seems to change. It changes as the Lord reminds David what is true. In our seasons of lament, we often feel things and say things that are not true.

They still matter because God cares about the way we feel, but at some point God will remind us of what is actually true. This is how lament works. We cry out to God with our honest feelings of despair, and God then reminds us of what is actually true. The result is that we begin to praise the Lord again.

As the Lord begins to minister to his desperate soul, David becomes aware of the good news of what is really true (vv. 6-8). Verses 1-5 must not be overlooked. God wants to hear our honest cries of desperation. Those cries of desperation led David to his awareness of God's help. Throughout this season God reminds David of one important truth: God helps those who cannot help themselves. This is the good news of Psalm 28. In many different ways, God helps us when we find ourselves in desperate situations. Those are the moments in which God loves to intervene. David experiences this in three different ways in Psalm 28. Each of these we need to remember when our hearts begin to cry for help.

The Lord Hears His People, So Call on Him

PSALM 28:6

One of the most encouraging lines in Psalm 28 is simply, "He has heard the sound of my pleading" (v. 6). Given that David just spent five verses pouring out his heart to God and crying out for help, it is good to know that none of that was in vain. He asked the Lord not to ignore him, and the Lord answered that prayer. That little line reminds us of a precious truth: the Lord listens to his people. When we speak, his ears are open to us. He hears the cries of our hearts (Ps 34:15; Isa 59:1).

We often take this truth for granted. We fail to marvel that the God of the universe gives us his undivided attention. The only reason this is true is because of the work of Jesus Christ on our behalf. Because Jesus has reconciled us to God, we can bring all our petitions to him. We can be confident that, through the intercession of Jesus on our behalf, the Lord hears our prayers (Rom 8:34). Because of that, the Father invites us to bring all our requests to him (Matt 7:10-11; Phil 4:6).

If the Lord hears when we call, if he invites us to bring every concern to him, if he promises to help us when we call, why would we not live in unceasing prayer? If you know he is listening, take every single concern to him in prayer. Are you regularly pouring out your heart to

God? Are you being honest with him in your moments of desperation? God is listening, so talk to him.

The Lord Helps His People, So Trust in Him

PSALM 28:7

When we find ourselves in moments of desperation and despair, one of the most important things we can do is say, "The LORD is . . ." and simply remind ourselves of what is true. David does this. His heart is encouraged by the awareness that "the LORD is my strength and my shield; my heart trusts in him, and I am helped" (v. 7). Verses 1-5 make clear that David needed strength. In verse 7 he is reminded of exactly where help comes from. Our God loves to give strength to those who are weary (Isa 40:29; Phil 4:13). He does it time and time again.

David also rejoices because God is his shield. This means that nothing will ever get to us without going through God first. Through our relationship with Jesus Christ, we can be confident that no one can succeed against us if God is for us (Rom 8:31). The Lord protects us and assures us that he will complete all the work he intends to accomplish in us (Phil 1:6). The poetic language of Psalm 28 is there to get us to picture the truth. Just think about the truth that the Lord is your shield. The Lord is standing in front of you, protecting you from anything that comes at you. Nothing gets to you without going through him first.

So if the Lord is your strength and your shield, then your heart should trust in him and his help. The one who believes these truths is helped by them. David already saw the Lord as a rock in verse 1, but it is as if now, after meditating on it and praying through it, that which he knew in his mind he now knows with his heart. He is now assured that the Lord, his rock and strength and shield, is helping him. That reality turned his despair into rejoicing. If the Lord loves to help you, then trust in him.

The Lord Holds His People, So Run to Him

PSALM 28:8-9

Psalm 28 ends with two precious images: the Lord is a stronghold and a shepherd.

The Hebrew word translated "stronghold" is related to the idea of strength and means "a strong place of safety" (Ross, *Psalms 1–41*, 648).

It means that the Lord is a safe place, a shelter in danger, and a place of protection. Proverbs 18:10 says, "The name of the LORD is a strong tower; the righteous run to it and are protected." David makes this personal when he refers to the Lord as "a stronghold of salvation for his anointed" (v. 8). David is saying that the Lord is not just a safe place; he is a safe place for him personally. These truths must not just be known; they must be applied and believed personally.

David also praises the Lord for being a shepherd to his people (v. 9). The Lord has carried his people over and over again and led them safely out of danger. He is a refuge who protects us and a shepherd who carries us. The last line of Psalm 28 demands our meditation. The Lord carries us forever. This is the same expression used in Isaiah 40:11, where God is said to carry his people close to his heart (Cole, *Thirsting*, 98). He carries his people and ensures that they make it safely home. Since the Lord holds his people, run to him!

Conclusion

Through the journey of Psalm 28, David goes from absolute despair to exuberant praise. He says in verse 7 that after all his despair, "my heart celebrates, and I give thanks to him with my song." From a prayer of desperation to a song of joy. The question is, How has his heart been transformed in this way? This question matters because most believers can relate to David's despair in verses 1-5 and wonder how to make the transition to songs of joy.

We learn from Psalm 28 that we make this movement toward joyful praise by remembering and responding. At the moment we begin to feel despair and desperation, we must remember the truth and respond to it. We cannot believe our own hearts and minds when they try to tell us there is no hope. Instead, like David in Psalm 28, we must remind ourselves of what we know is true. We must remind ourselves that God hears us, God helps us, and God holds us. Then, in response to those truths, we choose by faith in Jesus Christ and our position as children of God to call on him, trust in him, and run to him.

Our faith in Jesus Christ, and only our faith in Jesus Christ, gives us the assurance that these things are true. God has not promised these things to all people universally. God has promised these things to those who have come to him by faith through Jesus Christ. Our confidence is not based on anything other than who we are as the blood-bought children of God. So, as God's children, we take all our despair and moments of desperation and find the Lord to be a sufficient help.

Reflect and Discuss

1. In what areas of life do you currently need help? How do the truths of Psalm 28 encourage you in that?
2. In what areas of life do you need to either run to the Lord, trust in the Lord, or call on the Lord?
3. In your moments of trouble, do you tend to look inward, outward, or upward? How can the truths of Psalm 28 help you look upward more quickly?

Our God Is an Awesome God

PSALM 29

Main Idea: God's power over creation declares his status as King and calls all creatures in heaven and on earth to praise him.

I. Worship the Lord for His Glory (29:1-2).
  A. Acknowledge his power (29:1).
  B. Honor his name (29:2a).
  C. Praise his holiness (29:2b).
II. Worship the Lord for His Sovereignty (29:3-9).
  A. He is sovereign over the waters (29:3-4).
  B. He is sovereign over the mountains (29:5-7).
  C. He is sovereign over the wilderness (29:8-9).
III. Worship the Lord for His Majesty (29:10-11).
  A. Our Lord is the King in his position (29:10).
  B. Our Lord is the King by his promise (29:11a).
  C. Our Lord is the King with his peace (29:11b).

One of the most beloved and well-known Christian hymns, popularized by George Beverly Shea who would sing it at Billy Graham Evangelistic Crusades, is "How Great Thou Art." It is easy to imagine the writer of this magnificent hymn reflecting on Psalm 29 as he penned those words. Psalm 29 is "a grand hymn of praise" (VanGemeren, *Psalms*, 291), what James Boice calls "pure praise . . . pure poetry" (*Psalms 1–41*, 254).

The psalm praises the God of creation who sovereignly reigns as Lord over all things. Several literary and poetic features tie this majestic psalm together:

- The name "LORD" (*Yahweh*) occurs eighteen times.
- The phrase "the voice of the LORD" occurs seven times.
- The psalm uses the words of ancient Canaanite poetry, possibly as a polemic against the worship of Baal who was believed to be "lord of storms" (VanGemeren, *Psalms*, 292). Baal is not god; Yahweh is!

- The poem divides into three sections (vv. 1-2,3-9,10-11), with a movement from heaven to earth, as well as from west to east, and then possibly from north to south.

This psalm celebrates the God who is King, the God who is omnipotent, and the God who is the Lord above the storm. The psalm contains no prayer or petition, no lament or confession. Instead, it challenges us to acknowledge and worship with the mind and the heart our God who is an awesome God!

Worship the Lord for His Glory

PSALM 29:1-2

The psalm begins with a two-verse prologue of praise built around the verbs "ascribe" (or "give," KJV, NKJV) and "worship" (see Ps 96:1-2). The prologue highlights three truths that explain why and how we should worship the Lord for "the glory due his name" (v. 2).

Acknowledge His Power (29:1)

The word *ascribe* appears three times in rapid succession. Each is an imperative (Ross, *Psalms 1–41*, 655). "Heavenly beings" is literally "sons of gods" in Hebrew and denotes the angels in heaven. The psalm calls those who sang at the dawn of creation (Job 38:7) to lead the way in acknowledging the worth and omnipotence ("glory and strength") of the God who is the sovereign Lord. Tell the Lord there is no one like him. It honors him and instructs you.

Honor His Name (29:2a)

For the third time we see the word *ascribe*. For the second time we see the word *glory*. We are to give honor to the glory of Yahweh's "name." Yahweh's name is a constant theme in the Psalms. "His name" speaks of his nature and character, who he is, and all that he is as God.

Psalm 8:1 tells us his name is "magnificent." Psalm 9:10 says of God, "Those who know your name trust in you." Proverbs 18:10 tells us "the name of the Lord is a strong tower; the righteous run to it and are protected." Philippians 2:9-10 tells us there is a "name that is above every name . . . the name of Jesus." Our God has a name that we must honor.

Praise His Holiness (29:2b)

The verb now changes from "ascribe" to "worship," though the meanings are closely related. Derek Kidner writes,

> Both of the main notes of true adoration are heard here in the words *ascribe* (or "give") and *worship* (or "bow down"), for the former enlists the mind . . . while the latter enlists the will to take the humble attitude of a servant. (*Psalms 1–72,* 125)

Understanding leads to response. Angels bow down to the Lord and praise him in beauty, the "splendor of his holiness." It is unclear whether it is the Lord's holiness that is in view or the angels' (and our) holiness with which they are to come before him. If it is the angels', Allen Ross likes the translation, "Worship the LORD 'in holy array'" (Ross, *Psalms 1–41,* 657). However, the flow of the text points again to the character and nature of God. Angels (and we) are to bow down in worship, adoration, and praise because the awesome God of power and salvation is also an awesome God of beautiful or splendid holiness. No god is like this God. He is utterly unique and distinct. He is the God who is holy and true (Rev 3:7), the God who says, "Be holy because I am holy" (Lev 11:44,45; 19:2; 20:7; 1 Pet 1:16). Why? Because as Habakkuk 1:13 affirms of God, "Your eyes are too pure to look on evil, and you cannot tolerate wrongdoing." We who have been made holy through the blood of Christ are to worship the Lord who is holy.

Worship the Lord for His Sovereignty

PSALM 29:3-9

The Bible teaches us about the awesome power of the Word of God. In Genesis 1 our God speaks creation into existence. He speaks the word, and it happens. In John 1:1 we learn that the "Word," the *logos,* is a person. It is the Son of God, the Lord Jesus Christ. Through him, the Word, God created all things (John 1:3). Through him God sustains all things (Col 1:17; Heb 1:3).

Here in verses 3-9 the voice of that Word echoes in sovereign and awesome power and majesty. And he does so in nature by means of a tremendous and deafening thunderstorm.

He Is Sovereign over the Waters (29:3-4)

God's glory, strength, and splendor rest over all his creation. David reflects on how God's voice is heard in the claps of thunder. God is over all the waters—the waters in the sky and on earth. Yet something of his glory is uniquely experienced at the awesome sound of thunder in the thunderstorm. There is "glory" and "power" and "splendor" in his voice "above the vast water" (ESV, "many waters"). Martin Luther heard the voice of God in a storm of thunder and lightning (v. 7) in July 1805 and cried out, "St. Anne help me! I will become a monk" (Bainton, *Here I Stand*, 5). In a storm Luther began a spiritual pilgrimage that would lead him to become the father of the Reformation.

He Is Sovereign over the Mountains (29:5-7)

The storm building in the Mediterranean has moved east to the northern region of Israel, to the mountains of Lebanon and Sirion (or Mount Hermon, v. 6). These majestic mountains with their magnificent cedars are like twigs and small animals for entertainment in the presence of the Lord. He speaks, and the great trees break. They snap in two ("breaks" and "shatters"; v. 5). He speaks with thunder, and the mountains shake. They skip and tremble like a newborn "calf" or like a "young wild ox." These mighty mountains, rising to a height of ten thousand feet, are mere toys for great Yahweh. With thunder comes lightning, and verse 7 draws our attention to this spectacular and fascinating display of God's power. The pagan Canaanites were nature worshipers who believed the gods lived in the mountains (VanGemeren, *Psalms*, 295). The Lord has no respect for these puny gods and impotent deities. He shakes their house with thunder and banishes their darkness with "flames of fire" (v. 7) or "flashes of lightning" (NIV). God is not *in* nature; he is *over* nature. He is not *in* it; he *made* it. Enjoy nature, but do not worship it or turn it into some idol. Great as it is, it is nothing when compared to the God who created and controls it.

He Is Sovereign over the Wilderness (29:8-9)

The storm now moves farther east, or perhaps south, across the land of promise, the land of Israel. Moving from the majestic mountains, the storm reaches to the desert region, the wilderness of Kadesh. If the movement is South, images would recall the forty years of wandering in the wilderness. Yes, God was and is in control in the wilderness too!

The first part of verse 9 presents an interpretive challenge. The CSB, NKJV, ESV, and NASB have, "The voice of the LORD makes the deer give birth." In contrast, the NIV has, "The voice of the LORD twists the oaks." The NIV translation interprets the Hebrew phrase with influence from the next line, which reads "and strips the forest bare." The interpretive decision is not easy, but both ideas are true. In the face of such a display of sovereign power, what can we say? What can we do? The last part of verse 9 provides the answer: we gather together in the place of worship, and we shout with the angels in verses 1-2, "Glory!" Praise initiated in heaven among the voices of the angels now is heard on earth in the voices of men and women, boys and girls. "Glory" initially had the idea of weight. It is the opposite of light, trivial, or inconsequential. Ross says, "To speak of God's glory is to speak of his intrinsic value, what gives him his importance" (*Psalms 1–41*, 474). God is of supreme or ultimate importance. In response we give him praise, worship, and adoration. Mind and heart unite in humble recognition of the greatness and sovereignty of our God. As the chorus in "How Great Is Our God" by Chris Tomlin reminds us, God is a King clothed in majesty, splendor, and light. Darkness submits to him and cannot hide from him. Indeed, our God is a great God, so everyone on earth should shout for joy and praise him.

Worship the Lord for His Majesty

PSALM 29:10-11

As David considers the magnificent display of God's might and majesty in the storm, his mind travels to another majestic display of God's might: the Genesis flood. If ever there was an event that put on full display the majestic power of God over nature and in judgment, it was the flood. The flood, like the storm, shouts a clear and incontestable message: Yahweh, the Lord, is "King forever."

Our Lord Is the King in His Position (29:10)

David tells us, "The LORD sits enthroned over the flood." To build and expand on that truth, he declares, "The LORD sits enthroned, King forever." The word "flood" appears only here and in the flood narratives of Genesis 6–11. It is the ultimate and supreme example of Yahweh's glory, sovereignty, power, and majesty over the waters and over all creation. His majesty in power and judgment by means of a universal flood testifies to his position as King. Truly he is, as Revelation 19:16 proclaims, "KING OF KINGS AND LORDS OF LORDS."

Our Lord Is the King by His Promise (29:11a)

The God who has the strength to bring the flood of Genesis is the God who can give me strength for the day, for each and every moment. The phrase *his people* is crucial. To his people and only to his people does he promise strength. As he strengthened Noah and his family for the task of building the ark and surviving the flood, so he will strengthen us when the waters rise, the storms come, and we can only flee to him for strength. Through Christ we can do all things (Phil 4:13). Through Christ, the Word, the voice of God, the Lord will give us strength.

Our Lord Is the King with His Peace (29:11b)

The last phrase of verse 11 parallels the first but with a different and complementary emphasis. The phrase "his people" appears again. "Gives strength" finds a companion in "blesses his people with peace" (*shalom*). The storm has passed. The Lord is King over all. He is completely and majestically in control. God's people experience peace, *shalom*, wellness of life in all its aspects.

There is a quietness and rest for the people of God even in the storm. Why? Hear the Word of God:

> *Therefore, having been justified by faith, we have peace with God through our Lord Jesus Christ.* (Rom 5:1 NKJV)

> *And the peace of God, which surpasses all understanding, will guard your hearts and minds through Christ Jesus.* (Phil 4:7)

The God of glory is a God of grace. The God of majesty is a God of mercy. The God of power is a God of peace. Our God is an awesome God.

Conclusion

We can hear the voice of God in the powerful storm. However, we hear the voice of God best in the person of his Son, Jesus Christ. When our Lord was born, the angels, the heavenly beings sang a portion of Psalm 29. In Luke 2:13 we read, "Suddenly there was a multitude of the heavenly hosts . . . praising God and saying: Glory to God in the highest heaven [Ps 29:1], and peace on earth [Ps 29:11] to people he favors!"

When our Lord was baptized, Matthew 3:17 tells us, "And a voice from heaven said, 'This is my beloved Son, with whom I am well-pleased.'" When our Lord was gloriously transfigured, we read again in Matthew 17:5, "And a voice from the cloud said, 'This is my beloved Son, with whom I am well-pleased. Listen to him!'" The voice that witnessed and testified at each of these moments in history finds its embodiment in the personal voice of God, Jesus Christ, the Word of God (John 1:1). This is the one of whom Peter said, "You have the words of eternal life" (John 6:68). This is the one whose voice could calm the sea (Mark 4:38-41) because he is "the LORD who sits enthroned over the flood . . . King forever" (Ps 29:10). And it is concerning this one that the Bible says in Hebrews 3:7-8, "Today, if you hear his voice, do not harden your hearts" (see also Heb 3:15; Ps 95:7-11). Jesus, the voice of God, is speaking today. He says, "Come to me, all of you who are weary and burdened, and I will give you rest" (Matt 11:28). Jesus is speaking. Are you listening?

Reflect and Discuss

1. The psalm calls the heavenly beings to praise God. In what ways does this call draw us to praise God?
2. Should Christians have prayers that praise God without making requests? In what ways will our prayers of praise shape our prayers of request?
3. Why is praise and worship "due" to God (v. 2)?
4. How does praising God for his glory and strength, his worth and omnipotence, instruct you about him? How could the lack of this type of praise lead to an inaccurate view of God?
5. Think further about the poetic imagery used to describe the Lord. Why are these images useful to describe the Lord's power and glory?
6. Do you ever speak about God's glory with your family, friends, and coworkers? Why or why not? In what ways could you do this?
7. How do Christians sometimes speak about God in a way that diminishes another's view of his glory and power?
8. How is the story of the flood in Genesis a good example of both the Lord's justice and his mercy? What other examples in Scripture display God's justice and mercy in one event?

9. How can you use the power of God over creation to encourage other Christians in their faith? How could you use it to tell others about the gospel of Christ?
10. Why must someone submit to God as King if they desire to have the peace Psalm 29 speaks about?

Thanksgiving for the Grief and the Gladness

PSALM 30

Main Idea: God often humbles us with momentary grief so that he might exalt us with eternal gladness.

I. **God Humbles Us with Momentary Grief.**
II. **God Exalts Us with Eternal Gladness.**
III. **We Give Thanks for the Grief and the Gladness.**

For some reason, we don't naturally tend to be grateful people. Simple things like saying "thank you" or writing a thank-you note don't seem to come easily. Every mom has to remind her children over and over again to say thank you, often, and awkwardly, right in front of the person whom they should be thanking. Right alongside the never-ending parental reminder to turn off the lights is the never-ending reminder to say thank you. Apparently, this does not come naturally even as we get older. God the Father has to continually remind us!

One thing we do realize as we get older is that we become thankful for things we were never thankful for before. It takes us a long time to be truly grateful for how hard our parents worked, how many sacrifices they made, and how they tried to be good parents even if they didn't know how. Perspective certainly increases thanksgiving. That, in many ways, is the heart of Psalm 30. In this psalm David finds himself on the other side of suffering. On that other side, he has gained some new perspective. That new perspective has given him a new sense of gratitude for things he sees more clearly than he ever did before. David sees the kindness of the Lord in his times of grief and realizes that God often humbles us with momentary grief so that he might exalt us with eternal gladness. We can thank God for both.

God Humbles Us with Momentary Grief

David writes this psalm as a man who has just come out of a near-death experience. When he says, "You have lifted me up," he gives the mental picture of being stranded in the bottom of a well in which there was no way out. The fact that he was "lifted up" means that he must have first been cast down. Anyone who was a child of the 1980s remembers the story of Jessica McClure. In 1987, eighteen-month-old Jessica fell into a well in Midland Texas. The opening of the well was only eight inches, and she was stranded there for fifty-eight hours. The entire nation was glued to their TVs as rescuers tried to lift her out. Miraculously, they did. David feels as if the presence of his enemies and his own physical struggles have left him in a similar situation to Jessica's.

Many of us have felt that way. We have felt as if we have fallen into a pit that is so deep no one can hear us or rescue us. In those moments, what do we do? Well, David did the only thing he could do: he cried to the Lord for help. God heard his cry and responded with mercy. God "healed" him, brought him up, and spared him (vv. 1-3). In response, David invites the congregation to join him in praise (vv. 4-5). He calls the congregation to sing and praise the holy name of the Lord. David is giving his testimony of deliverance. Why? Because God's "anger lasts only a moment, but his favor, a lifetime. Weeping may stay overnight, but there is joy in the morning." When the Lord turns our weeping into rejoicing, there is a reason to praise the Lord. The congregation responds with joyful songs. At this moment in the psalm, it all seems pretty clear. We suffer, we pray, God delivers, and we rejoice. It's a great story. But verses 1-5 only give part of the story.

Verses 6-12 give the other side of the same story. These two accounts complement each other. David tells the story again but with more details. You could even say it this way: verses 1-5 is me (Josh) telling a story, and verses 6-12 is my wife telling the same story but with more details. Verses 1-5 give the facts while verses 6-12 give some more important insight. That is much what is happening here, but David gives the rest of the story.

Psalm 30:6 says, "When I was secure, I said, 'I will never be shaken.'" That is usually what you say right before you are shaken. This is a cringe-worthy statement. It is a statement of arrogance. His prosperity had led him to self-reliance, which then led him to sinful self-confidence. He feels invincible. We see this same pattern all the time in someone who feels invincible because of his own success. David had forgotten that only the favor of the Lord allowed him to be so prosperous (v. 7). And because of his pride and self-reliance, God hid his face from David, and David was terrified. At the end of verse 7, you could put an equal sign between those two statements. God hides his face = we are terrified.

We all know how one moment can change everything. One decision, one phone call, one email, one diagnosis. It is amazing how everything can be changed in one moment. In this moment David went from feeling invincible to feeling absolute terror because God hid his face. Verses 1-5 tell us that David was in the well of affliction. Verses 6-12 tell us why God put David in the well of affliction. God, a loving heavenly Father, afflicted David with momentary affliction as discipline for his self-reliance.

Psalm 30 reminds us that God, in his love, often disciplines us for our own good. God will make us experience troubles and calamities (Ps 71:20-21) in order to humble us and bring us back to himself. Because of God's love for us, we can be confident that all these troubles are for our good and his glory (Rom 8:28). God's heart in these troubles is kind, his motives are pure, and his purposes are good, but the truth still remains: God will often give us seasons of momentary grief. In order for us to walk through those seasons faithfully, we must see God's good purpose in them. Thankfully, Psalm 30 shows us this as well.

God Exalts Us with Eternal Gladness

The God who humbles is the God who also exalts. The God who gives troubles is also the God who revives (Ps 70:20-21). Psalm 30 shows us that God humbles so that he might exalt. Psalm 30 shows us an incredible reversal. David was in a pit; then he was lifted up. He cried, and he was healed. He was in Sheol, but he was restored. Anger was turned to favor. God longed to exalt David, but the pathway to the exaltation was humiliation. God wanted David to experience favor, joy, dancing, and gladness, but the journey to get there was painful.

This should not surprise us. This is the way the kingdom works. Jesus reminds us in the Beatitudes that God exalts those who are humble. The kingdom works a lot like a basketball. In order for a basketball to bounce up, it must first be thrown down. Imagine an insecure basketball that gets upset every time it is thrown down. What if the basketball said, "I'm so tired of being thrown to the ground! If you loved me, you wouldn't throw me down." What the basketball does not understand is that it is only useful when it is thrown down. It is the act of throwing it down that propels it into usefulness. So it is with us. God will often throw us down in order to propel us into usefulness. God often changes the trajectory of our lives by humbling us. God gives us momentary grief so that he might exalt us with eternal gladness. David had been thrown down, but now he is experiencing dancing and gladness (vv. 11-12).

We Give Thanks for the Grief and the Gladness

Thanksgiving really is the heart cry of Psalm 30. Both stanzas of the psalm include it. Verses 4-5 are an exclamation of joyful thanksgiving. Verses 11-12 are another outburst of thanksgiving. In both moments the personal story is turned into corporate celebration—a great model for how church gatherings should look week after week. The testimonies of God's individual celebrations should lead the church into corporate worship and celebration. But for David, the most overwhelming realization of this moment in his life is seen in verses 11-12. David declares, "You turned my lament into dancing; you removed my sackcloth and clothed me with gladness, so that I can sing to you and not be silent. LORD my God, I will praise you forever." David is giving thanks for this entire situation.

It is amazing how quick we can be to turn on God. A moment of grief can immediately make us question God's love and affection for us. The God we adore in the good times can become the God we disdain in the bad times. This is why we need Psalm 30. Psalm 30 reminds us that we must give thanks for both good and bad seasons because we can trust that God is behind both and is working them out for our good. Often, it is only as we look back that we can get this kind of perspective.

David, looking back, realized that if it were not for the discipline of the Lord, he would have remained in his proud state and would not have been useful to the Lord. So the Lord, in his kindness, threw him down in order to propel him into usefulness. When we see life with that kind of perspective, we too can give thanks for both the seasons of grief and the seasons of joy.

Conclusion

Psalm 30 tells us the story of David, and it calls us to rejoice with him. It's a great story. Psalm 30 resonates with us not because it's a great story but because it is *the* story. When we see Psalm 30 in light of the story of Scripture, we begin to see that Jesus was also thrown down by the Father. Jesus was put into the pit—not because of his sin but because of ours. God crushed him for our sins (Isa 53:10). Jesus endured the discipline we deserved; he endured the pain we deserved; he endured the humiliation we deserved. Jesus, like a basketball, was thrown down by the Father.

But that is not the end of the story. Because Jesus was willing to be thrown down, God propelled him up out of the grave and all the way to the right hand of the Father. Jesus experienced momentary grief so that he might be exalted to everlasting joy (Heb 12:1-2). He was humbled so that he might be exalted (Phil 2).

That story can become our own as we are united with Christ by faith. We can be crucified with him so that we might also be raised with him. God treats us like sons, which means he will often throw us down in order to raise us up (Heb 12:5-11). God, as he did with his Son Jesus, often humbles us with momentary grief so that he might exalt us with eternal gladness.

Reflect and Discuss

1. If you are a believer, you have a story like Psalm 30:1-3. Tell that story to someone. Take the time to reflect on the ways in which God has rescued you and share them.
2. Psalm 30 shows the way in which an individual story should lead to corporate celebration. We are to use our stories to invite people to praise the Lord. In so doing, God gets the glory. This week, invite someone to praise the Lord for the good thing he has done in your life.
3. Are there times in which you feel like God gives you momentary grief? If so, how did God use such a situation to give you more lasting joy? Why is it so difficult to trust God in times of grief? How did God see you through one?

Blessed Assurance

PSALM 31

Main Idea: God gives us sufficient assurance to fight the effects of our affliction.

I. **The Dramatic Effects of Our Afflictions (31:1-2,9-13)**
II. **We Have the Assurance of God's Sufficiency (31:1-2,3-5).**
III. **We Have the Assurance of God's Loyalty (31:7,16,21).**
IV. **We Have the Assurance of God's Goodness (31:19).**
V. **Using Our Assurance as a Weapon**

If there is one thing I (Josh) have learned from my own suffering and the suffering of others, it is that the brain and the body are intimately and inseparably intertwined. Our spiritual, psychological, and emotional suffering can produce dramatic physical effects. The name for this is "psychosomatic effects." Some doctors refer to this as a modern phenomenon, but that is only because they have never read the Bible carefully. The Bible is filled with this reality. The Bible, written by the one who created our minds and bodies, shows us that our afflictions, no matter the kind, affect the entire person. Afflictions affect us mentally, emotionally, spiritually, and physically. In other words, the effects of our afflictions are far-reaching. Psalm 31 makes this clear.

Psalm 31 reveals the deep and overarching effects of our own afflictions. It shows us how our afflictions can almost overwhelm us. But Psalm 31 also shows that there is a balm for these afflictions. In the midst of this heavy psalm, there is a settled assurance. Not only is David pouring out his heart and showing the reality of his afflictions, but he is also pouring out his heart and showing the reality of his assurance. There is so much back-and-forth between affliction and assurance it makes us wonder if he's crazy or if he's actually figured out something. The truth is, in his affliction David discovered that God has given sufficient assurance to fight its effects. This is good news for all those who are afflicted.

The Dramatic Effects of Our Afflictions

PSALM 31:1-2,9-13

Verses 1-2 set the tone for the entire psalm, and the tone is one of desperation. The cry for a refuge, a rescue, and a rock reveals the desperate need for strength, safety, and stability. David acknowledges his own "affliction" (v. 7) and "distress" (v. 9) and then goes on to describe just how dramatic the effects were. He suffered emotional affliction (v. 7), physical affliction (vv. 8,13), spiritual affliction (vv. 10,22), and relational affliction (vv. 11,13). Every area of his life was affected by his suffering. When he says that his "eyes are worn out" (v. 9), he is saying that his whole body is filled with grief. He feels as if he has been torn apart (Ross, *Psalms 1–41*, 692). In verse 10 he says that his "life is consumed with grief."

These verses, as difficult as they are to read, resonate with anyone who has gone through a season of intense suffering. There are times in all our lives when we feel consumed with grief. And what makes our own grief worse is when others speak against us in our affliction. While David was feeling as if his entire life was filled with grief, he is despised, rejected, forgotten, and talked about by those around him (vv. 11-13). Even though kids say, "Sticks and stones may break my bones, but words will never hurt me," this just simply is not true. The wounds caused by sticks and stones heal much quicker than the wounds caused by words. We are humans, and there is no way we can go through this kind of attack without feeling the effects.

One of the greatest lies of the enemy is that we are alone in our afflictions—that no one understands and no one has ever suffered like we have. If we believe this, instead of dealing honestly with our affliction, we will hide it and be overcome with shame and grief. This is never the way God intended for us to handle affliction. One of the most wonderful things about Psalm 31 is it shows us that instead of passively waiting for our afflictions to end, we must actively battle them. And the greatest weapon we have to fight the effects of affliction is the blessed assurance that is ours in Christ Jesus. Psalm 31 gives us three assurances God has given us to help us in our afflictions.

We Have the Assurance of God's Sufficiency

PSALM 31:1-2,3-5

Three of the most precious words in times of affliction are, "For you are" (v. 3). Our primary weapon to battle the effects of affliction is the confidence we have in who God is. When we don't have the strength to stand, each of us can stop and say, "I can stand, *for you are* my strength, Lord." This is exactly how David does battle. And this is exactly how we might fight. The problem is, we often don't want a God; we want a genie. We just want someone to grant our wishes. But that's not what we really need. What we need most is what only God can give—himself!

Psalm 31:3-4 reminds us that God in himself is sufficient. David already has what he needs most. David longs for a refuge, a rock, and a fortress (vv. 1-2), and then he immediately reminds himself that he already has all those things (vv. 3-4). God does not just *meet* our needs; God *is* what we need. He himself is sufficient. In our suffering we must learn to run to God to get God, not run to God to get something from God. In our suffering we remind ourselves that he is sufficient, and we run into his hands where we know he is enough (v. 5).

We Have the Assurance of God's Loyalty

PSALM 31:7,16,21

Three times in Psalm 31 David reminds himself of the faithful love of God. This is the *chesed* love of God. It is not just love; it is commitment. It is love that is based on God's faithfulness, not ours. There have been some great definitions written to describe the *chesed* love of God, but maybe the clearest is one written for children. Sally Lloyd-Jones defines this love as "a Never Stopping, Never Giving Up, Unbreaking, Always and Forever Love" (*Storybook Bible*, 36).

This kind of love is pictured throughout the Old Testament and clearly articulated in Romans 8. This is a love from which we cannot be separated. Through the sacrifice of Jesus Christ, God has invited us to come into a relationship with him in which he makes an unbreakable covenant with us. And when we come to faith in Christ, we can be assured that there is nothing in heaven or earth that could ever separate us from his love. In times of affliction, we need the assurance of his loyal love.

I like the way this assurance manifests itself in David's life. David, in the midst of his trouble, says, "I trust in the LORD" and "I will rejoice and be glad" (vv. 6-7). In his pain and sorrow, he is deeply assured by God's loyalty, and that confidence changes his response to the situation. In verses 7-8 David says, "You have seen my affliction," "You know the troubles of my soul," "[You] have not handed me over," and "You have set my feet in a spacious place." These four clauses are in the perfect tense in Hebrew, which is generally translated with the past tense in English. They are often referred to as "perfects of confidence" (Ross, *Psalms 1–41*, 692). This means that the psalmist is absolutely convinced that God sees and will deliver him. This confidence flows from God's loyal love.

We Have the Assurance of God's Goodness

PSALM 31:19

One of the most common refrains of the psalms is the declaration of God's goodness. Psalm 23:6 assures us that goodness and mercy will follow us all the days of our lives. Psalm 34:8 encourages us to taste and see that the Lord is good. Psalm 119:68 says that the Lord is good and all he does is good. And here again in Psalm 31:19 the psalmist declares, "How great is your goodness, which you have stored up for those who fear you."

What an amazing thought! God is storing up goodness for us. God is stockpiling goodness in order to pour it out on us. There is an unlimited amount of goodness that God has stored up to pour on us in Jesus. The rest of that verse sounds a bit obscure: "In the presence of everyone you have acted for those who take refuge in you." This means that not only has God stored up good things for us, but he has also demonstrated through past generations, in the sight of everyone, how good he has been (Goldingay, *Psalms 1–41*, 447). In other words, if you ever question God's goodness for the future, just look to his goodness in the past.

One of the best ways we can assure ourselves of God's goodness is by looking back to what has been done for us in Christ Jesus. God has given us the ultimate display of his goodness by sending his Son Jesus Christ to die on our behalf. When we come to faith in him, not only do we receive the assurance of salvation, but we also receive the assurance of eternal goodness. In the midst of our affliction, we must continue to look back to the cross and see his goodness so that we might be assured of his goodness in the future. God has been good, and he will continue to be good to all who are his.

Using Our Assurance as a Weapon

The resounding truth from Psalm 31 is this: God gives us sufficient assurance to fight the effects of our affliction. This assurance was enough for David, and it is enough for us. But that assurance only helps us when we rest on it. We must choose to use that assurance as a weapon against all the effects of our suffering. In the last verse of Psalm 31, David gives us three exhortations, each a call to use this assurance as a weapon.

First, we must be strong. Our afflictions expose our weakness, yet our weakness exposes God's strength. The call to be strong in Psalm 31:24 is the same call to be strong in 2 Corinthians 12:9-10. It is a call to allow the grace of God to give us sufficient strength in our weakness. As David says, God is our *rock* (vv. 2-3). That is just a poetic way to say God is strong and I can find strength in him. Be strong in him.

Second, we must be courageous. The first thing to creep in when we are afflicted is discouragement. We aggressively fight that by walking forward in courageous confidence and assurance in God. We don't stop. We don't despair. We don't just watch as the heaviness descends. We fight. We assure ourselves. We remind ourselves of what is true.

Finally, by implication, we must be patient. The final line of this psalm addresses those "who put [their] hope in the Lord." That means hold on. It means that God is working, he has not forgotten us, and he will manifest himself in his perfect timing. The affliction seems long, but if we are patient, God will show us that the best is yet to come.

Conclusion

Affliction is certain. Not only is it an inevitable reality of living in a broken world, but it is also an unavoidable way in which God molds us and makes us into the image of Jesus. At times, it will almost feel as if it is too much to bear, but when it comes, you have a choice: you can let the heaviness overtake you, or you can fight against it with the blessed assurance of God's sufficiency, loyalty, and goodness. Affliction without assurance always results in despair. But affliction with assurance always leads to hope. In your affliction, trust in the heart of God and assure your heart with his promises. The best is always yet to come.

Reflect and Discuss

1. Think back to a time of deep affliction. How did it affect your whole body? How did you feel in that moment? Were you ever tempted to give up? How did you fight for hope during that time of affliction?
2. Looking back on your affliction, how has God shown himself sufficient? What specific truths helped you during those moments?
3. Out of the three responses in verse 24, which one do you feel you need the most right now? How can you apply that today?

Can I Be Forgiven?

PSALM 32

Main Idea: Sin destroys us and our relationship to God, but godly confession and repentance bring healing and joy.

I. The Cleansing of Sin Is a Blessing (32:1-2).
- A. God will cover our sin (32:1).
- B. God will not count our sin (32:2).

II. The Cover-up of Sin Will Bring Discipline (32:3-4).
- A. Sin brings physical suffering (32:3).
- B. Sin brings spiritual suffering (32:4).

III. The Confession of Sin Brings Forgiveness (32:5).
- A. Acknowledge your sin.
- B. Confess your sin.

IV. The Cure for Sin Is Discovered through Prayer (32:6-7).
- A. You must seek the Lord (32:6).
- B. You will be secure in the Lord (32:7).

V. The Counsel about Sin Is Essential (32:8-9).
- A. Listen to the Lord's instruction (32:8).
- B. Submit to the Lord's direction (32:9).

VI. The Celebration concerning Sin's Forgiveness Rejoices the Heart (32:10-11).
- A. Trust in the Lord (32:10).
- B. Be glad in the Lord (32:11).

It will take you further than you want to go. It will keep you longer than you want to stay. It will cost you more than you want to pay. It will require of you more than you want to give. I am talking about sin, an absent word in our modern culture. To mention it is to draw a snicker if not run the risk of scorn and ridicule. It is not a word we bring up in polite company.

The Bible, however, speaks about sin often. Sin is the major obstacle that separates humans from God. Some form of the word *sin* occurs about six hundred times in the Bible (Blocker, "Sin," 782). A modern question may be, Whatever happened to sin? A biblical question is, What can be done about sin?

Psalm 32 is one of seven penitential psalms (Pss 6; 32; 38; 51; 102; 130; 143) (Ross, *Psalms 1–41*, 705). Grief, repentance, and sorrow over sin characterize the psalm. Yet "it is not a lament over sin [so much as it] is a thanksgiving for the forgiveness of sin" (Belcher, *Messiah*, 100). Psalm 32 is also the first of thirteen psalms to have the title *Maskil*. The meaning is uncertain, though it could have the idea of that which gives wisdom or understanding (Kidner, *Psalms 1–72*, 38).

It is probably correct to interpret this psalm in connection with Psalm 51. Both were written in the context of David's murder of Uriah and his power rape of Bathsheba (see 2 Sam 11–12). Psalm 32 was probably penned after Psalm 51, after a time of intense meditation and reflection. Leupold sees the psalm as "the fulfillment of the vow contained in Ps. 51:13, 'Then will I teach transgressors [your] ways, and sinners shall be converted unto [you]'" (*Exposition*, 269).

The Cleansing of Sin Is a Blessing

PSALM 32:1-2

Like Psalm 1 and the Beatitudes delivered by Jesus in the Sermon on the Mount (Matt 5:3-12), Psalm 32 begins with "blessed" (ESV) or "joyful" (CSB). The first word evokes celebration. David walked through the valley of deep, dark sin. So, how could he write—not once but twice—the word *joyful*?

God Will Cover Our Sin (32:1)

David uses three synonyms for sin and a threefold expression of deliverance from sin in verses 1-2. First, he speaks of forgiveness and sin's covering. "Transgression" (*peshah*) refers to open rebellion and disloyalty, a departure grounded in defiance. It is willful sin. David knew full well what he was doing was wrong (Ross, *Psalms 1–41*, 709).

"Sin" (*chatah*) means to miss the mark. It is an archery term. It is the idea of missing, often with willful intent, the clear and expressed will of God. David says it is a blessed and joyful man "whose transgression is forgiven" (lit. "carried away," "lifted off") and "whose sin is covered." The word "covered" conveys atonement language, affirming God's gracious act of atonement, or reconciliation, whereby the sinner's sin is no longer a basis for God's righteous anger and displeasure (VanGemeren, *Psalms*, 312). In his mercy and by means of our confession (v. 5) and trust (v. 10), God will cover, remove, and forgive our sins.

God Will Not Count Our Sin (32:2)

A third word for sin appears in verse 2. It is the word "iniquity" (*awon*), meaning a crooked or wrong act (VanGemeren, *Psalms*, 312). The Hebrew word carries the idea of "corrupt" or "twisted." It is a joyful person "whom the Lord does not charge with iniquity." Confession with the mouth is crucial to forgiveness, as verse 5 indicates, but so is the integrity of one's heart. In this person's spirit there "is no deceit!" There is nothing dishonest or duplicitous. With an honest and humble heart, this person owns up to all his sin and, in the process, receives the Lord's gracious and full forgiveness.

Steve Lawson points out how difficult it is for fallen humanity to see sin the way God sees sin. He rightly says that we need "straight talk about sin." His list is instructive:

> Man calls it an accident;
> God calls it an abomination.
> Man calls it a blunder;
> God calls it a blasphemy.
> Man called it a chance;
> God calls it a choice.
> Man calls it an error;
> God calls it an enmity.
> Man calls it a fascination;
> God calls it a fatality.
> Man calls it an infirmity;
> God calls it an iniquity.
> Man calls it luxury;
> God calls it leprosy.
> Man calls it a liberty;
> God calls it lawlessness.
> Man calls it a trifle;
> God calls it tragedy.
> Man calls it mistake;
> God calls it madness.
> Man calls it a weakness;
> God calls it willfulness. (*Psalms*, 175)

We need God's grace to see sin as he sees it so that we can confess it and receive grace.

The Cover-up of Sin Will Bring Discipline

PSALM 32:3-4

Sin has a simple, basic spiritual law: confess it and you will be blessed; conceal it and you will be disciplined. In David's life and in ours, the pain and sorrow of sin's cover-up can take several paths of punishment.

Sin Brings Physical Suffering (32:3)

David kept silent concerning his sin with Bathsheba. Not until the prophet Nathan confronted him did he acknowledge his sin (2 Sam 12:7,13). However, it appears that even before that dramatic confrontation David's cover-up ate away at him. He says, "My bones became brittle" (ESV, "wasted away"). His "groaning" was "all the day long." Physically he was drained. Emotionally he was at the end of himself. The word translated "groaning" is used "of a lion roaring" (see Job 4:10; Isa 5:29; Bratcher and Reyburn, *Handbook*, 304). Sin will do a job on you so that you roar like a lion in severe pain and agony. Like a cancer in the soul, sin consumes and destroys.

Sin Brings Spiritual Suffering (32:4)

God is the hound of heaven, the faithful Father who will not let us go. Proverbs 3:12 reminds us, "For the LORD disciplines the one he loves, just as a father disciplines the son in whom he delights." David's pain and anguish are not accidental. They are providential. Further, they are intense and heavy. He tells us they came "day and night." He also says such "was heavy on me," for God's hand was bringing the pressure of discipline. So great and severe was this chastening that David was all but destroyed. He cries out, "My strength was drained as in the summer's heat." Like a weakening body exposed for days to the searing Middle Eastern heat, David was dried up. He was nothing like the blessed person of Psalm 1:3, who is a fruitful tree planted by the rivers of water. Physically drained and emotionally distraught: this is the price paid for covering up sin.

The Confession of Sin Brings Forgiveness

PSALM 32:5

The discipline of God humbles us and should bring us to the point of repentance and confession of sin. This is what we see in verse 5. A great

God provides great forgiveness. It is complete, and it is immediate. Note the two steps involved.

Acknowledge Your Sin

David "acknowledged" (made known) his sin, and he did so to God. *All sin* is against God (Ps 51:4). He no longer attempted to hide, cover up, or conceal his iniquity and corruption. David now saw his sin as God saw it. He called his actions what God called them: sin, iniquity, and transgressions. Do not lie to God about your sin. You cannot fool him. You are only deceiving yourself.

Confess Your Sin

Like the prodigal son of Luke 15, David came to his senses and had a talk with himself. He said, "I will confess my transgressions to the LORD." Note the parallelism:

> *I acknowledged my sin to you*
> *I will confess my transgressions to the LORD*

The result: "You forgave the guilt of my sin." Proverbs 28:13 tells us, "The one who conceals his sins will not prosper, but whoever confesses and renounces them will find mercy." First John 1:9 adds, "If we confess our sins, he is faithful and righteous to forgive us our sins and to cleanse us from all unrighteousness." By our calling sin what God calls it and through the perfect atoning work of his Son, the Lord Jesus, God forgives and covers our sins, imputing them to the spotless and sinless Son of God. David kept silent to hide his sin. Our Savior, the Suffering Servant of the Lord, kept silent and bore our sin (Isa 53:7). Can you be forgiven? Yes, through the Savior sent from heaven, the Lord Jesus Christ.

The Cure for Sin Is Discovered through Prayer

PSALM 32:6-7

Prayer, in its most basic sense, is having a conversation with God. It is talking to him and listening to him. The problem for most of us is not that the Lord is unavailable; the problem is we do not go to him. We do not make ourselves available to spend time with our Lord and Savior. As James, the half-brother of our Lord Jesus, reminds us, "You do not have because you do not ask" (Jas 4:2).

You Must Seek the Lord (32:6)

The ones who are "joyful" (v. 1) are those who confess their sin and find the forgiveness of God. They run to the great forgiver of sin. Part of pursuing God is praying, seeking the Lord when he may be found (Isa 55:6-7). We should not take this privilege for granted.

Those who seek the Lord and draw near to him are promised, "When great floodwaters come, they will not reach [you]." Eugene Peterson, in *The Message*, writes, "When all hell breaks loose and the dam bursts we'll be on high ground, untouched."

You Will Be Secure in the Lord (32:7)

David makes three great declarations about *who* God is and *what* God will do for the faithful who pray immediately to the Lord. First, he will be our "hiding place." Second, he will "protect" (ESV, "preserve") us "from trouble." Third, he will "surround" us "with joyful shouts of deliverance" (ESV, "praise"). Protection, preservation, and praise! Selah! Pause and meditate on that.

The Counsel about Sin is Essential

PSALM 32:8-9

A sudden and dramatic shift occurs in verse 8. God now speaks directly to David. The emphasis is on the instruction, counsel, and understanding of the Lord. John Piper says,

> What good would it be if he [God] guarded us from destruction but did not tell us which way to go? Protection with direction, care with counsel, that is the happy condition of the person who prays to God and receives forgiveness for his sins. ("Go to God in Prayer")

Listen to the Lord's Instruction (32:8)

God promises three things in verse 8. He will "instruct," "teach" (ESV), and counsel you. He will do so "in the way you should go" (ESV). He also says, "With my eye on you, I will give counsel." The idea is that God will counsel and instruct us with a watchful eye on us. His omniscient eye never misses a thing. This is an awesome promise to comfort us, especially when "the great floodwaters" come (v. 6). Perfect wisdom comes by listening to this one who instructs us. Spurgeon says, "Practical teaching is the very best of instruction, and they are thrice happy who, although they . . . are ignorant of Aristotle, and the ethic of the schools, have nevertheless learned to follow the Lamb" (*Treasury*, 84).

Submit to the Lord's Direction (32:9)

Verse 9 introduces us to a portion of God's animal farm. It highlights two beasts for our edification: the horse and the mule. The text draws attention to their lack of understanding and stubborn disposition. What is God's point?

Don't be stubborn like a horse or mule. Be submissive to God's will. Don't be resistant. Be receptive to God's Word. Don't force God to "bit and bridle" you. He will if you force his hand. It is better to follow him gladly and willingly than stubbornly and forcibly. David acted like a mule, and God put the bit of suffering and the bridle of discipline in his life. He will do the same for you and me if necessary.

The Celebration concerning Sin's Forgiveness Rejoices the Heart

PSALM 32:10-11

Full and total forgiveness is a sweet experience and a precious gift. It is an occasion for joyful celebration. David knows well what he has received and what he did not deserve. With a heart overflowing in gratitude, he closes the psalm by contrasting the life of the wicked and the life of the righteous. He utters a final charge to all who have been bathed in the mercy and goodness of God and his forgiveness.

Trust in the Lord (32:10)

"Many pains" and sorrows are the life and destiny of "the wicked." Now, but especially at the judgment, no joy or happiness will exist for them. In stark contrast, "the one who trusts in the LORD will have faithful love surrounding him." "Faithful love" is a translation of the Hebrew word *chesed*, which describes the unfailing covenant love and loyalty the Lord showers on his children. Such a God can be trusted. As he promises, his eye is continually watching over you.

Be Glad in the Lord (32:11)

Three commands of praise conclude Psalm 32: "Be glad," "rejoice," and "shout for joy." Who can respond with such praise, worship, and adoration? It is the "righteous ones" and "upright in heart." It is those who now have a right standing before God and a heart turned toward the Lord. The godly who are mindful of all the benefits (forgiveness, protection, guidance) of the Lord will rejoice! These benefits are not indiscriminate gifts. They are given only to the "righteous," who are "upright in heart," descriptions that parallel the blessing in verse 2 on those "in whose spirit is no deceit."

Conclusion

The psalms point to Jesus, and Jesus could have prayed them all. But how does one who is sinless pray a psalm of confession and brokenness over sin he does not have? I think Richard Belcher Jr. provides wonderful theological and Christological insight into the answer:

> Jesus can affirm the blessedness of forgiveness because he knows that it is his work on the cross as our priest that is the basis of the forgiveness of sin. The burden of sin can be lifted off the sinner . . . because Jesus himself bore the weight of sin. Sin is covered because of his shed blood. Sin is not charged against a person because Jesus has paid the penalty for that sin (vv. 1-2). Jesus, as our sin bearer, felt the full impact of the negative consequences of sin on the cross, including all the emotional, spiritual, and physical ramifications of what suffering on the cross and bearing the judgment of God for our sin entailed. The psalmist tried to avoid sin by keeping silent about it and suffered consequences in his life until he came to confess his transgressions to the Lord (vv. 3-5). Jesus' silence does not relate to covering up his own sin, because he was sinless, but relates to his willingness to endure the punishment for the sins of others. . . . As our representative he confesses our sins so we can receive forgiveness.
>
> The turning point in verse 6 exhorts others to pray to God to be delivered. Jesus himself experienced the power of God's deliverance when he was raised from the dead on

> the third day. He experienced deliverance from the rush of great waters, the preservation from trouble, and the shouts of deliverance that come from the mighty power of God (vv. 6-7). Although there is some debate concerning who is speaking in verses 8-9, these verses make sense as the instruction of Jesus to his people because he is in a unique position to exhort us to submit ourselves to God's way. He is our faithful high priest who is able to sympathize with our weaknesses (Heb. 4:15). The one who trusted in God and was delivered now exhorts God's people to be glad and rejoice. He was able to see beyond the suffering of the cross to the joy that lay beyond ("who for the joy set before him endured the cross," Heb. 12:2), for he knew that the day of the forgiveness of sin lay on the other side of his work on the cross. He rejoices in his finished work that brings the forgiveness of our sin, and we who have experienced the relief of the forgiveness of sin should also rejoice in what he has done for us. (*Messiah,* 102–3)

Reflect and Discuss

1. In what ways will sin take you further than you want to go or cost you more than you want to pay?
2. Should people be concerned about their spiritual status if they are not affected by their sin in the way verses 3-4 describe? Why or why not?
3. Why is it difficult for us to see sin the way God sees it? How can we view sin correctly?
4. In what ways could you lie to God about your sin? Why do we lie about our sin or try to hide it?
5. What are the necessary parts of true confession? Should confession take place in both a vertical direction (you to God) and horizontal direction (you to others)?
6. This section teaches, "The problem for most of us is not that the Lord is unavailable; the problem is we do not go to him." In what ways do you refuse to go to the Lord to be healed from your sin?
7. Why do we need God's instruction (v. 8)? What does he instruct us to do?

8. How do we fight sin? What are proper and improper ways to fight sin? What is the church's role in helping believers fight sin?
9. How does sin affect our relationships with God, other people, and ourselves?
10. What must you believe in order to avoid sin? In what ways is sin a result of false beliefs?

The Joy of Trusting God

PSALM 33

Main Idea: Those who trust the Lord completely rejoice in the Lord fully.

I. Celebrate a Trustworthy God (33:1-5).
II. Trust Him because His Words Are Sure (33:6-9).
III. Trust Him because His Ways Are Perfect (33:10-12).
IV. Trust Him because His Love Is Unfailing (33:13-19).

In Proverbs 13:12 the wise man declares, "Hope delayed makes the heart sick, but desire fulfilled is a tree of life." Almost all of us can tell a story that exemplifies the truth of that verse. Hopes delayed (or deferred) make our hearts sick. There is almost no heart sickness like the sickness of a hope that is left unfulfilled. This is the reason so many people become cynical. I once had a church member tell me that he didn't like to let himself get happy about many things because he knows he will just be disappointed. What a sad way to live! But it's the way people live when their hopes have not been met.

The point of Proverbs 13:12 is not, "Don't get your hopes up or you will surely be disappointed." The goal of the verse is not to keep us from hoping. The goal of that verse is to get us to put our hopes in the right things. We must put our hopes in something that will not disappoint us. If you put your hopes in something that will never let you down, then your hopes will never be disappointed. That is really the point of Psalm 33.

Psalm 33 is a psalm of gladness. It begins with an outburst of praise. The reason for the joy is best summarized in verse 21: "For our hearts rejoice in [God] because we trust in his holy name." David rejoices because he has discovered that the Lord is trustworthy. In other words, David is rejoicing because the Lord never disappoints. When we place all our hopes in someone who never disappoints, our hearts will be glad. This deeply joyful psalm reminds us that those who trust the Lord completely will rejoice in the Lord fully. The more we trust the Lord, the more we will experience his joy.

Celebrate a Trustworthy God

PSALM 33:1-5

As we read Scripture, we must find not only the message of the text but also the tone of the text. The first three verses of Psalm 33 set the tone for the entire psalm. It is a psalm of gladness. In this call to worship, the worship leader invites all "you righteous ones" to join in celebration of the Lord. In many ways Psalm 33 is a response to Psalm 32. Psalm 33 does not even have a heading, and it is joined together with Psalm 32 as one psalm in ten Hebrew manuscripts (Craigie and Tate, *Psalms 1–50*, 272). Psalm 32 tells us to rejoice—Psalm 33 rejoices. It is almost as if Psalm 33 listened to Psalm 32 and responds by picking up the instruments and calling the people to sing. Psalm 33 is a call to worship for every person who trusts and follows Jesus.

Seven Hebrew words describe the kind of worship expected: *rejoice* (ESV, "shout for joy"), *praise*, *give thanks* (ESV), *make music*, *sing*, *play skillfully*, and *shout* (vv. 1-3). They call for outward, celebratory expressions of worship. They are also most likely exhortations to give this kind of praise in public, not just in private (Ross, *Psalms 1–41*, 728). Why is this kind of worship called for? Because "praise from the upright is beautiful" (v. 1). It is fitting for believers to praise the Lord this way. The Lord deserves this kind of genuine exultation.

The reason for this praise is the trustworthiness of the Lord (v. 21). When you know and experience what it is like to truly trust in the Lord, you will know what it is like to truly exult (or rejoice) in the Lord. Verses 4-5 summarize the rest of the psalm. These verses show us three reasons to trust the Lord: his "word," his "work," and his "unfailing love." The rest of the psalm focuses on those three themes and calls us to trust the Lord's word, work, and love and, as a result, come to know the Lord's joy.

Trust Him because His Words Are Sure

PSALM 33:6-9

Verses 6-9 celebrate that God's word is sure. His word is certain, settled, always right, and never in doubt. His word is always the final word. When he speaks, it happens. The evidence of this is found in the fact that the "heavens were made by the word of the LORD, and all the stars, by the breath of his mouth." His word is so strong that all the stars in the heavens came into existence simply by his breath (v. 6). There may be no element more powerful than water. Water can destroy a home or an entire city in a matter of moments. Yet all the waters of the sea are gathered into a heap by his words. He puts the depths of the water into his own storehouses (v. 7). Think about the times throughout the Bible in which God has used water for his purposes, calling it to stop flowing, start moving, or to come from a rock—all of this by the power of his word.

When you see God at work by the power of his word, you feel both fear and awe. All people should fear him and stand in awe of the power of his word (v. 8). There is nothing God is unable to accomplish with just a word. When he speaks, things happen (v. 9). You might have heard the old phrase, "God said it. I believe it. That settles it." But the reality is, if God said it, that settles it, whether you believe it or not. Everything God says is settled the moment he says it. The point of verses 6-9 is that God's word is powerful, effective, perfect, and sure (Ps 119).

In a time in which we are bombarded with constant news, it is often hard to know whom to believe. During the COVID-19 global pandemic, one of the most challenging things was knowing whom to believe. It was exhausting. In moments like these, we need our hearts settled on the sure foundation of the words of God. When we settle our own conviction that God's word is perfect and certain, we will find the heaviness of all the other voices lift and the joy of trust in God's word begin to settle. We can trust the Lord because his word is sure.

Trust Him because His Ways Are Perfect

PSALM 33:10-12

The words and works of God always go together. As James Boice said,

> How different it is with us. We say one thing and do another, so that we are inconsistent at best and hypocritical or blatantly dishonest at worst. God is utterly consistent, always upright, and consistently good. Thus, he is always to be praised for everything he says and for everything he does. (*Psalms 1–41*, 287)

It makes sense, then, that a celebration of God's word would lead to a celebration of God's works.

Verses 10-12 talk about the counsel and plans of the Lord and of those who oppose him. "The LORD frustrates the counsel of the nations;

he thwarts the plans of the peoples" (v. 10). All over the world, right now, powerful people are making important decisions. Many of those decisions will affect us or our loved ones. Yet all these decision makers are ultimately pawns in the hands of God (think about Pharaoh). There is a God in heaven whose counsel stands forever, and his plans are established through all generations (v. 11). This is God's world, and we just live in it. He runs it, he rules over it, and nothing frustrates his plans (Eph 1:11; Heb 6:7).

This confidence in God's sovereign control over all things is what makes verse 12 so special. This is not a verse about America, but it is an important kingdom principle. Simply stated, God blesses those who trust in him. Those who are on his side receive his blessing. Those who align themselves with God's purposes will experience God's best. God works for those who trust him (Rom 8:28). For us as Christians—his people, his kingdom—it is a call to be assured that the God who controls all things is looking out for us! It is a call to rejoice because the sovereign God of the universe is our God.

Trust Him because His Love Is Unfailing

PSALM 33:13-19

So far in Psalm 33 we have been given a picture of a magnificent God. His word and his works are powerful beyond measure. Nothing and no one can compare. Then, in verses 13-15 we are told that the one who created the world with the power of his word and who rules the world with his sovereign hand has his eye on us. The one who sits in heaven "looks down," "gazes" at, and "considers" all the works of people. In other words, God is not a passive onlooker; God is an active observer. And he is not just vaguely looking down at people; he is looking at you. Psalm 32:8 is simply amazing. God says, "With my eye on you, I will give counsel." As Psalm 33:18 says, "But look, the LORD keeps his eye on those who fear him." What an amazing thought!

Psalm 33:13-19 emphasizes that God is looking at us because he loves us (v. 18). His observing eye reflects his loving heart. He has committed his love to his people and has promised to love them perfectly and eternally. He is not distant; he is personal. He watches us out of a loving heart to ensure we are kept alive and cared for (v. 18). No king, no president, no nation can ensure our safety (v. 16). No amount of money we have saved and no amount of insurance we have purchased can ultimately save us. If we put our hopes in those things, it is impossible for us to rejoice because none of them are certain. But God has promised his unfailing love toward us, and for that reason our hearts can rejoice.

One of the reasons believers have such a hard time responding with joyful songs and shouts of praise as in verses 1-3 is because they have never stopped to ponder the power of God's word, God's works, and God's love. When we come to realize just how much God loves us and just how much he is working on our behalf, the burdens of our hearts will be lifted and his joy will permeate our lives. We do this by focusing on the gospel. The power of God's word, work, and love are all seen most clearly in what God has done for us in Christ Jesus (Rom 8). When we trust in Christ alone as the payment for our sins and we are brought into the family of God, God treats us like sons and daughters. And since we are his children, God commits himself to us and ensures that we will always be under his loving care. As we think more clearly about Christ, we will come to know more of his joy.

Conclusion

PSALM 33:20-22

How do we respond to the reality that God's word is sure, his works are perfect, and his love is unfailing? The answer is in the final three verses. First, we must stop worrying and start waiting. Anxiety and joy cannot coexist. Anxiety is the enemy of joy. Joy flows from faith, while anxiety flows from disbelief. The two cannot dwell in the same heart at the same time. Anxiety robs us of our joy. So we must fight our worries by reminding ourselves of the realities that are ours in Christ Jesus. As verse 20 says, "We wait for the LORD; he is our help and shield." God works for those who wait for him (Isa 64:4). As we look to Jesus, trust in him, and rest in his love, we will find that God's rest will lead us to a heart that rejoices in God.

Second, we must stop despairing and start rejoicing. Verse 21 says, "For our hearts rejoice in him because we trust in his holy name." Trust and gladness go together. The more we trust, the more our hearts rejoice. But faithlessness always leads to despair. We should memorize Psalm 33:21 and keep it close to our hearts. We need to be reminded that our lack of rejoicing is often rooted in a lack of faith.

One of the questions that is often asked from a passage like Psalm 33 is, "What do I do when I don't feel like rejoicing?" A word from Eugene Peterson might be helpful here:

> We are invited to bless the Lord; we are commanded to bless the Lord. And then someone says, "But I don't feel like it. And I won't be a hypocrite. I can't bless God if I don't feel like blessing God. It wouldn't be honest."
>
> The Biblical response to that is, "Lift up your praising hands to the holy place and bless God!" You can lift up your hands regardless of how you feel; it is simple motor movement. You may not be able to command your heart, but you can command your arms. Lift your arms in blessing; just maybe your heart will get the message and be lifted up also in praise. We are psychosomatic beings; body and spirit are intricately interrelated. Go through the motions of blessing God and your spirit will pick up the cue and follow along. (*Long Obedience* 2000, 54)

There are times when our mouths begin to rejoice because there is so much faith in our hearts. There are other times when we start rejoicing as an act of faith in hopes that our hearts will follow. Either way, those who trust the Lord completely can rejoice in the Lord fully. So let us fix our minds and hearts on Christ, put our faith firmly on him, and let our hearts rejoice.

Reflect and Discuss

1. What makes you hesitant to respond to God the way the psalmist did in verses 1-3? Have you had moments when you felt like responding that way? If so, what brought about those moments?
2. The psalmist says to sing a new song to God. New songs are written out of new moments—moments in which God has done something great for you. What are some of those new moments you have experienced recently that are causes for rejoicing?
3. What specific things weigh down your heart and keep you from trusting the Lord? In what areas of your life do you find it most difficult to trust him? Take the truths of Psalm 33 and remind yourself of why you should fully trust the Lord with every area of your life.

Taste and See

PSALM 34

Main Idea: God will fully satisfy those who trust him to satisfy the longings of their hearts.

I. We Are Invited to Personally Experience Him.
II. We Are Invited to Actively Pursue Him.
III. We Are Invited to Be Fully Satisfied in Him.

The gospel is not just a message; it's an invitation. The gospel, when fully presented, includes an invitation to come to Jesus by faith so that your sins may be forgiven. Jesus spent his life inviting people to himself. Jesus invited people to follow him, come to him, take up their cross, and drink from him. Even today, Jesus is inviting people to himself as his church preaches the gospel. From beginning to end, the Bible is an invitation. All those invitations flow from the heart of God who loves people and longs for them to know him. God is inviting people to himself.

Psalm 34 is a psalm of joy. It is about the joy of experiencing the goodness of God. But if Psalm 34 is anything, it is an invitation. David begins by inviting us to proclaim the goodness of the Lord with him. He invites us to exalt God's name together. Even more than that, David is inviting us to experience what he himself has experienced—namely, the goodness of God. This invitation can be summarized in the most familiar verse of Psalm 34. Verse 8 says, "Taste and see that the LORD is good. How happy is the person who takes refuge in him!" This is an invitation to see for ourselves what David has seen for himself. It is an invitation to experience the goodness of God. David pleads with us to accept this invitation because he knows that those who trust God to satisfy the longing of their hearts will be fully satisfied with God. That is the point of Psalm 34.

Psalm 34 is one of only fourteen psalms that give us the historical setting in which they were written (Johnston, *Psalms*, 347). The superscription says, "Concerning David, when he pretended to be insane in the presence of Abimelech, who drove him out, and he departed."

The specifics of this story are recorded in 1 Samuel 21, and it is one of the most interesting moments in David's life. While Saul was still king, David was rising in prominence. When David was seen, people would chant, "Saul has killed his thousands, but David his tens of thousands" (1 Sam 18:7). As a result, Saul became jealous and angry, and he was consumed with trying to kill David. As David was running for his life, he fled to Gath. This was an interesting place for David to hide because it was the hometown of Goliath, whom he had killed a few years prior. Everyone in Gath knew who David was.

David was recognized, and news got to the king that he was there. David, while trying to save his life, ran into a town filled with people who wanted to end his life. He was trapped, but he had an idea. He decided to act like he had lost his mind. He let his saliva run down his beard and he began to scratch at a doorpost. When the king saw him, he said, "Look! You can see the man is crazy!" And David left Gath unharmed. From that situation David wrote Psalm 34.

As you read this psalm with this situation in mind, you sense how overwhelmed David was by the goodness of God in sparing his life. Much of Psalm 34 is personal testimony (vv. 1-7,15-22). David sought the Lord, and God heard him and delivered him from all his fears (v. 4). When David looked to the Lord, his face was radiant, and he was not put to shame (v. 5). He cried to the Lord, and the Lord heard him and saved him from all his troubles (v. 6). In a moment in which his life was in danger, the angel of the Lord protected him and rescued him (v. 7). As David walks out of Gath alive, he cannot help but be overwhelmed by God's goodness. You feel his utter joy in the first two verses as he exclaims, "I will bless the Lord at all times; his praise will always be on my lips. I will boast in the Lord; the humble will hear and be glad." In other words, you could not stop him from praising the Lord if you tried.

Verse 3 shows us that Psalm 34 is more than just a testimony; it is an invitation. David says, "Proclaim the Lord's greatness with me; let us exalt his name together." He does not want to praise the Lord alone. He calls on all those who hear him to join in his praise of God's goodness. Verses 8-22 serve as a continual call to worship, and the theme is clearly God's goodness (vv. 8,10,12,14). This idea of goodness is important. Everyone longs for goodness. We all want good things in our lives. David wants us to know that our desire for goodness comes from God. God is good, and our craving for goodness can only be filled in him. David has experienced that. He has seen the goodness of God and seen that God is satisfying. Now David invites us to experience the same thing. That invitation is summarized in eight words: "Taste and see that the LORD is good." These words show us what it really means for us to come to know for ourselves just how good God is.

We Are Invited to Personally Experience Him

Psalm 34 does not invite us to know the Lord or to study the Lord or to see the Lord but to *taste* the Lord. Jesus used words like this all the time. Jesus invited people to eat his flesh and drink his blood. He invited people to come to him and drink. He invited people to feast on him. These words remind us that God is calling us to go beyond personal knowledge to personal experience. Taste is not easily described. Taste needs to be experienced.

Coffee companies are notorious for trying to describe their coffees with words like subtle, sweet, bold, rich, strong, nutty, and robust. But none of those descriptors can take the place of tasting. There is even a difference in reading the ingredients and tasting the product. Hearing the words *skim milk, milk fat, palm oil, lactose, egg whites, soy lecithin,* and *artificial flavors* is not nearly as great as tasting a Snickers bar. Certain things need to be tasted. They need to be personally experienced. God is one of them.

Every week when a pastor gets up to preach, he is essentially listing ingredients. Hopefully he does it so well that those who hear him long to taste for themselves. But the truth is, hearing the ingredients every week can never take the place of personally tasting. A person must taste for themselves and see that the Lord is good. Jesus is meaningless to so many churchgoers because they have never personally experienced him. To many Jesus is distant and impersonal. They know about God, but they don't know God. They have heard about him but never experienced him. But in Psalm 34 David is speaking from his own experience and pleading with us to have our own experiences.

David motivates us to experience God by affirming all the benefits. If you desire life and want to enjoy what is good, taste of the Lord (v. 12). If you want to have the listening ear of the Lord, taste of the Lord (v. 17). If you want to know the saving power of the Lord, taste of him (v. 19). If you want to have a refuge in times of trouble, taste of the

Lord (v. 22). An endless amount of blessings is reserved for those who will taste and see. God is inviting us to do just that.

We Are Invited to Actively Pursue Him

We are not only invited to personally experience God, but we are also invited to actively pursue him. "Taste" is a command that demands action. It is not something that happens passively or by accident. Those who really taste and see are those who have chosen to actively pursue the Lord. If you have ever tried to get a stubborn child to taste something he doesn't want to taste, then you know that forcing someone to taste just doesn't accomplish much. Every person must choose to taste. Each must choose to pursue the Lord. This is what David did. He walked with the Lord, he trusted the Lord, he pursued the Lord, and as a result, he experienced the Lord's goodness.

In Matthew 7:7 Jesus says, "Ask, and it will be given to you. Seek, and you will find. Knock, and the door will be opened to you." Jesus obviously longs for us to experience him. He is offering us himself. But he also makes clear that those who would experience him must first pursue him. There are those who will never experience specific answers to prayer because they have not prayed (Ross, *Psalms 1–41*, 752).

Verses 9-16 of this psalm give us many practical means by which we pursue the Lord. The call to "fear the LORD" is really a call to live in obedient devotion to him (v. 9). Verse 10 calls us to "seek the LORD" and assures us that those who do will in fact experience him. David calls us to keep our tongues from evil (v. 13), "turn away from evil" (v. 14), seek and pursue peace (v. 14), and walk in holiness before the Lord (vv. 15-16). God makes himself known to those who seek him and walk with him. There is unquestionably a connection between the level of someone's pursuit and the level of his or her experience. Those who fight sin and pursue holiness experience God.

One of the most discouraging things about the American church is how many people attend church each Sunday for their weekly dose of Jesus. To think about it in terms of "tasting," these people eat junk food all week and expect that Sunday salad to make them healthy. It doesn't work that way. One healthy meal does not negate twenty unhealthy meals. In order for people to truly experience all that God has to offer and to know his goodness, they must choose to satisfy the cravings of their hearts with God, not junk. Those who do will be rewarded.

We Are Invited to Be Fully Satisfied in Him

David invites us to personally experience the Lord, to actively pursue the Lord, and finally, to be fully satisfied in the Lord. David makes a guarantee. It is a guarantee he feels confident in making not only because of his own personal experience but also because of God's consistent promises. David guarantees that if you will taste, you will in fact see that the Lord is good. If a person will stop feasting on junk and instead feast on the Lord, he will certainly discover that there is nothing more satisfying than Jesus. The truth is, those who trust God to satisfy the longing of their hearts will be fully satisfied with God.

The reason we know the Lord will satisfy us if we seek him is because we were created to be satisfied only with him. God created us to experience life at its fullest only when we are walking in step with him. As we receive his invitation to trust and follow him and choose by faith to trust Christ alone as the payment for our sins, he brings us back into a right relationship with him that makes it possible for us to seek him better and know him. The moment we give our lives to Christ is the beginning of a new life in which we daily seek him because we know that he alone can satisfy.

The battle of life for every believer is that of believing every day that nothing will satisfy us like Jesus. This is a truth that we must believe. We must know for sure that everything else in life will leave us hungry, but Jesus will satisfy us fully. Then by faith we must seek to daily taste of him. To have the longings of our souls met in him, we must seek to experience him and pursue him in hope.

The Lord paints an amazing picture for us through the prophet Jeremiah. The Lord says,

> *For my people have committed a double evil: They have abandoned me, the fountain of living water, and dug cisterns for themselves—cracked cisterns that cannot hold water.* (Jer 2:13)

This is exactly what we are tempted to do every day. We are constantly tempted to leave the only one who can truly satisfy our souls for something that cannot satisfy us at all. Therefore, we must keep going back to Jesus, believing that he alone can satisfy the longings of our souls. And we must keep reminding ourselves of the truth of Psalm 34: God will fully satisfy those who trust him to satisfy the longings of their hearts.

Reflect and Discuss

1. Think about the invitations of Jesus. List as many as you can. What do those invitations tell you about Jesus? What do they tell you about people?
2. Discuss with someone a time when you, like David, really saw God work in your life. Discuss a time when you experienced the goodness of God. What did you learn about God from that moment?
3. Are you pursuing the Lord right now as if he is the only one who can truly satisfy you? If not, are there other things you are going to for satisfaction other than God? Why is it that only God can truly satisfy you?

A Longing for Justice

PSALM 35

Main Idea: We long for God's justice because we love God's glory.

I. The Persecution of God's People
II. The Prayer for God's Action
III. The Passion for God's Glory

David, the anointed king of Israel, is enduring life-threatening, unjust attacks and persecution. His enemies are hateful, angry, aggressive, and violent. They are doing all they can to destroy him. In the midst of it all, David feels as if God has forgotten him. He feels alone in his suffering.

If you have ever been falsely accused, bullied, or faced persecution while it seemed as if God had forgotten you, you may understand exactly what David is feeling. Although this psalm certainly speaks to those who have experienced those moments, this psalm goes well beyond that. The persecution David faces is not just about him. He is the anointed king who represents the Lord and has been given responsibility for God's people. This is about the people of God and the glory of God. So, feeling the weight of unjust persecution, David cries out to the Lord for justice in Psalm 35.

Most people have trouble with psalms like this. It is not only an individual lament (Ross, *Psalms 1–41*, 763), but it is also an imprecatory psalm. An imprecatory psalm is one in which the author curses his enemies (Johnston, *Psalms*, 357). It is a call for God to bring down his righteous judgment against those who have come against him. The fact that many believers have problems with psalms like these is understandable. These psalms seem to contradict the teaching of Jesus to bless those who curse us (Luke 6:28). They seem contrary to the goodness and kindness of God just spoken of in the previous psalm. But the primary reason people have problems with these psalms is because so many have never been in a situation like David's.

Imagine you are in North Korea and your neighbor finds out you are a Christian. He then tells another neighbor, who tells another neighbor, until finally the police are alerted. You hear a knock on your door, and police are standing there asking if the rumor is true. Upon confessing your belief in Jesus, you and your spouse are taken to a labor camp while your children are taken and sold as slaves.

Imagine you are a believer in Somalia where the violent Islamic group al-Shabab is trying to eradicate Christianity from the entire nation. You have watched as friends and family members have been executed on the spot for professing Christ. You have watched as radical Muslims have systematically destroyed churches, homes, and hospitals, all to remove any hint of Christianity.

Imagine being a believer in Nigeria where groups like Boko Haram are violently threatening Christians. One morning, you send your young daughter to her Christian school and find out that afternoon that she and more than three hundred of her female friends have been captured. Imagine knowing that most of them are being physically, spiritually, and sexually abused at the hands of Muslim men. Many of them are being sold as brides and sent away to Muslim villages.

All of these represent real-life scenarios, and one out of every nine Christians in the world is facing this kind of persecution (opendoorusa.com). If you watched a loved one executed, saw a family displaced and possessions burned, or had a nine-year-old daughter captured and sold into slavery, you would understand what David was feeling in Psalm 35. Every verse of this psalm would be the cry of your heart. This psalm not only brings much-needed perspective to American Christians, but it also gives a voice to our brothers and sisters around the world who are facing this kind of persecution. Psalm 35 is a cry for justice.

This psalm can be broken up into three sections. Section one is verses 1-10. Section two is verses 11-18. And section three is verses 19-28 (Futato, "Book of Psalms," 136). Each of these sections contains the same three elements: persecution, prayer, and passion. Each of these elements leads us to the wonderful truth of Psalm 35: we long for the justice of God because we love the glory of God.

The Persecution of God's People

Every section of Psalm 35 paints a picture of unrelenting attacks. In verse 1 David speaks of his "opponents." This is a legal term, painting the picture of a courtroom in which many false witnesses have risen against him (Johnston, *Psalms*, 262). His enemies are also fighting against him.

This points to the physical persecution and those who are coming after him to kill him. In verses 4-8 David says they "intend to take my life," "plan to harm me," "hid their net for me without cause," and "dug a pit for me without cause."

You see this same picture of suffering in the second section of the psalm (vv. 11-18). "Malicious witnesses" are bringing personal attacks and accusations. There are those who "gnash their teeth," revealing the depth of their anger and hatred. They come at him with "ravages" and like "young lions." The persecution is physical, emotional, and psychological.

In the third section of the psalm (vv. 19-28), the persecution is seen in even more intensity. Not only is David surrounded by those who rejoice at his misfortune (v. 26), but also their hatred and accusations are all unjust. Those who are coming after him hate him without cause (v. 19) and "contrive fraudulent schemes" against him and his people. He is not the only one suffering. They are clearly coming after him and those he is called to protect (vv. 10,20). They are taking advantage of those who cannot defend themselves. This is not just personal for David; this is also about those he has been charged to protect.

The Prayer for God's Action

Every verse of Psalm 35 is a prayer. Verse 1 makes clear that David is crying out to the "Lord." He is asking the Lord to "oppose" those who oppose him. He feels like a defendant in the courtroom without a defense attorney. The prosecution has carefully crafted their story and rehearsed their false narratives with their hundreds of witnesses, and on the other side of the courtroom David stands alone. He begs God to defend him. He also begs God to fight against those who fight against him (v. 1). He begs God to "come to [his] aid."

As you read the psalm, you will notice the constant repetition of the word "let." Every time that word is used, it is David begging God to come to his aid. "Let those who intend to take my life be disgraced and humiliated; let those who plan to harm me be turned back and ashamed" (v. 4); "Let them be like chaff in the wind" (v. 5); "Let their way be dark and slippery" (v. 6); and "Let ruin come on [them] unexpectedly" (v. 8).

The ultimate cry of his heart in Psalm 35 is in verses 22-26. He does not want the Lord to remain silent or be distant. He needs the Lord to be vocal and near. He begs the Lord to "wake up" and rise to his defense (v. 23). Ultimately, David longs for the Lord to "vindicate" him. He wants the Lord to defend him and make his righteousness known. He simply wants the Lord to do something!

David knows God. He knows God deeply and intimately. There may be no single figure in the Old Testament who knows God more intimately than David does. He knows the love, kindness, grace, and goodness of the Lord. David also knows that God is a just warrior, a deliverer, and a vindicator. David does not have a wrong view of God; he has a wholistic and accurate view of God, and he is asking God to bring his righteous justice.

But David is not just praying for God's swift justice. While David is being falsely accused and physically attacked, he is still concerned about their healing (vv. 11-14). Before we judge David for his desire to see the justice of God poured out on his enemies, note that he also prayed for them and mourned over them "like one mourning for a mother." When you think of the depth of their hatred, unjust accusations, and continual physical persecution, it is astonishing that David would fast, pray, and mourn over them to seek their good at all.

The Passion for God's Glory

One of the reasons we know Psalm 35 can be divided into three distinct sections is because each ends the same way—with a passion for God's glory. In verses 9-10 David declares, "I will rejoice in the LORD; I will delight in his deliverance." That word "delight" means to exult and be glad. David is not simply praising the Lord; he is declaring his passion for the glory of the Lord. He wants to declare the works and wonders of God.

In verse 10 David uses an important phrase as he begins to praise: "Who is like you?" That is a phrase taken from Exodus 15, right after God delivers his people from the Egyptians. You remember the situation. They had been enslaved and oppressed for 430 years. As the people finally fled Egypt and headed toward the promised land, they found themselves in a bind. They had the Red Sea in front of them and the Egyptian army behind them. When they called out to the Lord, the sea parted, the people crossed, and the entire Egyptian army was drowned when the sea closed. On the other side of the sea, the people declared, "LORD, who is like you among the gods? Who is like you, glorious in holiness, revered with praises, performing wonders?" (Exod 15:11). The people watched as God saved them and destroyed their enemies, and they rejoiced in both God's salvation and his judgment. This is what David is pointing us to here. David longs for God to manifest himself in his current situation in a way that God receives all the glory.

He continues his passion for God's glory as he praises and exalts the Lord among God's people (vv. 17-18). He longs for the people to see God move and then to see them shout for joy and be glad (v. 27). He wants the people to see the Lord exalted and his people saved (v. 27). He wants to proclaim the Lord's righteousness all day long (v. 28). David longs for God's glory.

The way David ends each section of this psalm helps us see the point of the whole psalm. His desire to praise the Lord shows us that David was more concerned with God's name than his own. He watched as God's king was threatened, God's people were oppressed, and God's name mocked, and David longed for God to act for the sake of his name. David longed for God's justice because he loved God's glory.

Conclusion

Anytime we read a psalm about the king, it points us beyond David to the ultimate anointed King, Jesus Christ. This is undoubtedly true about Psalm 35 because Jesus specifically tells us this psalm refers to him. In John 15:18-25 Jesus quotes this psalm and says that it is speaking of him. If you go back and read Psalm 35 with this in mind, it makes perfect sense. Jesus was the one who was ultimately hated without cause, falsely accused, mocked, and ridiculed.

When we see Jesus in Psalm 35, however, we must see him both in his first coming and in his second coming. Jesus is the Suffering Servant of Psalm 35. Jesus is also the just warrior David longed to see in Psalm 35. He will one day respond to the prayers of his persecuted people and, like a mighty warrior, come to make all things right. The only reason he is waiting is his desire to see all his enemies saved (2 Pet 3:9). But one day his patience will run out, and he will return as the just warrior to manifest the glory of his name.

When we see Jesus in Psalm 35, there are three necessary responses. First, we must submit to King Jesus. We must see Jesus in his gracious salvation and his just wrath. Psalm 34:8 is true—the Lord is good; blessed are those who take refuge in him. Psalm 35 is also true—God will manifest his righteous judgment toward those who rebel against him instead of taking refuge in him. We must accept the invitation of Jesus to trust and follow him now. As we do, we will taste and see that he is good.

Second, we must seek the good of our enemies. Psalm 35 does not conflict with Jesus's command to love our enemies. We know this because David loved his enemies in Psalm 35. He blessed them, fasted for them, and prayed for them. Even in the greatest moments of injustice, we must bless those who persecute us. The way we do that is to trust that the Lord will bring his righteous judgment in his time and in the perfect way (Rom 12:19). God will make all things right.

Finally, we must pray for God's kingdom to come. When we do, we are praying for both his reign in the hearts of all people now and his return to reign on earth. Praying for God's kingdom is praying Psalm 35. It is praying that people might be saved *and* that God might destroy his enemies and execute justice. We long for God's justice because we love God's glory.

Reflect and Discuss

1. How do the truths from Psalm 35 and the reality of persecution around the world help put your own life and struggles into perspective?
2. When you think about the injustice being done around the world to Christians, what does it stir up in you? Do you long for God to make things right? Pray that God would stir up in you a longing for his kingdom to come.
3. Have you ever had a time when you felt like David did in this psalm—a time when you were falsely accused or treated unjustly? If so, how did you deal with that? How could Romans 12:19 help you with that?
4. What is the difference between wanting God to vindicate your name and wanting him to vindicate his name? Why does that distinction matter? Look at Ezekiel 36:22-38 to see how God vindicates his holy name.

Inexhaustible Satisfaction

PSALM 36

Main Idea: Inexhaustible satisfaction is found in an inexhaustible God.

I. The Sad Reality of Ignoring God (36:1-4)
II. The Satisfying Reality of God (36:5-9)
III. The Longing to Be Satisfied by God (36:10-12)

Eugene Peterson says,

> There is a general assumption prevalent in the world that it is extremely difficult to be a Christian. But this is as far from the truth as the east is from the west. The easiest thing in the world is to be a Christian. What is hard is to be a sinner. Being a Christian is what we were created for. . . . In the course of Christian discipleship we discover that without Christ we were doing it the hard way and that with Christ we are doing it the easy way. It is not Christians who have it hard, but non-Christians. (*Long Obedience* 1980, 115)

At first glance that statement might seem odd, and even outright wrong, to us. I mean, being a Christians is hard, isn't it? Well, being a human is hard. Life in a broken world is hard. We often find ourselves, as believers, feeling overwhelmed by the suffering, pain, and grief in us and around us. But truthfully, living in this broken world without Jesus is harder. Living life with Jesus is the best possible life in this broken world. We were created to live life with God and only find fullness of life when we do.

In Psalm 36 David shows us the reality of those who live life with God and those who live without him. It is a picture of two different ways to live. More than that, it is the longing of a man who wants to experience the fullness of life with God—to experience the fullness of his goodness. Psalm 36 shows why every person should seek to experience the fullness of life with God—namely because there is inexhaustible satisfaction found in an inexhaustible God.

The Sad Reality of Ignoring God

PSALM 36:1-4

The first four verses of Psalm 36 paint a picture of the ungodly. It's a picture of everyone who has rejected and ignored God. It does not speak of the wicked as those who just do wicked things but as those who have wicked hearts. They are filled with transgression and have no fear of God in their hearts (Craigie, *Psalms 1–50*, 291). And right here, in the first verse, we are reminded of why we must have a proper understanding of salvation. The gospel is not a call to morality or a decision to do better. Salvation begins with regeneration. Regeneration is an internal work of God in which he makes us alive through the new birth. It is a radical change from the inside out (John 3; 2 Cor 5:17; Eph 2:4). This is the only solution for the wicked because their problem is internal, not external (Lawrence, *Conversion*, 23–24).

The wicked, as described in Psalm 36, flatter themselves in order to make themselves feel OK. They compare themselves to others and justify themselves in their own eyes (v. 2). They are convinced that their iniquity will not be found out and there will be no consequences if it is (v. 2). Their hearts grow hardened, and they stop acting wisely and doing good (v. 3). They reject the wisdom of God and are left to walk in the path of folly (vv. 3-4). They ignore God and wisdom, and they are self-centered and arrogant. Thus is the life of every one of us without Jesus.

The life of the unbeliever in verses 1-4 is a sad life. It is sad because it ignores all that is good and right in life. It is sad because it rejects wisdom and chooses instead the pathway of folly and destruction. It is sad because those who follow it grow increasingly hardened by sin and store up increasing punishment. Ultimately, it is sad because it misses all the goodness God provides. It is the sad life of the one who ignores God.

Some might respond to this by saying, "Well, I know a lot of lost people who aren't like this. They are great people. They are missing Jesus, but their lives are not sad." In reality, there are no people like that. They might appear that way, but that is not the reality. Without Christ, every person is spiritually dead, disobedient, and doomed (Eph 2:1-3). They are living lives void of all that is good.

If unbelievers heard us talk like this, they might immediately feel as if this confirms what they have always thought about believers—they are arrogant and think they have it all together. But the opposite is true.

Believers acknowledge that we are terrible sinners who deserve nothing more than an eternal hell. The only reason there is any good in us at all is because God, by a gracious miracle, has done a work in our hearts to show us our sinfulness and our need for a Savior, and he has made us born again. When believers talk about the real life they have, they are not magnifying themselves as great but magnifying God as great!

The Satisfying Reality of God

PSALM 36:5-9

In contrast to the sad reality of ignoring God, there is the satisfying reality of God himself. Verses 5-9 show a picture of the vastness of God. His faithful love reaches to heaven (v. 5). It is unfailing, personal, and without limit. His love cannot be measured. His faithfulness reaches to the clouds (v. 5). His reliability and dependability never stop. His righteousness is like the highest mountains and his judgments like the deepest sea (v. 6). He is perfect, just, fair. He is full of goodness and perfection. There is no way to measure the depth of his goodness and perfection. The clouds, mountains, and great deep reveal that God is full of inexhaustible goodness.

What is more amazing than that is that God is personal. His "faithful love" refers to the covenant love he has for his people. His love is priceless (v. 7) because it is personal. It is not just a fact to believe; it is a reality to experience. God offers us the opportunity to take refuge in him, to run and find safety and security and a home (v. 7). He not only tells us that there is an abundance in his house, but he also invites us to come and feast so that we might be filled and satisfied (v. 8). When you look closely, you will notice that verses 5-6 describe who God is and verses 7-9 reveal that he is offering all that he is to us. God is inviting us not only to marvel at the abundance of his goodness but also to feast on it (John 7:37).

In his book on the Psalms, C. S. Lewis says that God is the "all-satisfying object" (*Reflections* 1958, 92–93). That really is the point of Psalm 36. When comparing the sad life of the unbeliever with the satisfying reality of God, we come to see just how good God is and how good it is to know him. The reality is, inexhaustible satisfaction is found in an inexhaustible God. His goodness, faithfulness, and love cannot be measured, and all of it is offered to us through Jesus Christ.

The Longing to Be Satisfied by God

PSALM 36:10-12

This psalm ends with a prayer. It is a prayer of longing, a cry of deep desire. In light of the sad reality of the wicked compared to the satisfying reality of God, this prayer expresses the longing to find full satisfaction in God. Verse 10 mirrors verse 5. Verse 5 states the reality of God's love and faithfulness while verse 10 expresses a longing to personally experience it. It is one thing to know it; it is another to experience it. We must long to feast and drink for ourselves from the abundance of his goodness.

If we are honest, many of us are not daily experiencing the reality of God's love and goodness. We are not feasting on the abundance of his house and drinking from his refreshing streams (v. 8). Verse 11 shows us two reasons this might be the case. First, pride keeps us from experiencing the satisfying reality of God. When we choose to live independently of God and center our lives on ourselves, we miss all that God has to offer. So we pray that the "foot of the arrogant" would not come near us. We spend time daily in God's Word so that we might stay centered on him. We fight the constant pull of self-centeredness by re-centering ourselves on God.

Second, evil keeps us from experiencing the satisfying reality of God (v. 11). We cannot feast on the world and on Christ at the same time. Every time we say yes to sin, we say no to satisfaction in God. Sin is how we attempt to satisfy ourselves, while holiness expresses our belief that only God can truly satisfy us. We must, by faith, choose to believe that walking with Jesus is always the most satisfying way to live.

Conclusion

There is a sense in which we all need to be reminded of the sacrifices and suffering that come with following Jesus. Jesus promised it, and we cannot ignore it. It is undeniably true that the more we choose to follow Jesus the more it will cost us. But we must be careful, while being honest about the difficult realities of following Jesus, not to miss the satisfying realities of following Jesus. As Peterson says, it's not Christians who have it hard but non-Christians. Nothing in all of life is more satisfying than walking in daily intimacy with God. Once we begin to really get a taste of that, we will want more and more and more.

Reflect and Discuss

1. How have you seen the picture of the ungodly in verses 1-4 manifested in your life before you knew Christ?
2. How have you seen your life become inward focused instead of God focused?
3. Everything your soul longs for is found in God. How have you experienced the soul-satisfying reality of God? In what ways has he satisfied the longings of your heart?
4. According to verses 11-12, pride and evil keep us from experiencing the satisfying reality of God. What areas of pride or sin most often keep you from experiencing God's best?

Gospel Hope

PSALM 37

Main Idea: We must walk by faith in the promise that the righteous get their best lives later.

I. **Fight the Pull of Worldliness (37:1).**
II. **See the Whole Picture (37:2).**
III. **Walk by Faith in Gospel Hope (37:3).**
IV. **Pursue Joy in Jesus (37:4).**

When people think about the book of Psalms, they most often think of the raw, intimate heart cries to God. They think about the psalms that include the words "O Lord" as an indication that the words are an honest plea to God. Psalm 37 doesn't feel that way at all. Psalm 37 feels more like a proverb than a psalm. It feels like David, as an older man (37:25), is sharing some much-needed wisdom with a younger generation. This quality might be why this psalm includes so many well-known and much-loved verses.

One of the most important things to note about this psalm is that it is an alphabetic acrostic, meaning that each stanza begins with a successive letter of the Hebrew alphabet. We don't know all the reasons David would have chosen to write this psalm this way, but we do know that one of the most helpful aspects of an acrostic psalm is how much easier it is to memorize (for those who know the Hebrew alphabet and memorize the psalm in Hebrew). When you read this psalm, and you see the wisdom of David and his desire to instruct the next generation, it seems like exactly the kind of psalm we should memorize, a psalm that we need not only to read but also get deep into our souls.

In this psalm David is wrestling with this question: Why do the righteous struggle while the wicked thrive? He is also reflecting on the futility of expending emotional energy comparing your life with others, especially the wicked's. He warns us of the danger of comparison. He reveals that deeply rooted desire in each of us to see what others have and think it is better than what we have, and to allow that feeling to draw our hearts and minds away from devotion to Christ. As he wrestles, reflects, and warns us, he shows us that we make the most of this life for Jesus when we keep looking beyond this life to the next.

Psalm 37 has forty verses and almost a dozen commands. Although it might be difficult at first to see how they all fit together, the reality is that every verse in this psalm is summarized in the first four verses. It is helpful to see the four primary commands in verses 1-4 and then draw a line from those to the other verses in the psalm. Each of these commands show us how to stay faithful and grow in Christlikeness while surrounded by false appearances.

Fight the Pull of Worldliness

PSALM 37:1

Verse 1 is a call to guard our hearts. "Do not be agitated" is a great translation. It means not to burn hot with anger inside. It is not so much an outburst of anger but the kind of anger that dwells in our hearts unseen (Goldingay, *Psalms 1–41*, 519)—a kind of anger that stews in our hearts and causes us to sulk or get worked up. The command is mentioned three times in this psalm (vv. 1,7,8), and the reason for the anger is seen in verse 7. The internal anger is the result of watching the wicked prosper. Their prospering tends to affect our hearts if we stew on it.

When David talks about what the prosperity of the wicked tends to do to his heart, he shows us a deadly process that can take place in our hearts whenever we see others around us who appear to have it better. The process begins with comparing ourselves with others. This is exactly what we are warned about in verse 1. We are called to stop looking at the prosperity of others, comparing it to our own lives, and allowing any sense of injustice to eat us up. Comparison inevitably leads to coveting. This is why David immediately says, "Do not envy those who do wrong" (v. 1). Envy is the feeling of discontent when we want something someone else has. If we allow envy to germinate in our hearts, it will then lead to competition. The anger and agitation will eventually lead to "harm" (v. 8). It will lead us into working to get what someone else has. Comparing, coveting, and competing combine to form a deadly process. It is a process that will pull us away from a godly and content heart toward worldliness. It manifests itself in so many ways.

We see it when a teenage girl tries to live a pure, modest, and holy life but watches as other girls who walk in immorality and immodesty get all the attention; when a businessman chooses to balance his work and family and walk in ethical integrity but then watches as a coworker sacrifices his family, cheats the company, and gets the promotion; when a college student doesn't cheat on an exam while those who do cheat get a better grade and don't get caught. There are a thousand ways in which this manifests itself in our hearts.

But this deadly trap and this pull toward worldliness are most often subtler than that—when we get on social media and see a family, a house, a spouse, a life that feels so much better than ours. At that moment the comparing begins. This is exactly where David tells us to stop. Stop at the moment we begin to compare our lives with someone else's. "Do not be agitated by evildoers." Do not let these thoughts enter your heart and mind. Stop them immediately and avoid the pull of worldliness (Luke 21:34).

See the Whole Picture

PSALM 37:2

How do we avoid the comparison when it consistently appears that the wicked are prospering while the righteous are suffering? David's answer is simple: see the whole picture. We can keep from comparing and competing, "For they wither quickly like grass and wilt like tender green plants" (v. 2). When you see the wicked prospering, you are only seeing a part of the picture. When we see the whole picture, we will realize that everything they have is fleeting. "They wither quickly."

As was mentioned, every verse in Psalm 37 can be tied back to verses 1-4. Throughout the psalm David continues to emphasize the fleeting nature of the wicked (vv. 8-10,12-17,20,28,35-38). The evildoers, who appear to prosper, "will be destroyed" (v. 9), "will be no more" (v. 10), "will perish," and "will fade away like the smoke" (v. 20). So the questions we must ask are, Do we really want their lives? Do we really envy them? Do we really wish we had what they have?

In Luke 16 Jesus gives the parable of the rich man and Lazarus. Every day when the rich man would leave his gated home dressed in fine linen, he would pass a poor man covered with sores. All the poor man wanted were the crumbs that fell from the rich man's table—the crumbs the dogs would eat—but he got nothing. One day the poor man died and was taken to heaven ("Abraham's side") while the rich man died and was taken to hell. The rich man called out for mercy but was told, "Son, remember that during your life you received your good things" (Luke 16:25). The rich man, like those in Psalm 37, appeared to be blessed, but he soon perished. David wants us to see the whole picture and realize that the life we tend to covet is not the life we really want.

Walk by Faith in Gospel Hope

PSALM 37:3

Instead of getting agitated and worked up by the fleeting prosperity of the wicked, "trust in the LORD and do what is good; dwell in the land and live securely" (v. 3). Psalm 37 is filled with positive commands to replace the agitation (vv. 3,4,5,7,27,34). The feel of verse 3 is, "Hey, stop looking at them and being bothered. You just keep walking by faith, do good, cultivate a life of faithfulness, and God will reward you in due time!"

David says, "Trust in the LORD" (v. 3), meaning, put your confidence in the Lord and his promises. Walk in confidence that what God said, he will do—specifically, the promise that he will, in his timing, reward those who patiently walked with him. These promises run throughout the entire psalm (vv. 6,9,11,18,22,23-24,27-28,34,37,39-40). All these promises have one common theme—they are fulfilled later. Believe the promise that those who are obedient to the commands in Psalm 37:3 will in fact be rewarded. That is the key to fighting worldliness and pursuing Christlikeness. You live by faith in the promise of something better. That is called hope. Hope is the confidence that the best is yet to come.

The hope we must walk in is gospel hope, meaning it is rooted and grounded in what God has done for us in Christ Jesus. Because Jesus died, was buried, rose again, and ascended to the right hand of the Father, by faith in him we have hope that our lives too will end in resurrection. To walk by faith in gospel hope means not only believing the facts of the gospel but also living out the gospel daily, to live as if there is always something better for us because we are "in Christ." By faith we are assured that what we hope for will in fact come true (Heb 11:1). That is the point of Psalm 37:3. When we feel the pull of the world, we choose to walk by faith in gospel hope.

Pursue Joy in Jesus

PSALM 37:4

Finally, the way we remain faithful when it seems like the wicked around us are prospering is to pursue our joy in Jesus. One of the most precious promises in Psalm 37 comes in response to a command: "Take delight in the Lord, and he will give you your heart's desires." The way to "take delight in the Lord" is to make Jesus our greatest delight. It is a call to stop looking at everyone else around us and look to Jesus—to make him our greatest treasure and greatest pursuit. As John Piper says, this is a "radical call to pursue your fullest satisfaction in all that God promised to be for you in Jesus" (*Future Grace*, 399). When we make Jesus our greatest delight, we will find that there is no joy greater than the joy he gives. We will find that all the worldly things we once envied no longer appeal to us. As we pursue joy in Jesus, he will increasingly become our greatest longing.

Conclusion

There is an old hymn that says,

> Standing on the promises of Christ my King,
> Through eternal ages let His praises ring;
> "Glory in the highest," I will shout and sing,
> Standing on the promises of God. (R. Kelso Carter, "Standing on the Promises")

Essentially, that is what Psalm 37 calls us to do. It calls us to stand on the promise that even though it appears that the wicked are thriving while the righteous suffer, the Lord will reward the faithfulness of his people.

Reflect and Discuss

1. Take some time to think about and discuss with another believer the pull you feel toward worldliness. How does that manifest itself in your life? In what areas have you experienced comparison, coveting, and competition?
2. Hope is the confidence that the best is yet to come. Living with gospel hope is walking daily in a way that allows you to say no to temporary things for the sake of eternal things. What about that is the most challenging for you? Why is it so difficult to get your best life later when so many others seem like they are getting theirs now?
3. Throughout your Christian life, what has been your primary motivation for obedience? Consider the difference between obeying because we are indebted to God as opposed to obeying out of

delight in God. How does this thought change your motive for fighting sin, sacrificing for the Lord, and walking in obedience?

4. Are you taking practical steps to "delight in the LORD"? How are you seeking to find joy and satisfaction in him? Are you living as if Jesus is the greatest treasure?

The Discipline of the Lord

PSALM 38

Main Idea: Like a father with a son, the Lord disciplines those he loves for their good.

I. **Understanding the Lord's Discipline**
II. **There Is Love in the Discipline of the Lord (38:1-2).**
III. **There Is Pain in the Discipline of the Lord (38:3-20).**
IV. **There Is Hope in the Discipline of the Lord (38:21-22).**
V. **The Big Question**

In 1665 what is now known as the Great Plague hit London, England. In eighteen months, one-fourth of the entire population died. The graveyards were so overfilled that workers would drive carts through the city crying out, "Bring us your dead." Families would bring their dead, put them in the cart, and watch them be hauled off to mass graves.

In London during that time was a pastor named Ralph Venning. He was known not only as a faithful gospel preacher but also a man who loved and cared for the poor. He began writing a book that was almost finished before the plague began. Because of the plague, it was not finished and published till a few years after the plague. The book was a 250-page explanation of the seriousness of sin. Venning showed how sin went not only against the character of God but also against the good of man. He titled the book *The Plague of Plagues: The Sinfulness of Sin!* He made the case that there is no plague greater than the one called sin (Venning, *The Plague of Plagues*, 15). Venning also said,

> Sin is worse than affliction, than death, than Devil, than Hell. Affliction is not so afflictive, death is not so deadly, the Devil not so devilish, Hell not so hellish as sin is! . . . The four evils I have just named are truly terrible, and from all of them everyone is ready to say, Good Lord, deliver us! Yet none of these, nor all of them together, are as bad as sin. (*The Plague of Plagues*, 177)

It is hard to imagine any biblical truth that is preached or believed any less than that one. Yet with all that we face in these times, nothing we face is any more serious than sin itself. That is why we need Psalm 38. It reminds us of the plague of plagues.

Understanding the Lord's Discipline

Psalm 38 is about the discipline of the Lord.[5] David says, "LORD, do not punish me in your anger or discipline me in your wrath" (v. 1). We don't hear much about the discipline of the Lord, so we need some context in how to understand it. The Lord disciplines his children in two ways: instructive and corrective.

The **instructive discipline** of the Lord refers to the way God teaches us, trains us, and molds us into his image. It is the work the Lord does in our lives to grow us as disciples. A great example of this is John 15:2, where Jesus says that those who bear fruit are pruned so they might bear more fruit. Many times that pruning process is painful and even confusing. We wonder why we are experiencing the pain, the hurt, the struggle, or the difficult situations. We might even wonder if God is against us. In reality, the Lord is bringing instructive discipline. This is exactly the kind of discipline we see in Hebrews 12:7-11. The author of Hebrews says that the Lord disciplines us because he loves us and wants us to bear the fruit of righteousness. If he did not discipline us, we would be illegitimate children and not sons. This discipline is always for our holiness and for our good.

Corrective discipline is applied to us because of our continued rebellion toward the Holy Spirit's conviction of sin. In 1 Peter 4, Peter makes clear that some believers suffer for the sake of righteousness, and some suffer because of their sin. First Corinthians 11 tells us that some who took Communion in an unworthy manner had become ill and even died. This kind of discipline is not just the natural consequences of sin; it is God applying discipline for our good in order to bring us back to him. It is not penal, but it is discipline (Ross, *Psalms 1–41*, 823). David, the author of Psalm 38, serves as a great example of this. His sin with Bathsheba (2 Sam 11) brought on years of discipline from the Lord.

---

[5] I am indebted to John MacArthur, "The Discipline of God," for some general themes of this section.

It is the corrective discipline of the Lord that we see in Psalm 38. David acknowledges that his suffering is because of his sin, iniquity, and foolishness (vv. 3,4,5). We don't think much about the corrective discipline of the Lord, mainly because we find it hard to process in light of so many other gospel truths. This is where Psalm 38 helps us. Psalm 38 gives us three truths we must know about the corrective discipline of the Lord.

There Is Love in the Discipline of the Lord

PSALM 38:1-2

One of the most confusing things about Psalm 38 is the idea that believers could experience the "anger" or "wrath" of God (v. 1). But David is not saying he is experiencing the anger and wrath of God; he is saying that he *feels* like he is. He feels the heavy hand of the Lord on him (v. 2). The reality is, the discipline is not coming out of wrath but out of love. God's discipline for a believer is never punitive; it is corrective.

Proverbs 3:11-12 is helpful here. Solomon says,

> *Do not despise the Lord's instruction, my son, and do not loathe his discipline; for the Lord disciplines the one he loves, just as a father disciplines the son in whom he delights.*

This is exactly what Hebrews 12:7-11 affirms. The Lord's discipline is proof that we are his children and evidence of his love. His heart is always loving, and his motive is always our holiness. In the same way a father disciplines a child he loves, so God the Father disciplines his children whom he loves.

Often, when we feel like the Lord is against us or is angry with us, the reality is that he is just disciplining us for our own good. He is protecting us, correcting us, molding us, and working in us. If you are a child of God, there is always love in the discipline of the Lord.

There Is Pain in the Discipline of the Lord

PSALM 38:3-20

The more you read this psalm, the more you feel David's entire life seems to be falling apart. There is spiritual pain (vv. 1-2). David feels the heaviness of the Lord and weight of a strained relationship. There is emotional pain (vv. 4-6,8). He has a "burden too heavy" for him. His heart is filled with mourning, and he groans because of the anguish of his heart. The emotional pain seems unrelenting. And there is relational pain (vv. 11-12,19). His own family has turned against him and become distant. His enemies have risen up against him, and he feels under attack.

Anyone who has felt this kind of spiritual, emotional, and relational pain will know that it quickly affects the physical body. Eventually the body will manifest the pain of the heart. This seems to be an unrelenting reality in David's life. He says twice that there is "no soundness" in his body (vv. 3,7). There is no health in his bones, and his insides are filled with burning pain. David is feeling continual and painful physical problems because of his sin.

Of course, not all sickness is a result of specific unrepentant sin, but some pain is. Some pain is instructive discipline, like Paul's thorn in the flesh or Job's boils. And some is corrective like David's. We know that some people had become ill and even died in Corinth because they had taken the Lord's Supper in an unworthy manner and were under the corrective discipline of the Lord (1 Cor 11:30). As Hebrews 12:11 makes clear, all discipline is painful at the moment, but it yields the fruit of righteousness in those who are trained by it. Even the pain of discipline is for our good.

There Is Hope in the Discipline of the Lord

PSALM 38:21-22

In the midst of all the pain of Psalm 38, there is also intense hope. We first see it in verse 9 with the subtle reminder that the Lord sees all our suffering and is not unaware, nor is he uninvolved. He is lovingly working through all of it. In verse 15 David explicitly says, "For I put my hope in you, LORD; you will answer me, my Lord, my God." By "hope," David means that he anticipates that God will bring good out of this. No matter how the discipline might feel, the purpose is always good. God will bring something good out of it.

The psalm ends with resounding hope in God himself. David ends by praying to "the LORD," Yahweh, the God of the covenant who has promised never to forsake his people. He prays to "[his] God" who is sovereign over all things and is able to make all these things work together for good. And he prays to "[his] Lord, [his] salvation." He is aware of who he is and who God is. He knows that God is for him in all these things.

At the end of Psalm 38, the discipline is working. David is calling on the Lord, he has repented of his sins (v. 18), he longs for the presence of the Lord (v. 21), and he has placed his hope in the Lord (v. 15). God has applied the painful discipline, and David has responded by looking to the Lord.

The Big Question

When it comes to the discipline of the Lord, one question that often plagues us is, How do I know if I am experiencing corrective or instructive discipline? Two things help us here. First, if we are under the corrective discipline of the Lord, God will make that clear, as he does to David. Most corrective discipline is a result of ongoing willful disregard for the conviction of the Holy Spirit. In other words, this is the kind of rebellion you are aware of.

The second truth that helps us is that, in many ways, it does not matter what kind of discipline it is because God's motive is the same and our response should be, too. If, like the prodigal son, you experience the corrective discipline of the Lord, God is calling you closer, and your response should be to turn away from sin and turn toward him. If, like Job, you are experiencing the instructive discipline of the Lord, God is calling you closer, and your response should be to trust in him and come nearer. In both cases, God's motive is love; his desire is to draw us close.

Conclusion

The only reason we can walk through the discipline of the Lord with confidence is because of the truths of Romans 8. No matter how it might feel (Ps 38:1), there is no condemnation for those who are in Christ Jesus(Rom 8:1). God is working on you, he is for you, and nothing can separate you from his love. All of that is true because of what God has done for us in Christ. When we place our faith in him, God brings us into his family and treats us like his children. He is eternally for us, and because of that, he is eternally committed to doing what is best to conform us into his image and ensure we find our greatest joy in him.

Reflect and Discuss

1. Almost every believer struggles with the idea of being disciplined by God. Why do you think that is? Why is it so difficult to see his discipline as a sign of his being a loving Father to us?
2. Read Hebrews 12:7-11. What does this teach us about the character of God and the role of discipline in our lives? What hope and encouragement do we find in that text?
3. When it comes to discipline, what hope do we find in the gospel?
4. No matter the cause for the discipline, what does Psalm 38 teach us about our response to suffering? What should be our posture when we go through disciplinary moments like David did?

Hopeful Perspective in Suffering

PSALM 39

Main Idea: Jesus gives meaning to life when life appears meaningless.

I. **Our Lives Are Fleeting (39:4-6).**
II. **Our Hope Is Solid (39:7-11).**
III. **Our Home Is Heaven (39:12-13).**

In seasons of trials, when our hearts are heavy, we might feel as if one of the most difficult things to do is go to church, where everyone seems happy and the songs are all triumphant. We might walk in and wonder if anyone else even understands the kind of pain we are going through. We might assume that everyone else is fine and we are the only ones who are struggling with sorrow and despair. We might find it hard to sing the happy songs when our hearts feel sad. This is why we need the psalms of lament.

Many people read the psalms of lament and find them discouraging or even depressing. But if we can be honest with ourselves and honest with God, the psalms of lament are refreshing. They give us what the modern American church often doesn't—the freedom to express how we really feel. Many of these psalms are written by a man who knew and loved God deeply. Their existence reminds us that we are not alone in our pain. Psalm 39 specifically reminds us that God has actually provided songs for us to sing when our hearts feel heavy.

The superscription of Psalm 39 says, "For the choir director, for Jeduthun. A psalm of David." Jeduthun was one of the musicians appointed by David to lead worship in the tabernacle (1 Chron 16:41-42; Motyer, *Psalms by the Day*, 102). Apparently David, in one of his dark moments of the soul, wrote a lament and asked it to be put to music so the congregation could sing it. We might not want to sing it in church, but it is certainly a message the church needs. For those who feel as if life no longer has any meaning, Psalm 39 reminds us that Jesus gives meaning to life when life seems meaningless.

Context

PSALM 39:1-3

David is suffering because of his sin (vv. 10-11). This is a continuation of what David was experiencing in Psalm 38; he is under the loving yet painful discipline of the Lord. This discipline is not punitive; it is corrective, but it is painful nonetheless. And apart from the internal and external pain described in Psalm 38, there is the rising sense of discouragement and anger. David is struggling. He is wrestling. He is asking questions. He is doing what all of us do when our suffering seems unrelenting. His heart is heavy, his mind is spinning, yet he wants to make sure he remains faithful.

Although David's mind is increasingly filled with questions, he does not want to open his mouth and vent, especially in the presence of unbelievers (v. 1). He does not want his struggles to cause unbelievers to question the goodness of the Lord. So, while his heart is filled with discouragement, accusations, and frustrations, he tries his best to hold it in. He tries his best to "guard [his] mouth with a muzzle." It doesn't work.

While he was "speechless and quiet," his "pain intensified" and his "heart grew hot." The more he "mused," the harder it was to remain silent. Like a kettle on the stove that has reached its boiling point, David's top finally pops and his whistle blows. He can't contain his pain any longer. David tried to bury his pain. It didn't work. It never does. Burying our hurt and pain will lead to bitterness, which will eventually manifest itself in innumerable hurtful ways. The pain has got to come out. If we aren't careful, it can come out in ungodly bursts of anger. Often these outbursts of anger are addressed to those around us who will be damaged by them. So what should we do with all the boiling pain inside of us? We should take it to the Lord.

David's mouth finally opens, the pain is revealed, and he cries out, "LORD!" This is where we take our pain. We don't bury it and allow it to lead to outbursts of anger. As we take our pain to the Lord, the Lord gives clarity. He is not surprised or upset by our honesty. He already knows it, and when we are faithful to bring it to him, he will use it to give us new perspective—hopeful perspective. This is what David does, and the Lord gives him hopeful perspective in suffering. God gives him three realities that give us perspective when life gets hard.

Our Lives Are Fleeting

PSALM 39:4-6

In a moment of hopelessness, David cries out to the Lord: "LORD, make me aware of my end and the number of my days so that I will know how short-lived I am" (v. 4). He is feeling the futility and the fleeting nature of life. He feels that life is just a "vapor" (v. 5). This is the same word Solomon uses to open and close the book of Ecclesiastes, a word that Solomon uses thirty-eight times in that book. Solomon knew from experience (and probably from singing a song his dad wrote) that the things of this world are fleeting. The more he tried to grab on to them, the more he found them futile. David is feeling the same thing.

David feels like life itself is just a fleeting vapor (v. 5). We struggle and toil and work for nothing (v. 6). We store up wealth, and someday someone else will get it (v. 6). This type of futility is seen so clearly at an estate sale. At an estate sale you can purchase a person's possessions for about ten cents on the dollar. What a person worked hard for is eventually sold off with little or no regard for any real sentimental or monetary value. This is what happens to all the things we collect in this life.

David gets to the heart of what he is feeling with one word in verse 6—*shadow*. Like C. S. Lewis noted in *The Last Battle*, David is realizing that this earthly world is just a shadow. Yet that is not hopeless. The presence of the shadow points to the presence of a greater reality. God made it to be this way (v. 5). God made the world so that it might continually point us to something better. Life begins to feel futile when we start to live for the shadows instead of the substance. David, as he pours out his heart to God, begins to realize that everything that feels futile is just a shadow of a much greater reality. His hope is not in the shadows.

Our Hope Is Solid

PSALM 39:7-11

If life is fleeting and all is vanity, why does anything even matter? What is the meaning? David realizes that, contrary to the fleeting nature of the shadows and the vapor of life, there is something solid to hold on to. David immediately says, "My hope is in you" (v. 7). This indicates that even as he vents to the Lord, he begins to turn a corner. Hope emerges. This is what happens when we get honest with God.

There is an important shift in verse 7. David is asking "what" questions. He wants to know what the meaning of life is when everything seems like vanity. But his "what" question gets a "who" answer (Goldingay, *Psalms 1–41*, 559). Where do we find meaning in this life? In the Lord himself. David realized that when everything in life seems meaningless, the Lord gives meaning. The Lord is the greater reality behind the shadows. The Lord is the solid place to stand when life seems like a vapor. As Edward Mote reminds us, "All other ground is sinking sand" ("The Solid Rock"). But the good news is, there is a solid hope found in Jesus Christ. Jesus takes the shadows and helps us see the substance behind them.

This really is the power of the gospel. The gospel delivers us from living in such a way that all we do is grasp for the shadows. When we see our own sinfulness and are awakened to the reality of life and eternity without Christ, and when we see Jesus taking on himself all our sin so that we might have his righteousness, and then we turn by faith to him and ask him to save us, he not only saves us from sin and hell, but he also saves us from a meaningless existence. He opens our eyes to the true meaning of life. There truly is no meaning apart from him.

Our Home Is Heaven

PSALM 39:12-13

As David continues to pour out his heart to God and to experience the clarity that only God can bring, he moves from a sense of meaninglessness to real gospel hope. And gospel hope, rooted and grounded in a relationship with Jesus Christ, allows us to see beyond this life to the next life. In fact, we not only get to see it, but also find hope and joy in it. This is what happens to David as he ends the psalm.

David still feels pain. There is still sorrow in his heart. There are still tears in his eyes because even with solid gospel hope, sometimes life in this broken world is just hard. But the pain and suffering of this world are temporary. David reminds himself that, although the season of suffering seems unending, he is just an "alien, a temporary resident" in this world. He knew he didn't belong here. He knew this is temporary.

We must all, like the great saints of old, look beyond this life to the next if we want to find any real sense of meaning (Heb 11). We don't belong here. We are passing through. No matter how painful the moment is, in light of eternity, it is just a moment. We believers must continue to remind ourselves that our home is in heaven.

In this psalm of lament, there is such a precious and sweet ending. As the Lord continues to point us toward the hope of the next life as a way to endure the pain of this life, he still wants us to smile. David concludes with, "Turn your angry gaze from me so that I may be cheered up before I die and am gone" (v. 13). David wants to smile. This life is not intended to be all pain and suffering. There are smiles to be had.

While we look toward the next life, we still find joy in this one. God gives good gifts to be enjoyed. So we have great meals with friends, we take walks on the beach, we spend time in the mountains, we enjoy good films, we have our hearts stirred by great pieces of music, and we laugh and smile. We remember that all these little moments of joy God gives us in this life are just a shadow of the real substance. There will be a day in which we believers will experience the fullness of joy for all eternity (16:9-11). Until then, we pour out our hearts to God, we keep our hope in Jesus and our eyes toward heaven, and we enjoy the little pleasures God gives us on this earth as we wait for something better.

Conclusion

The presence of these types of psalms continues to remind us that for every human being, even those who are trusting in Christ, life in this broken world is difficult. We struggle with the brokenness around us and the brokenness within us. Yet, through Christ, there is always hope. But that hope does not become a living reality until we are able to see beyond the shadows and look continually to the substance. So we keep our eyes on Jesus, we hold on to hope, and we enjoy every beautiful moment of this life as a little glimpse of the joy that awaits those who trust Christ.

Reflect and Discuss

1. Psalms like this one give us what the church often doesn't: the freedom to express how we really feel. What hope and encouragement do you find in David's own struggles with sin, patience, and the seeming futility of life?
2. Life is a vapor. Why does that matter? If everything we store up in this life will eventually mean nothing, how should that change the

way you live? How might thinking about life as a shadow help you look beyond it to see the greater reality?

3. Our hope in Christ is solid. We tend to look for hope in things, but David finds hope in God himself. How does God make life worth living? How does the gospel give us daily hope?
4. Our real home is heaven. If we believers are, as verse 12 says, just temporary residents in this land, how should that change the way we live? How does the hope of heaven encourage us to stay faithful in the midst of daily trials and difficulties?

Sold Out to Do God's Will

PSALM 40

Main Idea: Trust the Lord, do his will, and proclaim his greatness while you patiently wait for him to rescue you.

I. Wait on the Lord with Confidence (40:1-3).
  A. He will hear you when you call (40:1).
  B. He will help you when you're down (40:2).
  C. He will honor you when you worship (40:3).
II. Trust in the Lord with Conviction (40:4-5).
  A. Trust the God who is true to you (40:4).
  B. Trust the God who thinks of you (40:5).
III. Delight in the Lord with Consecration (40:6-8).
  A. Do not become consumed with externals (40:6).
  B. Know that what counts is internal (40:7-8).
IV. Testify about the Lord with Courage (40:9-10).
  A. Tell of his righteousness (40:9-10).
  B. Tell of his faithfulness (40:10).
V. Plead with the Lord with Cause (40:11-15).
  A. Ask for the Lord's presence when ambushed (40:11-12).
  B. Ask for the Lord's protection when attacked (40:13-15).
VI. Rejoice in the Lord with Celebration (40:16-17).
  A. Remember he is your Savior (40:16).
  B. Remember he is your Deliverer (40:17).

When circumstances are difficult and situations weigh us down, we have a popular saying that sums up how we feel: "My life is in the pits." King David certainly felt this way at times in his life, and he expressed his thinking about it in Psalm 40.

Psalm 40 is similar to Psalm 27 in structure. It is composed of two sections: thanksgiving (vv. 1-10) and personal lament (vv. 11-17) (Broyles, *Psalms*, 190).[6] Despite two distinct sections, a remarkable unity and structure bind this song together so that the whole song

[6] Psalm 40:13-17 is also identical to Psalm 70.

anticipates a complete fulfillment in David's greater Son, Jesus of Nazareth. The author of Hebrews understands the song in this way. Hebrews 10:5-7 quotes Psalm 40:6-8 and applies it to the life of the Lord Jesus. Only the Lord Jesus, in fact, could say these verses with complete purity of heart and devotion.

Verse 8 captures the essence of this psalm and the heart of the Lord Jesus: "I delight to do your will, my God, and your instruction is deep within me." Here is a life sold out to do God's will. Here is the life God desires and expects of us. What does such a life look like? What will be its passions?

Wait on the Lord with Confidence

PSALM 40:1-3

Something happened to David that, figuratively speaking, put him in a "desolate pit" (v. 2), a "slimy pit" (NIV). Sinking in "muddy clay" (NKJV, "miry clay"), David realizes only one person can save him. It is "the LORD," Yahweh. What will the Lord do when his servant cries out?

He Will Hear You When You Call (40:1)

David "waited patiently for the LORD." He trusted God's timing, and the Lord came through. "He turned to me and heard my cry for help." My (Danny's) hero Adrian Rogers often said, "God is never early and he is never late; he is always right on time." He hears and responds when we call.

He Will Help You When You're Down (40:2)

Verse 2 expands on the thanksgiving of verse 1. God brought David out of a hopeless and desperate situation, "a desolate pit" and "muddy clay." He set his "feet on a rock," a solid and secure foundation (cf. 2 Cor 4:8-9). He made his "steps secure." The Lord provided both a foundation and direction, solid ground and guidance. This is the help Yahweh gives to those who are his.

He Will Honor You When You Worship (40:3)

Verse 3 continues the theme of thanksgiving. "A new song in my mouth" is a song of salvation, even vindication, and "a hymn of praise to our God" is a new song of worship, a hymn of exultation in the Lord. What follows is a surprise containing a startling evangelistic impulse. Three powerful verbs address the response of those who hear David's testimony. They will "see," "fear," and "trust in the LORD." John Piper says, "Let us never view our own song as the stopping place of God's mercies. God aims for us to sing others into the kingdom" ("In the Pits with a King").

A believer's testimony and experience of God's salvation will be a witness that will bring others to the Lord! Others will be saved when they see how great is the God of our salvation (Ps 27:1). David, no doubt, would affirm the words of the hymn writer Charles Gabriel:

> From sinking sand, he lifted me.
> With tender hand, he lifted me.
> From shades of night to plains of light,
> O praise his name, he lifted me! ("In Loving-Kindness
> Jesus Came")

Trust in the Lord with Conviction

PSALM 40:4-5

Standing on a solid and secure rock, David encourages those who "trust in the Lord" (vv. 3,4). Happiness or blessedness is on the way! VanGemeren says, "David blesses those who put their confidence in the covenantal God (v. 4), whose acts of protection are innumerable" (*Psalms*, 366).

Trust the Lord Who Is True to You (40:4)

The righteous person of Psalm 1 appears once again. He trusts in the Lord and is blessed by the Lord. He will not respect, trust in, or turn to the proud, those who foolishly trust in themselves instead of Yahweh. These people "run after lies!" They "turn aside to false gods" (NIV). To trust in yourself instead of Christ is to make yourself into a god and to commit the sin of idolatry. No, trust in the God who is trustworthy, reliable, and dependable. Trust the one whom 1 John 5:20 says "is the true God and eternal life" and the one Revelation 19:11 calls "Faithful and True."

Trust the God Who Thinks of You (40:5)

Our God is great and awesome, incomprehensible and beyond our full understanding. This is true on a cosmic level. It is true on a personal level too. David boldly confesses, "LORD [*Yahweh*] my God, you have done many things"—not a few things! David thinks of the Lord's "wondrous works and [his] plans for us." Meditating on all God's works, David confesses, "None can compare with you. If I were to report and speak of them, they are more than can be told." Spurgeon says, "Far beyond all human arithmetic they are multiplied . . . the list is too long for writing, and the value of the mercies too great for estimation" (*Treasury*, 237).

The past is full of the Lord's blessings, the present is complete with his care, and the future is abundant in his plans. This is the God we can trust with confidence and conviction. This is the God we can count on anytime, anyplace, in any and every moment of life.

Delight in the Lord with Consecration

PSALM 40:6-8

Here is the heart of this psalm, the pivotal point from which everything flows. Derek Kidner says verse 6 "anticipates the Servant prophecies and the New Covenant" (*Psalms 1–72*, 159). The author of Hebrews (10:5-7), using the interpretive key of Luke 24:25-27,44, sees these words fulfilled in the Messiah-King, Jesus Christ. Richard Belcher notes,

> The author of Hebrews placed these verses in the mouth of Christ. . . . Christ submitted himself fully to obey his Father's will and offered himself as the sacrifice on the cross so that he is able to affirm, "Behold I have come to do your will, O God." He presents himself to die on the cross. (*Messiah*, 176–77)

The words echo those of Samuel in his rebuke of Saul in 1 Samuel 15:22:

> *Does the Lord take pleasure in burnt offerings and sacrifices as much as in obeying the Lord? Look: to obey is better than sacrifice, and to pay attention is better than the fat of rams.*

Do Not Become Consumed with Externals (40:6)

Verses 6-8 present, in summation, the career of Jesus and provide believers a pattern for radical devotion and consecration to the will of God. Perhaps David had presented his sacrifice and offering before going into battle, atoning for his sin as well as the sin of the people whom the king often represented to God (VanGemeren, *Psalms*, 367). However, God desires more than mere formalism and routine ritualism. He wants you. He wants what the sacrifice and offering witness to. The psalmist responds in an interesting manner: "You open my ears to listen." A literal translation is, "Ears you have dug for me." Ross notes, "The focus is on the ears, but it refers to the whole person (a synecdoche); if God has the ear, it means the person is listening to God's instructions" (*Psalms 1–41*, 864). Hebrews 10:5, following the Septuagint, gives a paraphrase in terms of the meaning: "A body you have prepared for me." God has taken his servant as his own, opening his ears to hear, with a view to obeying the will of the Lord (v. 8). The servant's ears are open, not closed. Hearing God's word means he is available to the Lord in whole—not merely in terms of "sacrifice and offering," not merely in terms of "a whole burnt offering or a sin offering." David is the Lord's in body and soul. So was Jesus—perfectly! Here is the pattern for the sold-out and surrendered life to God (Rom 12:1-2). Calvin writes, "In token of his gratitude, [David] offers and consecrates himself entirely to God; as if he had said, I am now wholly devoted to God, because, having been delivered by his wonderful power, I am doubly indebted to him for my life" (*Psalms 36–92*, 98).

Know That What Counts Is Internal (40:7-8)

Because the servant of the Lord is committed to the Lord, finds his satisfaction in the Lord, and loves his Lord, he can simply say, "See, I have come" (NIV, "Here I am, I have come"). The idea is, "I am yours!" David writes, "In the scroll it is written about me." The Word of God is his manual, his guide, and the map of his life. David may have had in mind the royal charter for the conduct of a king found in Deuteronomy 17:14-20, which teaches us that the issues of the heart are paramount. These words also suggest the arrival of one whose coming is a fulfillment of Old Testament promise and expectation. Thus, Jesus can say in John 5:46, "Moses . . . wrote about me."

The servant of the Lord has a twofold declaration, a motto for life. First, "I delight to do your will, my God." Second, "Your instruction is deep within me." Here is the true new-covenant person of Jeremiah 31:31-34. All that matters in life is that he pleases God. He knows what pleases God because the Lord's law is in his heart. Oh, that our passion for God would be the passion of Christ who perfectly fulfilled these verses and who said in John 6:38, "For I have come down from heaven, not to do my own will, but the will of him who sent me."

Testify about the Lord with Courage

PSALM 40:9-10

John Piper says, "Our song is our evangelism . . . our joy in God is both our worship and our evangelism" ("Let All Who Seek Thee Rejoice and Be Glad in Thee"). The psalmist has experienced the "salvation" (v. 10) of the Lord. He cannot be silent about it. He must tell others, "The LORD is great!" (v. 16).

Tell of His Righteousness (40:9-10)

The salvation of the Lord is described in a fivefold manner: your "righteousness," your "faithfulness," your "salvation," your "constant love," and your "truth." David says, "I proclaim righteousness [i.e., God's righteous acts] in the great assembly [among those gathered for worship]; see, I do not keep my mouth closed. . . . I did not hide your righteousness in my heart." God had put a new song in David's heart (v. 3), which he now proclaims for all to hear. The righteous God saves and delivers! He redeems and he rescues! Those who trust him (vv. 3-4) will see his "wondrous works" (v. 5), his righteous acts of salvation, and they must tell others.

Tell of His Faithfulness (40:10)

Four additional aspects of good-news proclamation are now addressed, good news that "the great assembly" of God's people need to hear and never forget. David proclaimed God's righteousness in verse 9. Now he declares, "I did not hide your righteousness in my heart." Four wonderful attributes of the Lord are connected to this "righteousness:"

- Faithfulness—dependability, support, firmness
- Salvation—rescue, deliverance, safety, aid, help
- Constant love—(*chesed*) covenant love and loyalty
- Truth—reliability, trustworthiness to keep one's word

This is the awesome God of whom we testify among the people of God.

Plead with the Lord with Cause

PSALM 40:11-15

The tone now changes. It is as if a new crisis, a new situation of distress and danger, has arisen (VanGemeren, *Psalms*, 369). Even with the Lord's deliverance and direction, trouble is still lurking in the shadows where evil men operate. David prayed in verse 1 and was rescued. He will pray again and plead his cause with faith and confidence in the Lord. Given that "troubles without number have surrounded" him, he has no other hope than in the Lord. He has nowhere else to turn.

Ask for the Lord's Presence When Ambushed (40:11-12)

David asks for three things in verse 11: "compassion" (*racham*), "constant love" (*chesed*), and "truth" (*emet*). Note the prominence of the personal pronoun *your* indicating their source. Personally, and as the leader and representative of God's nation, David desperately needs all three of these to preserve (NIV, "protect") him. The Lord must not "withhold" them. He must "always guard" David with them. Why? Verse 12 has the answer.

First, "troubles without number have surrounded me." Second, "my iniquities have overtaken me." The result? David says, "I am unable to see." David was paralyzed and shut down as he bore the load of these sins. Third, "they are more than the hairs of my head," an intensification of the previous two declarations. Fourth, "my courage leaves me."

David did not see all this coming. So often we don't. We see neither where the attacks are coming from nor what will be their intensity. David knew his troubles were great, but he also knew God's compassion, love, and truth were greater.

Ask for the Lord's Protection When Attacked (40:13-15)

The theme of the Lord's protection develops in verses 13-15. When we are attacked, ambushed, and assaulted for doing the right thing in the right way, we can ask the Lord to protect us, putting the whole matter in his hands and refusing to take it on ourselves to render justice.

One can sense the urgency of David's prayer as well and his willingness to give things to the Lord. In verse 13 he cries, "Lord, be pleased to rescue me; hurry to help me." In verses 14-15 David makes his prayer specific. He again, in faith, entrusts the entire matter to the Lord. Note the repetition of the phrase *let those*. First, he says, "Let those who intended to take my life be disgraced and confounded." Foil their evil plans and show them their sin in what they do. Second, he says, "Let those who wish me harm be turned back and humiliated." This reinforces the first "let those." Third, David says, "Let those who say to me, 'Aha, aha!' be appalled because of their shame." "Aha" is a potshot, a slur of derision and contempt; it expresses malicious joy and delight over the misfortune of one's enemy (VanGemeren, *Psalms*, 371).

David asks God to shame and dishonor his foes, to confuse and confound them. David essentially says, "All they want is to take my life, do me evil, and ridicule me." Bottom-line, David says, "I want justice, what is right, but I will leave it all in your hands, Lord."

Rejoice in the Lord with Celebration

PSALM 40:16-17

In the final two verses we meet those, like David, who love, seek, rejoice in, and magnify the Lord. They display a beautiful balance. They know who God is, and they know who they are. One is mighty and magnificent. That is God. The other is "oppressed and needy." That is us.

Remember He Is Your Savior (40:16)

David prays that all who seek the Lord—a constant theme in the Psalms—will "rejoice and be glad." Further, those who love the Lord's salvation will respond in praise and declare, "The Lord is great [NASB, "exalted"]." Salvation moves us to praise the God who saves. To love his salvation is to love him. I do not love *the rock* (salvation) on which I stand. I love *the Lord* who put me on the rock!

Remember He Is Your Deliverer (40:17)

We have nothing to brag about or boast in when God saves. After all, we are "oppressed and needy." We have nothing and need everything. Amazingly, the Lord thinks about us (v. 17)—little, puny you and me—and does so with an intent to help and deliver. That is who he is. The Lord is "my helper." The Lord is "my deliverer." He is "my God." When we are in trouble and people would do us harm, we can plead, "My God, do not delay." Hurry! Come soon! Come quickly! But do it in your time, not mine, according to your plan and purpose, not mine. You were right on time on the third day with a glorious resurrection and an empty tomb for your Son. He trusted you. I believe I can trust you too.

Conclusion

What an amazing and delightful surprise Psalm 40 is! It portrays the career and commitment of Christ. Yet because we are in him, the psalm tells us a poignant and powerful word, a word of personal commitment and world evangelization. When we are in the pits and cry out to our King like helpless and hopeless children, he hears, and he answers. In response, we join our confession and declaration with that of King Jesus in verse 8: "I delight to do your will, my God." With a song in our hearts and a resolve of will to serve him anywhere, any way, and anytime, people will see him, fear him, and put their trust in him as they see lives sold out to do God's will. Is yours such a life? Will you say to King Jesus, "I delight to do your will, my God?" He died for us. We should be willing to do the same for him!

Reflect and Discuss

1. Describe some of the "wondrous works" God did for Israel (v. 5). What wondrous works has he done in your life? What happens if you forget God's past works for you?
2. How does one patiently wait on the Lord? What should you do as you wait?
3. In what ways does impatience indicate pride and unbelief?
4. Describe times in your life when God's timing was better than your timing.
5. If God did not allow his people to experience the "desolate pit" or the "muddy clay," how would their relationships with him be different?
6. If your testimony and experiences can be a witness that will bring others to the Lord, then how should you pray and think about your current experiences?
7. Can Christians voice trust in God but practically trust themselves? If yes, how so?
8. What externals are you most likely to be consumed with instead of being fully devoted to the Lord?
9. In what ways can joy lead to evangelism? How can this make evangelism seem less daunting?
10. Is it possible to be more focused on your salvation than on the God who saves you? If yes, how so?

The Blessing of Mercy

PSALM 41

Main Idea: God blesses those who exalt Jesus by giving and receiving his mercy.

I. You Will Be Blessed by Giving Mercy (41:1-3).
II. You Have Been Blessed by Receiving Mercy (41:4-13).

It is hard for us to understand the surprise, shock, and scandal of Jesus choosing Matthew. Out of all the twelve apostles, there was no more notorious sinner than Matthew (MacArthur, *Twelve Ordinary Men*, 151). The Jews were under the oppressive rule of the Romans, and one of the ways the Romans oppressed them was through taxation. A Jewish tax collector was someone who sided with the Romans in oppressing his own people. Beyond that, in order to line their own pockets, tax collectors notoriously collected more than was required. In other words, Matthew was a traitor and a crook. As has been pointed out,

> He was the worst of the worst. No self-respecting Jew in his right mind would ever choose to be a tax collector. He had effectively cut himself off not only from his own people, but also from his God. (MacArthur, *Twelve Ordinary Men*, 155)

We do not know for sure why Jesus chose Matthew, but Paul gives us a clue in 1 Corinthians 1. Paul tells us that God has chosen the foolish in order to shame the wise. That is exactly what we see with Matthew in Matthew 9. There is a party at Matthew's house, and it is filled with tax collectors and sinners. The Pharisees, in their normal passive-aggressive way, ask the disciples why Jesus would eat with people like this. Jesus, overhearing their question, answered them directly:

> *"It is not those who are well who need a doctor, but those who are sick. Go and learn what this means: I desire mercy and not sacrifice. For I didn't come to call the righteous, but sinners."* (Matt 9:12-13)

Jesus looked at the most learned religious leaders of the day and told them to go and learn something from Hosea 6. In all their religious education, they had missed something, and Jesus wanted them to go learn it. In all their training, they had missed mercy. They had missed the heart of God.

In his confrontation with the Pharisees, Jesus makes a profound statement: A head full of knowledge means nothing unless it comes with a heart full of mercy. There are many ways to define mercy, but mercy can be best understood in three words: seeing, feeling, and acting on behalf of undeserving people. It is compassion in action. It's exactly what Jesus showed to Matthew. Jesus saw him, felt for him, and acted on his behalf. The Pharisees had no category for mercy. They didn't receive it because they didn't think they needed it. They didn't give it because they didn't think anyone deserved it. Jesus made it very clear: if you miss mercy, you miss God. That is why we need Psalm 41.

Psalm 41 is about the blessing of mercy. It is about the blessing of giving and receiving mercy. Verses 1-3 function as instruction while verses 4-12 function as thanksgiving. They are bracketed in blessing. This reveals to us that mercy and blessing go together. More specifically, Psalm 41 shows us that God blesses those who give and receive mercy.

You Will Be Blessed by Giving Mercy

PSALM 41:1-3

Psalm 41 is the last psalm in the first book of the Psalms. This first book begins and ends with blessing. Psalm 1 and Psalm 41 both begin with a statement of the person who is "happy" or blessed. But what does the psalmist mean by the word *blessed* or *happy*? The blessing of the Psalms can best be understood as the joy, satisfaction, and benefits that come from walking with God (Futato, "Book of Psalms," 156). If you have walked closely with the Lord, you know exactly what that means. Even in the midst of struggle and uncertainty, joy and satisfaction come from walking in a right relationship with God. Being blessed is, as I (Josh) once heard a pastor say, a little taste of heaven on earth. It is a little taste of the life God intended for us to live. We will get the fullness of that blessing later, but God in his grace gives us a little taste of that joy, that satisfaction, and those benefits here on earth (Matt 5:3-10; Eph 1:3-14). That is blessing.

A life lived in surrender and obedience to the Lord has benefits. Psalm 1 makes this clear. The entire book of Proverbs makes this clear. Sin always complicates things. Anyone who has done just a little counseling will certainly have seen how sin makes everything messy. Deuteronomy 12:28 says it well: "Be careful to obey all these things I command you, so that you and your children after you may prosper forever." We must believe by faith that walking with God is the way of blessing.

Psalm 41:1 tells us that those who are "considerate of the poor" receive that kind of blessing from God. That word "considerate" means having compassionate concern and care. It means taking careful and thoughtful action (Johnston, *Psalms*, 419). It is not just a feeling; it is an act of sacrificial service. The "poor" who are referenced in that first verse are not just those who are financially poor but the weak, powerless, oppressed, overlooked, or marginalized (Motyer, *Psalms by the Day*, 108). This could be everyone from the poorest person in your community to the most overlooked person in your church. It is those who tend not to be seen—those who are not valued; the weak; the helpless.

My father loved the type of people who are mentioned in Psalm 41:1. It was almost as if he felt more at home with them than anyone else. Every church he pastored had a thriving bus ministry. When I was growing up, I distinctly remember our church filled with those who had been bused in from the poorest neighborhoods, the local cerebral palsy center, and the men's job corps. Although I didn't fully understand this when I was a child, looking back I realize how much Jesus loved to fill the house with those precious people. Matthew was like one of them. He was financially rich but poor in every other way. He, like the lepers, prostitutes, and lame, were not seen by the religious of the day. But Jesus saw them. He did not look past them; he looked at them. By seeing them, he placed value on them. That is because God is rich in mercy. He sees, feels, and acts on behalf of those who tend to be overlooked.

The call of Psalm 41:1 is to show mercy. The promise is that God blesses those who show this kind of mercy. God blesses those who really see those who are unseen. God blesses those who help the unseen know that they are loved by God and that the God who created them does see them. And the blessing of God is not just an internal satisfaction but has external benefits. God will "save [the merciful one] in a day of adversity," "keep him," "preserve him," "sustain him," and "heal him." This is not the promise of a life without trouble, but it is a promise that God will see and sustain us as we see others and show mercy to them.

We tend to take verses like this and spend most of our time talking about all the things they *don't* mean. When we do that, we often miss all that it *does* mean. One thing we can know for sure: God blesses those who bless others (Gen 12; Ps 67). According to the measure we show mercy, that same mercy will be shown back to us (Luke 6:38). It is not wrong to show mercy motivated by the promise of blessing. God blesses those who show mercy. But we should also be motivated by the fact all of us too are recipients of the same mercy.

You Have Been Blessed by Receiving Mercy

PSALM 41:4-13

David makes a transition in Psalm 41:4 and begins to reflect on his own neediness and poverty (Ps 40:17). He remembers his own season of suffering and the emotional, physical, relational, and spiritual toll it took on him (Pss 38–39). In that season David prayed for the Lord to be merciful to him, and in 41:4 he looks back on that time. He pleads for the Lord to see him, feel for him, and act on his behalf. David often prays this way. He often prays that God would give him what he does not deserve but what he so desperately needs. In verses 4-9 he recounts the way the Lord has done this for him.

When David was sick, God had mercy on him (v. 4). When David's enemies rose against him, God showed mercy to him (v. 5). When false rumors and hateful threats were coming at David, God had mercy (v. 6). When his enemies devised evil plans, and even those he trusted came against him, God showed mercy (vv. 7-9). In all these moments, the Lord showed mercy and raised him up (v. 10). Again and again God saw him, felt for him, and acted on his behalf. So now David remembers not only God's mercy but also the way God showed his delight in him. As he says in Psalm 18:19, "He brought me out to a spacious place; he rescued me because he delighted in me."

Psalm 41:10-12 is a great reminder that God does not save out of duty but out of delight. He is not obligated to save us; he loves saving us. He delights in our salvation. God sent his Son Jesus Christ so that our sins might be laid on him and our sinfulness might be exchanged for his righteousness. God saved us because he loves us and delights in us. From that moment on, God continues to show his mercy to us in a thousand different ways (Titus 3:4-7).

God's past work makes us confident about God's future work (Rom 8). The God who saved us and secured us is the God who will continue to do that until he takes us safely home. This is why David is confident that with God he will continue to walk in triumph (vv. 10-12). God treats us this way not because we deserve it but because God delights in showing mercy. We are what we are because we have been shown great mercy. We are recipients of a million mercies. In Christ, God saw us, felt for us, and acted on our behalf.

At the Last Supper, the night on which Jesus was betrayed, he alluded to Psalm 41:9 (Matt 26:20-25; Mark 14:18-21; Luke 22:21-23). Jesus was taking on himself the curse that we deserved so that we might get his blessing. He was being rejected in order that we might be eternally accepted. He felt the weight of our sin so that we might feel the full force of his blessing.

After both reflecting on the blessing of showing mercy and the blessing of receiving mercy, David cannot help but bless the Lord. He ends this psalm with praise to God for his everlasting kindness and mercy. In so doing, he reminds us just how blessed we are to have a God who continues to show us mercy in spite of our sins. How amazing to have a God who really sees us, who feels deeply for us, and who acts sacrificially on our behalf! God calls us to show the same mercy to others that we have received—not because we owe it to him or others but because in the same way God delights to show us mercy, we feel the blessing of God when we show mercy.

Conclusion

The Pharisees seemed to be blind to their own massive spiritual deficiencies. They didn't realize they had missed mercy and in turn were missing the Messiah. They seemed to be blind to the fact that in all their study, they missed the heart of God. That is a scary thing. It is frightening to think that we could study the Bible and yet miss the heart of God. One of the ways we fight the tendency to be like the Pharisees is to continually remind ourselves of just how much mercy we have been shown and then aggressively seek to show it to others. One way to continually test the condition of our hearts is to gauge how often we give thanks for the mercy we have received and how often we show others the mercy that has been shown to us.

Reflect and Discuss

1. Why do you think the Pharisees, despite all their knowledge of Scripture, missed the heart of God? How can we avoid the same fate?
2. Does the definition of blessing resonate with you? How have you experienced the joy, satisfaction, and benefits of walking with Jesus?
3. Have you ever had someone truly "see" you—someone who took the time to look beyond the surface and actually see how you are doing? If so, why is that such a powerful thing? Why is it so rare? Why don't we do the same more often?
4. This week, look for opportunities to show mercy. Take the time to see people, feel for them, and then act on their behalf. Right now, pray that God would open a door for you to show mercy.

When All Is Not Well with Your Soul

PSALMS 42–43

Main Idea: Since our souls are not always well, each must fight for a satisfied soul.

I. **Our Souls Are Not Always Well.**
II. **Each Must Fight for a Satisfied Soul.**

In 2018 a clinical study by the University of Portsmouth was published on a condition called "give-up-itis" (Leach, "Give-up-itis"). The real medical term for give-up-itis is "psychogenic death." It is when a person, after some major injury or tragedy, gives up the fight for life. Most of us have either seen or heard of someone who died after he or she just gave up the fight, and this clinical study shows us that there really is something medical behind it. The study showed that those who give up most often die within a matter of days. It also shows that a person who begins to give up goes through certain stages like withdrawal, apathy, and then emotional numbness. The most interesting part of the study is that it shows death is not inevitable for these people. At any stage they could reverse it, but they choose not to fight it.

As I (Josh) read the article on the study, I couldn't help but wonder how many believers struggle with give-up-itis of the soul. Maybe it starts with some kind of trauma, disappointment, heartbreak, or hurt. As a result, a person's soul begins to suffer, and he or she might even end up going through some of the same stages of withdrawal, apathy, and numbness. Slowly, such a person's soul feels like it is on life support, and the sufferer just starts slowly dying because he or she loses the desire to fight.

Over the years, I have seen this happen time and time again in people. But it doesn't have to be that way. It can be reversed. We can fight give-up-itis of the soul and flourish once again. That is why we need Psalms 42–43. These psalms, both addressing the condition of our souls, go together because of the repeated chorus. Psalms 42–43 are about the core of who we are—the most important part of us, the part from which everything flows. When a soul is unhappy, it affects everything else in life.

In 1871, Horatio Spafford, a wealthy business owner and faithful supporter of evangelist D. L. Moody, lost his entire livelihood as well as his four-year-old son in the Chicago fire. Not long after that event, as he began to rebuild his business, he boarded his wife and four daughters on a boat to head to Europe for vacation. He planned to finish up some business and meet them there shortly after. Tragically, he never saw his daughters again. The ship they were on wrecked, and his wife alone was saved. After that event, Spafford chose to write these words:

> When peace, like a river, attendeth my way,
> When sorrows like sea billows roll;
> Whatever my lot, Thou hast taught me to say,
> "It is well, it is well, with my soul."

The words of the hymn "It Is Well with My Soul" are some of the most comforting ever written. But what do we do when we find ourselves in a place of spiritual depression, when we feel totally unable to follow Spafford's example? Psalms 42–43 show us how spiritual depression happens and how we can fight it.

Our Souls Are Not Always Well

As you read these two psalms, notice the chorus that is repeated in 42:5,11 and 43:5: "Why, my soul, are you so dejected?" The word *dejected* means depressed, bent low, or in despair (Ross, *Psalms 42–89*, 22). The psalmist goes on to ask why his soul is in so much "turmoil." *Turmoil* means "disquiet" or "anxiety." In other words, his soul is not well. There is no "peace, like a river" attending his soul. In reality, it feels like his soul is raging like a sea (42:7). There is no peace, no sense of God's presence, no joy, and no rest.

Instead of just passively accepting this condition, he confronts it with a question: Why? It's an honest and important question. He is asking his soul why it feels this way. He honestly does not know why he finds himself in this condition. But he wants to know, and he wants to be restored. In that process of the psalmist asking the question and seeking to change the condition of his soul, we discover at least four potential reasons for this condition.

His soul may not be doing well because of **spiritual dryness and isolation**. Verses 1-2 are some of the most precious verses in the Psalms: "As a deer longs for flowing streams, so I long for you, God.

I thirst for God." Although this verse expresses a deep desire for God, it is also the cry of a longing soul. He is "thirsting" and "longing" like a deer that desperately needs water. In other words, this longing flows from a void. When we are thirsty, it is because our bodies are dehydrated. The longing of the soul flows from a sense that God is distant and the soul is parched. The psalmist expresses that at the end of verse 2 when he asks, "When can I come and appear before God?" Apparently, the psalmist has been unable to worship and has been separated from the assembly (42:4,9; 43:2-4). There has been a lack of corporate worship, a lack of fellowship, and a lack of joyful singing (43:4). Those seasons of spiritual isolation, without corporate worship, most often lead to spiritual dryness. And those seasons of spiritual dryness affect our souls.

His soul also might not be doing well because of **physical struggles**. When it comes to spiritual depression, it is difficult to know what is the cause and what is the symptom. Psalm 42:3 makes clear that he is not sleeping and not eating. No matter whether this is a cause or a symptom, such physical struggles affect our souls.

It could have also been **relational pressures**. There are those who are speaking against him (42:3) and those who are oppressing him (42:9). He has adversaries making life difficult for him (42:10). He also has enemies and deceitful persons coming after him (43:1-2). Few things can affect our souls more than relational tension and pressures.

His soul might also be struggling because of **his own natural disposition**. The Bible is filled with stories of men like David, Elijah, and Jeremiah who seemed to be more naturally disposed to fall into dark feelings. Church history tells of men like Martin Luther, William Cowper, and Charles Spurgeon who felt emotional struggles. The reality is, some people are more naturally disposed to them than others.

Apart from the spiritual, physical, relational, and personality contributors, unmet expectations, disappointment, hurt, or isolation may have led him into this season. The point is, our souls are not always well, and there can be many understandable and legitimate reasons for this. Life is hard, and things often pile up and snowball on us. A war is being waged for our souls (1 Pet 2:11), and these psalms remind us that we are not alone in seasons of spiritual depression. But the most helpful part of these psalms is the reality that we don't have to passively accept it; we can aggressively deal with it.

Each Must Fight for a Satisfied Soul

The psalmist is unquestionably and understandably struggling with a soul that is not well. This was not just in his mind; his soul was suffering. Thankfully, he not only noticed it, but he also decided to fight against it. He is not giving up. In reality, this entire psalm is a fight for a joyful and satisfied soul. It is as if the psalmist, feeling that he has fallen into what *Pilgrim's Progress* calls the "Slough of Despond," is clawing his way out of the pit. He refuses to stay there and wallow in his own spiritual depression. How do we fight for our souls when they are not well? These psalms give us three ways.

First, we fight for a satisfied soul by **stopping and asking**. The psalmist feels as if God has forgotten him (42:9). He knows it's not true (42:8), but he feels as if it's true. He does not ignore the feeling. He stops and asks why. Although most believers feel this way at some time, most fail to stop and simply ask the question, Why? When your soul is not well, be honest about it; don't ignore it. Tell it to God. Tell it to a trusted friend. As Psalm 42:4 says, pour out your heart to the Lord. Don't be afraid to be honest and ask the questions. Such seasons are a part of the process God is using to grow you and mold you and mature you. Stop and ask.

Second, we fight for a satisfied soul by **going after God**. When our souls are not well, we tend to ignore them or withdraw from God and others. In other words, we tend to be passive. But we must fight that temptation and instead go harder after God. The cry of Psalm 42:1 is a cry of longing and pursuit of God. It is interesting that in Psalm 42:7 the psalmist says, "Your breakers and your billows have swept over me." It implies that God has led him into this place in order to draw him nearer. Every disruption in our lives is an invitation to greater intimacy with God. Every time a soul pants for God, it's an invitation to drink and be satisfied. So when our souls are not well, we sing (42:8) and go to God's Word (43:3-4). We don't wallow in despair; we fight for our joy. We run after God.

Third, we must **preach to ourselves**. Three times the psalmist not only asks why his soul is in turmoil, but he also commands his soul to put its hope in God (42:5,11; 43:5). He starts with his feelings and then commands his soul to do what he knows is right. His own command for his soul to "hope in God" is a call to put his confidence in God, to believe in him, to trust in him. The opposite of hope in God is desperation in self.

When self-centered desperation sets in, we fight it with hope in God. We remind ourselves that we will once again praise him.

Martyn Lloyd-Jones deals with these two psalms and the idea of preaching to ourselves in these moments. He says,

> I suggest that the main trouble in this whole matter of spiritual depression in a sense is this—that we allow our self to talk to us instead of talking to our self. You have to take yourself in the hand, you have to address yourself, preach to yourself, question yourself. This self of ours, this other man within us, has got to be handled. Do not listen to him; turn to him; speak to him; condemn him; upbraid him; exhort him; encourage him; remind him of what you know, instead of listening placidly to him and allowing him to drag you down and depress you. (*Spiritual Depression*, 21)

We must preach to ourselves the truths of the gospel of Jesus Christ. Every moment we must continue to remind ourselves of the death, burial, and resurrection of Jesus Christ and the implications of that on our lives. We must teach ourselves to say with Horatio Spafford,

> My sin—oh, the bliss of this glorious thought:
> My sin—not in part but the whole
> Is nailed to the cross and I bear it no more,
> Praise the Lord, praise the Lord, O my soul!

We preach Ephesians 1 to ourselves and remind ourselves that we are blessed, loved, chosen, adopted, redeemed, and heirs of all the promises of God. We must preach Romans 8 to ourselves and remember that there is no condemnation for those who are in Christ Jesus, and there is nothing that can separate us from the love of God. The key to fighting spiritual depression is to daily remind ourselves of the truths of the gospel and who we are as the children of God.

Conclusion

Although the idea of "soul give-up-itis" might seem odd, it speaks of a constant temptation for every believer. Our souls are under constant attack, and our souls get tired and wounded. This is a normal part of the Christian life. As it happens, we have a sinful tendency to just passively sit by while our souls suffer. But when our souls suffer, everything else suffers. So instead of being passive, we must fight with all our might and in every moment for joyful and satisfied souls. We must tell ourselves the truth of the gospel and fight the good fight of faith. As each of us does, we all will be able to proclaim, "It is well with my soul."

Reflect and Discuss

1. Have you experienced moments in which you felt like the psalmist in Psalm 42:5? If so, can you identify anything that led to your soul feeling dejected?
2. What things in your life have a tendency to regularly wage war on your soul and make you depressed?
3. How have you responded in the past to seasons of spiritual depression?
4. Out of the three ways we fight spiritual depression, which one would be the most helpful for you right now?

More Than Conquerors

PSALM 44

Main Idea: Through the work of Jesus Christ on our behalf, we can be confident that all our suffering is a part of God's plan to do something great in our lives.

I. A Confusing Circumstance (44:1-22)
II. A Conflicting Conclusion (44:23-26)
III. A Christian's Clarity (Romans 8)

Do you know the feeling you get when you casually ask someone how they are doing and then, surprisingly, they respond in a way that is uncomfortably honest? Or that feeling you get when, in the middle of a lighthearted conversation mostly filled with small talk, the person you are talking to turns the conversation to something shockingly heavy? That's a bit of how you feel when you read Psalm 44.

When you first begin to read it, you get a feel for where you think the conversation is going. It is uplifting, encouraging, and full of praise. After Psalms 42–43, the change of tone is refreshing. The sons of Korah sing praise not only for what God has done for the people of God in the past but also for what God has done for them personally. The people are so filled with praise that they declare, "We boast in God all day long; we will praise your name forever" (v. 8).

Just when you think you have gotten the feel and direction of the psalm, it completely changes. In one verse it moves from "boasting all day long" and "prais[ing] your name forever" to "you have rejected and humiliated us" (v. 9) and "You sell your people for nothing" (v. 12). Seemingly out of nowhere, the song turns shockingly heavy. Psalm 44 is raw. It is honest. And it can feel a bit troubling.

Psalm 44 is just an honest expression of a common dilemma. Psalm 44 describes the moments in which life just does not make sense. It describes the times when our circumstances make it seem as if God has forgotten us or has turned against us. It is about those moments in life in which our situations do not seem to match our theology. If you have walked with Jesus very long, you have had moments like that. In those moments, we need Psalm 44.

We do not know the specific context of this psalm, but the situation is clear. It recounts the seasons of great victories, miracles, and supernatural moments (vv. 4-8). It remembers those wonderful seasons in which it just feels like God is blessing us, he is with us, and he is for us—those seasons in which we can almost feel the wind of the Spirit behind us. But then, in a moment, something happened and everything changed. Instead of victories, we have defeats (v. 9). Instead of feeling loved, we feel deserted (v. 12). Instead of feeling exalted, we feel humiliated (v. 14). Although such a new season is not nearly as enjoyable as the previous season, the pain of the moment is not the real issue. The real issue is the confusion of the moment. This new season is confusing. It does not match with our theology. And this psalm shows us how a confusing circumstance can lead to a conflicting conclusion if we are not confident in who we are in Christ.

A Confusing Circumstance

PSALM 44:1-22

The psalm begins with the sons of Korah remembering all the stories their parents taught them (vv. 1-3). Children need to hear the stories of what God has done in the past, and these children had heard them. They were told about Moses crossing the Red Sea, Joshua conquering Jericho, and David defeating Goliath. Those stories cultivated in them a deep conviction: our God can do what no one else can do (v. 3). They also understood that God did these things because the Lord was "favorable toward them" (v. 3).

If the stories from the saints of the past were not enough, they had their own stories of God's miraculous works. In verses 4-8 they move from "they" to "we." The children too had driven back their foes and trampled down their enemies (v. 5). Even in their own lives they understood that it was not them but the Lord who had done all these things on their behalf (vv. 5-8). Like their ancestors, they trusted in the Lord, the Lord blessed them, and he gave them the victory. Through these circumstances, they had become convinced that this is how it works with the Lord: as long as you trust the Lord, the Lord blesses you and always gives you the victory. That belief is what made this new season so confusing.

In verses 9-16 the psalm turns to their current circumstances, and instead of the praise going to God for the wonderful things he had done, the blame now goes to God for all their current defeats. The psalmist says,

> *You have rejected and humiliated us; you do not march out with our armies. You make us retreat from the foe. . . . You hand us over to be eaten like sheep. . . . You sell your people for nothing; you make no profit from selling them. . . . You make us a joke among the nations.* (vv. 9-12,14)

They were mad. They were confused (Lane, *Psalms 1–89*, 201).

A Conflicting Conclusion

PSALM 44:23-26

What made this current season of defeat so difficult is that, in their minds, they didn't deserve it. God had rejected them while they had been faithful to him. "All this happened to us, but we have not forgotten you or betrayed your covenant. Our hearts have not turned back; our steps have not strayed from your path. But you have crushed us" (vv. 17-19). In other words, this is not the way they expected to be treated. This experience does not match what they had seen in the past. They delight in God, but God does not seem to bless them or give them the victory. So now, instead of boasting in the Lord, they are complaining to the Lord.

It seems that somehow, in the midst of their learning of God's work in the distant past and experiencing God's work in the recent past, they had developed a certain understanding of how God works. It just made sense: if all their victories were because God delighted in them and was fighting for them, then all their defeats must be because God was angry with them and fighting against them. They simply did not know how else to process this difficult season. They did not have a category for it. They had not changed, but thought God had. They had remained faithful, but thought God had not. Their paradigm for how to gain victory was falling apart.

As a result of their paradigm crumbling, they were convinced that God was asleep or had rejected them (v. 23). They believed that God was either intentionally hiding from them or had just chosen to ignore them (v. 24). They were lying face down, clinging to the ground, filled with confusion (v. 23), and begging God to wake up and help them once again (vv. 25-26).

One of the most helpful things about the psalms is that they give us the freedom to be honest. The psalms remind us that we are not alone in how we are feeling. This situation here is familiar to most Christians—we all eventually face moments in which our circumstances don't seem to match up with our theology. We have been faithful, for instance, and as a result expected victories and blessings. Psalm 44 shows us that sometimes that formula does not prove out. Suffering is not always an indication that God has turned against us.

In one sense, there are a lot of psalms like this. There are many laments. But this one is different. Almost every psalm of lament ends with a resolution. The complaint will end with a statement of praise and trust. Psalms 42–43 are great examples of this. While feeling as if our souls are downcast, there is a settled confidence that we will once again praise the Lord. But we don't get that in Psalm 44. There is no resolution. It just leaves us with a believer who is facedown, begging God to wake up. Apart from the comfort of knowing someone else has felt like we have, there does not seem to be much help here. But as we look closer, we can find some deep encouragement from Psalm 44.

A Christian's Clarity

ROMANS 8

There is, in Psalm 44:22, a little glimmer of hope for these confusing moments that try to convince us that God has turned against us or forgotten us. In the darkest lines of this psalm, there is a strong accusation against the Lord. Verse 22 says, "Because of you we are being put to death all day long; we are counted as sheep to be slaughtered." If that verse sounds familiar, it is because the apostle Paul used it in Romans 8.

Paul had been building a case for the church in Rome—based on the fact that they had been justified by God, had peace with God, were alive to God, and released from slavery for God—that now God was eternally for them. Because of what has been done for us through the death and resurrection of Jesus Christ, there is now no condemnation for us believers. Through Christ we have new life in the Spirit and are made his children. The God who saved us is the God who secures us and ensures that we make it to glory. Because of Christ we know, if God is for us, no one and nothing can stand against us.

But what do we do with our suffering? How do we explain that? That is exactly what Paul addresses in Romans 8:31-35. He asks the question we are all asking: What about affliction or distress or persecution or famine or nakedness or the sword (8:35)? Can those things separate us from the love of God? Do those things mean that God has forgotten us or turned against us? Then Paul quotes Psalm 44:22. As Paul thought about how to help us process our suffering, he thought of Psalm 44. He brought us back to a blunt mention of the times in which it feels as if God has forgotten us—of the circumstances that are confusing and the conflicting conclusions that often follow. He knows we will all experience the feeling of Psalm 44.

After bringing our minds back to the confusion described there, Paul immediately says, "No, in all these things we are more than conquerors through him who loved us" (Rom 8:37). What does he mean by "these things"? He means all the Psalm 44 things. He means all the confusing moments in which we feel as if God has forgotten us. Even in those moments, we are not separated from the love of God in Christ Jesus. Here, in Romans 8, as Paul quotes Psalm 44, we find some Christian clarity. Seeing Psalm 44 as a New Testament believer, in light of Romans 8, tells us exactly what we do when "these things" come into our lives and tempt us to lose confidence in God (Schreiner, *Romans*, 464).

First, we must remember that "these things" are an inevitable reality of life. Paul uses Psalm 44:22 to describe our own Christian experience. We must be mentally and spiritually prepared for these situations, because we will experience some defeats and difficulties. We must not be surprised by these moments. They are an inevitable part of life in a broken world.

Second, we must remember that these things do not mean God is against us. Even in all those seasons, we must remember that as blood-bought believers, our suffering does not mean God has turned against us. Romans 8:37 makes clear that even in those things God is for us.

Third, we must remember that as believers, we will always prevail over these things. Psalm 44 ends without resolution; Romans 8 does not. Romans 8:37 tells us that in all those things we are more than conquerors. We are overwhelmingly conquerors. God will always use even the hardest, most tragic moments for our good and his glory.

Finally, we must remember that bad circumstances never mean that God has stopped loving us. Romans 8:37-39, using the experience of Psalm 44 as an example, reminds us that even in these confusing moments, in which God seems to have forgotten us, he is eternally committed to us and nothing can separate us from his love. In the moments we begin to doubt, we must remind ourselves of how God has shown us that kind of love through Christ.

Conclusion

One of the lessons God often teaches us in our suffering is that our theology of suffering needs to be strengthened. He often graciously exposes our unbiblical paradigm of how he works. God will remind us that our suffering is not an indication that he has fallen asleep, even if it feels like it at times. God will teach us a more helpful theological foundation. God will show us, in these moments, that through the work of Jesus Christ on our behalf, we can be confident that all our suffering is a part of God's plan to do something great in our lives. If we ever doubt it, we should stop and feast on the promises that are ours in Romans 8.

Reflect and Discuss

1. Have you ever had seasons of life in which you felt like the believers in Psalm 44? If so, how did those seasons make you question God?
2. Discuss with other believers how tough seasons have affected them and their own relationships with the Lord.
3. Make a list of the truths of Romans 8 and how they relate to those seasons of suffering. How do those truths encourage you?
4. Specifically, think about the way your relationship with Jesus brings clarity and hope to every season of suffering and share about that with a friend.

Our Wedding Song

PSALM 45

Main Idea: Jesus is the anointed King who will come and rescue his bride.

I. A Song for the Groom (45:1-9)
II. A Song for the Bride (45:10-17)
III. A Song for the Church

Have you ever wondered why generation after generation is drawn to the same fairy tales? The ones we love so much are the same ones that have been told and retold for centuries. Every year new movies tell the same stories in more sophisticated and dramatic ways. There are some obvious reasons we love these stories so much. For boys, there are battles to win, swords to wield, horses to ride, dragons to slay, and enemies to destroy. For girls, there are beautiful dresses to wear, a prince who rescues, and the perfect ending.

These stories resonate with us. They point to a larger story that we want to be a part of. They paint pictures of the people we want to be. And it's not just because they are compelling narratives. It's because God has created us to be a part of a story like Cinderella's, for instance. In some way, we long for her happy ending because God has put that story in our hearts. It's the story of the Bible, and it's the story of Psalm 45.

The superscription of Psalm 45 says that it's a love song. More specifically, it is a song that would have been sung at the wedding of a king. Verse 1 sets the tone. The writer of the love song says, "My heart is moved by a noble theme as I recite my verses to the king; my tongue is the pen of a skillful writer" (v. 1). The tone of joy, celebration, and anticipation is set. The king is about to get married, and the people cannot wait to sing this wedding song.

A Song for the Groom

PSALM 45:1-9

The first part of the song is a celebration of the king, the groom. The songwriter wants us to picture him in our minds. He's described in great detail in four primary ways. First, he is a man of commanding presence. Verse 2 says, "You are the most handsome of men." This might be better translated, "You are the most excellent of men" (Ross, *Psalms 42–89*, 67). This is certainly a reference to his physical appearance, but it is more than that. He is striking in his appearance. He is noticed when he walks into the room. He speaks with eloquence, authority, and grace. He appears to be obviously blessed by God.

Second, he is a man of great military strength. The sword strapped on his side is not just for show. He is a "mighty warrior" (v. 3). He is a warrior-king who is majestic in splendor and ready to do battle. When he fights, he wins (v. 5). He defeats his enemies, and he hits his targets. His acts of warfare are "awe-inspiring" (v. 4).

Third, he is a man of noble character. Not only does he fight, but he also fights for the right causes—"the cause of truth, humility, and justice" (v. 4). He loves what is right and hates what is wrong (v. 7). He defends his people and sacrifices on their behalf.

Finally, he is a joyful king. The psalmist talks about his throne, scepter, robes, palaces, kingdom, and anointing. This is certainly a song written for a king. Up to this point, given his commanding presence, military strength, and noble character, we might picture this man as a little stoic and stern. Verse 7 shatters that image. This king has been anointed "with the oil of joy more than [his] companions," meaning he has been given superabundant joy. Supernatural gladness has been poured out on him. Not only is this wedding a source of great joy, but the groom is also a man of contagious joy.

A Song for the Bride

PSALM 45:10-17

After a lengthy celebration in song over the groom, the attention turns to the bride in verses 10-17. Just picture this scene: the bride is in her chamber getting ready for her groom to arrive. Her friends are around her, the anticipation palpable. In that moment she receives some wedding advice (vv. 10-12). The advice can be summed up in three statements. First, she is told not to look back (v. 10). She is to leave and cleave. She is to let go of her family and give herself fully to her husband. Second, she is told to honor her husband (v. 11). She is to look to him, love him, bless him, and respect him. Finally, she is told to look ahead with hope (v. 12). She is to be encouraged and confident that the Lord will do good in her life. Now, having received the last bit of advice, she is beautifully adorned and ready for the wedding (v. 13).

At this point, it would be helpful to give some cultural context. In ancient times, the first step in the wedding would be the betrothal. This is different from a modern engagement. In a betrothal, two families would enter into an agreement that was viewed as more like an unbreakable covenant. Although the wedding was not official, nor would it have been consummated until the wedding day, the betrothal made the wedding as good as done. On the wedding day, the friends and family of the bride and groom would gather at their homes while they prepared for the ceremony. The groom would lead his friends and family on a joyful procession through the streets to the bride's house. He would then take his bride as well as her friends and family and lead them back in joyful procession to his home. They would feast for days (Boice, *Psalms 42–106*, 381). That is what is happening here. The groom will come and take his bride in joyful procession to enter the king's palace (v. 15).

Finally, a blessing is given to the couple that their marriage will produce offspring and that those children will rule throughout the land (v. 16). They will have a great name and be remembered for all generations (v. 17). They will be blessed and honored forever and ever. This is a fitting ending to a joyful moment of celebration.

A Song for the Church

Psalm 45 paints an impressive picture. From the glory of the groom to the beauty of the bride, every bit of this song is a worthy tribute to a joyful occasion. This psalm feels like a fairy tale, and we love it. We love it because God has put it in our hearts. We are drawn to stories like this because God is inviting us into a story like this. As strange as it might sound, this is not just a wedding song for a groom or a wedding song for a bride; this is a wedding song for the church. What makes this psalm significant is that this is not just their wedding song; this is our wedding song.

Psalm 45 is a messianic psalm, meaning it finds its ultimate fulfillment in the person of Jesus Christ. Any time a psalm gives praise and glory to a king, it is pointing forward to the ultimate King, Jesus Christ.

Even more than that, Psalm 45:6 says that this king is both God and man; it says, "Your throne, God, is forever and ever; the scepter of your kingdom is a scepter of justice." This is not just any king. This is pointing us to King Jesus. If that is not convincing enough, we know this is speaking of Jesus because in Hebrews 1, when the author talks about the superiority of Jesus, he quotes Psalm 45:6-7 (Heb 1:8-9). Jesus is in fact the ultimate anointed King who will come to take his bride.

When we read Psalm 45 with Jesus in mind, we are reminded that Jesus is in fact the one of commanding presence, military strength, and noble character. He is the joyful King who is waiting to come and take his bride. This is Jesus! And the church is his bride. The church—those who have become his by faith in his death and resurrection—is the bride who is awaiting the groom to come and take them home (Eph 5:32; Rev 19).

In his first coming, he came to rescue his bride from death, sin, and hell. He came to give his life as a ransom for many. As we come to him by faith, the Bible says we are betrothed to him (2 Cor 11:2). We are not married, but it is as good as done. The time of consummation has not yet arrived, but God has made a promise that it will. Now, like the bride of Psalm 45, we trust in his promise to return, and we prepare ourselves for the wedding. One day he will leave his throne, dressed for battle, and with a joyful procession he will rescue us and take us home, where we will feast with him at the marriage supper of the lamb. He will come, as verses 16-17 say, and bring many sons to glory who will rule and reign with him forever and ever.

How do we respond to this truth? The same way the bride in Psalm 45 responded. While we wait for Christ to return, we don't look back, we honor Christ, and we look ahead with hope. We, like the bride, leave and cleave. We turn from sin and follow Christ completely. Like the bride, we strive to submit to Christ, love him, and honor him above all others. We give ourselves fully to Christ and his kingdom. And we hold onto the hope that one day Christ will return and take us home, where our salvation will be complete and we will rule and reign with him forever.

Reflect and Discuss

1. When you imagine Jesus, how do you picture him? Does your picture fit with the image of Psalm 45? Do you see Jesus as a joyful King?

2. Out of the four descriptions of King Jesus in Psalm 45, which is most encouraging and helpful to you at this moment in your life? Why?
3. As the bride of Christ, we should heed the instruction given to the bride in Psalm 45:10-12. Which one of those three responses is the most challenging for you?
4. In what ways can you choose to trust and follow the Lord more faithfully as you await his return?

A Mighty Fortress

PSALM 46

Main Idea: God is a fortress from our greatest fears.

I. **His Protection Makes Us Courageous (46:1-3).**
II. **His Presence Makes Us Glad (46:4-6).**
III. **His Position Makes Us Rest (46:7-10).**
IV. **The Lord of Armies (46:7,11)**

One of the most precious and glorious promises ever given to the church is found in Matthew 16:18. Jesus said, "On this rock I will build my church, and the gates of Hades will not overpower it." That verse gives us the absolute confidence that Christ—along with his church—will ultimately prevail. We often fail to see in that verse that the promise of protection points to the possibility of danger. In other words, that promise also tells us that the gates of hell are going to try to prevail against us. Satan and all his minions will try, throughout every generation, to prevail against the church.

I don't know about you, but I feel it. I feel the darkness trying to overpower the light. At times the darkness around us can cause us to be afraid. Maybe this is why the most common command in all of Scripture is, "Fear not." The Lord knew that when the darkness tries to overtake us we could tend to be afraid. But, in God's glorious providence, he has taken one of our primary challenges—fear—and used it to continually drive us to himself, where we find him sufficient to meet every challenge and every fear we face. And, through the constant promises and assurances and commands of the Lord, we are reminded that even when the gates of hell try to prevail against us, we do not have to be afraid because the Lord is our fortress. That is the glorious promise of Psalm 46.

During the prophetic ministry of Isaiah, the entire Near East lived in fear of the Assyrians. They were a brutal and barbaric people, intent on taking over. The Assyrians used both psychological and physical threats to weaken and destroy their opponents. They would often surround cities and send messengers into them to taunt the people and encourage them to surrender. If the people did not, the Assyrians would then invade, setting houses on fire, and murdering or raping the inhabitants. Isaiah had already watched as this happened to Israel; now the Assyrians were looking to conquer Judah.

A messenger was sent from the king of Assyria to Hezekiah telling him to surrender (Isa 37:17-20). The king of Assyria also sent messengers to tell the people that no god had ever saved anyone from him, and they must not listen to King Hezekiah if he should tell them to trust the Lord (Isa 36:13-20). So King Hezekiah does the only thing he knows to do. When it seems the Assyrian king will soon prevail and even sends him a letter to assure him of that, Hezekiah lays it on the altar, gets on his face before God, and begs God for help. That night, after Hezekiah had prayed, the angel of the Lord went outside the gates of Jerusalem and killed 185,000 of the Assyrian soldiers.

Most commentators agree that out of that situation, the people of God wrote Psalm 46 (Boice, *Psalms 42–106*, 391). The hymn is three stanzas and one chorus. The chorus (vv. 7,11) speaks to the primary message of the psalm—the Lord is with us; God is our fortress. The message of the psalm is clear: God is a fortress from our greatest fears. When it feels as if the gates of hell have come against us and we are terribly afraid, the Lord is our fortress. When it appears that there is no way out and defeat is imminent—when you are backed into a corner and there is no escape—in those moments the Lord is our fortress. Psalm 46 gives us three truths to show us how the Lord saves us from all our fears.

His Protection Makes Us Courageous

PSALM 46:1-3

The first stanza of this song is a testimony to the Lord's protection. The Lord is first of all seen as a "refuge." This means that the Lord shields us when we are in danger (Motyer, *Psalms by the Day*, 121). It is significant that the text says, "God is our refuge," because our protection is only as good as a refuge is strong. There is a difference in finding refuge in a bounce house, a tree house, or a beach house. The fact that our refuge is God himself means that when we need shelter, safety, and strength, we find those things in the Lord!

God is also seen in verse 1 as a present helper in our time of need. Now the difficulty of having the Lord as our refuge is that you cannot physically see him, like you could a castle or fortress. Yet the benefit of having the Lord as our refuge is that he is always right there. You do not have to run far to find a refuge in the Lord. Our refuge is only good if we can get there in time, and since the Lord is "always found," we can run to him at any moment.

Our response to this reality should be that "we will not be afraid." The reality of God's strength combined with the reality of his nearness should cause us never to be afraid because we know we can run to him at any moment and be saved. When this truth settles in our hearts, it gives us an unshakable courage—a courage that can withstand the crumbling of the mountains around us and the sea welling up on top of us. When our whole world seems to be falling in around us, we can run to the Lord and find courage in the safety of his shelter.

The promises of Psalm 46:1-3 are much like the one Jesus gives in Matthew 16:18, that the gates of Hades will not overpower the church. The reality of the promise points to the possibility of danger. The reason we need a strong fortress we can run to at any moment is because our lives will often feel like verses 2-3. We will often feel as if the entire world is crashing in on us. Whether it's caused by a natural disaster, a global pandemic, or a devastating diagnosis, each of us will at times feel as if our entire world is falling apart. We will be afraid. But, even "though" (vv. 2-3) everything feels like chaos around us, there is a refuge where we can run to find courage. That refuge is great enough to handle any fear we might have. The protection of the Lord makes us courageous.

His Presence Makes Us Glad

PSALM 46:4-6

Not only does his protection make us courageous, but his presence makes us glad. The second stanza (vv. 4-6) contains a massive contrast in feelings. The nations are raging, the kingdoms are toppling, the earth is melting, but the people of God are assured by the presence of God. In the midst of all the raging and all the chaos and all the fears, there are a river and streams (v. 4). This river is a metaphor for the presence of God that brings refreshment and joy to his people (Goldingay, *Psalms 42–89*, 69).

Ever since Genesis 2, a river has been a symbol of God's presence. The rivers flowing into and out of the garden of Eden remind us that abundant life flows from the presence of God (Beale and Kim, *God Dwells*, 20). Psalm 46 gives us a picture of the presence of God like a calming river that flows through nations as they seem to be crumbling to the ground. The presence of God is like a calm river in the midst of turmoil. The presence of the Lord brings gladness to our hearts in the midst of danger. As Psalm 16:11 says of God, "In your presence is abundant joy." This is why there is emphasis on the "dwelling place of the Most High" (46:4). When it feels as if the world is falling apart around us, we must know that God is there, and his presence gives us joy in the midst of the chaos. We must go to the river and drink from the satisfying reality of his presence.

His Position Makes Us Rest

PSALM 46:8-10

The third stanza of this song focuses on the position of the Lord as the sovereign God. The simple words "I am God" in verse 10 are enough to give us rest. The Lord looks at us in our fears and says, "I am God." Our God is exalted and ruling and reigning over all things. Just so we might have our hearts filled with restful confidence in God's position, the psalmist invites us to "come, see the works of the LORD." This is an invitation to see for ourselves what God has done.

Think about this in terms of the threat of the Assyrians. After the angel of the Lord showed up, there were 185,000 dead soldiers outside the city walls. Their camp was filled with bows, spears, and empty wagons. The only way to dispose of the mess was to burn it. The psalmist invites us to come and see as the smoke is ascending to the sky—every billow a reminder that the Lord is the one who makes wars cease and shatters bows and cuts spears (v. 9). Every page of Scripture is an invitation to come and behold the works of the Lord. Time and time again the Lord has revealed his sovereign rule.

There is only one command in Psalm 46. It is found in verse 10. After affirming the Lord's protection, presence, and position, the psalmist commands us to "stop." Psalm 46:10 says, "Stop fighting, and know that I am God, exalted among the nations, exalted on the earth." This is not a call to silence. It is not a call to meditation. It is not a call just to be still. It is, as the CSB translates it, a call to stop! It is a call for the nations to stop fighting and rebelling against the Lord. And it is a call for the people of God to stop their worrying and fretting. It is a call to stop and know that the Lord of Armies is our God, and he will be exalted.

The Lord of Armies

PSALM 46:7,11

The psalm ends with the chorus. It has already been sung in verse 7, and now it is repeated in verse 11. The chorus says, "The LORD of Armies is with us; the God of Jacob is our stronghold." The idea of the "LORD of Armies"—or "LORD of Hosts" as it is often translated—is used over two hundred times in the Old Testament. It means that our God is a warrior, and he rules over all the armies of the world and in heaven. No commander is stronger, and nothing can come against him that has power greater than his. The Lord is working all things together according to his will (Rom 8:28). The fact that God is our stronghold means that the Lord is our place of safety. He is our fortress. This is Israel's testimony. They saw it. They experienced it. Psalm 46 is inviting us to learn from their testimony and live with the settled assurance that even if the gates of hell try to prevail against us, God is a fortress to protect us from all fears.

Reflect and Discuss

1. As a means of reflection, look up the lyrics to "A Mighty Fortress" by Martin Luther and meditate on them.
2. How have you seen the Lord show himself strong in your own life? How have you seen him deliver you from fear?
3. In what times have you supernaturally experienced gladness and rest when your situation seemed chaotic or terrifying?

The Sovereign Rule of King Jesus

PSALM 47

Main Idea: Jesus Christ is the sovereign King over the whole earth.

I. We Spread This Truth through Aggressive Missions (47:1-4).
II. We Celebrate This Truth through Joyful Worship (47:5-7).
III. We Rest in This Truth through Hopeful Expectation (47:8-9).

God has a marvelous way, as we walk with him, of taking us through certain experiences or circumstances in order for us to personally experience something we have known to be true of him. He will use these moments not only to reveal himself to us but also to make himself feel more real and more personal than he ever seemed before. Through those times we move beyond just *knowing about* God to actually *knowing* God. Everyone who has walked with God for any amount of time has experienced moments like that. Sometimes these experiences are joyful, and sometimes they are painful. It can be everything from the birth of a child to a surprising diagnosis. No matter what the circumstance is, there is something beautiful about these moments because, in them, God becomes more real in our minds.

The Bible is a record of those kinds of moments. The Bible tells us of real people who had real experiences with a real God. It tells us how God invades the lives of people in order to show them who he really is. One of those moments happened around 700 BC while Hezekiah was king of Judah. The entire known world lived under the threat of the brutal and barbaric Assyrians. Hezekiah had already watched as the Assyrians invaded the northern kingdom of Israel, and now the Assyrians set their sights on the southern kingdom of Judah. Outside of Jerusalem were more than 185,000 Assyrian soldiers ready to attack. To put that in perspective, that is almost the exact same size as the entire active duty United States Marine Corps.

The Assyrians were known not only for their brutal physical warfare but also for their taunting psychological warfare. In their normal style, they sent messengers to Jerusalem to taunt the people and to tell them it was useless to listen to King Hezekiah or to ever think that their God could save them (Isa 36:13-20). They mocked the people, their God, and their king. They assured the people that no king or any god had ever saved people from the power of the king of Assyria. Then they sent a letter directly to King Hezekiah telling him to spare the battle and surrender.

When Hezekiah received the letter, he did the only thing he knew to do. He took the letter, went to the temple, laid the letter before God, and prayed (Isa 37:14-20). He asked the Lord to save them for the sake of his own name so that all peoples might know that their God is in fact God over all things. That night, the angel of the Lord went into the Assyrian camp and killed 185,000 of the troops that were about to invade. The king of Assyria then went home, and while he was worshiping his god, his son killed him. In all this, Hezekiah and the nation saw God reveal himself as the all-powerful sovereign King over the whole earth. In that season they not only knew it; they had also experienced it. God's sovereign rule was personal to them. It was probably in response to that that the sons of Korah wrote Psalms 46–47.

Psalm 47 celebrates the sovereign rule of the King of the universe. As New Testament believers, we know that this King is in fact King Jesus, which means that Psalm 47 is actually celebrating the sovereign rule of King Jesus over the whole earth. Jesus rules over all things, and nothing is outside of his control. Psalm 47 not only reminds us of this foundational truth, but it also shows us how to respond to that truth. If it is true that our King, Jesus Christ, is in fact the King over the whole earth, how should that change the way we live? Psalm 47 gives us three appropriate responses to the rule and reign of King Jesus.

We Spread This Truth through Aggressive Missions

PSALM 47:1-4

When the Assyrian army came into Judah to warn the people, they taunted them and assured them that there has never been a god who could stand against the king of Assyria. Then, in one night, it was made clear that there is in fact no king who has ever stood against Israel's God. As you read that story, it just feels like their response should have at least contained a little bit of taunting and gloating. Maybe even a little "Na Na, Hey Hey, Kiss Them Goodbye!" Instead, they responded by calling the Assyrians, and all peoples, to respond to their God and be saved.

"Clap your hands, all you peoples; shout to God with a jubilant cry" is not just an invitation; it is a command. It is a command for all nations to celebrate and praise God. Why? "For the LORD, the Most High, is awe-inspiring, a great King over the whole earth." God has revealed his universal kingship; therefore, all peoples must respond to him (Futato, "Book of Psalms," 170). The call to fear the Lord is a call to submit to the authority of the Lord. This is a call to be saved!

The psalmist continues to urge the nations to respond to the Lord by building his case in verses 3-4. The Lord has revealed his sovereign rule by subduing peoples and putting nations under Israel's feet. God has made his sovereignty known; therefore, all people should submit to him and be saved. He cannot be ignored. He cannot be defeated. He alone can save. He alone is a safe refuge.

The authority of the Lord Jesus Christ is one of the truths that calls us into aggressive missions. In Matthew 28:18, before giving his commission, he establishes his authority. Among other reasons, he does this to remind us that the breadth of our mission should extend to the breadth of his authority. If Jesus has authority over all nations, then all nations must hear the gospel and respond. Psalm 47 also reminds us that the heartbeat of missions is to spread the true worship of God all over the world; as Psalm 67 says, we want to spread the joy of the Lord to the ends of the earth (Piper, *Let the Nations Be Glad*, 40).

God saved his people from the Assyrians in order that his name might be made known, and he has saved us for the same reasons. He has saved us that we might make his name known to all peoples. Since Jesus has established his authority over the whole earth, we must be aggressive to tell all people about King Jesus and call them to submit to him and be saved.

We Celebrate This Truth through Joyful Worship

PSALM 47:5-7

When reading and interpreting Scripture, it is imperative not only to understand the meaning of the text but also to sense the emotion of the text. The emotion of Psalm 47 is one of exuberant and joyful celebration. The people had just seen the supernatural salvation the Lord accomplished on their behalf, and in response they are clapping, shouting, and singing. Verses 3-7 are filled with personal pronouns because the sovereign rule of their King has become personal to them. So has their response. This psalm is an authentic and joyful celebration of God's revelation of himself to them.

In verses 5-7 there are five calls to sing praises to the Lord. The fourfold repetition of the call to "sing praise" indicates that the singing, clapping, dancing, and praising went on and on (Lane, *Psalms 1–89*, 216). This was not only their natural response to what they had experienced but also what they felt to be the appropriate response to what they experienced. While on the verge of utter destruction and in a situation in which there seemed to be no hope, God saved them, and the natural and appropriate response to that is joyful worship.

Should our worship services sound the same? Should we too respond to the truth of King Jesus's authority over the whole earth with the same joyful celebration? If they responded this way when God saved them from the Assyrians and imminent destruction, we should respond to an even greater degree when God saves us from the devil and eternal damnation. The proper response to our salvation by the sovereign King of the universe should be one of personal and corporate expressions of joyful worship. This type of worship is not only pleasing to the Lord; it is also a great testimony to a lost world. The world needs to see by means of our happy disposition and joyful celebration that it is good to know King Jesus. We must therefore fight for joyful hearts.

We Rest in This Truth through Hopeful Expectation

PSALM 47:8-9

Psalm 47 ends with the feel of hopeful expectation. This moment is not only a fulfillment of the Lord's promise to Abraham (Goldingay, *Psalms 42–89*, 80), but it is also a prophetic picture of how all the nations will submit to King Jesus. These verses remind us that one day all nations and all kings and all peoples will see the sovereign rule of King Jesus.

The picture of King Jesus in verse 8 is important. Jesus is not only ruling over the nations, but he is also seated on his throne. As Hebrews 1:3 reminds us, after Jesus completed his saving work, he ascended and sat down. Right now he is seated at the right hand of the Father (Eph 1:20). Even though the nations are raging and the peoples are plotting (Ps 2) and at times it feels as if the mountains are going to crumble into the sea (Ps 46), Jesus is not wringing his hands and pacing. He is seated because he is ruling and working all things according to the counsel of his will (Eph 1:11).

We must read Psalm 47 and see Jesus as a great Savior. We must read Psalm 47 and see Jesus as a great King. We must also read Psalm 47 and see Jesus as a sovereign Ruler who is in absolute control over all things. He has the whole world in his hands. He has you, your family, your diagnoses, your future, and every detail of your every moment in his hands. If it is true that our King, Jesus Christ, is in fact ruling over all things in heaven and earth, we must respond by resting in that truth with hopeful confidence.

Conclusion

Every Sunday morning church service should feel a little bit like a pep rally. If we have gathered around the name of Jesus Christ, the sovereign King of the universe, then there must be a proper response to that. The church gathers not only to celebrate this truth (as if at a pep rally) but also to prepare to respond to that truth with action (as after a pep rally). If a high school football team loses on Friday night by forty points, the coach does not comfort himself with the fact that they had a great pep rally. They have a new rally to prepare for the next game.

So it is that we should not only respond to the truths of Psalm 47 with joyful celebration and hopeful expectation, but we should also respond with aggressive missions. God wants us not only to know with our minds but also know with our hearts that he is the King of the universe. He wants that truth to compel us to share that news with all people, giving our lives for the sake of the great mission of God. God wants the reality of King Jesus to fill our minds, deeply affect our hearts, and move our feet to sacrificial action.

Reflect and Discuss

1. How does the authority of King Jesus, as seen in Psalm 47 and Matthew 28:18-20, affect the mission of God? How should it change our involvement in the mission and our sacrifices for the sake of the mission?
2. Why should the authority of King Jesus cause us to celebrate? Why is this kind of celebration appropriate? How does our response affect what outsiders think about Jesus?
3. Is anything in your life stealing your affections or quenching the fire of passion for King Jesus? If so, what? Is your worship, inside and outside the church building, a proper reflection of how good Jesus is?
4. How does seeing Jesus as sovereign Ruler bring rest to your anxious heart? How can this truth help you trust the Lord in every situation?

A Celebration of God's Presence

PSALM 48

Main Idea: In God's presence we find our only satisfaction and our primary mission.

I. Everything Flows from the Presence of the Lord.
II. In His Presence We Find Our Only Satisfaction.
III. In His Presence We Find Our Primary Mission.

Early in my ministry I (Josh) worked with a pastor who used to repeat one phrase over and over again. It felt like his life message. In one way or another, it came out in every sermon and every conversation. It even ended up being a theme of a book he wrote. At first, the phrase seemed so simple that I didn't give it much thought, but the longer I have walked with Jesus, the more deeply profound the statement has become to me. Now, it seems to flow out of my mouth as often as it did his. The phrase is this: "Everything flows from the presence of the Lord" (Elliff, *Presence Centered Church*, 10).

We were not only created *by* God, but we were also created *for* God. We were created to really live only when we live proceeding from his presence. The answer to all of life's greatest questions is found in the presence of the Lord. Everything our hearts long for is found in the presence of the Lord. It's what Jesus meant in John 15 when he said that he is the vine and we are the branches. We were created to be completely dependent on his presence. And, as Jesus also clarifies in John 15, our experience of his life is dependent on our daily proximity to Jesus. In all my life I have never met anyone who walked intimately with Jesus who was disappointed. That is because in his presence we find everything our hearts long for.

Psalm 48 is a celebration of God's presence. It is a reminder of the centrality of God's presence. It reminds us that everything flows out of his presence. More specifically, it shows us that our only source of life and our primary mission are found in the presence of the Lord.

Psalm 48 begins with an exclamation of praise: "The Lord is great and highly praised." With this line, the tone of the psalm is immediately set. This is a psalm of exuberant worship. Much like Psalms 46 and 47, this song celebrates the greatness of God and calls for all within earshot to join in singing praise to the God who alone deserves it. Psalm 48:1 reminds us that the degree of our praise is determined by the degree of God's greatness. If God is infinitely great, then he deserves our greatest praise. As verse 10 reminds us, "Like your name, God, so your praise reaches to the ends of the earth." God's name is great, and our praise should reflect that.

What is bringing about this exclamation of praise? To the modern reader, this might come as a surprise. The praise seems to be rooted in a love for the "city of [Israel's] God" (v. 1). The entire psalm is clearly a reflection on the glory of Mount Zion (v. 2). This song praises the "citadels" (v. 3), the "towers" (v. 12), and "ramparts" (v. 13) of this glorious place. The sons of Korah exclaim, "His holy mountain, rising splendidly, is the joy of the whole earth. Mount Zion—the summit of Zaphon—is the city of the great King" (vv. 1-2). To those who have seen Mount Zion, this praise of this mountain might be a bit surprising. Mount Zion is not that high, nor is it that beautiful. It would not normally be called "the joy of the whole earth." It could not compare to some of our national parks like Acadia, Arches, or Glacier. Those places are majestic. So why all of the hyperbole about Mount Zion?

The sons of Korah are not rejoicing in a place; they are rejoicing in a person. There is a celebration of Zion, not because of Zion's natural beauty but because the temple was there. If the temple was there, the presence of the Lord was there. The exuberant praise in Psalm 48 flowed from the joy and sense of significance that come from the presence of the Lord. The sons of Korah had tasted the presence of the Lord and found their greatest satisfaction and their greatest significance there.

Everything Flows from the Presence of the Lord

If we know the story line of the Bible, this praise of God's presence should not be surprising. God has always revealed the centrality of his presence in our lives. From the first creation to the new creation, God's presence has been a central theme (Lister, *Presence of God*, 20–22). When you trace the theme of God's presence throughout the Bible, two truths emerge, both of which we see in Psalm 48.

First, we were created to find our life and satisfaction in his presence. The glory of Eden is that Adam and Eve were able to live in the uninterrupted presence of God. The great effect of sin is that Adam and Eve were removed from the presence of God. But God has always desired his people to experience his presence. He established the tabernacle so that no matter where his people went, God's presence would go with them (Exod 33). It was not just *symbolic* of God's presence among them; it *was* God's presence among them, and they knew that their only hope in life was his presence. After the people entered the promised land, God gave them the temple so that his presence might dwell among them permanently. When the temple was dedicated, the glory of the Lord filled the temple (2 Chr 5).

In the New Testament, the glory of the Lord was in Jesus Christ, as he came to tabernacle among us and display God's glory (John 1:14). He declared that true life and satisfaction are only found in him (John 7:37). After Jesus's ascension, the presence of the Lord descended on the early church, and they were filled with his presence (Acts 2). Now, God's people are the temple of God, and his presence dwells in us (1 Cor 6:19). In the new heavens and new earth, God will restore us back to a life in which we live fully in his presence (Rev 21). The emphasis of the Bible has always been on the truth that all our life and satisfaction come from his presence. There is no life outside of his presence.

Second, the emphasis has always been on God's desire to see his presence spread to the ends of the earth (Beale and Kim, *God Dwells*, 29ff). Even before sin entered the picture, God's desire was that his presence would spread from Eden so that the whole world might be filled with his glory. From the tabernacle to the temple to the filling of the church in Acts 2, God's desire has always been that his presence spread to all people (Hab 2:14). So the emphasis on God's presence is both our own satisfaction and our own mission. In his presence, both of these things become clearer. What flows from his presence is our own satisfaction—found as we experience him, and our own significance—found as we fulfill his mission. Psalm 48 celebrates both of these working together. In his temple God makes himself known (v. 3).

In His Presence We Find Our Only Satisfaction

Since we were created not only by God but also for God, we can only find true satisfaction in God. Psalm 48 reminds us that everything the heart truly longs for is found in the presence of the Lord. Verse 3 says that the Lord is a "stronghold," which means that our protection is found in him. Verse 8 says the Lord's kingdom is established forever, which means that our hope is found in him. Verse 9 says in his presence we discover his "faithful love," which means that love, acceptance, approval, and affirmation are found in him. Verse 11 says, "Mount Zion is glad. Judah's villages rejoice," which means that our joy is found in him. And verse 14 says, "This God, our God forever and ever—he will always lead us," which means that our direction is found in him. Everything we need is found in him.

Not only does Psalm 48 give us an important reminder about the source of our true satisfaction, but it also contains an important warning about the substitutes for our true satisfaction. In verse 2 we read of Mount Zaphon. In pagan mythology, Mount Zaphon is known as the dwelling place of the chief god of the pantheon (Ross, *Psalms 42–89*, 123). Zaphon is also the place where Baal was worshiped. The psalmist says that Mount Zion is the uppermost peak of Mount Zaphon, which geographically speaking is laughable (Goldingay, *Psalms 42–89*, 86). Zaphon was larger and more majestic in every way. But theologically speaking, Zion is much greater than Zaphon because the Lord is greater than all the gods of the nations. The psalmist knows that the Lord is the true sovereign King of the world, and no other god compares. The psalmist also knows that only the Lord, not the gods of the nations, can truly satisfy us.

In Psalm 48 Zaphon stands for all the idols in our lives that try to steal away our hearts and affections. Externally they might appear more glorious, but in reality they are just empty promises. Only Mount Zion, where the presence of the Lord dwells, can truly satisfy. Mount Zaphon is always there, trying to take the heart, mind, and affections away from the Lord. This is a reminder and a warning that all of us need. The enemy constantly tries to lead us away from true satisfaction in Christ by showing us the "glory" of Zaphon. We must see beyond the external beauty, and by faith we must continue to give our hearts to the Lord alone. Jesus alone is the sovereign and satisfying reality of life.

In His Presence We Find Our Primary Mission

Psalm 48, in all its talk about the satisfying reality that is found in God's presence, also reveals to us the central mission that is found in God's presence. It is God's presence in which we have our hearts captured by the mission of God and find our place in that mission. In verse 10 the psalmist says, "Like your name, God, so your praise reaches to the ends of the earth." This is the mission of God: that the praise of God be spread to all peoples.

The compelling vision of every church should be the one found in Revelation 7. It is the vision of every nation, tribe, people, and language gathered as a great choir, standing before the throne and worshiping the Lamb. In that vision the church finds its true mission: to make sure that the praise of Jesus "reaches to the ends of the earth" (Ps 48:10). In God's presence we discover that Zion alone, and not Zaphon, is worthy of our lives and our praise. That discovery should compel us to spend our lives making sure that the ends of the earth know that Jesus alone can save and satisfy.

Emphasis on enjoying the presence of God is not at conflict with emphasis on the mission of God. These two go hand in hand. Those who have experienced the satisfying reality of God's presence will be the most compelled by God's mission. In God's presence our hearts begin to beat with his. In his presence we are motivated to make sure that every nation, tribe, and language hear about the death, burial, and resurrection of Jesus Christ and are given an opportunity to respond (Rom 10:8-18). We exist not only to enjoy his presence but also to invite all peoples to come and enjoy his presence (Ps 67).

Conclusion

As we see this picture of Mount Zion contrasted with Mount Zaphon, we are first confronted with a crucial question: Is Christ, the King of Zion, the center of our lives, or have we been led astray into the worship of something inferior (Zaphon)? Which one has our minds, hearts, and affections? Psalm 48 confronts us with the reality that our hearts are easily led astray into worshiping something of lesser value than Christ. This psalm calls us to believe by faith that only Jesus can satisfy us and, in response, to give ourselves fully to him.

Second, this text calls us into the mission of God. Psalm 48 reminds us that the heartbeat of our God is to see all people worshiping him. As John Piper reminds us, "Missions exists because worship doesn't" (*Let the Nations Be Glad*, 11). We were created to enjoy him and to make him known. May God's grand vision of the whole earth praising King Jesus propel us into aggressive missions.

Reflect and Discuss

1. If Mount Zaphon is a symbol of idols and false gods that steal away our affection from Christ, what are the Mount Zaphons in your life? What are the things that tend to become idols in your heart?
2. To discover what you truly worship, look at what controls your heart, mind, and will. Look carefully at those three areas and see if you are truly worshiping Christ daily.
3. How does time in the presence of God compel us into the mission of God? Is the vision of Revelation 7 compelling to you? How are you engaging in God's mission on a regular basis? How can you more faithfully engage in the mission?

What Money Cannot Buy

PSALM 49

Main Idea: Jesus alone can save you from the eternal darkness of hell.

I. **An Invitation to Wisdom (49:1-4)**
II. **Wealth Is a Terrifying Confidence (49:5-9).**
III. **Wealth Is a Temporary Currency (49:10-12).**
IV. **Jesus Is a Triumphant Contrast (49:13-15).**
V. **A Concluding Plea (49:16-20)**

In Luke 12, while so many people are gathered around Jesus that they begin trampling one another, he begins to teach his disciples. While he is teaching, a man from the crowd decides to ask Jesus to help him with something. What a wonderful opportunity! Jesus is there. You are there. You can ask him to help you with anything! The man takes advantage of this amazing opportunity and says to Jesus, "Teacher, tell my brother to divide the inheritance with me" (v. 13). You immediately get the sense that this man did not make the most of his opportunity. Jesus responds by saying, "Friend, who appointed me a judge or arbitrator over you?" (v. 14). Then Jesus decides to make an example out of him.

Jesus looks at the crowd and says, "Watch out and be on guard against all greed, because one's life is not in the abundance of his possessions" (v. 14). Then Jesus tells the crowd a story. The story is about a rich man whose land was so productive that he didn't know what to do with all his produce. So he tore down all his barns and built new, bigger barns. He then assured himself that he had enough stored up for the rest of his life so he could just eat, drink, and enjoy himself. But God said to him, "You fool! This very night your life is demanded of you. And the things you have prepared—whose will they be?" (v. 20). Jesus then sums up the story by saying, "That's how it is with the one who stores up treasure for himself and is not rich toward God" (v. 21).

With that little story, Jesus gives a tremendously strong warning against a tremendously subtle enemy. Jesus warns against the subtle enemy of covetousness, and the story reminds us of how easily our wealth can deceive us and give us a false sense of confidence. The man's abundance was not the issue; the man's heart was the issue. He was a fool because his wealth had captured his heart and made him lose his soul. That is exactly the point of Psalm 49 (Boice, *Psalms 42–106*, 408).

Psalm 49 is about the foolishness of trusting in your riches. It is about the inevitability of death and the inability of wealth to save you from it. It is a reminder that wealth has an awful ability to give us a false sense of confidence that will ultimately lead us to hell. And just like the story in Luke 12, Psalm 49 is a strong warning against a subtle enemy. Ultimately, Psalm 49 reminds us that only Jesus, not our material wealth, can save us from eternal darkness in hell.

An Invitation to Wisdom

PSALM 49:1-4

Psalm 49 begins with a universal invitation to hear the wisdom of this song. It is a call for all people, rich and poor, wise and unwise, no matter their ethnicity, nationality, or economic class, to take heed and listen (vv. 1-2). Why? Because what is about to be said is universally true. What is about to be said has been pondered and comes from the voice of wisdom (v. 3). The person who has written this song has also listened, and now he is going to solve one of life's greatest riddles (v. 4). This song is going to address one of the great questions of life regarding wealth and the universal desire for it. In this song, there are three statements of wisdom regarding possessions and eternity.

Wealth Is a Terrifying Confidence

PSALM 49:5-9

Psalm 49:5-9 shows us why those who place their trust in wealth should be terrified. But it begins with the wise songwriter stating that his hearers, on the other hand, should never be fearful. "Why should I fear in times of trouble?" the psalmist asks. The words of verse 5 remind us of the obvious temptation to fear when we are in trouble or are surrounded by enemies and lack the resources to help ourselves. Verse 6 gets a little more specific (Goldingay, *Psalms 42–89*, 100). Those who have wealth don't seem troubled at all. It may even be that those who are wealthy bring the fear upon those who are less fortunate. The point, though, seems to be that while poverty tends to increase people's worries, wealth tends to increase people's confidence (v. 6).

When someone becomes wealthy, he or she is tempted to "trust" and "boast" in that wealth (v. 6). Again, wealth is not the problem, but wealth does tend to give our hearts a false confidence and an arrogant boast. The wealthy tend to trust their wealth, meaning it causes them to rest easy. They also tend to boast in their wealth, meaning they want everyone to know about it. Their boasting points to the real condition of their hearts and shows that much of their identity is wrapped up in their wealth. Such trusting and boasting tend to create a sense of superiority, arrogance, and elitism (Alcorn, *Money*, 51; 1 Cor 4:7; 1 Tim 6:17).

The psalmist points out the major problem with all of this false confidence: the deep and dark pit of death awaits everyone (v. 9), and no amount of wealth can save anyone from it (vv. 7-8). A person cannot use money to rescue himself from death, nor can his money buy anyone else out of death. As verse 8 reminds us, "The price of redeeming him is too costly, one should forever stop trying." And while these verses begin with the awareness that the poor are often the ones most tempted to be terrified, the wealthy should be most terrified. We should not be terrified by a lack of wealth but by the false confidence wealth can bring. The false confidence of the wealthy is a terrifying reality. Their wealth cannot save them from the darkness of death.

Wealth Is a Temporary Currency

PSALM 49:10-12

As the psalmist continues this universal call to wisdom, we are reminded that this monetary currency everyone seeks is a temporary currency. Death is the great leveler (v. 10). The wise man, the foolish man, and the ignorant man all have the same fate awaiting them: death. Everyone will pass away. As for all the wealth of the rich man, he will leave it all to others when he dies (v. 10). All the currency that was accumulated throughout life that gave him so much confidence and arrogance will not help him at all in death because that currency is temporary and does not help with eternal matters.

The Message gives so much clarity on this point: "They leave their prowess behind, move into their new home, The Coffin, the cemetery their permanent address. And to think they named counties after themselves" (v. 11). The wealthy, in an attempt to continue their influence, named towns and cities after themselves, but nothing they did kept them from losing everything at death. Their mansions were replaced by their coffins. This is why Jesus said in Matthew 6:19 that we should not store up treasures on earth. No matter what, these treasures do not last because they are purchased with a currency that is temporary.

This section ends with a refrain in verse 12 that is essentially repeated in verse 20. It says, "But despite his assets, mankind will not last; he is like the animals that perish." What a depressing refrain! What a true refrain! We are not immortal. Like dogs, we will get old and die. The contrast between amassing assets (or "pomp" as the ESV says) and perishing like an animal is stark. All the assets accumulated with their wealth will come to an end just like their animals. And like animals, these people who placed their hope in wealth lived only for their appetites and not for eternity. Their wealth is a currency that can get them a lot, but it is temporary.

Jesus Is a Triumphant Contrast

PSALM 49:13-15

Verses 13-15 paint a picture of massive contrast. They speak of "the way of those who are arrogant, and of their followers, who approve of their words." This is those who have trusted and boasted in their wealth. The reason this is such a tempting way to live is because this way tends to get the applause and approval of the crowd (v. 13). It did for the wealthy in Psalm 49. But the other side of the story is that those who live for their wealth are actually being shepherded by death.

Whether intentional or not, Psalm 49:14 sets up a great contrast with Psalm 23. In Psalm 23 those who know the Lord are shepherded by the Lord. As a result, they are led in the paths of righteousness and will dwell in the house of the Lord forever. In Psalm 49 those who trust in their wealth are shepherded by death, and although they graze in lush pastures, they are being led to the slaughter (v. 14).

Do you remember the story of the rich man and Lazarus that Jesus tells in Luke 16? There was a rich man who flaunted his wealth through his expensive clothes and lavish home. But one of the frustrating things in his life was that outside the gates to his home was a poor man covered in sores and always begging for money. It was a disgusting nuisance. Every day the rich man would step over the poor man, and every day the poor man would just ask for the scraps from the table of the rich man. But the rich man ignored him. Soon both died. The poor man was taken to heaven where he reclined on Abraham's bosom. The rich man was taken to hell where, agonizing in the flames, he begged for the poor man to put a drop of water on his tongue. But Abraham responded to him, "Son, remember that during your life you received your good things, just as Lazarus received bad things, but now he is comforted here, while you are in agony" (Luke 16:25).

This is what Psalm 49:14 means when it says, "The upright will rule over them in the morning, and their form will waste away in Sheol." The reality is, those who have lived for their wealth and trusted in it have already received their good things. Those who trust in the Lord will rule over them in the light while they remain in the dark, "far from their lofty abode" (v. 14).

In contrast to all of that, there is another option. There is a triumphant contrast to the dark future of those who trusted in their wealth. Verse 15 says, "But God will redeem me from the power of Sheol, for he will take me." This verse can be named with all of the marvelous "but God" statements throughout the Bible. "Redeem" is a financial word. It means the price that is paid to ransom someone. Here, it refers to the price that is paid in order to ransom someone from death.

The question is, What could a person pay to ransom someone from death? We have already been told that this price is too costly and the wealthy should forever stop trying (v. 8). A person cannot pay that price, but God can. What price does God pay to ransom us from death? The price of his own Son, Jesus Christ. Jesus has come and redeemed us from darkness by giving his own life as the payment for our sins (Col 1:13). No person can buy his own way into eternal life; he must be bought in order to receive eternal life. And the wealthy must release their pride and humbly ask for Jesus to pay the price for them. Only Jesus can save us from the eternal darkness of hell.

One of the most important phrases in Psalm 49 is found at the end of verse 15: "For he will take me." That is the phrase used to refer to Enoch and Elijah when God took them up from the earth (Gen 5:24; 2 Kgs 2:3-10; Goldingay, *Psalms 42–89*, 104). The use of this phrase reminds us that the good news of the gospel is not only that believers are saved from the meaningless earthly existence of those who trust in riches but also that we are saved from the deep eternal darkness of hell. God, through Christ, has guaranteed that we, like the poor man in Luke 16, will be taken up to dwell with him. In other words, while those who trust in their wealth have their best life now, those who trust in Christ get their best lives later.

A Concluding Plea

PSALM 49:16-20

This psalm ends with a series of ways that the wise, who have heard and received this warning, should respond. First, we should not be afraid (v. 16). Those who trust in Christ should not fear anything in this life or the next because we are assured of the price that has been paid for our redemption. Also, we should never fear the wealthy, even if they, in their arrogance, seek to oppress us.

Second, we should not be envious. It is easy to envy the wealth of another as we see "his house increases." Even though we believers have chosen to live for the next life, it can bother us when those who live for this life seem blessed and are applauded for how well they have done for themselves (v. 18). But we must remember the reality: when they die, they will take nothing with them (v. 17). Those who have trusted in their wealth will be buried with their fathers and will "never see the light" (v. 19). Don't envy their wealth.

Finally, those who trust in the Lord should continue to look to Jesus. As the final refrain of Psalm 49 reminds that the wicked perish, we are reminded that through Christ we will be saved by his blood forevermore. We have a kingdom that cannot be shaken and a hope that is eternal. While our hearts might be tempted to fear and our eyes might tend to be envious of the wicked, we must keep our hearts and minds on Jesus and all that is promised to us in the life to come.

Reflect and Discuss

1. Why would the psalmist call all people, regardless of location or class, to listen to the wisdom of this psalm? Why does this apply to everyone?
2. How do you feel this psalm applies to you? Do you struggle with the desire for monetary wealth? If so, what do you see that desire doing to your heart?
3. How can the hope we have in Christ deliver us from the desire for wealth? What actions do you need to take to ensure that you are not led away by the deceitfulness of riches?

Judgment Must Begin with the House of God

PSALM 50

Main Idea: God condemns false and hypocritical worship, but he saves and accepts those who repent and worship him rightly.

I. **The Righteous Judge Issues a Summons (50:1-6).**
   A. Our mighty God comes to judge his people (50:1-3).
   B. Our mighty God calls creation to witness his judgment (50:4-6).
II. **True Worship Reflects the Truth that We Need God (50:7-15).**
   A. We can do the right things but for the wrong reasons (50:7-13).
   B. We need to do the right things for the right reasons (50:14-15).
III. **Hypocritical Worship Is Condemned; Genuine Worship Is Honored (50:16-23).**
   A. God will call out the wicked for their hypocrisy (50:16-22).
   B. God is honored by those who come rightly before him (50:23).

The New Testament has a verse that every serious Christian must stop and carefully reflect on. We must not run past it too quickly. The verse is 1 Peter 4:17. The ominous words are these: "For the time has come for judgment to begin with God's household." It would not surprise me if the apostle Peter had been reflecting on Psalm 50 when he wrote those words.

Psalm 50 presents a courtroom scene. A trial will start soon. "The Mighty One, God, the Lord [Yahweh]" will be the sovereign Judge (v. 1). All of creation, "heaven and earth" (v. 4), will be called as witnesses. None of this is surprising. Then the psalm names the accused. The identity of the defendants catches us off guard. We are unprepared for whom we see called to stand before the Judge. It is the people of God (v. 4), the Lord's "faithful ones," those he says, "made a covenant with me by sacrifice" (v. 5).

VanGemeren gives us a clear and concise description of this psalm. He writes, "This psalm is concerned with true loyalty to God. Loyalty is antithetical to formalism and hypocrisy" (*Psalms*, 426). The song was written by Asaph, David's director of "sanctuary music" (see 1 Chr 6:39; 15:17,19; 16:4-7; 2 Chr 29:30), a man who could also write prophetically (Ross, *Psalms 42–89*, 158). Asaph is credited with twelve psalms (Pss 50; 73–83), but it is possible some of the psalms attributed to him "refer to the family or guild from Asaph" (Ross, *Psalms 42–89*, 159).

The psalm is easy to divide. In verses 1-6 God assembles the court. In verses 7-15 he gives his first indictment: heartless formalism in worship. Finally, in verses 16-23 he gives the second indictment: hypocrisy in their actions. In their worship and in their lives, God is displeased with what he sees, and he will not look the other way. He calls his people to give an account for their brazen sin. He offers hope for forgiveness and reconciliation, but the time is now. They cannot delay. Neither can we.

The Righteous Judge Issues a Summons

PSALM 50:1-6

Our God is concerned with why we do what we do. To simply do the right thing, at the right time, at the right place, and in the right way is not enough. In fact, he finds such things detestable and unacceptable as acts of worship and service. What we do, whether in worship or everyday activity, must be the *right thing* done for the *right reason.* God says in Isaiah 29:13, "These people approach me with their speeches to honor me with lip-service, yet their hearts are far from me, and human rules direct their worship of me." In Micah 6:6-8 the prophet writes,

What should I bring before the LORD
when I come to bow before God on high?
Should I come before him with burnt offerings,
with year-old calves?
Would the LORD be pleased with thousands of rams
or with ten thousand streams of oil?
Should I give my firstborn for my transgression,
the offspring of my body for my own sin?
Mankind, he has told each of you what is good
and what it is the LORD requires of you;
to act justly,
to love faithfulness,
and to walk humbly with your God.

Jesus would also call out the hypocritical worship of the religious leaders of his day in Matthew 15:8-9, quoting Isaiah 29:13. God will not tolerate dishonest, hypocritical acts. He will deal with them, especially when his people are guilty.

Our Mighty God Comes to Judge His People (50:1-3)

God's people are always in a dangerous place when they forget who God is and what he can do. The psalm begins by addressing both concerns. The one to whom we are accountable is "The Mighty One, God, the Lord" (v. 1). He is the all-powerful, covenant God of Israel who "speaks." As Francis Schaeffer says so well, "He is there and he is not silent." Here "he summons the earth from the rising of the sun to its setting." He calls on the whole earth (from east to west) to appear as witnesses in his courtroom.

Since he will judge his people, he calls all to come to Zion, the holy mountain where the temple stands (v. 2). Because Zion is the place the Lord designated that he would meet his people, it is called "the perfection of beauty." God had designed Zion, and it cannot help but be perfect and beautiful. It is here that "God appears in radiance" (ESV, "shines forth"). This appearance is described in sober, if not terrifying, words in verse 3: "Our God is coming." This is not some distant, unknown deity who is calling his people out. No, he is "our God." He is "coming" to judge, and "he will not be silent!" He will show up for this judicial hearing, and he will speak.

Oh, what an appearance he makes! "Devouring fire precedes him, and a storm rages around him." This is the language of theophanic judgment, communicating the seriousness of this courtroom case. Throughout Scripture we are reminded that "the Lord your God is a consuming fire, a jealous God" (Deut 4:24; 9:3; Isa 66:15-16; Heb 12:29). God's people forget—or worse ignore—this at their great peril. Like a raging storm, "a mighty tempest" (ESV), our God will visit us in righteous judgment for our disrespect of him. He will not tolerate it. His patience has its limits.

Our Mighty God Calls Creation to Witness His Judgment (50:4-6)

God takes worship of himself seriously. The first three of the Ten Commandments make this abundantly clear (see Exod 20:3-7; Deut 5:7-11). The formalism and hypocrisy of his people displease him, and he wants the whole of his creation to see his displeasure. "On high, he summons heaven and earth in order to judge his people" (v. 4). God calls his witnesses just as he commanded his people to do (Deut 19:15), but these witnesses are unlike all others. Alec Motyer points out that the witnesses of this imaginary court scene "are always present all the time, seeing everything" (*Psalms by the Day*, 131).

Verse 5 commands the defendants to appear before God "the Judge" (v. 6). They are the Lord's "faithful ones . . . those who made a covenant with [him] by sacrifice." Leupold writes, "Those individuals who are specifically to be gathered are first described as his 'saints.' The term could be rendered 'My loyal ones.' It implies that they are, or at least should be, devoted to him" (*Exposition*, 391). As recipients of the Lord's covenant graces, their responsibility is all the greater. Scripture teaches that revelation brings responsibility. The more we know, the greater is our responsibility (see Matt 11:20-24).

Verse 6 provides an appropriate climax to the opening stanza: "The heavens proclaim his righteousness; for God is the Judge. *Selah.*" The righteous Judge of heaven who will judge the covenant people of the Lord is none other than the Lord himself. He summons all creation to attend this trial. The scene is set. The trial is about to begin. The great theophany of Exodus 19:16-19 looms in the background. Serious business is about to take place between God and his people.

Those of us who approach our Lord with frivolity in the twenty-first century should be warned. Do we ask the Lord to prepare our hearts and minds for worship? Do we read Scripture well? Do we sing for his praise or ours? Do our songs have biblical and theological integrity? Are our prayers rote repetition or sincere from careful meditation and preparation? Not to carefully weigh questions like these is to approach our great God in an unworthy manner and at our own risk. God is not our buddy in the sky or the man upstairs. He is the Mighty One, the Lord, the righteous Judge.

True Worship Reflects the Truth that We Need God

PSALM 50:7-15

A basic truth of orthodox theology is this: God has no deficiency. He is perfect in who he is and all that he does. Therefore, God does not depend on us for anything. He does not need us, but we do need him. That is why we worship. Matthew Barrett is right: "True, biblical worship is due to God not because he needs us, but because we need him" ("The Gospel Depends on a God Who Does Not Depend on You."). John Piper adds these convicting words:

> Simply put, God does not need you or me. He is altogether self-sufficient, dependent on no one. He is, in fact, the one who is responsible for the existence and preservation of all life, yours and mine. Therefore, he cannot be "served" as if he were needy or exhausted or weak or lacking something that only you and I and the people of your church can supply.
>
> To arrive on a Sunday morning and declare to God, "We are here for you," in the sense that you believe there is something you can give to God that he doesn't already have, or that you can shore up a weakness, or fill a gap or overcome a deficiency, is to insult God to the very core of his being. ("Are You Insulting God in Worship?")

Israel was guilty of insulting God because they had forgotten who God is, who they were, and how to rightly enter his presence to worship. Two important lessons emerge as our Lord exposes their sin.

We Can Do the Right Things but for the Wrong Reasons (50:7-13)

God begins his trial against "my people . . . Israel" (v. 7). He is both judge and prosecutor. He calls his people to "listen" as he "speak[s]" and "testif[ies]" against them. He does so based on the covenant relationship that exists between them: "I am God, your God."

The Lord wants to be clear why he charges them with crimes against their God. He begins by telling them, "I do not rebuke you for your sacrifices or for your burnt offerings, which are continually before me" (v. 8). Their acts of worship, in and of themselves, were not the problem. The problem, he says, is that they think he needs them and that they are doing him a favor. The Lord says, "I will not take a bull from your household or male goats from your pens" (v. 9). Today God would say, "I don't need your money, not a single cent!" Why? Verses 10-11 provide the answer as the case unfolds: "For every animal of the forest is mine, the cattle on a thousand hills. I know every bird on the mountains, and the creatures of the field are mine." He is the Creator, and all creation is his to do with as he pleases. It all belongs to him!

The Lord then resorts to using divine sarcasm in verse 12 to reveal Israel's folly and foolishness. He says, "If I were hungry," and of course the all-sufficient Father is never hungry, "I would not tell you." In case you have forgotten, he adds, "the world and everything in it is mine." Do you think, he asks them, that I, like the pagan gods and idols you once worshiped, "eat the flesh of bulls or drink the blood of goats" (v. 13)? How foolish have you become? How blind to true worship are you? Motyer sums up the situation well:

> Their devotion to offering sacrifice was aimed at doing God a favour. The direction of their religion was from man to God, a religion of "brownie points," of getting into God's good books, of human meritorious works. (*Psalms by the Day*, 131)

Yes, they were doing the right things, but they were doing them for the wrong reasons. Their theology of worship was pagan, not biblical.

We Need to Do the Right Things for the Right Reasons (50:14-15)

Proper, God-acceptable worship is always our biblically informed response to who God is and what he has done on behalf of his people who rightly recognize his value and worth. "Biblically informed" means they are acts of thanksgiving, not acts of appeasement or atonement. We "sacrifice a thank offering to God" (HCSB). We "pay [our] vows to the Most High" (v. 14). Leviticus 3 and 7, which give guidelines for offerings, inform this verse. As Ross writes, these are "an act of worship in the sanctuary that expresses publicly what God has done for them" (*Psalms 42–89*, 166). Hebrews 13:15 provides a New Testament complement: "Therefore, through him let us continually offer up to God a sacrifice of praise, that is, the fruit of lips that confess his name." Spurgeon summarizes:

> No longer look at your sacrifices as in themselves gifts pleasing to me, but present them as the tributes of your gratitude; it is then that I will accept them, but not while your souls have no love and no thankfulness to offer me. (*Treasury*, 387)

God has been faithful. He has lived up to his covenant promises. Fulfill your vows of offering praise and thanksgiving for what he has done. God delights in this worship.

Verse 15 brings stanza 2 to a close with full recognition that the people need God; God does not need them. "Call on me in a day of trouble," the Lord says, "I will rescue [ESV, "deliver"] you, and you will honor [ESV, "glorify"] me." I love the flow of this verse: Call when you are in trouble → I will rescue you → you will respond with proper worship by honoring me. The church father Augustine (AD 354–430) comments on this verse:

> For thou oughtest not to rely on thy powers, all thy aids are deceitful . . . but when thou art troubled, thou callest on Me; when thou callest upon Me, I will draw thee forth; when I shall draw thee forth, thou shalt glorify Me, that thou mayest no more depart from Me. (*Expositions*, 186)

Hypocritical Worship Is Condemned; Genuine Worship Is Honored

PSALM 50:16-23

When I (Danny) was in my early twenties, I was in a worship service where the music pastor tried to motivate our people to sing with more passion by saying, "What we do on Sunday is all that matters! What we do Monday–Saturday counts for nothing. It does not matter at all!" Although I believe his remarks were well intended, they are wrong. What we do every day does matter to God. We are to give ourselves to God 24/7 as a living sacrifice, which is our "true worship" (Rom 12:1). Yes, what we do on Sunday when we gather to worship and celebrate the death and resurrection of King Jesus matters a lot. But do not be deceived into thinking how you live the rest of the time does not matter to God. It does matter, and it matters a lot. The covenant people of Israel, like so many today, had forgotten that proper living and proper worship are connected. The results were spiritually and morally catastrophic. Derek Kidner says it well: "These men are not the heathen but the nominally orthodox, those who combine 'wickedness and worship'" (*Psalms 1–72*, 187). Michael Wilcock helpfully points out, in this final stanza,

> The seventh, eighth, and ninth commandments are explicitly mentioned (vv. 18-19), and the rest of the second table of the law is implied, in this scathing indictment not of pagans and unbelievers but of the wicked who recite God's laws and take his covenant on their lips (v. 16). These are people who in our day are known as Christians, but for whom religion

> and morality are two separate areas of life, with the former as God's real sphere of interest; the latter, in their view, he takes no more seriously than they do (v. 21a). (*Message*, 182)

These pseudo-worshipers could not have been more in error, as verses 16-23 reveal.

God Will Call Out the Wicked for Their Hypocrisy (50:16-22)

God speaks directly as prosecutor and judge: "[He] says to the wicked, 'What right do you have to recite my statutes and to take my covenant on your lips'" (v. 16)? In other words, he says, how dare you claim to be my people when your lives are such a contradiction to your confession! You claim to love me, but your lives betray your words. "You hate instruction and fling my words behind you" (v. 17). *The Message* renders verses 16-17 this way: "What are you up to, quoting my laws, talking like we are good friends? You never answer the door when I call; you treat my words like garbage."

Three specific examples of their hypocrisy and disregard for God's Word are given in verses 18-20: stealing, adultery, and slander. First, they were involved in stealing or thievery (see Exod 20:15). The text says, "When you see a thief, you make friends with him." When they see those who are getting wealthy by exploiting others, they cozy right up to them and try to get in on their game (cf. Jas 5:4-6). Second, "You associate with adulterers" (see Exod 20:14). They are comfortable hanging out with those who are unfaithful to their marriage vows. One has to wonder: Did they cover for their friends? Did they also participate in this sin? Third, their wagging tongues were off the leash! The psalmist writes, "You unleash your mouth for evil" (v. 19). The ESV reads, "You give your mouth free rein for evil." You also "harness your tongue for deceit." The GNT says, "You never hesitate to tell lies." The idea is that "they were fabricating the deceit, they were weaving a web of deceit" (Ross, *Psalms 42–89*, 169). But it gets worse. Verse 20 informs us they were weaving these webs of lies about their own families! "You sit, maligning your brother, slandering your mother's son." The Hebrew parallelism of reinforcing the first line with the second adds an extra punch to the indictment. They betray their own flesh and blood and feel no guilt or remorse.

Foolishly, they convinced themselves that their righteous and just God did not care because he was patient in bringing their discipline and judgment. When they did all these evil things, God says, "I kept silent." They "thought [he] was just like [them]" (v. 21). Motyer makes an interesting observation from the Hebrew text: a literal translation of "you thought I was just like you" is "you thought I AM to be like you." He then says, "Very likely there is an intentional recalling of 'I AM,' the Exodus name (Exodus 3:13-15)" (*Psalms by the Day*, 132). The ESV has a marginal reading that also makes this observation. If this is correct, and it certainly may be, then the words of condemnation that follow are even more weighty. I AM "will rebuke you and lay out the case before you" (v. 21). And "understand this, you who forget God, or I will tear you apart" (v. 22). The warning is stern and severe, but it is wrapped in mercy and grace. Forgetters of God can still find forgiveness if they remember, repent, and return (see Rev 2–3). Otherwise, terrible judgment awaits, and "there will be no one to rescue" them. No one!

God Is Honored by Those Who Come Rightly before Him (50:23)

The harsh warning of verses 21-22 finds a companion of hope in our final verse. True worshipers, repentant worshipers, are always welcomed and received by "the Mighty One" (v. 1). He says, "Whoever offers a thanksgiving sacrifice honors [ESV, "glorifies"] me, and whoever orders his conduct, I will show him the salvation of God." A humble heart and a holy life are always acceptable to our Lord. He gives us the former, making the latter possible. An acceptable life will inevitably emerge from a humble heart transformed by the gospel. Patrick Reardon is right:

> For all its ritual and ceremony, the religion of the Bible is ultimately a matter of the heart. This theme in our present psalm prepares for that important line in the psalm which is to follow: "The sacrifice to God is a contrite spirit; a broken and contrite heart, O God, You will not despise." (*Christ in the Psalms*, 98).

Conclusion

We are never more like the lost, those who are spiritually dead and "without hope and without God in the world" (Eph 2:12), than when we think we can do something for God instead of realizing we need God to do something for us, when we think saving power comes from our sacrifices for God instead of his sacrifice for us! No, our sacrifices are sacrifices of thanksgiving (Ps 50:14,23) that honor the Lord for what he has done for us in his Son, the Lord Jesus Christ. Then, and only then, will the Lord "show [us] the salvation of God" (v. 23). A single sacrifice can make mankind right with God, but it is not a sacrifice any human can make. It is the one made by the God-man, Jesus Christ, on the cross. Hebrews 9:26 is exactly what we need to hear: "But now [Jesus] has appeared one time, at the end of the ages, for the removal of sin by the sacrifice of himself." This sacrifice makes our thanksgiving sacrifices acceptable and pleasing to God, the living sacrifice of ourselves in grateful, heartfelt response to the mercies of God that flow from the fountain filled with blood located on Golgotha's hill (Rom 12:1).

Reflect and Discuss

1. Why is God concerned that we worship him for the right reasons?
2. How can you judge whether you are doing something for the right or wrong reasons?
3. How can forgetting who God is (v. 1) lead you to worship him without the right motives or in unworthy ways?
4. How can you prepare your heart and mind to sing, to pray, and to hear his Word? How can you do this before, during, and after you approach him alone and with God's people?
5. What is pseudo-worship? What are some subtle and obvious examples of it?
6. How is God's name profaned and the church's witness hurt when people are pseudo-worshipers?
7. What things may we begin to believe God needs from us? What creates these false beliefs?
8. Why are proper living and proper worship intimately connected? In what ways have you previously failed to properly link the two?
9. Can Christians be overly concerned with the sins of those outside the church? Why or why not? How does this psalm give the right perspective?
10. What could lead a worshiper of God to eventually hate God's instruction (v. 17)?

WORKS CITED

Adams, James E. *War Psalms of the Prince of Peace: Lessons from the Imprecatory Psalms.* Second edition. Phillipsburg, NJ: P&R Publishing, 2016.

Alcorn, Randy. *Money, Possessions, and Eternity.* Wheaton: Tyndale, 2003.

Allender, Dan B., and Tremper Longman III. *The Cry of the Soul.* Colorado Springs: Navpress, 1994.

Anderson, A. A. *Psalms 1–72.* Grand Rapids: Eerdmans, 1972.

Anderson, Courtney. *To the Golden Shore: The Life of Adoniram Judson.* Boston: Little, Brown & Company, 1956.

Augustine. *Augustine: Expositions on the Psalms.* Edited by Philip Schaff, vol. 8. Peabody: Hendrickson, 1994.

———. *Confessions: Books 1–8.* Translated by Carolyn J.-B. Hammond. Cambridge: Harvard University Press, 2014.

Bacon, Francis. *The Advancement of Learning.* Auckland, New Zealand: The Floating Press, 2010.

Bainton, Roland H. *Here I Stand: A Life of Martin Luther.* Illustrated edition. Nashville: Abingdon, 2013.

Barrett, Matthew. "The Gospel Depends on a God Who Does Not Depend on You." The Gospel Coalition, March 17, 2011, https://www.thegospelcoalition.org/article/the-gospel-depends-on-a-god-who-does-not-need-you.

Bavinck, Herman. *Doctrine of God.* Edinburgh: Banner of Truth, 1978.

Beale, G. K., and Mitchell Kim. *God Dwells among Us.* Downers Grove: IVP Academic, 2014.

Begg, Alistair. "*How Majestic Is Your Name.*" June 16, 1991, https://www.truthforlife.org/resources/sermon/how-majestic-is-your-name.

Belcher, Richard P., Jr. *The Messiah and the Psalms: Preaching Christ from All the Psalms.* Fearn, Ross-shire: Mentor, 2006.

Blocker, H. A. G. "Sin." Pages 781–88 in *New Dictionary of Biblical Theology.* Edited by Brian S. Rosner et al. Downers Grove: IVP Academic, 2000.

Boice, James Montgomery. *Psalms Volume I: Psalms 1–41.* An Expositional Commentary. Grand Rapids: Baker Books, 2005.

———. *Psalms Volume II: Psalms 42–106.* An Expositional Commentary. Grand Rapids: Baker Books, 2005.

Bonhoeffer, Dietrich. *Life Together and Prayerbook of the Bible.* Translated by Daniel W. Bloesch and James H. Burtness. Philadelphia: Fortress, 1995.

Bratcher, Robert G., and William D. Reyburn. *A Handbook on Psalms.* New York: United Bible Societies, 1993.

Bright, Bill. *A Handbook for Christian Ministry.* Orlando: New Life, 1994.

Broyles, Craig C. *Psalms.* Grand Rapids: Baker Books, 1999.

Bunyan, John. *The Pilgrim's Progress.* Chicago: Moody, 2007.

Calvin, John. *Psalms 1–35.* Calvin's Commentaries Vol. 4. Grand Rapids: Baker Books, 1996.

———. *Psalms 36–92.* Calvin's Commentaries Vol. 5. Grand Rapids: Baker Books, 1996.

Cole, C. Donald. *Thirsting for God.* Westchester: Crossway, 1986.

Cole, Robert. "Psalm 3: Of Whom Does David Speak, of Himself or Another?" Paper presented at the Annual Meeting of the Evangelical Theological Society, San Antonio, TX, November 2004.

Craigie, Peter C. *Psalms 1–50.* Word Biblical Commentary. Nashville: Thomas Nelson, 1983.

Craigie, Peter C., and Marvin E. Tate. *Psalms 1–50.* Second edition. Grand Rapids: Zondervan Academic, 2018.

Davidson, Richard M. "Psalm 22, 23, and 24: A Messianic Trilogy?" Paper presented at the Annual Meeting of the Evangelical Theological Society, San Diego, CA, 2019.

Dawkins, Richard. *A Devil's Chaplain: Reflections on Hope, Lies, Science, and Love.* Boston: Mariner, 2004.

"Editorial: A Scientist's Case against God." *The Independent* (London) April 20, 1992: 17. Quoting Richard Dawkins's speech at the Edinburgh International Science Festival (April 15, 1992).

Edwards, Jonathan. *The Works of Jonathan Edwards. Volume 13, The "Miscellanies."* Edited by Thomas Schafer. New Haven: Yale University Press, 1994.

Elliff, Bill. *The Presence Centered Church.* Little Rock: Grace and Truth, 2015.

Feinberg, P. D. "Atheism." Pages 112–13 in *Evangelical Dictionary of Theology*. Edited by Daniel J. Treier and Walter A. Elwell. 3rd edition. Grand Rapids: Baker Academic, 2001.

Feuerbach, Ludwig. *Lectures on the Essence of Religion*. Translated by Ralph Manheim. Eugene, OR: Wipf and Stock, 2018.

Fritch, Tara. "'Do You Believe in God?' The Response Continues." *Newport News*. October 15, 1995.

Futato, Mark D. "The Book of Psalms." *Cornerstone Biblical Commentary*. Carol Stream, IL: Tyndale House, 2009.

Gaebelein, Arno C. *The Book of Psalms: A Devotional and Prophetic Commentary*. 5th edition. New York: Loizeaux Brothers, 1965.

Geljon, Albert-Kees. "Didymus the Blind: Commentary on Psalm 24 (23 LXX): Introduction, Translation and Commentary." *Vigiliae Christianae* 65 (2011): 50–73.

Goldingay, John. *Psalms Volume I: Psalms 1–41*. Baker Commentary on the Old Testament Wisdom and Psalms. Grand Rapids: Baker Academic, 2006

———. *Psalms Volume II: Psalms 42–89*. Baker Commentary on the Old Testament Wisdom and Psalms. Grand Rapids: Baker Academic, 2006.

Greidanus, Sidney. *Preaching Christ from Psalms: Foundations for Expository Sermons in the Christian Year*. Grand Rapids: Eerdmans, 2016.

Henry, Matthew. *Matthew Henry's Commentary on the Whole Bible: Job to Song of Solomon*. Old Tappan, NJ: Fleming H. Revell, 1935.

Hornok, Marcia. "Antithesis." *Discipleship Journal* 60 (1990): 23.

Huxley, Aldous. *Ends and Means*. London: Chatto & Windus, 1937.

Johnston, James. *The Psalms: Volume 1—Psalms 1 to 41*. Wheaton: Crossway, 2015.

Kidner, Derek. *Psalms 1–72: An Introduction and Commentary on Books I and II of the Psalms*. Tyndale Old Testament Commentaries. Downers Grove: InterVarsity Press, 1973.

Lane, Eric. *Psalms 1–89: The Lord Saves*. Focus on the Bible. Scotland: Christian Focus, 2006.

Lawrence, Michael. *Conversion: How God Creates a People*. Wheaton: Crossway, 2017.

Lawson, Steven. *Psalms 1–75*. Nashville: Holman Reference, 2004.

Leach, John. "'Give-up-itis' Is a Medical Condition That Can Kill." University of Portsmouth. https://researchportal.port.ac.uk/en/clippings/give-up-itis-is-a-medical-condition-that-can-kill.

Leupold, H. C. *Exposition of the Psalms.* 1959; reprint, 1979, Grand Rapids: Baker Books.

Lewis, C. S. *The Last Battle.* New York: Harper Collins, 2000.

———. *Reflections on the Psalms.* San Francisco: HarperOne, 1958; reprint, 2017.

Lister, Ryan. *The Presence of God: Its Place in the Storyline of Scripture and the Story of Our Lives.* Wheaton: Crossway, 2014.

Lloyd-Jones, D. Martyn. *Spiritual Depression: Its Causes and Its Cure.* Grand Rapids: Eerdmans, 1965.

Lloyd-Jones, Sally. *The Jesus Storybook Bible.* Grand Rapids: Zonderkidz, 2007.

Luther, Martin. *First Lectures on the Psalms I: Psalms 1–75.* Edited by Hilton C. Oswald. St. Louis: Concordia, 1974.

———. *A Manual of the Book of Psalms: Or, the Subject-Contents of All the Psalms.* Translated by Henry Cole. London: R. B. Seeley and W. Burnside, 1837.

MacArthur, John. "The Discipline of God." April 8, 1973. https://www.gty.org/library/sermons-library/1636/the-discipline-of-god.

———. *Twelve Ordinary Men.* Nashville: Thomas Nelson, 2002.

McBeth, J. P. *Twenty-Third Psalm.* Dallas, TX: Self-published, 1952.

Moore, Russell. "Where the Wild Things Are, Part One." Russell Moore. November 27, 2006. https://www.russellmoore.com/2006/11/27/where-the-wild-things-are-part-one.

Motyer, Alec. *Psalms by the Day: A New Devotional Translation.* Fearn, Ross-shire: Christian Focus, 2016.

Nagel, Thomas. *The Last Word.* New York: Oxford University Press, 1997.

Packer, J. I. *Engaging the Written Word of God.* Peabody: Hendrickson, 2012.

Pascal, Blaise. *The Thoughts, Letters and Opuscules of Blaise Pascal.* Translated by A. M. Wight. New York: Hurd and Houghton, 1869.

Peterson, Eugene. *A Long Obedience in the Same Direction.* Downers Grove: InterVarsity Press, 1980, 2000.

Piper, John. "Are You Insulting God in Worship?" Desiring God. June 7, 2015. https://www.desiringgod.org/articles/are-you-insulting-god-in-worship.

———. *Future Grace: The Purifying Power of the Promises of God.* Sisters, OR: Multnomah, 1995.

———. "Go to God in Prayer: How Not to Be a Mule." Desiring God, 4 August 1980. https://www.desiringgod.org/messages/go-to-god-in-prayer.

———. "The Heart You Know and the Heart You Don't." Desiring God. September 2, 1990. https://www.desiringgod.org/messages/the-heart-you-know-and-the-heart-you-dont.

———. "In the Pits with a King." Desiring God. August 17, 1980. https://www.desiringgod.org/messages/in-the-pits-with-a-king.

———. "Let All Who Seek Thee Rejoice and Be Glad in Thee; Let Those Who Love Thy Salvation Say Continually, 'The Lord Be Magnified.'" Desiring God. March 17, 1996. https://www.desiringgod.org/messages/let-all-who-seek-thee-rejoice-and-be-glad-in-thee-let-those-who-love-thy-salvation-say-continually-the-lord-be-magnified.

———. *Let the Nations Be Glad.* Grand Rapids: Baker Books, 1993.

———. "The Shepherd, the Host, and the Highway Patrol." Desiring God. September 8, 1980. https://www.desiringgod.org/messages/the-shepherd-the-host-and-the-highway-patrol.

———. "Sweeter than Honey, Better than Gold." Desiring God. January 6, 1991. https://www.desiringgod.org/messages/sweeter-than-honey-better-than-gold.

———. "What Is Man? Reflections on Abortion and Racial Reconciliation." Desiring God. January 16, 1994. https://www.desiringgod.org/messages/what-is-man.

———. *When I Don't Desire God: How to Fight for Joy.* Wheaton: Crossway, 2013.

Reardon, Patrick Henry. *Christ in the Psalms.* Ben Lomond, CA: Conciliar, 2000.

"Religion: German Martyrs." *Time.* December 23, 1940. http://content.time.com/time/subscriber/article/0,33009,765103,00.html. Accessed November 4, 2021.

"Rose, Darlene." *The Chattanoogan.* February 29, 2004. https://www.chattanoogan.com/2004/2/29/47410/Rose-Darlene.aspx.

Rose, Darlene Deibler. *Evidence Not Seen: A Woman's Miraculous Faith in the Jungles of World War II.* Reprint edition. San Francisco: HarperCollins, 1990.

Ross, Allen. *A Commentary on the Psalms: 1–41.* Grand Rapids: Kregel Academic, 2012.

———. *A Commentary on the Psalms: 42–89.* Grand Rapids: Kregel Academic, 2013.

Sagan, Carl. *Broca's Brain: Reflections on the Romance of Science.* Reprint edition. New York: Ballantine, 1980.

Sailhamer, John H. *NIV Compact Bible Commentary*. Grand Rapids: Zondervan Academic, 1999.

Schaeffer, Francis A. "He Is There and He Is Not Silent." *The Complete Works of Francis Schaeffer*, volume 1. Wheaton: Crossway, 1988.

Schreiner, Thomas R. *Romans*. Baker Evangelical Commentary on the New Testament. Grand Rapids: Baker Academic, 1998.

Spurgeon, Charles. *The Metropolitan Tabernacle Pulpit: Sermons Preached and Revised*, volume 31. London: Passmore & Alabaster, 1885.

———. *The Treasury of David: Psalms 1–57*. Grand Rapids: Zondervan, 1979.

Storms, Sam. "The Agony and the Ecstasy (Psalm 22)." Sam Storms: Enjoying God. October 30, 2006. https://www.samstorms.org/all-articles/post/the-agony-and-the-ecstasy–psalm-22-.

———. "Those Troubling Psalms of Imprecation (1) (Psalm 35, Etc.)." Sam Storms. https://www.samstorms.org/all-articles/post/those-troubling-psalms-of-imprecation–1—psalm-35–etc–. Accessed December 20, 2021.

Stott, John. "The Living God Is a Missionary God." Pages 3–9 in *Perspectives on the World Christian Movement: A Reader*. Edited by Darrell R. Dorr et al. 4th edition. Pasadena: William Carey Library, 2009.

Taylor, William R. Psalms. The Interpreter's Bible, vol. 4. Nashville: Abingdon Press, 1955.

"Timothy McVeigh Dead." CNN. June 11, 2001. https://www.cnn.com/2001/LAW/06/11/mcveigh.01.

VanGemeren, Willem A. *The Expositors Bible Commentary*, volume 5. Grand Rapids: Zondervan, 1991.

———. *Psalms*. Grand Rapids: Zondervan, 2008.

Venning, Ralph. *The Plague of Plagues: The Sinfulness of Sin*. Edinburgh: Banner of Truth, 1993.

Wilcock, Michael. *The Message of Psalms 1–72: Songs for the People of God*. Downers Grove: IVP Academic, 2001.

Wilson, Gerald H. *Psalms Volume 1*. NIV Application Commentary. Grand Rapids: Zondervan Academic, 2002.

Wolde, Ellen Van. "A Network of Conventional and Deliberate Metaphors in Psalm 22." *Journal for the Study of the Old Testament*, vol. 44, no. 4: pp. 642–66.

"Yogi Berra's Most Memorable Sayings." MLB.com, September 23, 2015. https://www.mlb.com/news/yogisms-yogi-berras-best-sayings/c-151217962.

SCRIPTURE INDEX

Copyright Page (Continued)